北京市高等学校教育教学改革立项项目
大学英语四级后课程建设研究

英语名著与电影系列二

英美戏剧与电影
English and American Drama and Film

张桂珍　张红波　编

图书在版编目(CIP)数据

英美戏剧与电影 / 张桂珍, 张红波编 . —北京: 北京大学出版社, 2018.7
ISBN 978-7-301-29725-4

Ⅰ.①英… Ⅱ.①张…②张… Ⅲ.①英语—高等学校—教材 ②戏剧文学—英国 ③戏剧文学—美国 ④电影—鉴赏—英国 ⑤电影—鉴赏—美国 Ⅳ.① H319.39

中国版本图书馆 CIP 数据核字(2018)第 168670 号

书　　名	英美戏剧与电影 YINGMEI XIJU YU DIANYING
著作责任者	张桂珍　张红波　编
责任编辑	李　娜
标准书号	ISBN 978-7-301-29725-4
出版发行	北京大学出版社
地　　址	北京市海淀区成府路 205 号　100871
网　　址	http://www.pup.cn　新浪微博:@北京大学出版社
电子邮箱	编辑部 pupwaiwen@pup.cn　总编室 zpup@pup.cn
电　　话	邮购部 010-62752015　发行部 010-62750672　编辑部 010-62759634
印刷者	北京虎彩文化传播有限公司
经销者	新华书店
	720 毫米 ×1020 毫米　16 开本　23 印张　540 千字 2018 年 7 月第 1 版　2024 年 1 月第 2 次印刷
定　　价	49.00 元

未经许可, 不得以任何方式复制或抄袭本书之部分或全部内容。
版权所有, 侵权必究
举报电话: 010-62752024　电子邮箱: fd@pup.cn
图书如有印装质量问题, 请与出版部联系, 电话: 010-62756370

前言

《英美戏剧与电影》是"英语名著与电影"系列教材中的第二部,是为以非英语专业学生为教学对象的"英美戏剧与电影"方面的课程编写的。编者在多年的教学实践中了解到,非英语专业的学生虽然有着十多年的英语学习经历,但他们中绝大多数人从未读过英美文学经典的原著,而他们中有相当多的人希望在学完了大学基础英语之后,能有相关的课程指导他们读些原汁原味的文学作品,尤其是那些他们渴望了解却又望而却步的英美文学经典作品。但是他们的专业课业较重,没有很多时间用于英语学习,因此如何为他们开设这样的课程就一度成了我反复思考的问题。后来我为他们开出的专题课"英美小说与电影",终于使这个难题在一定程度上得到了解决。这门课的基本思路就是借助电影介绍名著,结合原著讲解电影,使名著的主要内容和成就在与电影的这种双重结合中得到生动、有效的呈现。在讲授"英美小说与电影"时,我又了解到学生们对英美经典戏剧知之甚少,就又为学生们开设了"英美戏剧与电影"。这两门课都受到学生们的热情欢迎和支持。学生们感到通过此课的学习,无论在文学素养、语言水平还是在为人处世等方面,都有很大的收获。我退休后,请我教研室有着多年英美文学教学经验的青年教师张红波接任了这门课。这里我和张红波老师把我们的讲义和经验整理成教材,希望能进一步推进此课的教学。

本教材由上下篇六个单元组成,可用于一个学期的教学,也可根据具体情况灵活掌握。上篇介绍三位英国剧作家及其代表作品;下篇介绍三位美国剧作家及其代表作品。每个单元包括作家作品介绍、剧本选读以及多种练习。本教材所选的对象都是英美文学史上影响广泛而非英语专业的许多学生却所知甚少的作家作品。当然,之所以最后选定这六位剧作家的六部作品,还由于它们都有着观赏性较强的相应电影。选读包括剧本中与电影重要场景相关的段落(Excerpts)和可以在讲解电影时作为参考的重要段落。选读中超过大学英语四级词汇的生词较多,非常影响阅读速度,因此本书对选读中的这些词汇提供了解释。在练习的设计上,本书力求难度适中,既有一般性的问题,也有启发思考的问题,希望能在帮助学生拓展知识的同时,增强英语归纳和表述的能力以及自主学习的能力。

教材中所选的经典戏剧基本上都有不止一个版本的电影,我们在课上使用的多是较忠实于原著的版本。但我们也会介绍不同的版本,鼓励学生课下观看其他版本,互为补充,增进对电影和原著的理解。这些异同以及相关信息可以进一步激发学生们观赏电影、阅读原著的兴趣,提高他们对作品的理解和欣赏水平。

在教学和教材的编写过程中,很多老师、朋友和学生给予了宝贵的鼓励和支持,在此表示真挚的谢意。感谢英国米德尔塞克斯大学的图书馆、音像馆、英美文学课、英美文化课为此课选材打下的基础;感谢美国伊利诺伊大学和内布拉斯加大学的图书馆和音像馆为我确定教学内容提供的帮助;感谢内布拉斯加大学英语系主任里奇(Joy S. Ritchie)教授为我的研究所提供的方便;感谢张红波老师的积极合作和为本书的编写所付出的努力;感谢北京大学出版社的支持;感谢李娜编辑为此书所付出的辛勤劳动;我还想感谢我的丈夫和女儿的理解、鼓励和支持。由于我们的精力和水平有限,本书难免有这样那样的不足,这里真诚希望使用它的教师和学生提出宝贵意见,使它更加完善,更适合非英语专业学生的使用。

张桂珍

2018年7月

于北京大学

目 录

Volume One English Drama and Film

Unit 1 William Shakespeare and *Romeo and Juliet* 2

  1.1 William Shakespeare: Life and Works 2
      1.1.1 About the Playwright 2
      1.1.2 William Shakespeare's Major Plays 3
  1.2 *Romeo and Juliet* 4
      1.2.1 About the Play 4
      1.2.2 Characters 5
      1.2.3 Selected Readings from the Play 6
      1.2.4 Exercises 55

Unit 2 Oscar Wilde and *An Ideal Husband* 60

  2.1 Oscar Wilde: Life and Works 60
      2.1.1 About the Playwright 60
      2.1.2 Oscar Wilde's Major Plays 62
  2.2 *An Ideal Husband* 62
      2.2.1 About the Play 62
      2.2.2 Characters 63
      2.2.3 Selected Readings from the Play 64
      2.2.4 Exercises 113

Unit 3 George Bernard Shaw and *Pygmalion* 119

  3.1 George Bernard Shaw: Life and Works 119
      3.1.1 About the Playwright 119
      3.1.2 George Bernard Shaw's Major Plays 121
  3.2 *Pygmalion* 121
      3.2.1 About the Play 121

3.2.2　Characters 122
3.2.3　Selected Readings from the Play 123
3.2.4　Exercises 172

Volume Two　American Drama and Film

Unit 4　Tennessee Williams and *A Streetcar Named Desire* 180
4.1　Tennessee Williams: Life and Works 180
　4.1.1　About the Playwright 180
　4.1.2　Tennessee Williams's Major Plays 182
4.2　*A Streetcar Named Desire* 183
　4.2.1　About the Play 183
　4.2.2　Characters 184
　4.2.3　Selected Readings from the Play 185
　4.2.4　Exercises 234

Unit 5　Arthur Miller and *The Crucible* 240
5.1　Arthur Miller: Life and Works 240
　5.1.1　About the Playwright 240
　5.1.2　Arthur Miller's Major Plays 243
5.2　*The Crucible* 243
　5.2.1　About the Play 243
　5.2.2　Characters 244
　5.2.3　Selected Readings from the Play 246
　5.2.4　Exercises 295

Unit 6　Lorraine Hansberry and *A Raisin in the Sun* 301
6.1　Lorraine Hansberry: Life and Works 301
　6.1.1　About the Playwright 301
　6.1.2　Lorraine Hansberry's Major Plays 303
6.2　*A Raisin in the Sun* 303
　6.2.1　About the Play 303
　6.2.2　Characters 305
　6.2.3　Selected Readings from the Play 305
　6.2.4　Exercises 355

主要参考书目 360

Volume One

English Drama and Film

Unit 1

William Shakespeare and *Romeo and Juliet*

1.1 William Shakespeare: Life and Works

1.1.1 About the Playwright

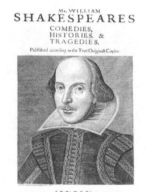

William Shakespeare (1564—1616) was an English poet and playwright widely regarded as the greatest writer of the English language, and the world's preeminent dramatist. He wrote approximately 37 plays and 154 sonnets, as well as a variety of other poems. His plays are categorized into comedies, tragedies, and histories.

Shakespeare's works have been translated into every major living language, and his plays are continually performed all around the world. In addition, Shakespeare is the most quoted writer in the literature and history of the English-speaking world, and many of his quotations and neologisms have passed into everyday usage in English and other languages.

William Shakespeare was born in April 1564 to a successful middle-class glove-maker in Stratford-upon-Avon, England. Shakespeare attended grammar school, but his formal education proceeded no further. In 1582 he married Anne Hathaway, when he was eighteen and she twenty-six, and had a daughter Susanna and twins, Judith and Hamnet. Hamnet, his only son, died at age eleven. He has no direct descendants today.

Around 1590 he left his family behind and traveled to London to work as an actor and playwright. Public and critical success quickly followed, and Shakespeare eventually became the most popular playwright in England and part-owner of the Globe Theater. His career bridged the reigns of Elizabeth I (ruled 1558—1603) and James I (ruled 1603—1625), and he was a favorite of both monarchs.

Wealthy and renowned, Shakespeare retired to Stratford and died in April 1616 at the age of fifty-two, and was buried inside the chancel of Holy Trinity Church in Stratford. At the time of Shakespeare's death, literary luminaries such as Ben Jonson hailed his works as timeless.

Throughout his plays, Shakespeare regularly demonstrated and celebrated the ideas and ideals of Renaissance humanism, and often presented characters who embodied humanistic principles. His style varied in accord with the status and personality of the characters and suited different tastes of his audiences. He was skilled in many poetic forms, varied rhetorical devices, and diverse moods.

Shakespeare created hundreds of living, believable "round characters" of complicated personalities, all of the different individuals showing the rich diversity of humanity. His plays were often set in other countries or in the past, but they represented people and life in England of his own time.

1.1.2 William Shakespeare's Major Plays

(1) Histories:
Henry IV, part 1 《亨利四世上篇》
Henry IV, part 2 《亨利四世下篇》
Henry V 《亨利五世》
Henry VI, part 1 《亨利六世上篇》
Henry VI, part 2 《亨利六世中篇》
Henry VI, part 3 《亨利六世下篇》
Henry VIII 《亨利八世》
King John 《约翰王》
Richard II 《理查二世》
Richard III 《理查三世》

(2) Comedies:
All's Well That Ends Well 《终成眷属》
As You Like It 《皆大欢喜》
The Comedy of Errors 《错误的喜剧》
Cymbeline 《辛白林》
Love's Labours Lost 《爱的徒劳》
Measure for Measure 《一报还一报》
The Merry Wives of Windsor 《温莎的风流娘儿们》
The Merchant of Venice 《威尼斯商人》

A Midsummer Night's Dream《仲夏夜之梦》
Much Ado About Nothing《无事生非》
Pericles, Prince of Tyre《泰尔亲王配力克里斯》
Taming of the Shrew《驯悍记》
The Tempest《暴风雨》
Troilus and Cressida《特洛伊罗斯与克瑞西达》
Twelfth Night《第十二夜》
Two Gentlemen of Verona《维洛那二绅士》
Winter's Tale《冬天的故事》

(3) Tragedies:
Antony and Cleopatra《安东尼与克莉奥佩特拉》
Coriolanus《科利奥兰纳斯》
Hamlet《哈姆雷特》
Julius Caesar《裘力斯·恺撒》
King Lear《李尔王》
Macbeth《麦克白》
Othello《奥赛罗》
Romeo and Juliet《罗密欧与朱丽叶》
Timon of Athens《雅典的泰门》
Titus Andronicus《泰特斯·安德洛尼克斯》

1.2 *Romeo and Juliet*

1.2.1 About the Play

Romeo and Juliet, Shakespeare's first romantic tragedy, is one of the best known and best loved of Shakespeare's plays though it is not among the most perfect in its poetry nor among the most complex in its characterization or dramatic structure. Called a "tragedy," it cannot be classed with *Macbeth*, *Hamlet*, *Othello*, and *King Lear*, the great works of Shakespeare's maturity as a playwright. *Romeo and Juliet* conforms rather to the simplest, most basic definition of the term "tragedy"—"a play or other literary work of a serious or sorrowful character, with a fatal or disastrous conclusion." Ballet, opera, and countless stage productions have demonstrated

Unit 1
William Shakespeare and *Romeo and Juliet*

the constant appeal of its story of love, separation, and death, and to call a young man a "Romeo" is to make him recognizable throughout the western world as a romantic young lover.

The play was probably written in 1594 or 1595 and was first published in 1597, entitled *An Excellent Conceited Tragedie of Romeo and Juliet*. The story of *Romeo and Juliet* was already familiar when Shakespeare gave it the form by which our world knows it. There is little doubt that he was influenced in the writing of his play by Arthur Brooke's long blank-verse poem of a generation earlier, *The Tragicall Historye of Romeus and Juliet* (1562). Brooke's poem is over three thousand lines long, and it covers some nine months in time. The background of warring families is similar as, in general, is the course of the action and the names and functions of the characters, notably excepting Mercutio, who is Shakespeare's own, unique creation.

Romeo and Juliet begins with a sonnet spoken by the chorus and in its poetry, language, and plot reflects the sonnet craze of the 1590s, from which Shakespeare's own sequence dates. The play is set in Renaissance Verona, where a long-standing feud between two houses, the Capulets and the Montagues, provides the violent milieu in which the ill-fated lovers are destroyed.

Shakespeare was evidently quite sympathetic toward Romeo and Juliet, and in attributing their tragedy to fate, rather than to a flaw in their characters, he raised them to heights near perfection. They are both sincere, kind, brave, loyal, virtuous, and desperately in love, and their tragedy is greater because of their innocence. The feud between the lovers' families represents the fate which Romeo and Juliet are powerless to overcome. The lines capture in poetry the youthful and simple passion which characterizes the play.

1.2.2 Characters

(1) The ruling house of Verona

Escalus, Prince of Verona. He provides for law and order.

Paris, a young nobleman, kinsman to the Prince; a suitor of Juliet.

Mercutio, kinsman to the Prince, and friend to Romeo. He is moody and witty.

(2) The house of Montague

Romeo, son to Montague. He is romantic and a bit rash.

Montague, father of Romeo.

Lady Montague, mother of Romeo.

Benvolio, nephew to Montague, cousin and friend to Romeo. He is a calm, peaceful man.

Abraham, servant to Montague.

Balthasar, servant to Romeo.

(3) The house of Capulet

Juliet, daughter to Capulet. She is about fourteen years old.

Capulet, father of Juliet. He is usually a pleasant man, but can be domineering when his authority is challenged.

Lady Capulet, mother of Juliet.

Tybalt, cousin to Juliet. He is aggressive and revengeful.

Nurse, servant to Juliet. She is a comic figure, being talkative and telling vulgar jokes.

Samson, servant to Capulet.

Gregory, servant to Capulet.

Peter, servant to Juliet's nurse.

(4) Other characters

Friar Lawrence, a Franciscan monk, Romeo's friend and confessor. He is wise and knowledgeable about herbal medicines.

Friar John, a Franciscan monk, sent by Friar Lawrence to tell Romeo of his sleeping potion plan for Juliet.

Apothecary, a poverty-stricken chemist, who illegally sells poison to Romeo.

1.2.3 Selected Readings from the Play

Notes on Shakespeare's English

Shakespeare's English belongs to a form of early Modern English (since 1500) with holdovers from Middle English (1066—1500). Here are a few rules.

1. Some personal pronouns were different. For example:

thou=you (subject), thee=you (object), ye=you (plural), thy=your, thyself=yourself, thine=yours

2. The conjugation of verbs was also different. Usually, the second person singular verbs ended with "-(e)st", and the third person singular verbs ended with "-(e)th". For example:

thou givest=you give, thou hearest=you hear

she giveth=she gives, he speaketh=he speaks

But there were some exceptions. For example:

thou art=you are, thou hast=you have, thou wilt=you will, thou shalt=you shall, thou canst=you can, thou dost=you do, thou wert=you were

he hath=he has, he doth=he does

3. Some words had special meanings or are considered obsolete today. For example:

soft=wait, still=always, want=lack

anon=soon, ere=before, ay(e)=yes, nay=no, wherefore=why

Unit 1
William Shakespeare and *Romeo and Juliet*

4. Contractions and inversions were frequently used. For example:
   wi'=with, o'=of/on, 'tis=it is, e'en=even, speak'st=speakest
   To strike him dead I hold it not a sin.=I hold it not a sin to strike him dead.
5. Shakespeare's plays were written in poetry. Usually each line had ten syllables with the stress falling on every other syllable. This pattern is called iambic pentameter. For example:
   But '**soft**! What '**light** through '**yon**der '**win**dow '**breaks**?

Excerpt 1 (from Act 1, Scene 1)

Another street fight has broken out between servants from the Montagues and the Capulets, two feuding families in Verona. While attempting to stop the fight, Benvolio, a Montague relative, is drawn into the fray by Tybalt, kinsman of the Capulets. The fight rapidly escalates as more citizens become involved and soon the heads of both households appear on the scene. At last, Prince Escalus arrives and angrily stops the riot.

Enter Prince Escalus with his train（随行人员）.

PRINCE
  Rebellious subjects（臣民）, enemies to peace,
  Profaners（滥用者） of this neighbor-stainèd（沾染邻居鲜血的） steel—
  Will they not hear?—What ho! You men, you beasts,
  That quench（熄灭） the fire of your pernicious（恶毒的） rage
  With purple fountains issuing from your veins（静脉，血管）:
  On pain of（违则以……处罚） torture, from those bloody hands
  Throw your mistempered（凶险的） weapons to the ground,
  And hear the sentence（判决） of your movèd（震怒的） prince.
  Three civil brawls（争斗） bred of（由……酿成） an airy（轻率的） word
  By thee, old Capulet, and Montague,
  Have thrice disturbed the quiet of our streets
  And made Verona's ancient citizens
  Cast by their grave-beseeming ornaments[①]
  To wield（挥舞） old partisans（戟） in hands as old,
  Cankered（锈蚀的） with peace, to part your cankered（恶毒的） hate.
  If ever you disturb our streets again,
  Your lives shall pay the forfeit（罚金） of the peace.
  For this time all the rest depart away.

---

① Cast … ornaments: throw aside appurtenances (like staffs) suitable for grave old age.

You, Capulet, shall go along with me,
And, Montague, come you this afternoon
To know our farther pleasure（意见） in this case,
To old Free-town, our common judgment-place.
Once more, on pain of death, all men depart.

All but Montague, Lady Montague,
and Benvolio exit.

MONTAGUE, *to Benvolio*
Who set this ancient quarrel new abroach（开口的）?
Speak, nephew, were you by when it began?

BENVOLIO
Here were the servants of your adversary（对手）,
And yours, close fighting ere（在……之前） I did approach.
I drew to part them. In the instant came
The fiery（暴躁的） Tybalt with his sword prepared,
Which, as he breathed defiance（藐视，挑战） to my ears,
He swung about his head and cut the winds,
Who, nothing hurt withal, hissed（发嘘声） him in scorn.
While we were interchanging thrusts and blows
Came more and more and fought on part and part（各为一方）,
Till the Prince came, who parted either part.

LADY MONTAGUE
O, where is Romeo? Saw you him today?
Right glad I am he was not at this fray（争斗）.

BENVOLIO
Madam, an hour before the worshiped sun
Peered（隐现） forth the golden window of the east,
A troubled mind drove me to walk abroad（在室外）,
Where underneath the grove（小树林） of sycamore
That westward rooteth（生根） from this city side,
So early walking did I see your son.
Towards him I made, but he was 'ware of me
And stole into the covert（隐秘处） of the wood.
I, measuring his affections（意向） by my own
(Which then most sought where most might not be found,
Being one too many（多余的一个） by my weary self),
Pursued my humor（心情）, not pursuing his,
And gladly shunned（回避） who gladly fled from me.

MONTAGUE
Many a morning hath he there been seen,

With tears <u>augmenting</u>（增加）the fresh morning's dew,
Adding to clouds more clouds with his deep sighs.
But all so soon as the all-cheering sun
Should in the farthest east begin to draw
The shady curtains from Aurora①'s bed,
Away from light steals home my heavy son
And private in his chamber <u>pens</u>（囚禁） himself,
Shuts up his windows, locks fair daylight out,
And makes himself an <u>artificial</u>（人造的） night.
Black and <u>portentous</u>（不详的） must this humor prove,
Unless good counsel may the cause remove.

BENVOLIO

My noble uncle, do you know the cause?

MONTAGUE

I neither know it nor can learn of him.

BENVOLIO

Have you <u>importuned</u>（强求，追问） him by any means?

MONTAGUE

Both by myself and many other friends.
But he, his own affections' <u>counselor</u>（顾问），
Is to himself—I will not say how true,
But to himself so secret and so <u>close</u>（保密的，沉默的），
So far from <u>sounding</u>（试探） and discovery,
As is the bud bit with an envious worm
Ere he can spread his sweet leaves to the air
Or dedicate his beauty to the sun.
Could we but learn from whence his sorrows grow,
We would as willingly give cure as know.

Enter Romeo.

BENVOLIO

See where he comes. So please you, step aside.
I'll know his <u>grievance</u>（苦衷） or be much denied.

MONTAGUE

I would thou wert so <u>happy</u>（幸运的） by thy stay
To hear true <u>shrift</u>（坦白）.—Come, madam, let's away.

Montague and Lady Montague exit.

BENVOLIO

Good <u>morrow</u>（早上）, cousin.

---

① Aurora: the ancient Roman goddess of the dawn.

ROMEO Is the day so young?

BENVOLIO

    But new struck nine.

ROMEO Ay me, sad hours seem long.

    Was that my father that went hence so fast?

BENVOLIO

    It was. What sadness lengthens Romeo's hours?

ROMEO

    Not having that which, having, makes them short.

BENVOLIO

    In love?

ROMEO

    Out—

BENVOLIO

    Of love?

ROMEO

    Out of her favor where I am in love.

BENVOLIO

    Alas that love, so gentle in his view（外表）①,

    Should be so tyrannous and rough in proof（实际）!

ROMEO

    Alas that love, whose view（视线） is muffled（蒙住） still（总是）,

    Should without eyes see pathways to his will（目的）!

    Where shall we dine?—O me! What fray（争斗） was here?

    Yet tell me not, for I have heard it all.

    Here's much to do with hate, but more with love.

    Why then, O brawling（爱争吵的） love, O loving hate,

    O anything of nothing first create!

    O heavy lightness, serious vanity,

    Misshapen chaos of well-seeming forms,

    Feather of lead, bright smoke, cold fire, sick health,

    Still-waking sleep that is not what it is!

    This love feel I, that feel no love in this.

    Dost thou not laugh?

BENVOLIO

    No, coz（=cousin）, I rather weep.

---

① gentle ... view: Love is often personified as Cupid, a cute boy, who is sometimes blindfolded to signify the idea that love is blind.

ROMEO

    Good heart, at what?

BENVOLIO

    At thy good heart's oppression（苦恼）.

ROMEO

    Why, such is love's transgression（罪过）.
    Griefs of mine own lie heavy in my breast,
    Which thou wilt propagate（增加） to have it pressed
    With more of thine（你的）. This love that thou hast shown
    Doth add more grief to too much of mine own.
    Love is a smoke made with the fume（烟） of sighs;
    Being purged[①], a fire sparkling in lovers' eyes;
    Being vexed[②], a sea nourished with loving tears.
    What is it else? A madness most discreet（审慎的）,
    A choking gall（苦味）, and a preserving sweet.
    Farewell, my coz.

BENVOLIO

    Soft（稍等）, I will go along.
    An if you leave me so, you do me wrong.

ROMEO

    Tut（啧啧）, I have lost myself. I am not here.
    This is not Romeo. He's some other where.

BENVOLIO

    Tell me in sadness（真诚）, who is that you love?

ROMEO

    What, shall I groan and tell thee?

BENVOLIO

    Groan? Why, no. But sadly tell me who.

ROMEO

    A sick man in sadness（悲伤） makes his will—
    A word ill urged（使用不当的） to one that is so ill.
    In sadness, cousin, I do love a woman.

BENVOLIO

    I aimed（猜测） so near when I supposed you loved.

ROMEO

    A right good markman（射手）! And she's fair I love.

---

① purged: cleared of smoke.
② vexed: stirred up.

BENVOLIO

A right fair mark（靶子）, fair coz, is soonest hit.

ROMEO

Well in that hit you miss. She'll not be hit
With Cupid's arrow. She hath Dian①'s wit,
And, in strong proof（铠甲） of chastity（贞洁） well armed,
From love's weak childish bow she lives uncharmed（不受魅惑）.
She will not stay（忍受） the siege of loving terms（甜言蜜语）,
Nor bide（承受） th' encounter（交战） of assailing eyes（灼灼逼人的目光）,
Nor ope（打开） her lap to saint-seducing（使圣人动心的） gold.
O, she is rich in beauty, only poor
That, when she dies, with beauty dies her store（资本）.

BENVOLIO

Then she hath sworn that she will still live chaste（贞洁的）?

ROMEO

She hath, and in that sparing（节约） makes huge waste;
For beauty, starved with her severity（严苛）,
Cuts beauty off from all posterity（后代）.
She is too fair, too wise, wisely too fair,
To merit bliss（赢得上天的赐福） by making me despair.
She hath forsworn to love, and in that vow
Do I live dead, that live to tell it now.

BENVOLIO

Be ruled by（听从） me. Forget to think of her.

ROMEO

O, teach me how I should forget to think!

BENVOLIO

By giving liberty unto（放纵） thine eyes.
Examine other beauties.

ROMEO

'Tis the way
To call hers, exquisite, in question（对……进行考量） more.
These happy（幸运的） masks that kiss fair ladies' brows（额头）,
Being black, puts us in mind（使……想起） they hide the fair.
He that is strucken blind cannot forget
The precious treasure of his eyesight lost.
Show me a mistress that is passing fair（超凡的美人）;
What doth her beauty serve but as a note（提醒）

---

① Dian: or Diana, is the Roman goddess of moon, hunting and chastity.

Where I may read who passed that passing fair?
Farewell. Thou canst not teach me to forget.

BENVOLIO

I'll pay that doctrine（教诲） or else die in debt.

> **Excerpt 2 (from Act 1, Scene 5)**
>
> *Paris, a relative of the Prince, asks Capulet for his daughter Juliet's hand in marriage. Capulet thinks Juliet is too young to marry but agrees to let the two meet at a party he is hosting that night. By accident, Romeo and Benvolio find out about the Capulet party. Benvolio encourages Romeo to go there with him. In the Capulet house, Romeo, disguised, sees Juliet and falls instantly in love.*

ROMEO, *to a Servingman*

What lady's that which doth enrich the hand
Of yonder knight?

SERVINGMAN

I know not, sir.

ROMEO

O, she doth teach the torches to burn bright!
It seems she hangs upon the cheek of night
As a rich jewel in an Ethiope's（黑人） ear—
Beauty too rich for use, for Earth too dear.
So shows a snowy dove trooping（成群结队而行） with crows
As yonder lady o'er her fellows shows.
The measure（舞） done, I'll watch her place of stand
And, touching hers, make blessèd my rude（粗糙的） hand.
Did my heart love till now? Forswear（否认） it, sight,
For I ne'er saw true beauty till this night.

TYBALT

This, by his voice, should be a Montague.—
Fetch me my rapier, boy. *Page*（侍从） *exits.*
What, dares the slave（奴才）
Come hither（这里） covered with an antic face（奇形怪状的面具）
To fleer（嘲笑） and scorn at our solemnity（庄重的仪式）?
Now, by the stock（血统） and honor of my kin（家族），
To strike him dead I hold it not a sin.

CAPULET

Why, how now, kinsman? Wherefore（为何） storm（暴怒） you so?

TYBALT

    Uncle, this is a Montague, our <u>foe</u>（敌人）,

    A <u>villain</u>（恶棍） that is hither come in <u>spite</u>（恶意）

    To scorn at our solemnity this night.

CAPULET

    Young Romeo is it?

TYBALT

    'Tis he, that villain Romeo.

CAPULET

    <u>Content</u>（镇定） thee, gentle coz. Let him alone.

    He <u>bears him</u>（表现） like a <u>portly</u>（尊贵的） gentleman,

    And, to say truth, Verona brags of him

    To be a virtuous and well-governed youth.

    I would not for the wealth of all this town

    Here in my house do him <u>disparagement</u>（不敬）.

    Therefore be patient. Take no note of him.

    It is my will, the which if thou respect,

    Show a <u>fair presence</u>（友好的举止） and put off these frowns,

    An <u>ill-beseeming semblance</u>（不合适的表情） for a feast.

TYBALT

    It fits when such a villain is a guest.

    I'll not endure him.

CAPULET

    He shall be endured.

    What, goodman boy? I say he shall. <u>Go to</u>（得啦）.

    Am I the master here or you? Go to.

    You'll not endure him! <u>God shall mend my soul</u>（老天爷）,

    You'll make a <u>mutiny</u>（叛乱） among my guests,

    You will <u>set cock-a-hoop</u>（闹事）, you'll <u>be the man</u>（充好汉）!

TYBALT

    Why, uncle, 'tis a shame.

CAPULET

    Go to, go to.

    You are a <u>saucy</u>（无礼的） boy. Is 't so indeed?

    This <u>trick</u>（胡闹） may chance to <u>scathe</u>（伤害） you. I know what.

    You must <u>contrary</u>（和……作对） me. <u>Marry</u>（叹词：真是）, 'tis time—

    [to dancing Guests] Well said, my hearts.—

    [to Tybalt] You are a <u>princox</u>（浑小子）, go. Be quiet, or—

    [to Servants] More light, more light!—

    [to Tybalt] for shame, I'll make you quiet.—

Unit 1
William Shakespeare and *Romeo and Juliet*

[going to dancing Guests] What, cheerly, my hearts!

TYBALT

Patience perforce（强迫地） with willful choler（愤怒） meeting
Makes my flesh tremble in their different greeting（两种不同力量的冲撞）.
I will withdraw, but this intrusion（闯入） shall,
Now seeming sweet, convert to bitt'rest gall.

He exits.

ROMEO, *taking Juliet's hand*

If I profane（亵渎） with my unworthiest hand
This holy shrine, the gentle sin is this:
My lips, two blushing pilgrims, ready stand
To smooth（拂去） that rough touch with a tender kiss.

JULIET

Good pilgrim, you do wrong your hand too much,
Which mannerly（得体的） devotion shows in this;
For saints have hands that pilgrims' hands do touch,
And palm（手掌） to palm is holy palmers'（朝圣者） kiss.

ROMEO

Have not saints lips, and holy palmers too?

JULIET

Ay, pilgrim, lips that they must use in prayer.

ROMEO

O then, dear saint, let lips do what hands do.
They pray: grant（许可） thou, lest faith turn to despair.

JULIET

Saints do not move（主动施恩）, though grant for prayers' sake.

ROMEO

Then move not（别动） while my prayer's effect I take.

He kisses her.

Thus from my lips, by thine, my sin is purged（清洗）.

JULIET

Then have my lips the sin that they have took（沾染）.

ROMEO

Sin from my lips? O trespass（罪过） sweetly urged（提出）!
Give me my sin again（退还）.

He kisses her.

JULIET

You kiss by th' book（很有一套）.

NURSE

Madam, your mother craves（渴望） a word with you.

Juliet moves toward her mother.

ROMEO

    What is her mother?

NURSE

    Marry, bachelor,

    Her mother is the lady of the house,

    And a good lady, and a wise and virtuous.

    I nursed her daughter that you talked withal.

    I tell you, he that can lay hold of（得到）her

    Shall have the chinks（叮当声，指钱币）.   *Nurse moves away.*

ROMEO, *aside*（旁白）

    Is she a Capulet?

    O dear account! My life is my foe's debt.

BENVOLIO

    Away, begone（离开）. The sport（娱乐）is at the best.

ROMEO

    Ay, so I fear. The more is my unrest.

CAPULET

    Nay, gentlemen, prepare not to be gone.

    We have a trifling foolish（微不足道的）banquet towards（马上就到）.—

    Is it e'en so（一定要走吗）? Why then, I thank you all.

    I thank you, honest gentlemen. Good night.—

    More torches here.—Come on then, let's to bed.—

    Ah, sirrah（小子）, by my fay（千真万确）, it waxes（变得）late.

    I'll to my rest.

                                  All but Juliet and the Nurse begin to exit.

JULIET

    Come hither, nurse. What is yond gentleman?

NURSE

    The son and heir of old Tiberio.

JULIET

    What's he that now is going out of door?

NURSE

    Marry, that, I think, be young Petruchio.

JULIET

    What's he that follows here, that would not dance?

NURSE

    I know not.

JULIET

    Go ask his name. *The Nurse goes.* If he be married,

    My grave is like to（可能）be my wedding bed.

NURSE, *returning*

His name is Romeo, and a Montague,
The only son of your great enemy.

JULIET

My only love <u>sprung</u>（发源） from my only hate!
Too early seen unknown, and known too late!
<u>Prodigious</u>（不祥的） birth of love it is to me
That I must love a <u>loathèd</u>（可恨的） enemy.

NURSE

What's this? What's this?

JULIET

A <u>rhyme</u>（歌谣） I learned <u>even now</u>（刚刚）
Of one I danced withal.

One calls within "Juliet."

NURSE

Anon, anon.
Come, let's away. The strangers all are gone.

They exit.

✤ Excerpt 3 (from Act 2, Scene 2)

After the party is over, Romeo hopes to see Juliet again, so he climbs a wall to hide in the Capulet orchard. His friends try to find him, but Romeo will not respond to their calls. Exasperated, Mercutio mocks Romeo's lovesickness in a bawdy speech. Then Benvolio persuades Mercutio to leave the scene, knowing Romeo's love of solitude. In the orchard, Romeo hears Mercutio's teasing.

ROMEO

He <u>jests at</u>（嘲笑） scars that never felt a wound.

Enter Juliet above.

But soft, what light through yonder window breaks?
It is the East, and Juliet is the sun.
Arise, fair sun, and kill the envious moon[①],
Who is already sick and pale with grief
That thou, her <u>maid</u>（女信徒）, art far more fair than she.
Be not her maid since she is envious.

---

① moon: Diana, the goddess of moon and chastity.

Her vestal（处女的） livery（制服） is but sick and green,
　　And none but fools do wear it. Cast it off.
　　It is my lady. O, it is my love!
　　O, that she knew① she were!
　　She speaks, yet she says nothing. What of that?
　　Her eye discourses（谈话）; I will answer it.
　　I am too bold（鲁莽）. 'Tis not to me she speaks.
　　Two of the fairest stars in all the heaven,
　　Having some business, do entreat（恳求） her eyes
　　To twinkle in their spheres（运行轨道） till they return.
　　What if her eyes were there, they in her head?
　　The brightness of her cheek would shame those stars
　　As daylight doth a lamp; her eye in heaven
　　Would through the airy region（天空） stream（闪耀） so bright
　　That birds would sing and think it were not night.
　　See how she leans her cheek upon her hand.
　　O, that I were a glove upon that hand,
　　That I might touch that cheek!
JULIET
　　Ay me.
ROMEO, *aside*
　　She speaks.
　　O, speak again, bright angel, for thou art
　　As glorious to this night, being o'er my head,
　　As is a wingèd messenger（天使） of heaven
　　Unto the white-upturnèd（翻白眼的） wond'ring（惊叹的） eyes
　　Of mortals（凡人） that fall back to gaze on him
　　When he bestrides（跨骑） the lazy puffing clouds
　　And sails upon the bosom of the air.
JULIET
　　O Romeo, Romeo, wherefore art thou Romeo?
　　Deny thy father and refuse thy name,
　　Or, if thou wilt not, be but sworn my love,
　　And I'll no longer be a Capulet.
ROMEO, *aside*
　　Shall I hear more, or shall I speak at this?
JULIET
　　'Tis but thy name that is my enemy.

---

① that ... knew: if only she knew.

Thou art thyself, though not a Montague.
What's Montague? It is nor hand, nor foot,
Nor arm, nor face, nor any other part
Belonging to a man. O, be some other name!
What's in a name? That which we call a rose
By any other word would smell as sweet.
So Romeo would, were he not Romeo called,
Retain that dear perfection which he <u>owes</u>（拥有）
Without that title. Romeo, <u>doff</u>（抛弃） thy name,
And, for thy name, which is no part of thee,
Take all myself.

ROMEO

I take thee at thy word.
Call me but love, and I'll be new <u>baptized</u>（受洗命名）.
Henceforth I never will be Romeo.

JULIET

What man art thou that, thus <u>bescreened</u>（遮掩） in night,
So <u>stumblest on</u>（意外撞见或听到） my <u>counsel</u>（心里话）?

ROMEO

By a name
I know not how to tell thee who I am.
My name, dear saint, is hateful to myself
Because it is an enemy to thee.
Had I it written, I would tear the word.

JULIET

My ears have yet not drunk a hundred words
Of thy tongue's uttering, yet I know the sound.
Art thou not Romeo, and a Montague?

ROMEO

Neither, fair maid, if either thee <u>dislike</u>（使……不悦）.

JULIET

How camest thou hither, tell me, and wherefore?
The orchard walls are high and hard to climb,
And the place death, considering who thou art,
If any of my kinsmen find thee here.

ROMEO

With love's light wings did I <u>o'erperch</u>（翻越） these walls,
For <u>stony limits</u>（石墙） cannot hold love out,
And what love can do, that dares love attempt.
Therefore thy kinsmen are no stop to me.

JULIET

If they do see thee, they will murder thee.

ROMEO

Alack（哎）, there lies more peril in thine eye

Than twenty of their swords. Look thou but sweet,

And I am proof against（能抵御……的） their enmity（敌意）.

JULIET

I would not for the world（无论如何） they saw thee here.

ROMEO

I have night's cloak to hide me from their eyes,

And, but thou love me, let them find me here.

My life were better ended by their hate

Than death prorogued（延期）, wanting（缺乏） of thy love.

JULIET

By whose direction found'st thou out this place?

ROMEO

By love, that first did prompt me to inquire.

He lent me counsel（建议）, and I lent him eyes.

I am no pilot; yet, wert thou as far

As that vast shore washed with the farthest sea,

I should adventure for such merchandise（货物）.

JULIET

Thou knowest the mask of night is on my face,

Else would a maiden blush bepaint（着色） my cheek

For that which thou hast heard me speak tonight.

Fain（宁愿） would I dwell on（遵守） form（礼制）; fain, fain deny

What I have spoke. But farewell compliment（客套话）.

Dost thou love me? I know thou wilt say "Ay（是），"

And I will take thy word. Yet, if thou swear'st,

Thou mayst prove false. At lovers' perjuries（假誓），

They say, Jove① laughs. O gentle Romeo,

If thou dost love, pronounce it faithfully.

Or, if thou thinkest I am too quickly won,

I'll frown and be perverse（倔强任性） and say thee nay（不），

So thou wilt woo（求爱）, but else not for the world.

In truth, fair Montague, I am too fond（痴心），

And therefore thou mayst think my havior（举止） light（轻佻）.

But trust me, gentleman, I'll prove more true

---

① Jove: also called Jupiter, is the supreme deity of the ancient Romans.

Than those that have more coying（忸怩作态） to be strange（冷淡）.
I should have been more strange, I must confess,
But that thou overheard'st（无意听到） ere I was ware,
My true-love passion. Therefore pardon me,
And not impute（归咎） this yielding to light love,
Which the dark night hath so discoverèd（揭示）.

ROMEO

Lady, by yonder blessèd moon I vow,
That tips（覆盖） with silver all these fruit-tree tops—

JULIET

O, swear not by the moon, th' inconstant（变化无常的） moon,
That monthly changes in her circled orb（轨道），
Lest that thy love prove likewise variable（多变的）.

ROMEO

What shall I swear by?

JULIET

Do not swear at all.
Or, if thou wilt, swear by thy gracious self,
Which is the god of my idolatry（偶像崇拜），
And I'll believe thee.

ROMEO

If my heart's dear love—

JULIET

Well, do not swear. Although I joy in thee,
I have no joy of this contract（盟誓） tonight.
It is too rash（冒进）, too unadvised（轻率）, too sudden,
Too like the lightning, which doth cease to be
Ere one can say "It lightens." Sweet, good night.
This bud of love, by summer's ripening breath,
May prove（成为） a beauteous flower when next we meet.
Good night, good night. As sweet repose（睡眠） and rest
Come to thy heart as that within my breast.

ROMEO

O, wilt thou leave me so unsatisfied?

JULIET

What satisfaction canst thou have tonight?

ROMEO

Th' exchange of thy love's faithful vow for mine.

JULIET

I gave thee mine before thou didst request it,

And yet I would it were to give again.

ROMEO

Wouldst thou withdraw it? For what purpose, love?

JULIET

But to be <u>frank</u>（慷慨的） and give it thee again.

And yet I wish but for the thing I have.

My <u>bounty</u>（慷慨） is as <u>boundless</u>（无边无际） as the sea,

My love as deep. The more I give to thee,

The more I have, for both are infinite.

Nurse calls from within.

I hear some noise within. Dear love, <u>adieu</u>（再会）.—

<u>Anon</u>（就来）, good nurse.—Sweet Montague, be true.

Stay but a little; I will come again.   *She exits.*

ROMEO

O blessèd, blessèd night! I am afeard,

Being in night, all this is but a dream,

Too <u>flattering</u>（令人喜爱） sweet to be <u>substantial</u>（切实）.

Reenter Juliet above.

JULIET

Three words, dear Romeo, and good night indeed.

If that thy <u>bent</u>（意图） of love be honorable,

Thy purpose marriage, send me word tomorrow,

By one that I'll procure to come to thee,

Where and what time thou wilt perform the <u>rite</u>（仪式）,

And all my fortunes at thy foot I'll lay

And follow thee my lord throughout the world.

NURSE, *within*

Madam.

JULIET

I come anon.—But if thou meanest not well,

I do <u>beseech</u>（恳求） thee—

NURSE, *within*

Madam.

JULIET

<u>By and by</u>（不久）, I come.—

To cease thy <u>strife</u>（求爱） and leave me to my grief.

Tomorrow will I <u>send</u>（派人来）.

Unit 1

William Shakespeare and *Romeo and Juliet*

ROMEO

So thrive my soul（我以灵魂起誓）—

JULIET

A thousand times good night. *She exits.*

ROMEO

A thousand times the worse to want thy light.

Love goes toward love as schoolboys from their books,

But love from love, toward school with heavy looks.

Going.

Enter Juliet above again.

JULIET

Hist（嘘）, Romeo, hist! O, for① a falc'ner's（falconer放鹰人） voice

To lure this tassel-gentle（雄鹰） back again!

Bondage（拘束） is hoarse（嘶哑） and may not speak aloud,

Else would I tear the cave where Echo② lies

And make her airy（无形的） tongue more hoarse than mine

With repetition of "My Romeo!"

ROMEO

It is my soul that calls upon my name.

How silver-sweet sound lovers' tongues by night,

Like softest music to attending（聆听） ears.

JULIET

Romeo.

ROMEO

My dear.

JULIET

What o'clock tomorrow

Shall I send to thee?

ROMEO

By the hour of nine.

JULIET

I will not fail. 'Tis twenty year till then.

I have forgot why I did call thee back.

ROMEO

Let me stand here till thou remember it.

---

① for: If only I had.

② Echo: a nymph in Greek mythology who, scorned by Narcissus, wasted away with grief until only a voice remained to haunt empty caves.

JULIET

    I shall forget, to have thee still stand there,

    Rememb'ring how I love thy <u>company</u>（陪伴）.

ROMEO

    And I'll still stay, to have thee still forget,

    Forgetting any other home but this.

JULIET

    'Tis almost morning. I would have thee gone,

    And yet no farther than a <u>wanton</u>'s（顽皮孩子） bird,

    That lets it hop a little from his hand,

    Like a poor prisoner in his <u>twisted</u>（缠绕的） <u>gyves</u>（脚镣），

    And with a silken thread <u>plucks</u>（扯） it back again,

    So <u>loving-jealous of</u>（因为爱恋所以嫉恨） his liberty.

ROMEO

    I would I were thy bird.

JULIET

    Sweet, so would I.

    Yet I <u>should</u>（可能会） kill thee with much cherishing.

    Good night, good night. Parting is such sweet sorrow

    That I shall say "Good night" till it be morrow.

She exits.

ROMEO

    Sleep <u>dwell</u>（停留） upon thine eyes, peace in thy breast.

    Would I were sleep and peace so sweet to rest.[①]

    Hence will I to my <u>ghostly friar</u>'s（神父） close <u>cell</u>（房间），

    His help to crave, and my <u>dear hap</u>（好运） to tell.

He exits.

✂ Excerpt 4 (from Act 2, Scene 3)

Romeo arrives at Friar Lawrence's cell as day breaks. The Friar is collecting herbs and flowers while he muses on their powers to medicate and to poison. He speaks of how good may be perverted to evil and evil may be purified by good. Then Romeo enters and tries to persuade Friar Lawrence to marry him and Juliet.

---

①   Would ... rest: If only I were sleep and peace, to rest in such sweet places!

Unit 1
William Shakespeare and *Romeo and Juliet*

ROMEO

    Good morrow, father.

FRIAR LAWRENCE

    <u>Benedicite</u>（上帝保佑你）.

    What early tongue so sweet saluteth me?

    Young son, it argues a <u>distempered</u>（不安的） head

    So <u>soon</u>（早） to bid "Good morrow" to thy bed.

    <u>Care</u>（忧愁） keeps his <u>watch</u>（守夜） in every old man's eye,

    And, where care lodges, sleep will never lie;

    But where <u>unbruisèd</u>（未经沧桑的） youth with <u>unstuffed</u>（无烦恼充塞的） brain

    <u>Doth</u> <u>couch</u>（使……躺卧） his limbs, there golden sleep doth reign.

    Therefore thy earliness doth me assure

    Thou art <u>uproused</u>（唤醒） with some distemp'rature,

    Or, if not so, then here I <u>hit it right</u>（说中了）:

    Our Romeo hath not been in bed tonight.

ROMEO

    That last is true. The sweeter rest was mine.

FRIAR LAWRENCE

    God pardon sin! Wast thou with Rosaline?

ROMEO

    With Rosaline, my ghostly father? No.

    I have forgot that name and that name's woe.

FRIAR LAWRENCE

    That's my good son. But where hast thou been then?

ROMEO

    I'll tell thee ere thou ask it me again.

    I have been feasting with mine enemy,

    Where on a sudden one hath wounded me

    That's by me wounded. Both our remedies

    Within thy help and holy <u>physic</u>（药品） lies.

    I bear no hatred, blessèd man, for, <u>lo</u>（看）,

    My <u>intercession</u>（求情） likewise <u>steads</u>（对……有利） my foe.

FRIAR LAWRENCE

    Be plain, good son, and <u>homely</u>（简单） in thy <u>drift</u>（含义）.

    <u>Riddling</u>（谜一般的） confession finds but riddling <u>shrift</u>（赦罪）.

ROMEO

    Then plainly know my heart's dear love is set

    On the fair daughter of rich Capulet.

As mine on hers, so hers is set on mine,
And all combined, save（只缺） what thou must combine
By holy marriage. When and where and how
We met, we wooed, and made exchange of vow
I'll tell thee as we pass（行走）, but this I pray,
That thou consent to marry us today.

FRIAR LAWRENCE

Holy Saint Francis, what a change is here!
Is Rosaline, that thou didst love so dear,
So soon forsaken（忘却）? Young men's love then lies
Not truly in their hearts, but in their eyes.
Jesu Maria, what a deal of brine（盐水）
Hath washed thy sallow（灰黄色的） cheeks for Rosaline!
How much salt water thrown away in waste
To season（给……调味） love, that of it doth not taste（毫无味道）!
The sun not yet thy sighs from heaven clears,
Thy old groans yet ringing in mine ancient ears.
Lo, here upon thy cheek the stain（污迹） doth sit（遗留）
Of an old tear that is not washed off yet.
If e'er thou wast thyself, and these woes thine,
Thou and these woes were all for Rosaline.
And art thou changed? Pronounce this sentence（格言） then:
Women may fall when there's no strength in men.

ROMEO

Thou chid'st（责骂） me oft（经常） for loving Rosaline.

FRIAR LAWRENCE

For doting（溺爱，发痴）, not for loving, pupil mine.

ROMEO

And bad'st（吩咐） me bury love.

FRIAR LAWRENCE

Not in a grave
To lay one in, another out to have.

ROMEO

I pray thee, chide me not. Her I love now
Doth grace for grace and love for love allow.
The other did not so.

FRIAR LAWRENCE

O, she knew well
Thy love did read by rote（机械地）, that could not spell.

But come, young waverer(摇摆不定的人), come, go with me.
In one respect I'll thy assistant be,
For this alliance may so happy prove
To turn your households' rancor(深仇) to pure love.

ROMEO

O, let us hence. I stand on(坚持，依赖) sudden haste.

FRIAR LAWRENCE

Wisely and slow. They stumble(跌倒) that run fast.

Excerpt 5 (from Act 3, Scene 1)

With the help of Friar Lawrence and the Nurse, the wedding of Romeo and Juliet is accomplished. Later that day, Benvolio and Mercutio are walking on the street when they encounter Tybalt with his men. Mercutio and Tybalt soon get into a war of words. Then Romeo appears. Tybalt loses no time to provoke him into a fight, but Romeo will not fight because, although unknown to the others, he and Tybalt are now relatives by marriage.

Enter Romeo.

TYBALT

Well, peace be with you, sir. Here comes my man.

MERCUTIO

But I'll be hanged, sir, if he wear your livery(男仆的制服).
Marry, go before to field(决斗场), he'll be your follower(追随你).
Your Worship(阁下) in that sense may call him "man."(仆人)

TYBALT

Romeo, the love I bear(怀有) thee can afford
No better term(名称) than this: thou art a villain.

ROMEO

Tybalt, the reason that I have to love thee
Doth much excuse the appertaining(相应的) rage
To such a greeting. Villain am I none.
Therefore farewell. I see thou knowest me not.

TYBALT

Boy, this shall not excuse the injuries
That thou hast done me. Therefore turn and draw(拔剑).

ROMEO

I do protest I never injured thee
But love thee better than thou canst devise(设想)

Till thou shalt know the reason of my love.

And so, good Capulet, which name I tender（尊重）

As dearly as mine own, be satisfied.

MERCUTIO

O calm, dishonorable, vile（卑劣的） submission（屈服）!

Alla stoccato[①] carries it away.   *He draws.*

Tybalt, you rat-catcher[②], will you walk?

TYBALT

What wouldst thou have with me?

MERCUTIO

Good king of cats, nothing but one of your nine lives[③], that I mean to make bold withal（拿取）, and, as（根据） you shall use（对待） me hereafter, dry-beat（痛打） the rest of the eight. Will you pluck your sword out of his pilcher（皮套） by the ears? Make haste, lest mine be about your ears ere it be out.

TYBALT

I am for you.   *He draws.*

ROMEO

Gentle Mercutio, put thy rapier up（收起）.

MERCUTIO

Come, sir, your *passado*[④].   *They fight.*

ROMEO

Draw, Benvolio, beat down their weapons.

        Romeo draws.

Gentlemen, for shame forbear（克制） this outrage（恶行）!

Tybalt! Mercutio! The Prince expressly（清楚地） hath

Forbid this bandying（斗殴） in Verona streets.

Hold, Tybalt! Good Mercutio!

        Romeo attempts to beat down their rapiers.
        Tybalt stabs（捅）*Mercutio.*

PETRUCHIO

Away, Tybalt!

        Tybalt, Petruchio, and their followers exit.

MERCUTIO

I am hurt.

---

① Alla Stoccato: literally, at the thrust (fencing term). Mercutio means that Tybalt's onslaught has apparently unarmed Romeo.

② rat-catcher: alluding to his name Tybalt. In *Reynard the Fox*, a popular tale, the Prince of Cats is named Tibalt, similar to Tybalt.

③ nine lives: According to a myth in many cultures, cats have multiple lives.

④ passado: forward thrust (fencing term).

A plague（瘟疫）o' both houses! I am sped（完了）.
Is he gone and hath nothing?

BENVOLIO

What, art thou hurt?

MERCUTIO

Ay, ay, a scratch（划伤）, a scratch. Marry, 'tis enough.
Where is my page?—Go, villain, fetch a surgeon.

Page exits.

ROMEO

Courage, man, the hurt cannot be much.

MERCUTIO

No, 'tis not so deep as a well, nor so wide as a church door, but 'tis enough. 'Twill serve（起作用）. Ask for me tomorrow, and you shall find me a grave man. I am peppered（完蛋）, I warrant, for this world. A plague o' both your houses! Zounds（见鬼）, a dog, a rat, a mouse, a cat, to scratch a man to death! A braggart（吹牛者）, a rogue, a villain that fights by the book of arithmetic（根据书本）! Why the devil came you between us? I was hurt under your arm.

ROMEO

I thought all for the best.

MERCUTIO

Help me into some house, Benvolio,
Or I shall faint. A plague o' both your houses!
They have made worms'（蠕虫） meat of me.
I have it, and soundly（彻底）, too. Your houses!

All but Romeo exit.

ROMEO

This gentleman, the Prince's near ally（近亲）,
My very friend, hath got this mortal hurt
In my behalf. My reputation stained
With Tybalt's slander（诋毁）—Tybalt, that an hour
Hath been my cousin! O sweet Juliet,
Thy beauty hath made me effeminate（软弱）
And in my temper softened valor's（勇猛） steel.

Enter Benvolio.

BENVOLIO

O Romeo, Romeo, brave Mercutio is dead.
That gallant（英勇的） spirit hath aspired the clouds（升天）,
Which too untimely（过早） here did scorn the earth（厌弃尘世）.

ROMEO

This day's black fate on more days doth depend（笼罩）.

This but begins the woe others（他日）must end.

Enter Tybalt.

BENVOLIO

Here comes the furious Tybalt back again.

ROMEO

Alive in triumph, and Mercutio slain（杀死）!
Away to heaven, respective（毕恭毕敬的）lenity（慈悲），
And fire-eyed fury be my conduct（向导） now. —
Now, Tybalt, take the "villain" back again
That late thou gavest me, for Mercutio's soul
Is but a little way above our heads,
Staying（等待） for thine to keep him company.
Either thou or I, or both, must go with him.

TYBALT

Thou wretched（该死的） boy that didst consort（陪伴） him here
Shalt with him hence.

ROMEO

This shall determine that.

They fight. Tybalt falls.

BENVOLIO

Romeo, away, begone!
The citizens are up, and Tybalt slain.
Stand not amazed（发呆）. The Prince will doom（判决） thee death
If thou art taken. Hence, be gone, away.

ROMEO

O, I am Fortune's fool!

BENVOLIO

Why dost thou stay?

Romeo exits.

✂ Excerpt 6 (from Act 3, Scene 5)

After Romeo flees, Prince Escalus arrives and banishes him from Verona. Romeo learns of the order and almost commits suicide when he realizes he may not be able to see Juliet again. Friar Lawrence comforts Romeo, and advises him to visit Juliet that night and then before daybreak, flee to Mantua. Meanwhile, Juliet's parents decide to marry her to Paris. At dawn the next day, Romeo and Juliet make their final exchanges of love before Romeo leaves for Mantua.

Unit 1

William Shakespeare and *Romeo and Juliet*

Enter Romeo and Juliet <u>aloft</u>（在高处）.

JULIET
    Wilt thou be gone? It is not yet near day.
    It was the nightingale, and not the <u>lark</u>（云雀）,
    That pierced the fearful hollow of thine ear.
    Nightly she sings on yond <u>pomegranate</u>（石榴） tree.
    Believe me, love, it was the nightingale.

ROMEO
    It was the lark, the <u>herald</u>（报信者） of the morn,
    No nightingale. Look, love, what envious <u>streak</u>s（光芒）
    Do <u>lace</u>（饰以花边） the severing clouds in yonder east.
    Night's candles are burnt out, and <u>jocund</u>（欢乐的） day
    Stands <u>tiptoe</u>（踮着脚） on the <u>misty</u>（雾蒙蒙的） mountain-tops.
    I must be gone and live, or stay and die.

JULIET
    Yond light is not daylight, I know it, I.
    It is some meteor that the sun exhaled
    To be to thee this night a <u>torchbearer</u>（火炬手）
    And light thee on thy way to Mantua.
    Therefore stay yet. Thou need'st not to be gone.

ROMEO
    Let me be ta'en; let me be put to death.
    I am content, so thou wilt have it so.
    I'll say yon gray is not the morning's eye;
    'Tis but the pale <u>reflex</u>（反光） of Cynthia[①]'s brow.
    Nor that is not the lark whose <u>notes</u>（啼叫声） do beat
    The vaulty heaven so high above our heads.
    I have more <u>care</u>（愿望） to stay than will to go.
    Come death and welcome. Juliet wills it so.
    How is 't, my soul? Let's talk. It is not day.

JULIET
    It is, it is. <u>Hie</u>（赶快） hence, begone, away!
    It is the lark that sings so out of tune,
    Straining harsh <u>discords</u>（不协和和弦） and unpleasing <u>sharps</u>（半升调）.
    Some say the lark makes sweet <u>division</u>（变奏）.
    This doth not so, for she divideth us.
    Some say the lark and loathèd toad changed eyes.

---

① Cynthia: another name of Artemis, an ancient Greek goddess, characterized as a virgin huntress and associated with the moon. The name comes from her birthplace Mt. Cynthus, on Delos.

O, now I would they had changed voices too,
Since arm from arm that voice doth us <u>affray</u>（古语：恐吓），
Hunting thee hence with <u>hunt's-up</u>（出猎号声） to the day.
O, now begone. More light and light it grows.

ROMEO
More light and light, more dark and dark our woes.

Enter Nurse.

NURSE
Madam.

JULIET
Nurse?

NURSE
Your lady mother is coming to your chamber.
The day is broke; be wary; look about. *She exits.*

JULIET
Then, window, let day in, and let life out.

ROMEO
Farewell, farewell. One kiss and I'll descend.

They kiss, and Romeo descends.

JULIET
Art thou gone so? Love, lord, ay husband, friend!
I must hear from thee every day in the hour,
For in a minute there are many days.
O, by this count I shall be much in years
Ere I again behold my Romeo.

ROMEO
Farewell.
I will omit no opportunity
That may convey my greetings, love, to thee.

JULIET
O, think'st thou we shall ever meet again?

ROMEO
I doubt it not; and all these woes shall serve
For sweet discourses in our times to come.

JULIET
O God, I have an <u>ill-divining</u>（预兆不详的） soul!
Methinks I see thee, now thou art so low,
As one dead in the bottom of a tomb.
Either my eyesight fails or thou lookest pale.

ROMEO

And trust me, love, in my eye so do you.
Dry sorrow drinks our blood. Adieu, adieu. *He exits.*

JULIET

O Fortune, Fortune, all men call thee <u>fickle</u>（变化无常的）.
If thou art fickle, what dost thou with him
That is renowned for faith? Be fickle, Fortune,
For then I hope thou wilt not keep him long,
But send him back.

Enter Lady Capulet.

LADY CAPULET

Ho, daughter, are you up?

JULIET

Who is 't that calls? It is my lady mother.
Is she not <u>down</u>（睡下） so late or up so early?
What <u>unaccustomed</u>（特殊的） cause <u>procures</u>（导致） her hither?

Juliet descends.

LADY CAPULET

Why, how now, Juliet?

JULIET

Madam, I am not well.

LADY CAPULET

<u>Evermore</u>（始终） weeping for your cousin's death?
What, wilt thou wash him from his grave with tears?
An if thou couldst, thou couldst not make him live.
Therefore <u>have done</u>（停止）. Some grief shows much of love,
But much of grief shows still some want of wit.

JULIET

Yet let me weep for such a <u>feeling</u>（痛心的） loss.

LADY CAPULET

So shall you feel the loss, but not the friend
Which you weep for.

JULIET

Feeling so the loss,
I cannot choose but ever weep the friend.

LADY CAPULET

Well, girl, thou weep'st not so much for his death
As that the villain lives which slaughtered him.

JULIET

    What villain, madam?

LADY CAPULET

    That same villain, Romeo.

JULIET, *aside*

    Villain and he be many miles <u>asunder</u>（相离）.—

    God pardon him. I do with all my heart,

    And yet no man like he doth <u>grieve</u>（使……悲伤） my heart.

LADY CAPULET

    That is because the <u>traitor</u>（背信弃义者） murderer lives.

JULIET

    Ay, madam, from the reach of these my hands.

    <u>Would</u>（但愿） none but I might <u>venge</u>（为……报仇） my cousin's death!

LADY CAPULET

    We will have <u>vengeance</u>（报复） for it, fear thou not.

    Then weep no more. I'll send to one in Mantua,

    Where that same banished <u>runagate</u>（逃亡者） doth live,

    Shall give him such an unaccustomed <u>dram</u>（少量烈酒）

    That he shall soon keep Tybalt company.

    And then, I hope, thou wilt be satisfied.

JULIET

    Indeed, I never shall be satisfied

    With Romeo till I behold him—dead—

    Is my poor heart, so for a kinsman <u>vexed</u>（苦恼的）.

    Madam, if you could find out but a man

    To bear a poison, I would <u>temper</u>（调制；稀释） it,

    That Romeo should, upon <u>receipt</u>（收到） thereof,

    Soon sleep in quiet. O, how my heart <u>abhors</u>（憎恶）

    To hear him named and cannot come to him

    To <u>wreak</u>（发泄） the love I bore my cousin

    Upon his body that hath slaughtered him.

LADY CAPULET

    Find thou the means, and I'll find such a man.

    But now I'll tell thee joyful <u>tidings</u>（消息）, girl.

JULIET

    And joy comes well in such a needy time.

    What are they, <u>beseech</u>（恳求） your Ladyship?

LADY CAPULET

    Well, well, thou hast a <u>careful</u>（体贴的） father, child,

> One who, to put thee from thy heaviness（愁闷），
> Hath sorted out（挑选出） a sudden day of joy
> That thou expects not, nor I looked not for.

JULIET
> Madam, in happy time! What day is that?

LADY CAPULET
> Marry, my child, early next Thursday morn
> The gallant, young, and noble gentleman,
> The County（=count伯爵） Paris, at Saint Peter's Church
> Shall happily make thee there a joyful bride.

JULIET
> Now, by Saint Peter's Church, and Peter too,
> He shall not make me there a joyful bride!
> I wonder at this haste, that I must wed
> Ere he that should be husband comes to woo.
> I pray you, tell my lord and father, madam,
> I will not marry yet, and when I do I swear
> It shall be Romeo, whom you know I hate,
> Rather than Paris. These are news indeed!

LADY CAPULET
> Here comes your father. Tell him so yourself,
> And see how he will take it at your hands.

Enter Capulet and Nurse.

CAPULET
> When the sun sets, the earth doth drizzle（飘下） dew,
> But for the sunset（陨落） of my brother's son
> It rains downright.
> How now, a conduit（喷泉）, girl? What, still in tears?
> Evermore show'ring? In one little body
> Thou counterfeits（仿制） a bark（船）, a sea, a wind.
> For still thy eyes, which I may call the sea,
> Do ebb and flow（潮涨潮落） with tears; the bark thy body is,
> Sailing in this salt flood; the winds thy sighs,
> Who, raging（激荡） with thy tears and they with them,
> Without（若没有） a sudden calm, will overset（倾覆）
> Thy tempest-tossèd（风吹浪打的） body.—How now, wife?
> Have you delivered to her our decree（决定）?

LADY CAPULET
> Ay, sir, but she will none, she gives you thanks.

I would the fool were married to her grave.
CAPULET
Soft, take me with you（讲明白点）, take me with you, wife.
How, will she none? Doth she not give us thanks?
Is she not proud（满意的）? Doth she not count her blessed,
Unworthy（低贱的） as she is, that we have wrought
So worthy a gentleman to be her bride（=bridegroom新郎）?
JULIET
Not proud you have, but thankful that you have.
Proud can I never be of what I hate,
But thankful even for hate that is meant love.
CAPULET
How, how, how, how? Chopped logic（诡辩）? What is this?
"Proud," and "I thank you," and "I thank you not,"
And yet "not proud"? Mistress minion（娇美的） you,
Thank me no thankings, nor proud me no prouds,
But fettle（保养） your fine joints（身子骨） 'gainst Thursday next
To go with Paris to Saint Peter's Church,
Or I will drag thee on a hurdle（囚笼） thither（去那儿）.
Out, you green-sickness carrion（腐尸）! Out, you baggage（婊子）!
You tallow face（蜡黄脸）!
LADY CAPULET
Fie（呸）, fie, what, are you mad?
JULIET, *kneeling*
Good father, I beseech you on my knees,
Hear me with patience but to speak a word.
CAPULET
Hang（该死） thee, young baggage, disobedient wretch（家伙）!
I tell thee what: get thee to church o' Thursday,
Or never after look me in the face.
Speak not; reply not; do not answer me.
My fingers itch（痒）.—Wife, we scarce thought us blessed
That God had lent us but this only child,
But now I see this one is one too much,
And that we have a curse in having her.
Out on her（见鬼去）, hilding（贱货）.
NURSE
God in heaven bless her!
You are to blame, my lord, to rate（责骂） her so.

CAPULET

And why, my Lady Wisdom? Hold your tongue.
Good Prudence（精明）, smatter（闲扯）with your gossips（长舌妇）, go.

NURSE

I speak no treason（叛逆）.

CAPULET

O, God 'i' g' eden（老天爷）!

NURSE

May not one speak?

CAPULET

Peace, you mumbling（叽里咕噜的）fool!
Utter your gravity（大道理）o'er a gossip's bowl（大酒杯）,
For here we need it not.

LADY CAPULET

You are too hot.

CAPULET

God's bread, it makes me mad.
Day, night, hour, tide（季节）, time, work, play,
Alone, in company, still my care（忧虑）hath been
To have her matched. And having now provided
A gentleman of noble parentage（出身）,
Of fair demesnes（地产）, youthful, and nobly liened（有背景）,
Stuffed, as they say, with honorable parts（品质）,
Proportioned（相称）as one's thought would wish a man—
And then to have a wretched puling（哭哭啼啼的）fool,
A whining mammet（傀儡）, in her fortune's tender（好运临头的时候）,
To answer "I'll not wed. I cannot love.
I am too young. I pray you, pardon me."
But, if you will not wed, I'll pardon you!
Graze（觅食）where you will, you shall not house with me.
Look to 't; think on 't. I do not use to（向来不）jest.
Thursday is near. Lay hand on heart; advise（考虑）.
If you be mine, I'll give you to my friend.
If you be not, hang, beg, starve, die in the streets,
For, by my soul, I'll ne'er acknowledge thee,
Nor what is mine shall never do thee good.
Trust to 't, bethink you. I'll not be forsworn（背弃誓言的）.

He exits.

JULIET

Is there no pity sitting in the clouds

That sees into the bottom of my grief?—
O sweet my mother, cast me not away.
Delay this marriage for a month, a week,
Or, if you do not, make the bridal bed（婚床）
In that dim monument（坟墓） where Tybalt lies.

LADY CAPULET
Talk not to me, for I'll not speak a word.
Do as thou wilt, for I have done with thee.

She exits.

JULIET, *rising*
O God! O nurse, how shall this be prevented?
My husband is on Earth, my faith in heaven.
How shall that faith return again to Earth
Unless that husband send it me from heaven
By leaving Earth? Comfort me; counsel me.—
Alack, alack, that heaven should practice stratagems（计谋）
Upon so soft a subject as myself.—
What sayst thou? Hast thou not a word of joy?
Some comfort, nurse.

NURSE
Faith, here it is.
Romeo is banished, and all the world to nothing
That he dares ne'er come back to challenge you,
Or, if he do, it needs must be by stealth（偷偷摸摸地）.
Then, since the case so stands as now it doth,
I think it best you married with the County.
O, he's a lovely gentleman!
Romeo's a dishclout（抹布） to him. An eagle, madam,
Hath not so green, so quick, so fair an eye
As Paris hath. Beshrew（诅咒） my very heart,
I think you are happy in this second match,
For it excels your first, or, if it did not,
Your first is dead, or 'twere as good（几乎一样） he were
As living here and you no use of him.

JULIET
Speak'st thou from thy heart?

NURSE
And from my soul too, else beshrew them both.

Unit 1

William Shakespeare and *Romeo and Juliet*

JULIET
    Amen.
NURSE
    What?
JULIET
    Well, thou hast comforted me marvelous much.
    Go in and tell my lady I am gone,
    Having displeased my father, to Lawrence' cell
    To make confession and to be absolved（赦罪）.
NURSE
    Marry, I will; and this is wisely done.   *She exits.*
JULIET
    Ancient damnation, O most wicked fiend!
    Is it more sin to wish me thus forsworn
    Or to dispraise（毁谤） my lord with that same tongue
    Which she hath praised him with above compare（无与伦比）
    So many thousand times? Go, counselor.
    Thou and my bosom henceforth shall be twain（两不相干）.
    I'll to the Friar to know his remedy.
    If all else fail, myself have power to die.
                                                                                 She exits.

Excerpt 7 (from Act 4, Scene 1)

Facing great pressure from her parents to get married, Juliet desperately turns to Friar Lawrence for help. When she arrives at the Friar's cell, Lawrence is speaking with Paris about the latter's impending marriage to Juliet.

                              Enter Friar Lawrence and County Paris.

FRIAR LAWRENCE
    On Thursday, sir? The time is very short.
PARIS
    My father Capulet will have it so,
    And I am nothing slow to slack（减缓） his haste.
FRIAR LAWRENCE
    You say you do not know the lady's mind?
    Uneven is the course. I like it not.

PARIS

    Immoderately（无节制地） she weeps for Tybalt's death,
    And therefore have I little talk of love,
    For Venus[①] smiles not in a house of tears.
    Now, sir, her father counts it dangerous
    That she do give her sorrow so much sway（势力），
    And in his wisdom hastes our marriage
    To stop the inundation（泛滥） of her tears,
    Which, too much minded by herself alone,
    May be put from her by society（伴侣）.
    Now do you know the reason of this haste.

FRIAR LAWRENCE, *aside*

    I would I knew not why it should be slowed.—
    Look, sir, here comes the lady toward my cell.

                          Enter Juliet.

PARIS

    Happily met, my lady and my wife.

JULIET

    That may be, sir, when I may be a wife.

PARIS

    That "may be" must be, love, on Thursday next.

JULIET

    What must be shall be.

FRIAR LAWRENCE

    That's a certain（肯定的） text.

PARIS

    Come you to make confession to this father?

JULIET

    To answer that, I should confess to you.

PARIS

    Do not deny to him that you love me.

JULIET

    I will confess to you that I love him.

PARIS

    So will you, I am sure, that you love me.

JULIET

    If I do so, it will be of more price

---

① Venus: an ancient Italian goddess of gardens and spring, identified by the Romans with Aphrodite as the goddess of love and beauty.

Being spoke behind your back than to your face.

PARIS

Poor soul, thy face is much abused with tears.

JULIET

The tears have got small victory by that,

For it was bad enough before their spite（恶意伤害）.

PARIS

Thou wrong'st it more than tears with that report.

JULIET

That is no slander（诽谤）, sir, which is a truth,

And what I spake, I spake it to my face.

PARIS

Thy face is mine, and thou hast slandered it.

JULIET

It may be so, for it is not mine own.—

Are you at leisure, holy father, now,

Or shall I come to you at evening Mass（弥撒）?

FRIAR LAWRENCE

My leisure serves me, pensive（忧伤的） daughter, now.—

My lord, we must entreat the time alone.

PARIS

God shield（阻止） I should disturb devotion（祈祷）!—

Juliet, on Thursday early will I rouse you.

Till then, adieu, and keep this holy kiss. *He exits.*

JULIET

O, shut the door, and when thou hast done so,

Come weep with me, past（没有） hope, past cure, past help.

FRIAR LAWRENCE

O Juliet, I already know thy grief.

It strains me past（超出） the compass（范围） of my wits.

I hear thou must, and nothing may prorogue（延期） it,

On Thursday next be married to this County.

JULIET

Tell me not, friar, that thou hearest of this,

Unless thou tell me how I may prevent it.

If in thy wisdom thou canst give no help,

Do thou but call my resolution wise,

And with this knife I'll help（避免） it presently（立即）.

She shows him her knife.

God joined my heart and Romeo's, thou our hands;
And ere this hand, by thee to Romeo's <u>sealed</u>（确立关系），
Shall be the <u>label</u>（印章）to another <u>deed</u>（婚约），
Or my true heart with <u>treacherous</u>（悖逆的） <u>revolt</u>（反叛）
Turn to another, this shall <u>slay</u>（杀死）them both.
Therefore out of thy long-experienced time
Give me some present counsel, or, <u>behold</u>（看），
'Twixt my <u>extremes</u>（绝境）and me this bloody knife
Shall play the <u>umpire</u>（仲裁）, <u>arbitrating</u>（裁定）that
Which the <u>commission</u>（权威）of thy years and <u>art</u>（技能，学识）
Could to no <u>issue</u>（结局）of true honor bring.
Be not so long to speak. I long to die
If what thou speak'st speak not of remedy.

FRIAR LAWRENCE

Hold, daughter, I do <u>spy</u>（看到）a kind of hope,
Which craves as desperate an <u>execution</u>（执行）
As that is desperate which we would prevent.
If, rather than to marry County Paris,
Thou hast the strength of will to slay thyself,
Then is it likely thou wilt undertake
A thing like death to chide away this shame,
That cop'st with death himself to 'scape from it;
And if thou darest, I'll give thee remedy.

JULIET

O, bid me leap, rather than marry Paris,
From off the <u>battlements</u>（城垛）of any tower,
Or walk in <u>thievish</u>（盗贼出没的）ways, or bid me <u>lurk</u>（潜藏）
Where <u>serpents</u>（巨蛇）are. Chain me with <u>roaring</u>（咆哮的）bears,
Or hide me nightly in a <u>charnel</u>（停尸房）house,
O'ercovered quite with dead men's <u>rattling</u>（嘎嘎作响的）bones,
With <u>reeky</u>（发臭的） <u>shank</u>s（小腿）and yellow <u>chapless</u>（掉了下巴的）skulls.
Or bid me go into a new-made grave
And hide me with a dead man in his <u>shroud</u>（裹尸布）
(Things that to hear them told have made me tremble),
And I will do it without fear or doubt,
To live an <u>unstained</u>（无瑕的）wife to my sweet love.

FRIAR LAWRENCE

Hold, then. Go home; be merry; give consent

To marry Paris. Wednesday is tomorrow.
Tomorrow night look that thou lie alone;
Let not the Nurse lie with thee in thy chamber.

Holding out a vial.

Take thou this <u>vial</u>（药水瓶）, being then in bed,
And this <u>distilling</u>（渗透躯体的） liquor drink thou off;
When presently through all thy veins shall run
A cold and <u>drowsy</u>（催眠的） <u>humor</u>（体液）; for no pulse
Shall keep his <u>native</u>（自然的） progress, but <u>surcease</u>（停止）.
No warmth, no breath shall <u>testify</u>（证明） thou livest.
The <u>roses</u>（玫瑰色） in thy lips and cheeks shall fade
To <u>paly ashes</u>（灰白）, thy <u>eyes' windows</u>（眼睑） fall
Like death when he shuts up the day of life.
Each part, deprived of <u>supple</u>（灵活的） <u>government</u>（运动能力）,
Shall, stiff and <u>stark</u>（僵硬的） and cold, appear like death,
And in this borrowed likeness of shrunk death
Thou shalt continue two and forty hours
And then awake as from a pleasant sleep.
Now, when the bridegroom in the morning comes
To rouse thee from thy bed, there art thou dead.
Then, as the manner of our country is,
In thy best robes uncovered on the <u>bier</u>（尸架）
Thou shalt be borne to that same ancient <u>vault</u>（地下墓室）
Where all the <u>kindred</u>（族人） of the Capulets lie.
In the meantime, against thou shalt awake,
Shall Romeo by my letters know our <u>drift</u>（意图）,
And hither shall he come, and he and I
Will watch thy waking, and that very night
Shall Romeo bear thee hence to Mantua.
And this shall free thee from this present shame,
If no <u>inconstant toy</u>（临时变卦） nor womanish fear
<u>Abate</u>（减弱） thy valor in the acting it.

JULIET

Give me, give me! O, tell not me of fear!

FRIAR LAWRENCE, *giving Juliet the vial*

Hold, get you gone. Be strong and <u>prosperous</u>（顺利的）
In this resolve. I'll send a friar with speed
To Mantua with my letters to thy lord.

JULIET

    Love give me strength, and strength shall <u>help afford</u>（提供帮助）.
    Farewell, dear father.

They exit in different directions.

> ✂ **Excerpt 8 (from Act 5, Scene 3)**
>
> *Friar Lawrence's plan goes wrong. On the one hand, when Juliet tells her father that she agrees to marry Paris, Capulet is so pleased that he moves up the wedding to the next morning. On the other hand, Romeo does not get the Friar's message; instead, he receives the news of Juliet's death from his servant. He immediately buys poison from an apothecary and rushes back to Verona, determined to die beside Juliet. Before he arrives at the Capulet tomb, however, Paris is already there.*

Enter Paris and his Page.

PARIS

    Give me thy torch, boy. Hence and stand <u>aloof</u>（远离）.
    Yet put it out, for I would not be seen.
    Under yond <u>yew</u>（紫杉） trees lay thee all along,
    Holding thy ear close to the hollow ground.
    So shall no foot upon the <u>churchyard</u>（教堂墓地） tread
    (Being loose, unfirm, with digging up of graves)
    But thou shalt hear it. Whistle then to me
    As signal that thou hearest something approach.
    Give me those flowers. Do as I bid thee. Go.

PAGE, *aside*

    I am almost afraid to stand alone
    Here in the churchyard. Yet I will adventure.

He moves away from Paris.

PARIS, *scattering flowers*

    Sweet flower, with flowers thy bridal bed I <u>strew</u>（撒满）
    (O woe, thy <u>canopy</u>（顶篷） is dust and stones!)
    Which with sweet water nightly I will <u>dew</u>（浇洒），
    Or, wanting that, with tears distilled by moans.
    The <u>obsequies</u>（葬礼） that I for thee will keep
    Nightly shall be to strew thy grave and weep.

Page whistles.

    The boy gives warning something doth approach.

Unit 1

William Shakespeare and *Romeo and Juliet*

What cursèd foot wanders this way tonight,
To cross my obsequies and true love's rite?
What, with a torch? <u>Muffle</u>（遮蔽） me, night, awhile.

He steps aside.

Enter Romeo and Balthasar.

ROMEO
Give me that <u>mattock</u>（鹤嘴锄） and the wrenching iron.
Hold, take this letter. Early in the morning
See thou deliver it to my lord and father.
Give me the light. Upon thy life I charge thee,
Whate'er thou hearest or seest, stand all aloof
And do not interrupt me in my course.
Why I descend into this bed of death
Is partly to behold my lady's face,
But chiefly to take thence from her dead finger
A precious ring, a ring that I must use
In dear employment. Therefore hence, begone.
But, if thou, <u>jealous</u>（猜疑的）, dost return to <u>pry</u>（窥探）
In what I farther shall intend to do,
By heaven, I will tear thee joint by joint
And <u>strew</u>（撒满） this hungry churchyard with thy limbs.
The time and my <u>intents</u>（意图） are savage-wild,
More fierce and more <u>inexorable</u>（无情的） far
Than <u>empty</u>（空腹的） tigers or the roaring sea.

BALTHASAR
I will be gone, sir, and not trouble you.

ROMEO
So shalt thou show me friendship. Take thou that.

Giving money.

Live and be prosperous, and farewell, good fellow.

BALTHASAR, *aside*
<u>For all this same</u>（仍然）, I'll hide me hereabout.
His looks I fear, and his intents I doubt.

He steps aside.

ROMEO, *beginning to force open the tomb*
Thou detestable <u>maw</u>（动物的胃）, thou <u>womb</u>（娘胎） of death,
<u>Gorged with</u>（吞噬了） the dearest <u>morsel</u>（佳肴） of the earth,
Thus I <u>enforce</u>（强使） thy rotten jaws to open,
And in <u>despite</u>（憎恨） I'll <u>cram</u>（塞满） thee with more food.

PARIS

    This is that banished haughty Montague
    That murdered my love's cousin, with which grief
    It is supposèd the fair creature died,
    And here is come to do some villainous shame（恶行）
    To the dead bodies. I will apprehend（逮捕） him.

Stepping forward.

    Stop thy unhallowed toil（邪恶的勾当）, vile Montague.
    Can vengeance be pursued further than death?
    Condemnèd（该死的） villain, I do apprehend thee.
    Obey and go with me, for thou must die.

ROMEO

    I must indeed, and therefore came I hither.
    Good gentle youth, tempt（激怒） not a desp'rate man.
    Fly hence and leave me. Think upon these gone.
    Let them affright（惊吓） thee. I beseech thee, youth,
    Put not another sin upon my head
    By urging me to fury. O, begone!
    By heaven, I love thee better than myself,
    For I come hither armed against myself.
    Stay not, begone, live, and hereafter say
    A madman's mercy bid thee run away.

PARIS

    I do defy thy commination（威吓）
    And apprehend thee for a felon（重罪犯） here.

ROMEO

    Wilt thou provoke me? Then have at thee（看剑）, boy!

They draw and fight.

PAGE

    O Lord, they fight! I will go call the watch（巡夜卫队）.

He exits.

PARIS

    O, I am slain! If thou be merciful,
    Open the tomb; lay me with Juliet.

He dies.

ROMEO

    In faith, I will.—Let me peruse（细看） this face.
    Mercutio's kinsman, noble County Paris!
    What said my man when my betossèd（烦扰的） soul
    Did not attend（注意听） him as we rode? I think

He told me Paris should have married Juliet.
Said he not so? Or did I dream it so?
Or am I mad, hearing him talk of Juliet,
To think it was so?—O, give me thy hand,
One writ with me in sour misfortune's book!
I'll bury thee in a triumphant grave.—

He opens the tomb.

A grave? O, no. A <u>lantern</u>（灯塔）, slaughtered youth,
For here lies Juliet, and her beauty makes
This vault a <u>feasting presence</u>（欢宴场） full of light.—
Death, lie thou there, by a dead man <u>interr</u>ed（埋葬）.

Laying Paris in the tomb.

How oft when men are at the point of death
Have they been merry, which their <u>keepers</u>（看护人） call
<u>A light'ning before death</u>!（回光返照） O, how may I
Call this a light'ning?—O my love, my wife,
Death, that hath sucked the honey of thy breath,
Hath had no power yet upon thy beauty.
Thou art not conquered. Beauty's <u>ensign</u>（旗帜） yet
Is <u>crimson</u>（深红） in thy lips and in thy cheeks,
And death's pale flag is not <u>advanc</u>èd（进占） there.—
Tybalt, liest thou there in thy bloody sheet?
O, what more favor can I do to thee
Than with that hand that cut thy youth in <u>twain</u>（两截）
To <u>sunder</u>（切断） his that was thine enemy?
Forgive me, cousin.—Ah, dear Juliet,
Why art thou yet so fair? Shall I believe
That <u>unsubstantial</u>（无形体的） death is <u>amorous</u>（多情）,
And that the lean <u>abhorr</u>èd（可憎的） monster keeps
Thee here in dark to be his <u>paramour</u>（情妇）?
For fear of that I still will stay with thee
And never from this palace of dim night
Depart again. Here, here will I remain
With worms that are thy <u>chambermaids</u>（婢女）. O, here
Will I set up my everlasting rest
And shake the <u>yoke</u>（束缚） of <u>inauspicious stars</u>（厄运）
From this <u>world-wearied</u>（厌世的） flesh! Eyes, look your last.
Arms, take your last embrace. And, lips, O, you
The doors of breath, seal with a righteous kiss

A dateless <u>bargain</u>（契约）to <u>engrossing</u>（包罗一切的） death.

Kissing Juliet.

Come, bitter conduct, come, <u>unsavory</u>（难吃的） guide!
Thou desperate pilot, now at once run（使……冲向） on
The <u>dashing</u>（撞碎） rocks thy <u>seasick</u>（厌倦航行的） weary bark!
Here's to my love. *Drinking.* O true <u>apothecary</u>（药剂师），
Thy drugs are quick. Thus with a kiss I die.

He dies.

Enter Friar Lawrence with lantern, <u>crow</u>（撬棍）, and spade.

FRIAR LAWRENCE

Saint Francis be my <u>speed</u>（保佑）! How oft tonight
Have my old feet stumbled at graves!—Who's there?

BALTHASAR

Here's one, a friend, and one that knows you well.

FRIAR LAWRENCE

Bliss be upon you. Tell me, good my friend,
What torch is yond that <u>vainly</u>（徒然） lends his light
To <u>grubs</u>（蛆） and eyeless skulls? As I discern,
It burneth in the Capels' monument.

BALTHASAR

It doth so, holy sir, and there's my master,
One that you love.

FRIAR LAWRENCE

Who is it?

BALTHASAR

Romeo.

FRIAR LAWRENCE

How long hath he been there?

BALTHASAR

Full half an hour.

FRIAR LAWRENCE

Go with me to the vault.

BALTHASAR

I dare not, sir.
My master knows not but I am gone hence,
And fearfully did menace me with death
If I did stay to <u>look on</u>（旁观） his intents.

FRIAR LAWRENCE

Stay, then. I'll go alone. Fear comes upon me.

Unit 1
William Shakespeare and *Romeo and Juliet*

O, much I fear some ill <u>unthrifty</u>（不幸的） thing.

BALTHASAR

As I did sleep under this yew tree here,

I dreamt my master and another fought,

And that my master slew him.

FRIAR LAWRENCE, *moving toward the tomb*

Romeo!—

Alack, alack, what blood is this which stains

The stony entrance of this <u>sepulcher</u>（坟茔）?

What mean these masterless and <u>gory</u>（血淋淋的） swords

To lie discolored by this place of peace?

Romeo! O, pale! Who else? What, Paris too?

And <u>steep</u>ed（浸透） in blood? Ah, what an <u>unkind</u>（凶险的） hour

Is guilty of this <u>lamentable</u>（可悲的） <u>chance</u>（意外）!

The lady stirs.

JULIET

O <u>comfortable</u>（令人欣慰的） friar, where is my lord?

I do remember well where I should be,

And there I am. Where is my Romeo?

FRIAR LAWRENCE

I hear some noise.—Lady, come from that nest

Of death, <u>contagion</u>（疫病）, and unnatural sleep.

A greater power than we can <u>contradict</u>（抗拒）

Hath <u>thwarted</u>（阻挠） our intents. Come, come away.

Thy husband in thy bosom there lies dead,

And Paris, too. Come, I'll <u>dispose of</u>（安排） thee

Among a sisterhood of holy nuns.

Stay not to question, for the watch is coming.

Come, go, good Juliet. I dare no longer stay.

JULIET

Go, get thee hence, for I will not away.

He exits.

What's here? A cup <u>closed</u>（紧握） in my true love's hand?

Poison, I see, hath been his <u>timeless</u>（永久的） end.—

O <u>churl</u>（吝啬鬼）, drunk all, and left no friendly drop

To help me after! I will kiss thy lips.

<u>Haply</u>（或许） some poison yet doth hang on them,

To make me die with a <u>restorative</u>（滋补剂）. *She kisses him.*

Thy lips are warm!

Enter Paris's Page and Watch.

FIRST WATCH
　　Lead, boy. Which way?

JULIET
　　Yea, noise? Then I'll be brief. O, happy <u>dagger</u>（短刀）,
　　This is thy <u>sheath</u>（刀鞘）. There rust, and let me die.

　　　　　　　　She takes Romeo's dagger, stabs herself, and dies.

PAGE
　　This is the place, there where the torch doth burn.

FIRST WATCH
　　The ground is bloody.—Search about the churchyard.
　　Go, some of you; whoe'er you find, <u>attach</u>（抓捕）.

　　　　　　　　　　　　　　　　　Some watchmen exit.

　　Pitiful sight! Here lies the County slain,
　　And Juliet bleeding, warm, and newly dead,
　　Who here hath lain this two days burièd.—
　　Go, tell the Prince. Run to the Capulets.
　　Raise up the Montagues. Some others search.

　　　　　　　　　　　　　　　　　　　　　Others exit.

　　We see the ground whereon these woes do lie,
　　But the true <u>ground</u>（原因）of all these piteous woes
　　We cannot without <u>circumstance</u>（证据）<u>descry</u>（发现）.

　　　　　Enter Watchmen with Romeo's man Balthasar.

SECOND WATCH
　　Here's Romeo's man. We found him in the churchyard.

FIRST WATCH
　　Hold him in safety till the Prince come hither.

　　　　　Enter Friar Lawrence and another Watchman.

THIRD WATCH
　　Here is a friar that trembles, sighs, and weeps.
　　We took this mattock and this spade from him
　　As he was coming from this churchyard's side.

FIRST WATCH
　　A great suspicion. <u>Stay</u>（看押）the Friar too.

　　　　　　　Enter the Prince with Attendants.

PRINCE
　　What misadventure is so early up
　　That calls our person from our morning rest?

Unit 1

William Shakespeare and *Romeo and Juliet*

Enter Capulet and Lady Capulet.

CAPULET
    What should it be that is so shrieked abroad?

LADY CAPULET
    O, the people in the street cry "Romeo,"
    Some "Juliet," and some "Paris," and all run
    With open outcry toward our monument.

PRINCE
    What fear is this which startles in our ears?

FIRST WATCH
    <u>Sovereign</u>（君主）, here lies the County Paris slain,
    And Romeo dead, and Juliet, dead before,
    Warm and new killed.

PRINCE
    Search, seek, and know how this foul murder comes.

FIRST WATCH
    Here is a friar, and slaughtered Romeo's man,
    With instruments upon them fit to open
    These dead men's tombs.

CAPULET
    O heavens! O wife, look how our daughter bleeds!
    This dagger hath mista'en, for, lo, his house
    Is empty on the back of Montague,
    And it mis-sheathèd in my daughter's bosom.

LADY CAPULET
    O me, this sight of death is as a bell
    That warns my old age to a sepulcher.

Enter Montague.

PRINCE
    Come, Montague, for thou art early up
    To see thy son and heir now early down.

MONTAGUE
    Alas, my <u>liege</u>（君主）, my wife is dead tonight.
    Grief of my son's exile hath stopped her breath.
    What further woe <u>conspires</u>（合谋）against mine age?

PRINCE Look, and thou shalt see.

MONTAGUE, *seeing Romeo dead*
    O thou untaught! What manners is in this,
    To <u>press</u>（争抢）before thy father to a grave?

PRINCE

    Seal up the mouth of outrage for awhile,

    Till we can clear these ambiguities

    And know their spring, their head, their true descent,

    And then will I be general of your woes

    And lead you even to death. Meantime forbear,

    And let <u>mischance</u>（不幸，灾难） be slave to patience.—

    Bring forth the parties of suspicion.

FRIAR LAWRENCE

    I am the greatest, able to do least,

    Yet most suspected, as the time and place

    Doth make against me, of this <u>direful</u>（悲惨的） murder.

    And here I stand, both to <u>impeach</u>（控告） and <u>purge</u>（洗雪）

    Myself condemnèd and myself excused.

PRINCE

    Then say at once what thou dost know in this.

FRIAR LAWRENCE

    I will be brief, for my short date of breath

    Is not so long as is a tedious tale.

    Romeo, there dead, was husband to that Juliet,

    And she, there dead, that Romeo's faithful wife.

    I married them, and their stol'n marriage day

    Was Tybalt's doomsday, whose untimely death

    Banished the new-made bridegroom from this city,

    For whom, and not for Tybalt, Juliet <u>pined</u>（悲伤憔悴）.

    You, to remove that siege of grief from her,

    <u>Betrothed</u>（许配） and would have married her perforce

    To County Paris. Then comes she to me,

    And with wild looks bid me devise some mean

    To rid her from this second marriage,

    Or in my cell there would she kill herself.

    Then gave I her (so <u>tutored</u>〈指导〉 by my art)

    A sleeping potion, which so took effect

    As I intended, for it wrought on her

    The form of death. Meantime I writ to Romeo

    That he should hither come as this dire night

    To help to take her from her borrowed grave,

    Being the time the potion's force should cease.

    But he which bore my letter, Friar John,

Unit 1
William Shakespeare and *Romeo and Juliet*

  Was <u>stayed</u>（阻碍） by accident, and yesternight
  Returned my letter back. Then all alone
  At the prefixèd hour of her waking
  Came I to take her from her kindred's vault,
  Meaning to keep her <u>closely</u>（秘密地） at my cell
  Till I conveniently could send to Romeo.
  But when I came, some minute ere the time
  Of her awakening, here untimely lay
  The noble Paris and true Romeo dead.
  She wakes, and I entreated her come forth
  And bear this work of heaven with patience.
  But then a noise did scare me from the tomb,
  And she, too desperate, would not go with me
  But, as it seems, did violence on herself.
  All this I know, and to the marriage
  Her nurse is <u>privy</u>（私下知情的）. And if <u>aught</u>（任何事） in this
  <u>Miscarried</u>（失败） by my fault, let my old life
  Be sacrificed some hour before his time
  Unto the <u>rigor</u>（严厉） of severest law.

PRINCE
  We still have known thee for a holy man.—
  Where's Romeo's man? What can he say to this?

BALTHASAR
  I brought my master news of Juliet's death,
  And then in post he came from Mantua
  To this same place, to this same monument.
  This letter he early bid me give his father
  And threatened me with death, going in the vault,
  If I departed not and left him there.

PRINCE
  Give me the letter. I will look on it.—

              He takes Romeo's letter.

  Where is the County's page, that raised the watch?—
  Sirrah, what made your master in this place?

PAGE
  He came with flowers to strew his lady's grave
  And bid me stand aloof, and so I did.
  Anon comes one with light to ope the tomb,
  And by and by my master drew on him,

And then I ran away to call the watch.

PRINCE

This letter doth make good the Friar's words,
Their course of love, the tidings of her death;
And here he writes that he did buy a poison
Of a poor 'pothecary, and <u>therewithal</u>（随即）
Came to this vault to die and lie with Juliet.
Where be these enemies?—Capulet, Montague,
See what a <u>scourge</u>（灾祸） is laid upon your hate,
That heaven finds means to kill your joys with love,
And I, for <u>winking at</u>（纵容） your <u>discord</u>s（不和） too,
Have lost <u>a brace of</u>（一双） kinsmen. All are punished.

CAPULET

O brother Montague, give me thy hand.
This is my daughter's jointure①, for no more
Can I demand.

MONTAGUE

But I can give thee more,
For I will raise her statue in pure gold,
That whiles Verona by that name is known,
There shall no figure at such <u>rate</u>（等级） be set
As that of true and faithful Juliet.

CAPULET

As rich shall Romeo's by his lady's lie,
Poor sacrifices of our <u>enmity</u>（仇恨）.

PRINCE

A glooming peace this morning with it brings.
The sun for sorrow will not show his head.
Go hence to have more talk of these sad things.
Some shall be pardoned, and some punishèd.
For never was a story of more woe
Than this of Juliet and her Romeo.

All exit.

---

① jointure: an estate or property settled on a woman in consideration of marriage, to be owned by her after her husband's death.

Unit 1

William Shakespeare and *Romeo and Juliet*

1.2.4 Exercises

❶ Give a brief answer to each of the following questions.

Act 1

1) What is the Prince's sentence for the street fray between the Montagues and the Capulets?
2) Why is Romeo so depressed at the beginning of the play?
3) Why does Romeo go to the Capulet feast?
4) What's Romeo's first impression of Juliet? What does he compare her to?
5) Why does Capulet prevent Tybalt from attacking Romeo? What does Tybalt threaten to do?
6) What do Romeo and Juliet say after they learn the identity of each other?

Act 2

7) What does Juliet think of the fact that Romeo is a family enemy?
8) What does Juliet ask Romeo to do at the end of their meeting at the balcony?
9) How does Friar Lawrence respond to Romeo's intention to marry Juliet at first? Why does he agree to marry Romeo and Juliet in the end?

Act 3

10) Why is Romeo exiled?
11) What does Romeo think of his decreed banishment? What plan does Friar Lawrence set forth for him?
12) What advice does the Nurse give Juliet concerning her marriage with Paris? How does Juliet respond?

Act 4

13) What plan does Friar Lawrence propose to Juliet?
14) What does Capulet do when Juliet feigns obedience? What disastrous effect might this have for Friar Lawrence's plan?
15) What do Juliet's parents think is the cause of her supposed death?

Act 5

16) What does Romeo do in Mantua after he receives the news of Juliet's death?
17) Why does Friar John fail to deliver Friar Lawrence's message to Romeo?
18) Why does Romeo kill Paris? What does Paris ask Romeo to do as he is dying?
19) What does Romeo think when he sees Juliet's body in the tomb?
20) How does Romeo kill himself? How does Juliet kill herself?

❷ Identify the following characters.

1) _____ falls in love with the son of her family's foe, and asks him to prove his sincerity by marrying her. When her husband kills her cousin, she sides with the former and demonstrates so much strength that she risks her life in order to get united

with him.

2) _____ loves his daughter very much but makes the mistake of trying to impose his opinion on her. He is usually an easygoing man, but when his authority is challenged, he can be tyrannical.

3) _____ tries to preserve order by declaring death sentence on anyone of the two feuding families who disturbs public peace. However, he shows mercy on Romeo after the young man violates his decree.

4) _____ marries Romeo and Juliet in the hope of reconciling the two families. However, when his plan goes wrong, it leads to the death of the young couple.

5) _____ often teases Romeo with bawdy jokes. He is quick to respond to attacks, and is ready to fight Tybalt when the latter insults Romeo. Unfortunately, he is killed by Tybalt when Romeo tries to separate them.

6) _____ finds out the reason for Romeo's melancholy and encourages him to go to the Capulet feast, where Romeo meets Juliet.

7) _____ is torn between extreme joy, when he falls in love and gets married, and extreme despair, when he kills his wife's cousin and is banished. Desperate, he claims that he is "Fortune's fool".

8) _____ helps Juliet marry Romeo, but when Romeo is banished, she advises Juliet to marry another man, which Juliet considers as an act of betrayal.

9) _____ is unaware that he is in the middle of two lovers. He loves Juliet sincerely and comes to mourn her after her burial. He is killed in the ensuing fight with Romeo.

10) _____ views Romeo's visit to the Capulet feast as an intrusion and spares no effort taking revenge on Romeo for the insult.

❸ Plot Review

In the streets of Verona servants from two 1) _____ families, the Montagues and the Capulets, start a chaotic fight. To prevent further violence, the ruler of the city, Prince Escalus, decrees a 2) _____ penalty for anyone who disturbs public order in future.

Romeo, son of old Montague, is 3) _____ because a beautiful girl, Rosaline, does not return his affection. Meanwhile, Juliet, daughter of old Capulet, has a 4) _____, the young and rich Paris. Old Capulet agrees to let him meet Juliet at a party to be held that night. Romeo learns Rosaline is also invited to the party. Concealing his identity behind a 5) _____, he goes there as well, where he is spotted by Tybalt, a fiery member of the Capulet clan. Tybalt desires to fight Romeo, but is required by old Capulet to keep 6) _____. During the party, Romeo sees Juliet, and the two fall in love at first 7) _____. Later, they learn the

Unit 1
William Shakespeare and *Romeo and Juliet*

8) _____ of each other from Juliet's nurse, and both are deeply dismayed. That night Romeo, too much in love to go home to sleep, steals to Juliet's house, discovers her alone leaning on the balcony and overhears her words of 9) _____ for him. Excited, Romeo reveals himself. The two exchange vows of love and decide to 10) _____ the next day.

Romeo then seeks help from Friar Lawrence who, hoping their union will dissolve the 11) _____ between the two families, promises to marry the two that afternoon. Meanwhile, Tybalt sends Romeo a 12) _____ to fight, but Romeo refuses because he knows that Tybalt is Juliet's cousin. Romeo's friend Mercutio, however, takes his sword and rushes to his friend's 13) _____. Romeo tries to break up the fight, but in the process Tybalt gives Mercutio a mortal 14) _____ under Romeo's arm. Enraged at the death of his friend, Romeo kills Tybalt. As a result, the Prince 15) _____ Romeo from Verona. The news 16) _____ Romeo who then follows the Friar's advice to flee to Mantua at dawn next day. Before leaving, he spends the wedding night with Juliet.

After Romeo's departure, Juliet learns that her father has arranged for her to marry Paris in an effort to make her 17) _____. After futile resistance, Juliet goes to Friar Lawrence for help. The Friar gives her a 18) _____ that will cause her to appear dead until Romeo can come to rescue her. Juliet then pretends 19) _____ to her parents and agrees to marry Paris. Old Capulet is so pleased that he brings the wedding 20) _____ to the following morning, which forces Juliet to take action that night.

In Mantua, Romeo receives the news of Juliet's 21) _____ before the arrival of Friar Lawrence's messenger, who has been delayed by an outbreak of 22) _____. Not knowing the Friar's scheme, Romeo buys 23) _____ from an apothecary and determines to go to Verona to die beside Juliet's body. Reaching the Capulet vault at night, Romeo is confronted by Paris, who has come to 24) _____ his lost bride and mistakenly believes that Romeo has come to take 25) _____ on the dead bodies. In a fight that ensues, Romeo kills Paris and enters the vault. After bidding farewell to Juliet with a 26) _____, he drinks the poison and dies by her side. Soon Friar Lawrence arrives to deliver Juliet from the tomb, but Juliet awakens, finds Romeo dead, and refuses to 27) _____ with the Friar. Left alone, Juliet kisses Romeo and plunges his 28) _____ into her breast. Then the Prince, the Capulets and the Montagues all arrive. After the Friar tells them of the unhappy 29) _____ which has befallen Romeo and Juliet, the two families are finally 30) _____ with each other.

英美戏剧与电影
English and American Drama and Film

4 **Identify the speakers of the following lines, briefly tell the situation in which each of them is uttered, and explain its significance.**

1) From forth the fatal loins of these two foes
   A pair of star-crossed lovers take their life;
   Whose misadventured piteous overthrows
   Doth with their death bury their parents' strife.
2) If ever you disturb our streets again,
   Your lives shall pay the forfeit of the peace.
3) Tut, man, one fire burns out another's burning.
   One pain is lessened by another's anguish.
   Turn giddy, and be helped by backward turning.
   One desperate grief cures with another's languish.
   Take thou some new infection to thy eye,
   And the rank poison of the old will die.
4) And, to say truth, Verona brags of him
   To be a virtuous and well-governed youth.
   I would not for the wealth of all this town
   Here in my house do him disparagement.
5) O dear account! My life is my foe's debt.
6) My only love, sprung from my only hate!
   Too early seen unknown, and known too late!
7) He jests at scars that never felt a wound.
8) But soft, what light through yonder window breaks?
   It is the east, and Juliet is the sun.
9) O Romeo, Romeo, wherefore art thou Romeo?
   Deny thy father and refuse thy name,
   Or if thou wilt not, be but sworn my love,
   And I'll no longer be a Capulet.
10) What's in a name? That which we call a rose
    By any other word would smell as sweet.
11) Is Rosaline, that thou didst love so dear,
    So soon forsaken? Young men's love then lies
    Not truly in their hearts, but in their eyes.
12) In one respect I'll thy assistant be,
    For this alliance may so happy prove
    To turn your households' rancor to pure love.
13) Therefore love moderately: long love doth so;
    Too swift arrives as tardy as too slow.

14) A plague o' both your houses!
   They have made worms' meat of me.
15) O, I am Fortune's fool!
16) Wilt thou be gone? It is not yet near day.
   It was the nightingale, and not the lark,
   That pierced the fearful hollow of thine ear.
17) Thank me no thankings, nor proud me no prouds.
18) Death, that hath sucked the honey of thy breath,
   Hath had no power yet upon thy beauty.
19) Yea, noise? Then I'll be brief. O, happy dagger,
   This is thy sheath. There rust, and let me die.
20) Go hence to have more talk of these sad things.
   Some shall be pardoned, and some punishèd.
   For never was a story of more woe
   Than this of Juliet and her Romeo.

❺ Questions for essay or discussion

1) What do you think are the themes of this play?
2) What are the forces contributing to the tragedy of Romeo and Juliet?
3) How do different characters in the play represent different views of love?
4) Both Romeo and Juliet commit suicide in the end. Is it a sudden choice that they make on impulse, or have they thought about death before? How are their deaths foreshadowed in the play?
5) You must have had a general idea of the story before. How has the reading of the original play enriched your feeling or understanding of it? Give some examples.

Unit 2

Oscar Wilde and *An Ideal Husband*

2.1 Oscar Wilde: Life and Works

2.1.1 About the Playwright

Oscar Wilde (1854—1900) was a celebrity wit, aesthete, poet, novelist, philosophical essayist, dramatist, and prison convict. He was a spokesman for the late 19th-century Aesthetic Movement in England, which advocated art for art's sake. Oscar Wilde has been identified as a key figure within gay criticism. He is now recognized as a highly professional writer, acutely aware of his readership at a variety of levels, and also one who deliberately and systematically explored the oral dimension.

Oscar Wilde was born on October 10, 1854 in Dublin, Ireland to two accomplished parents, his father being a famous eye surgeon and his mother, known by her literary name as Speranza, noted for collecting Irish folk stories in the western hills in the late 1870s. His father's passion for Ireland's past, and his mother's campaigns for the future of a nation (which did not come to fruition until 1922 when Ireland gained independence from colonial rule of Great Britain), assured a political awareness for Wilde.

Wilde was a brilliant classics scholar at Trinity College, Dublin. After Trinity, he went to Magdalen College, Oxford, where he took a distinguished degree. Among his influences in Oxford was Professor of Art John Ruskin, who had published important books on northern Gothic art and on Italian art, especially the art of Venice. Ruskin's commitment to the social practice of aestheticism—the ideal of making life beautiful for all—had a lasting impact. Art was one of Wilde's primary passions, and his special passion seemed to have been for decoration and the decorative arts. He agreed with Walter Pater, a contemporary art critic, that art must best serve the needs of art. He felt, for example, that poetry did not serve religious, political, social, or biographical goals. Its ends were aesthetic and its pleasures were in its sounds, images, and thoughts.

Partly because of his brilliance and partly because he was one of the age's greatest conversationalists, Wilde was soon in the company of the famous and amusing people of his generation. Some of his conversational gift is apparent in his plays.

The period from 1890 to 1895 brought Wilde to the height of his writing career. His best-known novel, *The Picture of Dorian Gray*, appeared in 1891, which is the story of a young man whose sensual life eats away at him and eventually destroys him. The novel's failure led Wilde to try the stage, where he was a signal success. Wilde's first comedy, *Lady Windermere's Fan* (1892), was his first supreme success on the London stage. A little more than a year later, on April 19, 1893, Wilde's second comedy, *A Woman of No Importance*, opened in a production by Herbert Beerbohm Tree. It centres on the discovery of a dire secret and is at its most animated and conspicuously Wildean in the witty speeches of a dandified male aristocrat. Both plays have a noticeable feminist bias in that they stress the innate strength of their central female characters, a strength which draws on, and finally masters, a certain Puritanism. In April 1895, at the time of Wilde's arrest, charged with illegal homosexual practices, both the carefully plotted *An Ideal Husband* and *The Importance of Being Earnest* were playing to large London audiences. As the scandal developed, first Wilde's name was removed from the hoardings outside the theatres, then the runs of both plays were abruptly terminated.

By his own admission, his life was marked by an overindulgence in sensuality: "What paradox was to me in the sphere of thought, perversity became to me in the sphere of passion." He married Constance Lloyd in 1884 and soon had two sons. But by 1891 he had already had several homosexual liaisons, one of which was to bring him to ruin. His relationship with the much younger Lord Alfred Douglas, nicknamed "Bosie", ended with Douglas's father, the Marquess of Queensberry, publicly denouncing Wilde as a sodomite. Urged on by Bosie, Wilde sued for libel but lost. As a result, in 1895 he was tried for sodomy, convicted, and sentenced to hard labor for two years. In London, Wilde's crime and trial were scandal of the decade, perhaps of the century. He was bankrupt. His wife divorced him. He was denied the chance to see his sons. Public outrage, registered by the press, at how the darling of the aristocracy and prince of aesthetes had conned their admiration and respect, was astonishing. Journalists reported every detail of the libel case as it was tried. Vilification did not stop at Wilde; the entire literary school with which Wilde was associated fell instantly into the same disrepute. Wilde's actions have been seen as self-destructive, but they are also consistent with his efforts to force society to examine its own hypocrisy. Unfortunately, his efforts in court and prison ruined him and he died in exile in Paris on November 30, 1900, evidently of an infection of the inner ear three years after his release. Wilde's reputation as playwright was made and broken in a matter of a few years, and it was not restored until after his death.

2.1.2 Oscar Wilde's Major Plays

Salomé (French version) (1891, first performed in Paris 1896)《莎乐美》
Lady Windermere's Fan (1892)《温夫人的扇子》
A Woman of No Importance (1893)《无足轻重的女人》
An Ideal Husband (1895)《理想丈夫》
The Importance of Being Earnest (1895)《认真的重要性》

2.2 *An Ideal Husband*

2.2.1 About the Play

An Ideal Husband is one of the most serious of Wilde's social comedies. The plot turns on the exposure of discrepancies between the public role and private reality of a distinguished politician. The pressure of high-minded public opinion, exercised by the press, threatens to topple the career of Sir Robert Chiltern, who is blackmailed by the unscrupulous Mrs. Cheveley, for the corruption in which he engaged to launch his career 18 years earlier.

In the play, Wilde combines scintillating wit with both farce and melodrama, creating a piece that, over the course of its four acts, offers biting social and political commentary while espousing a philosophy that has the primacy of love and compassion as its focal point. Taken together, these elements compel Wilde's audience to consider what, exactly, makes a person truly moral.

Wilde's wit is on display throughout the play. Seemingly without effort, he produces one epigram after another. These concise, pithy, often paradoxical statements are uttered by minor and major characters alike and give *An Ideal Husband* an entirely playful sheen. George Bernard Shaw lavished praise on the play when it first hit the stage, declaring: "In a certain sense Mr. Wilde is to me our only thorough playwright. He plays with everything: with wit, with philosophy, with drama, with actors and audience, with the whole theatre."

Structurally, *An Ideal Husband* is a formulaic well-made play. The four-act drama unfolds in an orderly fashion, beginning with "exposition" through Society gossip, moving to the "complication" when the woman with a past turns up, building to the climactic *"scène à faire"* in Lord Goring's rooms where misunderstanding and malevolence peak, before settling it all in a "denouement" that restores the political and domestic *status quo*. Sir Robert Chiltern's career and his marriage are not just saved but enhanced by the end of the play; the wicked woman, Mrs. Cheveley, has been hounded out; the dandy, philosopher and *raisonneur* Lord Goring, is to be married into the fold.

2.2.2 Characters

Sir Robert Chiltern, baronet, Under-Secretary for Foreign Affairs in the English government. He is considered as an upright politician by the public and an ideal husband by his wife.

Lady Gertrude Chiltern, Sir Robert's wife. She is a woman with strict moral principles.

Mabel Chiltern, Sir Robert's younger sister. She is a pretty, witty young woman who falls in love with Lord Goring.

Lord Goring, viscount, is the best friend of the Chilterns. He is an idle man but turns out to be very helpful to his friends.

Lord Caversham, earl, father to Lord Goring. He is an aristocrat with traditional views on life.

Phipps, Lord Goring's servant. He is characterized by his impassivity and is described as an ideal butler.

Mrs. Cheveley, a woman with a past who has recently returned from abroad. Ambitious and cunning, she is the villain of the story.

Lady Markby, Mrs. Cheveley's friend. She is a pleasant and popular woman in upper society.

The Countess of Basildon and **Mrs. Marchmont**, high society women who frivolously banter on a number of topics at Sir Robert's dinner party.

Vicomte de Nanjac, Attaché at the French Embassy in London.

Tommy Trafford, Sir Robert's secretary, a man with a "brilliant future". He makes innumerable proposals to Mabel Chiltern but is foiled in all his attempts. He does not appear on stage.

2.2.3 Selected Readings from the Play

Excerpt 1 (from Act 1)

Sir Robert Chiltern is holding a political party in his house. His guests are genteel people who generally talk in a witty, polished manner. Among these are Lady Basildon and Mrs. Marchmont, who speak to each other languidly and cleverly, and Lord Caversham, father of Lord Goring, who bemoans the idleness of his son and the excesses of London Society. The most important arrival, however, is Mrs. Cheveley, who has come to speak specifically to Sir Robert.

[SIR ROBERT CHILTERN *enters. A man of forty, but looking somewhat younger. Clean-shaven, with finely-cut features, dark-haired and dark-eyed. A personality of mark. Not popular—few personalities are. But intensely admired by the few, and deeply respected by the many. The note of his manner is that of perfect <u>distinction</u>（卓越）, with a slight touch of pride. One feels that he is conscious of the success he has made in life. A nervous temperament, with a tired look. The firmly-<u>chiselled</u>（雕琢） mouth and chin contrast strikingly with the romantic expression in the deep-set eyes. The <u>variance</u>（差异） is suggestive of an almost complete separation of passion and intellect, as though thought and emotion were each isolated in its own sphere through some violence of will-power. There is nervousness in the nostrils, and in the pale, thin, pointed hands. It would be inaccurate to call him <u>picturesque</u>（优美如画的）. Picturesqueness cannot survive the House of Commons*[1]. *But Vandyck*[2] *would have liked to have painted his head.*]

SIR ROBERT CHILTERN: Good evening, Lady Markby! I hope you have brought Sir John with you?

LADY MARKBY: Oh! I have brought a much more charming person than Sir John. Sir John's temper since he has taken seriously to politics has become quite unbearable. Really, now that the House of Commons is trying to become useful, it does a great deal of harm.

SIR ROBERT CHILTERN: I hope not, Lady Markby. At any rate we do our best to waste the public time, don't we? But who is this charming person you have been kind enough to bring to us?

---

[1] House of Commons: the lower house of the UK parliament. The upper house is the House of Lords.
[2] Vandyck: or Sir Anthony van Dyck (1599–1641), a Flemish Baroque artist who became the leading court painter in England. He is most famous for his portraits of Charles I of England and his family and court, painted with a relaxed elegance that was to be the dominant influence on English portrait-painting for the next 150 years.

Unit 2

Oscar Wilde and *An Ideal Husband*

LADY MARKBY: Her name is Mrs. Cheveley! One of the Dorsetshire[①] Cheveleys, I suppose. But I really don't know. Families are so mixed nowadays. Indeed, as a rule, everybody turns out to be somebody else.

SIR ROBERT CHILTERN: Mrs. Cheveley? I seem to know the name.

LADY MARKBY: She has just arrived from Vienna.

SIR ROBERT CHILTERN: Ah! yes. I think I know whom you mean.

LADY MARKBY: Oh! she goes everywhere there, and has such pleasant scandals about all her friends. I really must go to Vienna next winter. I hope there is a good chef at the Embassy.

SIR ROBERT CHILTERN: If there is not, the Ambassador will certainly have to be recalled （召回）. Pray （请） point out Mrs. Cheveley to me. I should like to see her.

LADY MARKBY: Let me introduce you. *[To MRS. CHEVELEY.]* My dear, Sir Robert Chiltern is dying to know you!

SIR ROBERT CHILTERN *[bowing]*: Every one is dying to know the brilliant Mrs. Cheveley. Our attachés （随员） at Vienna write to us about nothing else.

MRS. CHEVELEY: Thank you, Sir Robert. An acquaintance that begins with a compliment is sure to develop into a real friendship. It starts in the right manner. And I find that I know Lady Chiltern already.

SIR ROBERT CHILTERN: Really?

MRS. CHEVELEY: Yes. She has just reminded me that we were at school together. I remember it perfectly now. She always got the good conduct prize. I have a distinct recollection of Lady Chiltern always getting the good conduct prize!

SIR ROBERT CHILTERN *[smiling]*: And what prizes did you get, Mrs. Cheveley?

MRS. CHEVELEY: My prizes came a little later on in life. I don't think any of them were for good conduct. I forget!

SIR ROBERT CHILTERN: I am sure they were for something charming!

MRS. CHEVELEY: I don't know that women are always rewarded for being charming. I think they are usually punished for it! Certainly, more women grow old nowadays through the faithfulness of their admirers than through anything else! At least that is the only way I can account for the terribly haggard （憔悴的） look of most of your pretty women in London!

SIR ROBERT CHILTERN: What an appalling philosophy that sounds! To attempt to classify you, Mrs. Cheveley, would be an impertinence （鲁莽）. But may I ask, at heart, are you an optimist or a pessimist? Those seem to be the only two fashionable religions left to us nowadays.

MRS. CHEVELEY: Oh, I'm neither. Optimism begins in a broad grin, and Pessimism ends with blue spectacles. Besides, they are both of them merely poses.

---

① Dorsetshire: a county in southern England.

SIR ROBERT CHILTERN: You prefer to be natural?

MRS. CHEVELEY: Sometimes. But it is such a very difficult pose to keep up.

SIR ROBERT CHILTERN: What would those modern psychological novelists, of whom we hear so much, say to such a theory as that?

MRS. CHEVELEY: Ah! the strength of women comes from the fact that psychology cannot explain us. Men can be analysed, women... merely adored.

SIR ROBERT CHILTERN: You think science cannot grapple with the problem of women?

MRS. CHEVELEY: Science can never grapple with the irrational. That is why it has no future before it, in this world.

SIR ROBERT CHILTERN: And women represent the irrational.

MRS. CHEVELEY: Well-dressed women do.

SIR ROBERT CHILTERN [with a polite bow]: I fear I could hardly agree with you there. But do sit down. And now tell me, what makes you leave your brilliant Vienna for our gloomy London—or perhaps the question is indiscreet?

MRS. CHEVELEY: Questions are never indiscreet. Answers sometimes are.

SIR ROBERT CHILTERN: Well, at any rate, may I know if it is politics or pleasure?

MRS. CHEVELEY: Politics are my only pleasure. You see nowadays it is not fashionable to flirt till one is forty, or to be romantic till one is forty-five, so we poor women who are under thirty, or say we are, have nothing open to us but politics or philanthropy. And philanthropy seems to me to have become simply the refuge of people who wish to annoy their fellow-creatures. I prefer politics. I think they are more…becoming!

SIR ROBERT CHILTERN: A political life is a noble career!

MRS. CHEVELEY: Sometimes. And sometimes it is a clever game, Sir Robert. And sometimes it is a great nuisance.

SIR ROBERT CHILTERN: Which do you find it?

MRS. CHEVELEY: I? A combination of all three.

[Drops her fan.]

SIR ROBERT CHILTERN [picks up fan]: Allow me!

MRS. CHEVELEY: Thanks.

SIR ROBERT CHILTERN: But you have not told me yet what makes you honour London so suddenly. Our season is almost over.

MRS. CHEVELEY: Oh! I don't care about the London season（社交季）! It is too matrimonial（与婚姻有关的）. People are either hunting for husbands, or hiding from them. I wanted to meet you. It is quite true. You know what a woman's curiosity is. Almost as great as a man's! I wanted immensely to meet you, and... to ask you to do something for me.

SIR ROBERT CHILTERN: I hope it is not a little thing, Mrs. Cheveley. I find that little things are so very difficult to do.

MRS. CHEVELEY [*after a moment's reflection*]: No, I don't think it is quite a little thing.

SIR ROBERT CHILTERN: I am so glad. Do tell me what it is.

MRS. CHEVELEY: Later on. [*Rises.*] And now may I walk through your beautiful house? I hear your pictures are charming. Poor <u>Baron</u>（男爵） Arnheim—you remember the Baron?—used to tell me you had some wonderful Corots①.

SIR ROBERT CHILTERN [*with an almost imperceptible start*]: Did you know Baron Arnheim well?

MRS. CHEVELEY [*smiling*]: Intimately. Did you?

SIR ROBERT CHILTERN: At one time.

MRS. CHEVELEY: Wonderful man, wasn't he?

SIR ROBERT CHILTERN [*after a pause*]: He was very remarkable, in many ways.

MRS. CHEVELEY: I often think it such a pity he never wrote his memoirs. They would have been most interesting.

SIR ROBERT CHILTERN: Yes: he knew men and cities well, like the old Greek②.

MRS. CHEVELEY: Without the dreadful disadvantage of having a Penelope③ waiting at home for him.

MASON: Lord Goring.

> [*Enter LORD GORING. Thirty-four, but always says he is younger. A well-bred, expressionless face. He is clever, but would not like to be thought so. A <u>flawless</u>（完美无瑕的） <u>dandy</u>（纨绔子弟，花花公子）, he would be annoyed if he were considered romantic. He plays with life, and is on perfectly good <u>terms</u>（关系） with the world. He is fond of being misunderstood. It gives him a post of vantage.*]

SIR ROBERT CHILTERN: Good evening, my dear Arthur! Mrs. Cheveley, allow me to introduce to you Lord Goring, the idlest man in London.

MRS. CHEVELEY: I have met Lord Goring before.

LORD GORING [*bowing*]: I did not think you would remember me, Mrs. Cheveley.

MRS. CHEVELEY: My memory is under <u>admirable</u>（极好的） control. And are you still a bachelor?

LORD GORING: I...believe so.

MRS. CHEVELEY: How very romantic!

LORD GORING: Oh! I am not at all romantic. I am not old enough. I leave romance to my seniors.

---

① Corots: works by Jean-Baptiste-Camille Corot (1796–1875), a French landscape painter.
② old Greek: a reference to Odysseus, one of the heroes of the *Iliad* and protagonist of the *Odyssey*.
③ Penelope: the wife of Odysseus, who remained faithful to him during his long absence from home during the Trojan War.

SIR ROBERT CHILTERN: Lord Goring is the result of Boodle's Club[①], Mrs. Cheveley.

MRS. CHEVELEY: He reflects every credit on the institution.

LORD GORING: May I ask are you staying in London long?

MRS. CHEVELEY: That depends partly on the weather, partly on the cooking, and partly on Sir Robert.

SIR ROBERT CHILTERN: You are not going to plunge us into a European war, I hope?

MRS. CHEVELEY: There is no danger, at present!

> [She nods to LORD GORING, with a look of amusement in her eyes, and goes out with SIR ROBERT CHILTERN. LORD GORING saunters over to MABEL CHILTERN.]

MABEL CHILTERN: You are very late!

LORD GORING: Have you missed me?

MABEL CHILTERN: Awfully!

LORD GORING: Then I am sorry I did not stay away longer. I like being missed.

MABEL CHILTERN: How very selfish of you!

LORD GORING: I am very selfish.

MABEL CHILTERN: You are always telling me of your bad qualities, Lord Goring.

LORD GORING: I have only told you half of them as yet, Miss Mabel!

MABEL CHILTERN: Are the others very bad?

LORD GORING: Quite dreadful! When I think of them at night I go to sleep at once.

MABEL CHILTERN: Well, I delight in your bad qualities. I wouldn't have you part with one of them.

LORD GORING: How very nice of you! But then you are always nice. By the way, I want to ask you a question, Miss Mabel. Who brought Mrs. Cheveley here? That woman in heliotrope, who has just gone out of the room with your brother?

MABEL CHILTERN: Oh, I think Lady Markby brought her. Why do you ask?

LORD GORING: I haven't seen her for years, that is all.

MABEL CHILTERN: What an absurd reason!

LORD GORING: All reasons are absurd.

MABEL CHILTERN: What sort of a woman is she?

LORD GORING: Oh! a genius in the daytime and a beauty at night!

MABEL CHILTERN: I dislike her already.

LORD GORING: That shows your admirable good taste.

---

① Boodle's Club: a London gentlemen's club, founded in January 1762. It is regarded as one of the most prestigious clubs in London, and counts many British aristocrats and notable politicians among its members.

VICOMTE DE NANJAC [approaching]: Ah, the English young lady is the dragon① of good taste, is she not? Quite the dragon of good taste.

LORD GORING: So the newspapers are always telling us.

VICOMTE DE NANJAC: I read all your English newspapers. I find them so amusing.

LORD GORING: Then, my dear Nanjac, you must certainly read between the lines.

VICOMTE DE NANJAC: I should like to, but my professor objects. [To MABEL CHILTERN.] May I have the pleasure of escorting you to the music-room, Mademoiselle（法语：小姐）?

MABEL CHILTERN [looking very disappointed]: Delighted, Vicomte, quite delighted! [Turning to LORD GORING.] Aren't you coming to the music-room?

LORD GORING: Not if there is any music going on, Miss Mabel.

MABEL CHILTERN [severely]: The music is in German. You would not understand it. [Goes out with the VICOMTE DE NANJAC. LORD CAVERSHAM comes up to his son.]

LORD CAVERSHAM: Well, sir! what are you doing here? Wasting your life as usual! You should be in bed, sir. You keep too late hours! I heard of you the other night at Lady Rufford's dancing till four o'clock in the morning!

LORD GORING: Only a quarter to four, father.

LORD CAVERSHAM: Can't make out how you stand London Society. The thing has gone to the dogs（堕落）, a lot of damned nobodies talking about nothing.

LORD GORING: I love talking about nothing, father. It is the only thing I know anything about.

LORD CAVERSHAM: You seem to me to be living entirely for pleasure.

LORD GORING: What else is there to live for, father? Nothing ages（衰老）like happiness.

LORD CAVERSHAM: You are heartless, sir, very heartless!

LORD GORING: I hope not, father. Good evening, Lady Basildon!

LADY BASILDON [arching two pretty eyebrows]: Are you here? I had no idea you ever came to political parties!

LORD GORING: I adore political parties. They are the only place left to us where people don't talk politics.

LADY BASILDON: I delight in talking politics. I talk them all day long. But I can't bear listening to them. I don't know how the unfortunate men in the House stand these long debates.

LORD GORING: By never listening.

LADY BASILDON: Really?

LORD GORING [in his most serious manner]: Of course. You see, it is a very

---

① dragon: A case of malapropism (the ludicrous misuse of words). The French diplomat confuses the English word "paragon" with "dragon".

dangerous thing to listen. If one listens one may be convinced; and a man who allows himself to be convinced by an argument is a thoroughly unreasonable person.

LADY BASILDON: Ah! that accounts for so much in men that I have never understood, and so much in women that their husbands never appreciate in them!

MRS. MARCHMONT [with a sigh]: Our husbands never appreciate anything in us. We have to go to others for that!

LADY BASILDON [emphatically]: Yes, always to others, have we not?

LORD GORING [smiling]: And those are the views of the two ladies who are known to have the most admirable husbands in London.

MRS. MARCHMONT: That is exactly what we can't stand. My Reginald is quite hopelessly faultless. He is really unendurably so, at times! There is not the smallest element of excitement in knowing him.

LORD GORING: How terrible! Really, the thing should be more widely known!

LADY BASILDON: Basildon is quite as bad; he is as domestic（恋家的）as if he was a bachelor.

MRS. MARCHMONT [pressing LADY BASILDON'S hand]: My poor Olivia! We have married perfect husbands, and we are well punished for it.

LORD GORING: I should have thought it was the husbands who were punished.

MRS. MARCHMONT [drawing herself up]: Oh, dear no! They are as happy as possible! And as for trusting us, it is tragic how much they trust us.

LADY BASILDON: Perfectly tragic!

LORD GORING: Or comic, Lady Basildon?

LADY BASILDON: Certainly not comic, Lord Goring. How unkind of you to suggest such a thing!

MRS. MARCHMONT: I am afraid Lord Goring is in the camp of the enemy, as usual. I saw him talking to that Mrs. Cheveley when he came in.

LORD GORING: Handsome woman, Mrs. Cheveley!

LADY BASILDON [stiffly]: Please don't praise other women in our presence. You might wait for us to do that!

LORD GORING: I did wait.

MRS. MARCHMONT: Well, we are not going to praise her. I hear she went to the Opera on Monday night, and told Tommy Rufford at supper that, as far as she could see, London Society was entirely made up of dowdies（邋遢女人；衣着过时者）and dandies.

LORD GORING: She is quite right, too. The men are all dowdies and the women are all dandies, aren't they?

MRS. MARCHMONT [after a pause]: Oh! do you really think that is what Mrs. Cheveley meant?

LORD GORING: Of course. And a very sensible remark for Mrs. Cheveley to make, too.

[Enter MABEL CHILTERN. She joins the group.]

MABEL CHILTERN: Why are you talking about Mrs. Cheveley? Everybody is talking about Mrs. Cheveley! Lord Goring says—what did you say, Lord Goring, about Mrs. Cheveley? Oh! I remember, that she was a genius in the daytime and a beauty at night.

LADY BASILDON: What a horrid combination! So very unnatural!

MRS. MARCHMONT *[in her most dreamy manner]*: I like looking at geniuses, and listening to beautiful people.

LORD GORING: Ah! that is morbid（病态）of you, Mrs. Marchmont!

MRS. MARCHMONT *[brightening to a look of real pleasure]*: I am so glad to hear you say that. Marchmont and I have been married for seven years, and he has never once told me that I was morbid. Men are so painfully unobservant!

LADY BASILDON *[turning to her]*: I have always said, dear Margaret, that you were the most morbid person in London.

MRS. MARCHMONT: Ah! but you are always sympathetic, Olivia!

MABEL CHILTERN: Is it morbid to have a desire for food? I have a great desire for food. Lord Goring, will you give me some supper?

LORD GORING: With pleasure, Miss Mabel.

[Moves away with her.]

MABEL CHILTERN: How horrid you have been! You have never talked to me the whole evening!

LORD GORING: How could I? You went away with the child-diplomatist.

MABEL CHILTERN: You might have followed us. Pursuit would have been only polite. I don't think I like you at all this evening!

LORD GORING: I like you immensely.

MABEL CHILTERN: Well, I wish you'd show it in a more marked way!

[They go downstairs.]

Excerpt 2 (from Act 1)

As the other guests go to dinner, Sir Robert and Mrs. Cheveley return to the Octagon room, and shift their conversation to more practical subjects.

SIR ROBERT CHILTERN: And are you going to any of our country houses before you leave England, Mrs. Cheveley?

MRS. CHEVELEY: Oh, no! I can't stand your English house-parties. In England people actually try to be brilliant at breakfast. That is so dreadful of them! Only dull people are brilliant at breakfast. And then the family skeleton（骨瘦如柴的人）is always reading family prayers. My stay in England really depends on you, Sir Robert.

[Sits down on the sofa.]

SIR ROBERT CHILTERN [taking a seat beside her]: Seriously?

MRS. CHEVELEY: Quite seriously. I want to talk to you about a great political and financial scheme（规划，方案）, about this Argentine（阿根廷的）Canal（运河）Company, in fact.

SIR ROBERT CHILTERN: What a tedious, practical subject for you to talk about, Mrs. Cheveley!

MRS. CHEVELEY: Oh, I like tedious, practical subjects. What I don't like are tedious, practical people. There is a wide difference. Besides, you are interested, I know, in International Canal schemes. You were Lord Radley's secretary, weren't you, when the Government bought the Suez（苏伊士）Canal shares（股份）?

SIR ROBERT CHILTERN: Yes. But the Suez Canal was a very great and splendid undertaking. It gave us our direct route to India. It had imperial value. It was necessary that we should have control. This Argentine scheme is a commonplace Stock Exchange swindle（骗局）.

MRS. CHEVELEY: A speculation（投机生意）, Sir Robert! A brilliant, daring speculation.

SIR ROBERT CHILTERN: Believe me, Mrs. Cheveley, it is a swindle. Let us call things by their proper names. It makes matters simpler. We have all the information about it at the Foreign Office. In fact, I sent out a special Commission to inquire into the matter privately, and they report that the works are hardly begun, and as for the money already subscribed（赞助）, no one seems to know what has become of it. The whole thing is a second Panama[①], and with not a quarter of the chance of success that miserable affair ever had. I hope you have not invested in it. I am sure you are far too clever to have done that.

MRS. CHEVELEY: I have invested very largely in it.

SIR ROBERT CHILTERN: Who could have advised you to do such a foolish thing?

MRS. CHEVELEY: Your old friend—and mine.

SIR ROBERT CHILTERN: Who?

MRS. CHEVELEY: Baron Arnheim.

SIR ROBERT CHILTERN [frowning]: Ah! yes. I remember hearing, at the time of his death, that he had been mixed up in the whole affair.

MRS. CHEVELEY: It was his last romance. His last but one, to do him justice.

---

① Panama: a reference to the Panama scandals, a corruption affair that broke out in the French Third Republic in 1892, linked to the building of the Panama Canal.

Unit 2

Oscar Wilde and *An Ideal Husband*

SIR ROBERT CHILTERN [*rising*]: But you have not seen my Corots yet. They are in the music-room. Corots seem to go with music, don't they? May I show them to you?

MRS. CHEVELEY [*shaking her head*]: I am not in a mood tonight for silver twilights, or rose-pink dawns. I want to talk business.

[*Motions to him with her fan to sit down again beside her.*]

SIR ROBERT CHILTERN: I fear I have no advice to give you, Mrs. Cheveley, except to interest yourself in something less dangerous. The success of the Canal depends, of course, on the attitude of England, and I am going to lay the report of the Commissioners before the House tomorrow night.

MRS. CHEVELEY: That you must not do. In your own interests, Sir Robert, to say nothing of mine, you must not do that.

SIR ROBERT CHILTERN [*looking at her in wonder*]: In my own interests? My dear Mrs. Cheveley, what do you mean?

[*Sits down beside her.*]

MRS. CHEVELEY: Sir Robert, I will be quite frank with you. I want you to withdraw the report that you had intended to lay before the House, on the ground that (以……为理由) you have reasons to believe that the Commissioners have been prejudiced or misinformed, or something. Then I want you to say a few words to the effect (大意是) that the Government is going to reconsider the question, and that you have reason to believe that the Canal, if completed, will be of great international value. You know the sort of things ministers say in cases of this kind. A few ordinary platitudes (陈词滥调) will do. In modern life nothing produces such an effect as a good platitude. It makes the whole world kin (同类的). Will you do that for me?

SIR ROBERT CHILTERN: Mrs. Cheveley, you cannot be serious in making me such a proposition!

MRS. CHEVELEY: I am quite serious.

SIR ROBERT CHILTERN [*coldly*]: Pray allow me to believe that you are not.

MRS. CHEVELEY [*speaking with great deliberation and emphasis*]: Ah! but I am. And if you do what I ask you, I…will pay you very handsomely!

SIR ROBERT CHILTERN: Pay me!

MRS. CHEVELEY: Yes.

SIR ROBERT CHILTERN: I am afraid I don't quite understand what you mean.

MRS. CHEVELEY [*leaning back on the sofa and looking at him*]: How very disappointing! And I have come all the way from Vienna in order that you should thoroughly understand me.

SIR ROBERT CHILTERN: I fear I don't.

MRS. CHEVELEY [*in her most nonchalant manner*]: My dear Sir Robert, you are a man of the world, and you have your price, I suppose. Everybody has nowadays.

The drawback（缺点，障碍） is that most people are so dreadfully expensive. I know I am. I hope you will be more reasonable in your terms（条件）.

SIR ROBERT CHILTERN *[rises indignantly]*: If you will allow me, I will call your carriage for you. You have lived so long abroad, Mrs. Cheveley, that you seem to be unable to realise that you are talking to an English gentleman.

MRS. CHEVELEY *[detains him by touching his arm with her fan, and keeping it there while she is talking]*: I realise that I am talking to a man who laid the foundation of his fortune by selling to a Stock Exchange speculator a Cabinet（内阁） secret.

SIR ROBERT CHILTERN *[biting his lip]*: What do you mean?

MRS. CHEVELEY *[rising and facing him]*: I mean that I know the real origin of your wealth and your career, and I have got your letter, too.

SIR ROBERT CHILTERN: What letter?

MRS. CHEVELEY *[contemptuously]*: The letter you wrote to Baron Arnheim, when you were Lord Radley's secretary, telling the Baron to buy Suez Canal shares—a letter written three days before the Government announced its own purchase.

SIR ROBERT CHILTERN *[hoarsely]*: It is not true.

MRS. CHEVELEY: You thought that letter had been destroyed. How foolish of you! It is in my possession.

SIR ROBERT CHILTERN: The affair to which you allude was no more than a speculation. The House of Commons had not yet passed the bill; it might have been rejected.

MRS. CHEVELEY: It was a swindle, Sir Robert. Let us call things by their proper names. It makes everything simpler. And now I am going to sell you that letter, and the price I ask for it is your public support of the Argentine scheme. You made your own fortune out of one canal. You must help me and my friends to make our fortunes out of another!

SIR ROBERT CHILTERN: It is infamous（无耻的）, what you propose—infamous!

MRS. CHEVELEY: Oh, no! This is the game of life as we all have to play it, Sir Robert, sooner or later!

SIR ROBERT CHILTERN: I cannot do what you ask me.

MRS. CHEVELEY: You mean you cannot help doing it. You know you are standing on the edge of a precipice（悬崖）. And it is not for you to make terms. It is for you to accept them. Supposing you refuse—

SIR ROBERT CHILTERN: What then?

MRS. CHEVELEY: My dear Sir Robert, what then? You are ruined, that is all! Remember to what a point your Puritanism（清教主义） in England has brought you. In old days nobody pretended to be a bit better than his neighbours. In fact, to be a bit better than one's neighbour was considered excessively vulgar and middle-class. Nowadays, with our modern mania（狂热） for morality, every one has to pose as a paragon of purity, incorruptibility（清廉）, and all the other seven deadly virtues—and what is the result? You all go over like ninepins（横七竖八地倒下）—one after the other. Not a year passes in England without somebody disappearing. Scandals used to lend charm, or at least interest, to a man—now they crush him. And yours is a very nasty scandal. You couldn't survive it. If it were known that as a young man, secretary to a great and important minister, you sold a Cabinet secret for a large sum of money, and that that was the origin of your wealth and career, you would be hounded（追猎） out of public life, you would disappear completely. And after all, Sir Robert, why should you sacrifice your entire future rather than deal diplomatically with your enemy? For the moment I am your enemy. I admit it! And I am much stronger than you are. The big battalions（部队） are on my side. You have a splendid position, but it is your splendid position that makes you so vulnerable. You can't defend it! And I am in attack. Of course I have not talked morality to you. You must admit in fairness（公平而论） that I have spared（免除） you that. Years ago you did a clever, unscrupulous（寡廉鲜耻的） thing; it turned out a great success. You owe to it your fortune and position. And now you have got to pay for it. Sooner or later we have all to pay for what we do. You have to pay now. Before I leave you tonight, you have got to promise me to suppress your report, and to speak in the House in favour of this scheme.

SIR ROBERT CHILTERN: What you ask is impossible.

MRS. CHEVELEY: You must make it possible. You are going to make it possible. Sir Robert, you know what your English newspapers are like. Suppose that when I leave this house I drive down to some newspaper office, and give them this scandal and the proofs of it! Think of their loathsome（可恶的） joy, of the delight they would have in dragging you down, of the mud and mire they would plunge you in. Think of the hypocrite（伪君子） with his greasy smile penning（书写） his leading article, and arranging the foulness of the public placard（标语牌）.

SIR ROBERT CHILTERN: Stop! You want me to withdraw the report and to make a short speech stating that I believe there are possibilities in the scheme?

MRS. CHEVELEY [sitting down on the sofa]: Those are my terms.

SIR ROBERT CHILTERN [in a low voice]: I will give you any sum of money you want.

MRS. CHEVELEY: Even you are not rich enough, Sir Robert, to buy back your past. No man is.

SIR ROBERT CHILTERN: I will not do what you ask me. I will not.

MRS. CHEVELEY: You have to. If you don't…

[Rises from the sofa.]

SIR ROBERT CHILTERN [bewildered and unnerved（胆怯的）]: Wait a moment! What did you propose? You said that you would give me back my letter, didn't you?

MRS. CHEVELEY: Yes. That is agreed. I will be in the Ladies' Gallery[①] tomorrow night at half-past eleven. If by that time—and you will have had heaps of opportunity—you have made an announcement to the House in the terms I wish, I shall hand you back your letter with the prettiest thanks, and the best, or at any rate the most suitable, compliment I can think of. I intend to play quite fairly with you. One should always play fairly... when one has the winning cards. The Baron taught me that... amongst other things.

SIR ROBERT CHILTERN: You must let me have time to consider your proposal.

MRS. CHEVELEY: No; you must settle now!

SIR ROBERT CHILTERN: Give me a week—three days!

MRS. CHEVELEY: Impossible! I have got to telegraph to Vienna tonight.

SIR ROBERT CHILTERN: My God! what brought you into my life?

MRS. CHEVELEY: <u>Circumstances</u>（机缘，命运）.

   [Moves towards the door.]

SIR ROBERT CHILTERN: Don't go. I consent. The report shall be withdrawn. I will arrange for a question to be put to me on the subject.

MRS. CHEVELEY: Thank you. I knew we should come to an amicable agreement. I understood your nature from the first. I analysed you, though you did not adore me. And now you can get my carriage for me, Sir Robert. I see the people coming up from supper, and Englishmen always get romantic after a meal, and that bores me dreadfully.

   [Exit SIR ROBERT CHILTERN.]

✂ Excerpt 3 (from Act 1)

Before she leaves, Mrs. Cheveley triumphantly announces to Lady Chiltern that she has succeeded in winning her husband's support for the canal scheme. Then Mabel Chiltern, bantering with Lord Goring, comes upon a diamond brooch on the sofa. Mysteriously, Goring takes the brooch and puts it in his pocket, claiming he gave it to someone many years ago. Once all the guests have exited, Lady Chiltern confronts Sir Robert on the topic of the canal scheme.

SIR ROBERT CHILTERN: How beautiful you look tonight, Gertrude!

LADY CHILTERN: Robert, it is not true, is it? You are not going to lend your support to this Argentine speculation? You couldn't!

SIR ROBERT CHILTERN *[starting]*: Who told you I intended to do so?

---

① Ladies' Gallery: a separated space created in 1834 in the Houses of Parliament, which provided a means of viewing debates for a small number of well-connected women.

LADY CHILTERN: That woman who has just gone out, Mrs. Cheveley, as she calls herself now. She seemed to taunt（讥讽）me with it. Robert, I know this woman. You don't. We were at school together. She was untruthful, dishonest, an evil influence on every one whose trust or friendship she could win. I hated, I despised her. She stole things, she was a thief. She was sent away for being a thief. Why do you let her influence you?

SIR ROBERT CHILTERN: Gertrude, what you tell me may be true, but it happened many years ago. It is best forgotten! Mrs. Cheveley may have changed since then. No one should be entirely judged by their past.

LADY CHILTERN [sadly]: One's past is what one is. It is the only way by which people should be judged.

SIR ROBERT CHILTERN: That is a hard saying, Gertrude!

LADY CHILTERN: It is a true saying, Robert. And what did she mean by boasting that she had got you to lend your support, your name, to a thing I have heard you describe as the most dishonest and fraudulent scheme there has ever been in political life?

SIR ROBERT CHILTERN [biting his lip]: I was mistaken in the view I took. We all may make mistakes.

LADY CHILTERN: But you told me yesterday that you had received the report from the Commission, and that it entirely condemned the whole thing.

SIR ROBERT CHILTERN [walking up and down]: I have reasons now to believe that the Commission was prejudiced, or, at any rate, misinformed（向……提供错误信息）. Besides, Gertrude, public and private life are different things. They have different laws, and move on different lines.

LADY CHILTERN: They should both represent man at his highest. I see no difference between them.

SIR ROBERT CHILTERN [stopping]: In the present case, on a matter of practical politics, I have changed my mind. That is all.

LADY CHILTERN: All!

SIR ROBERT CHILTERN [sternly]: Yes!

LADY CHILTERN: Robert! Oh! it is horrible that I should have to ask you such a question—Robert, are you telling me the whole truth?

SIR ROBERT CHILTERN: Why do you ask me such a question?

LADY CHILTERN [after a pause]: Why do you not answer it?

SIR ROBERT CHILTERN [sitting down]: Gertrude, truth is a very complex thing, and politics is a very complex business. There are wheels within wheels（错综复杂的情况）. One may be under certain obligations to people that one must pay. Sooner or later in political life one has to compromise（妥协）. Every one does.

LADY CHILTERN: Compromise? Robert, why do you talk so differently tonight from the way I have always heard you talk? Why are you changed?

SIR ROBERT CHILTERN: I am not changed. But circumstances alter things.

LADY CHILTERN: Circumstances should never alter principles!

SIR ROBERT CHILTERN: But if I told you—

LADY CHILTERN: What?

SIR ROBERT CHILTERN: That it was necessary, vitally necessary?

LADY CHILTERN: It can never be necessary to do what is not honourable. Or if it be necessary, then what is it that I have loved! But it is not, Robert; tell me it is not. Why should it be? What gain would you get? Money? We have no need of that! And money that comes from a tainted source is a degradation（堕落，耻辱）. Power? But power is nothing in itself. It is power to do good that is fine—that, and that only. What is it, then? Robert, tell me why you are going to do this dishonourable thing!

SIR ROBERT CHILTERN: Gertrude, you have no right to use that word. I told you it was a question of rational compromise. It is no more than that.

LADY CHILTERN: Robert, that is all very well for other men, for men who treat life simply as a sordid（肮脏的） speculation; but not for you, Robert, not for you. You are different. All your life you have stood apart from others. You have never let the world soil（玷污） you. To the world, as to myself, you have been an ideal always. Oh! be that ideal still. That great inheritance throw not away—that tower of ivory do not destroy. Robert, men can love what is beneath them—things unworthy, stained, dishonoured. We women worship when we love; and when we lose our worship, we lose everything. Oh! don't kill my love for you, don't kill that!

SIR ROBERT CHILTERN: Gertrude!

LADY CHILTERN: I know that there are men with horrible secrets in their lives—men who have done some shameful thing, and who in some critical moment have to pay for it, by doing some other act of shame—oh! don't tell me you are such as they are! Robert, is there in your life any secret dishonour or disgrace? Tell me, tell me at once, that—

SIR ROBERT CHILTERN: That what?

LADY CHILTERN [*speaking very slowly*]: That our lives may drift（漂泊） apart.

SIR ROBERT CHILTERN: Drift apart?

LADY CHILTERN: That they may be entirely separate. It would be better for us both.

SIR ROBERT CHILTERN: Gertrude, there is nothing in my past life that you might not know.

LADY CHILTERN: I was sure of it, Robert, I was sure of it. But why did you say those dreadful things, things so unlike your real self? Don't let us ever talk about the subject again. You will write, won't you, to Mrs. Cheveley, and tell her that you cannot support this scandalous（可耻的） scheme of hers? If you have given her any promise you must take it back, that is all!

SIR ROBERT CHILTERN: Must I write and tell her that?

LADY CHILTERN: Surely, Robert! What else is there to do?

SIR ROBERT CHILTERN: I might see her personally. It would be better.

LADY CHILTERN: You must never see her again, Robert. She is not a woman you should ever speak to. She is not worthy to talk to a man like you. No; you must write to her at once, now, this moment, and let your letter show her that your decision is quite irrevocable（不可撤销的）!

SIR ROBERT CHILTERN: Write this moment!

LADY CHILTERN: Yes.

SIR ROBERT CHILTERN: But it is so late. It is close on twelve.

LADY CHILTERN: That makes no matter. She must know at once that she has been mistaken in you—and that you are not a man to do anything base or underhand（偷偷摸摸的） or dishonourable. Write here, Robert. Write that you decline to support this scheme of hers, as you hold it to be a dishonest scheme. Yes—write the word dishonest. She knows what that word means. *[SIR ROBERT CHILTERN sits down and writes a letter. His wife takes it up and reads it.]* Yes; that will do. *[Rings bell.]* And now the envelope. *[He writes the envelope slowly. Enter MASON.]* Have this letter sent at once to Claridge's Hotel[①]. There is no answer. *[Exit MASON. LADY CHILTERN kneels down beside her husband, and puts her arms around him.]* Robert, love gives one an instinct to things. I feel tonight that I have saved you from something that might have been a danger to you, from something that might have made men honour you less than they do. I don't think you realise sufficiently, Robert, that you have brought into the political life of our time a nobler atmosphere, a finer attitude towards life, a freer air of purer aims and higher ideals—I know it, and for that I love you, Robert.

SIR ROBERT CHILTERN: Oh, love me always, Gertrude, love me always!

LADY CHILTERN: I will love you always, because you will always be worthy of love. We needs must love the highest when we see it!

[Kisses him and rises and goes out.]

[SIR ROBERT CHILTERN walks up and down for a moment; then sits down and buries his face in his hands. The Servant enters and begins pulling out the lights. SIR ROBERT CHILTERN looks up.]

SIR ROBERT CHILTERN: Put out the lights, Mason, put out the lights!

[The Servant puts out the lights. The room becomes almost dark. The only light there is comes from the great chandelier（吊灯） that hangs over the staircase and illumines（照亮） the tapestry（挂毯） of the Triumph of Love.]

---

① The place where Mrs. Cheveley stays while she is in London.

Excerpt 4 (from Act 2)

At the Chiltern residence the next morning, Sir Robert tells his trouble to his good friend Lord Goring, who then advises him on a plan of action.

LORD GORING: My dear Robert, it's a very awkward business, very awkward indeed. You should have told your wife the whole thing. Secrets from other people's wives are a necessary luxury in modern life. So, at least, I am always told at the club by people who are bald enough to <u>know better</u>（变聪明，明事理）. But no man should have a secret from his own wife. She <u>invariably</u>（总是） finds it out. Women have a wonderful instinct about things. They can discover everything except the obvious.

SIR ROBERT CHILTERN: Arthur, I couldn't tell my wife. When could I have told her? Not last night. It would have made a life-long separation between us, and I would have lost the love of the one woman in the world I worship, of the only woman who has ever stirred love within me. Last night it would have been quite impossible. She would have turned from me in horror... in horror and in contempt.

LORD GORING: Is Lady Chiltern as perfect as all that?

SIR ROBERT CHILTERN: Yes; my wife is as perfect as all that.

LORD GORING *[taking off his left-hand glove]*: What a pity! I beg your pardon, my dear fellow, I didn't quite mean that. But if what you tell me is true, I should like to have a serious talk about life with Lady Chiltern.

SIR ROBERT CHILTERN: It would be quite useless.

LORD GORING: May I try?

SIR ROBERT CHILTERN: Yes; but nothing could make her alter her views.

LORD GORING: Well, at the worst it would simply be a psychological experiment.

SIR ROBERT CHILTERN: All such experiments are terribly dangerous.

LORD GORING: Everything is dangerous, my dear fellow. If it wasn't so, life wouldn't be worth living.... Well, I am bound to say that I think you should have told her years ago.

SIR ROBERT CHILTERN: When? When we were engaged? Do you think she would have married me if she had known that the origin of my fortune is such as it is, the basis of my career such as it is, and that I had done a thing that I suppose most men would call shameful and dishonourable?

LORD GORING *[slowly]*: Yes; most men would call it ugly names. There is no doubt of that.

SIR ROBERT CHILTERN *[bitterly]*: Men who every day do something of the same kind themselves. Men who, each one of them, have worse secrets in their own lives.

LORD GORING: That is the reason they are so pleased to find out other people's secrets. It distracts public attention from their own.

SIR ROBERT CHILTERN: And, after all, whom did I wrong by what I did? No one.

LORD GORING [*looking at him steadily*]: Except yourself, Robert.

SIR ROBERT CHILTERN [*after a pause*]: Of course I had private information about a certain transaction contemplated by the Government of the day, and I acted on it. Private information is practically the source of every large modern fortune.

LORD GORING [*tapping his boot with his cane*]: And public scandal invariably the result.

SIR ROBERT CHILTERN [*pacing up and down the room*]: Arthur, do you think that what I did nearly eighteen years ago should be brought up against me now? Do you think it fair that a man's whole career should be ruined for a fault done in one's boyhood almost? I was twenty-two at the time, and I had the double misfortune of being well-born and poor, two unforgiveable things nowadays. Is it fair that the folly, the sin of one's youth, if men choose to call it a sin, should wreck（破坏） a life like mine, should place me in the pillory（颈手枷）, should shatter all that I have worked for, all that I have built up. Is it fair, Arthur?

LORD GORING: Life is never fair, Robert. And perhaps it is a good thing for most of us that it is not.

SIR ROBERT CHILTERN: Every man of ambition has to fight his century with its own weapons. What this century worships is wealth. The god of this century is wealth. To succeed one must have wealth. At all costs one must have wealth.

LORD GORING: You underrate yourself, Robert. Believe me, without wealth you could have succeeded just as well.

SIR ROBERT CHILTERN: When I was old, perhaps. When I had lost my passion for power, or could not use it. When I was tired, worn out, disappointed. I wanted my success when I was young. Youth is the time for success. I couldn't wait.

LORD GORING: Well, you certainly have had your success while you are still young. No one in our day has had such a brilliant success. Under-Secretary for Foreign Affairs at the age of forty—that's good enough for any one, I should think.

SIR ROBERT CHILTERN: And if it is all taken away from me now? If I lose everything over a horrible scandal? If I am hounded from public life?

LORD GORING: Robert, how could you have sold yourself for money?

SIR ROBERT CHILTERN [*excitedly*]: I did not sell myself for money. I bought success at a great price. That is all.

LORD GORING [*gravely*]: Yes; you certainly paid a great price for it. But what first made you think of doing such a thing?

SIR ROBERT CHILTERN: Baron Arnheim.

LORD GORING: Damned scoundrel（恶棍）!

SIR ROBERT CHILTERN: No; he was a man of a most subtle and refined intellect. A man of culture, charm, and distinction. One of the most intellectual men I ever met.

LORD GORING: Ah! I prefer a gentlemanly fool any day. There is more to be said for stupidity than people imagine. Personally I have a great admiration for stupidity. It is a sort of fellow-feeling, I suppose. But how did he do it? Tell me the whole thing.

SIR ROBERT CHILTERN [*throws himself into an armchair by the writing-table*]: One night after dinner at Lord Radley's the Baron began talking about success in modern life as something that one could reduce to an absolutely definite science. With that wonderfully fascinating quiet voice of his he expounded to us the most terrible of all philosophies, the philosophy of power, preached to us the most marvellous of all gospels（信条）, the gospel of gold. I think he saw the effect he had produced on me, for some days afterwards he wrote and asked me to come and see him. He was living then in Park Lane, in the house Lord Woolcomb has now. I remember so well how, with a strange smile on his pale, curved lips, he led me through his wonderful picture gallery, showed me his tapestries, his enamels, his jewels, his carved ivories, made me wonder at the strange loveliness of the luxury in which he lived; and then told me that luxury was nothing but a background, a painted scene in a play, and that power, power over other men, power over the world, was the one thing worth having, the one supreme pleasure worth knowing, the one joy one never tired of, and that in our century only the rich possessed it.

LORD GORING [*with great deliberation*]: A thoroughly shallow creed（信条）.

SIR ROBERT CHILTERN [*rising*]: I didn't think so then. I don't think so now. Wealth has given me enormous power. It gave me at the very outset（开端） of my life freedom, and freedom is everything. You have never been poor, and never known what ambition is. You cannot understand what a wonderful chance the Baron gave me. Such a chance as few men get.

LORD GORING: Fortunately for them, if one is to judge by results. But tell me definitely, how did the Baron finally persuade you to—well, to do what you did?

SIR ROBERT CHILTERN: When I was going away he said to me that if I ever could give him any private information of real value he would make me a very rich man. I was dazed at the prospect he held out to me, and my ambition and my desire for power were at that time boundless. Six weeks later certain private documents passed through my hands.

LORD GORING [*keeping his eyes steadily fixed on the carpet*]: State documents?

SIR ROBERT CHILTERN: Yes.

[*LORD GORING sighs, then passes his hand across his forehead and looks up.*]

LORD GORING: I had no idea that you, of all men in the world, could have been so weak, Robert, as to yield to such a temptation as Baron Arnheim held out to you.

SIR ROBERT CHILTERN: Weak? Oh, I am sick of hearing that phrase. Sick of using it about others. Weak? Do you really think, Arthur, that it is weakness that yields to temptation? I tell you that there are terrible temptations that it requires strength, strength and courage, to yield to. To stake all one's life on a single moment, to risk everything on one throw, whether the stake be power or pleasure, I care not—there is no weakness in that. There is a horrible, a terrible courage. I had that courage. I sat down the same afternoon and wrote Baron Arnheim the letter this woman now holds. He made three-quarters of a million over the transaction.

LORD GORING: And you?

SIR ROBERT CHILTERN: I received from the Baron 110,000 pounds.

LORD GORING: You were worth more, Robert.

SIR ROBERT CHILTERN: No; that money gave me exactly what I wanted, power over others. I went into the House immediately. The Baron advised me in finance from time to time. Before five years I had almost trebled（使……成三倍） my fortune. Since then everything that I have touched has turned out a success. In all things connected with money I have had a luck so extraordinary that sometimes it has made me almost afraid. I remember having read somewhere, in some strange book, that when the gods wish to punish us they answer our prayers.

LORD GORING: But tell me, Robert, did you ever suffer any regret for what you had done?

SIR ROBERT CHILTERN: No. I felt that I had fought the century with its own weapons, and won.

LORD GORING [sadly]: You thought you had won.

SIR ROBERT CHILTERN: I thought so. [After a long pause.] Arthur, do you despise me for what I have told you?

LORD GORING [with deep feeling in his voice]: I am very sorry for you, Robert, very sorry indeed.

SIR ROBERT CHILTERN: I don't say that I suffered any remorse. I didn't. Not remorse in the ordinary, rather silly sense of the word. But I have paid conscience money many times. I had a wild hope that I might disarm（消除……的敌意） destiny. The sum Baron Arnheim gave me I have distributed twice over in public charities since then.

LORD GORING [looking up]: In public charities? Dear me! what a lot of harm you must have done, Robert!

SIR ROBERT CHILTERN: Oh, don't say that, Arthur; don't talk like that!

LORD GORING: Never mind what I say, Robert! I am always saying what I shouldn't say. In fact, I usually say what I really think. A great mistake nowadays. It makes one so liable to be misunderstood. As regards this dreadful business, I will help you in whatever way I can. Of course you know that.

SIR ROBERT CHILTERN: Thank you, Arthur, thank you. But what is to be done? What can be done?

LORD GORING [*leaning back with his hands in his pockets*]: Well, the English can't stand a man who is always saying he is in the right, but they are very fond of a man who admits that he has been in the wrong. It is one of the best things in them. However, in your case, Robert, a confession would not do. The money, if you will allow me to say so, is... awkward. Besides, if you did make a clean breast of（完全承认）the whole affair, you would never be able to talk morality again. And in England a man who can't talk morality twice a week to a large, popular, immoral audience is quite over as a serious politician. There would be nothing left for him as a profession except Botany or the Church. A confession would be of no use. It would ruin you.

SIR ROBERT CHILTERN: It would ruin me. Arthur, the only thing for me to do now is to fight the thing out.

LORD GORING [*rising from his chair*]: I was waiting for you to say that, Robert. It is the only thing to do now. And you must begin by telling your wife the whole story.

SIR ROBERT CHILTERN: That I will not do.

LORD GORING: Robert, believe me, you are wrong.

SIR ROBERT CHILTERN: I couldn't do it. It would kill her love for me. And now about this woman, this Mrs. Cheveley. How can I defend myself against her? You knew her before, Arthur, apparently.

LORD GORING: Yes.

SIR ROBERT CHILTERN: Did you know her well?

LORD GORING [*arranging his necktie*]: So little that I got engaged to be married to her once, when I was staying at the Tenbys'. The affair lasted for three days... nearly.

SIR ROBERT CHILTERN: Why was it broken off?

LORD GORING [*airily*]: Oh, I forget. At least, it makes no matter. By the way, have you tried her with money? She used to be confoundedly fond of money.

SIR ROBERT CHILTERN: I offered her any sum she wanted. She refused.

LORD GORING: Then the marvellous gospel of gold breaks down sometimes. The rich can't do everything, after all.

Unit 2

Oscar Wilde and *An Ideal Husband*

✂ Excerpt 5 (from Act 2)

As their first step of counterattack, Sir Robert decides to write the Vienna embassy to investigate Mrs. Cheveley's life. Lady Chiltern then comes back from a meeting of the Woman's Liberal Association. After Sir Robert exits, she talks to Lord Goring about her husband's mysterious dealings with Mrs. Cheveley. Goring tries to make her recognize that even the most upstanding people sometimes suffer moments of moral frailty. He then pledges his assistance to Lady Chiltern, who is amazed by his sudden seriousness. After he leaves, Lady Markby and Mrs. Cheveley are announced.

LADY MARKBY *[turning to LADY CHILTERN]*: Dear Gertrude, we just called to know if Mrs. Cheveley's diamond brooch（胸针） has been found.

LADY CHILTERN: Here?

MRS. CHEVELEY: Yes. I missed it when I got back to Claridge's, and I thought I might possibly have dropped it here.

LADY CHILTERN: I have heard nothing about it. But I will send for the butler and ask.

  [Touches the bell.]

MRS. CHEVELEY: Oh, pray don't trouble, Lady Chiltern. I dare say I lost it at the Opera, before we came on here.

LADY MARKBY: Ah yes, I suppose it must have been at the Opera. The fact is, we all scramble（抢夺） and jostle（推挤） so much nowadays that I wonder we have anything at all left on us at the end of an evening. I know myself that, when I am coming back from the Drawing Room, I always feel as if I hadn't a shred（碎布） on me, except a small shred of decent reputation, just enough to prevent the lower classes making painful observations through the windows of the carriage. The fact is that our Society is terribly over-populated. Really, someone should arrange a proper scheme of assisted emigration. It would do a great deal of good.

MRS. CHEVELEY: I quite agree with you, Lady Markby. It is nearly six years since I have been in London for the Season, and I must say Society has become dreadfully mixed. One sees the oddest people everywhere.

LADY MARKBY: That is quite true, dear. But one needn't know them. I'm sure I don't know half the people who come to my house. Indeed, from all I hear, I shouldn't like to.

  [Enter MASON.]

LADY CHILTERN: What sort of a brooch was it that you lost, Mrs. Cheveley?

MRS. CHEVELEY: A diamond snake-brooch with a ruby（红宝石）, a rather large ruby.

LADY MARKBY: I thought you said there was a sapphire（蓝宝石） on the head, dear?

MRS. CHEVELEY [*smiling*]: No, lady Markby—a ruby.

LADY MARKBY [*nodding her head*]: And very <u>becoming</u>（相称的）, I am quite sure.

LADY CHILTERN: Has a ruby and diamond brooch been found in any of the rooms this morning, Mason?

MASON: No, my lady.

MRS. CHEVELEY: It really is of no consequence, Lady Chiltern. I am so sorry to have put you to any inconvenience.

LADY CHILTERN [*coldly*]: Oh, it has been no inconvenience. That will do, Mason. You can bring tea.

　　[*Exit MASON.*]

LADY MARKBY: Well, I must say it is most annoying to lose anything. I remember once at Bath, years ago, losing in the Pump Room an exceedingly handsome <u>cameo</u>（多彩浮雕宝石） bracelet that Sir John had given me. I don't think he has ever given me anything since, I am sorry to say. He has sadly degenerated. Really, this horrid House of Commons quite ruins our husbands for us. I think the Lower House by far the greatest blow to a happy married life that there has been since that terrible thing called the Higher Education of Women was invented.

LADY CHILTERN: Ah! it is <u>heresy</u>（异端邪说） to say that in this house, Lady Markby. Robert is a great <u>champion</u>（拥护者） of the Higher Education of Women, and so, I am afraid, am I.

MRS. CHEVELEY: The higher education of men is what I should like to see. Men need it so sadly.

LADY MARKBY: They do, dear. But I am afraid such a scheme would be quite unpractical. I don't think man has much capacity for development. He has got as far as he can, and that is not far, is it? With regard to women, well, dear Gertrude, you belong to the younger generation, and I am sure it is all right if you approve of it. In my time, of course, we were taught not to understand anything. That was the old system, and wonderfully interesting it was. I assure you that the amount of things I and my poor dear sister were taught not to understand was quite extraordinary. But modern women understand everything, I am told.

MRS. CHEVELEY: Except their husbands. That is the one thing the modern woman never understands.

LADY MARKBY: And a very good thing too, dear, I dare say. It might break up many a happy home if they did. Not yours, I need hardly say, Gertrude. You have married a <u>pattern</u>（模范） husband. I wish I could say as much for myself. But since Sir John has taken to attending the debates regularly, which he never used to do in the good old days, his language has become quite impossible. He always seems to think that he is addressing the House, and consequently whenever he discusses the state of the agricultural labourer, or the Welsh Church, or something quite improper of that kind, I am obliged to send all the servants out of the room. It is not pleasant to see one's own butler（男管家）, who has been with one for twenty-three years, actually blushing at the side-board, and the footmen（男仆）making contortions（脸部或身体的扭曲） in corners like persons in circuses. I assure you my life will be quite ruined unless they send John at once to the Upper House. He won't take any interest in politics then, will he? The House of Lords is so sensible. An assembly of gentlemen. But in his present state, Sir John is really a great trial（讨厌的人）. Why, this morning before breakfast was half-over, he stood up on the hearthrug, put his hands in his pockets, and appealed to the country at the top of his voice. I left the table as soon as I had my second cup of tea, I need hardly say. But his violent language could be heard all over the house! I trust, Gertrude, that Sir Robert is not like that.

LADY CHILTERN: But I am very much interested in politics, Lady Markby. I love to hear Robert talk about them.

LADY MARKBY: Well, I hope he is not as devoted to Blue Books（蓝皮书，官方报告） as Sir John is. I don't think they can be quite improving reading for anyone.

MRS. CHEVELEY [languidly]: I have never read a Blue Book. I prefer books…in yellow covers.

LADY MARKBY [genially unconscious]: Yellow is a gayer（欢快的） colour, is it not? I used to wear yellow a good deal in my early days, and would do so now if Sir John was not so painfully personal（人身攻击的） in his observations, and a man on the question of dress is always ridiculous, is he not?

MRS. CHEVELEY: Oh, no! I think men are the only authorities on dress.

LADY MARKBY: Really? One wouldn't say so from the sort of hats they wear? would one?

   [The butler enters, followed by the footman. Tea is set on a small table close to LADY CHILTERN.]

LADY CHILTERN: May I give you some tea, Mrs. Cheveley?

MRS. CHEVELEY: Thanks.

   [The butler hands MRS. CHEVELEY a cup of tea on a salver.]

LADY CHILTERN: Some tea, Lady Markby?

LADY MARKBY: No thanks, dear. [The servants go out.] The fact is, I have promised to go round for ten minutes to see poor Lady Brancaster, who is in very great trouble. Her daughter, quite a well-brought-up girl, too, has actually become engaged to be married to a curate（助理牧师） in Shropshire. It is very sad, very sad indeed. I can't understand this modern mania for curates. In my time we girls saw them, of course, running about the place like rabbits. But we never took any notice of them, I need hardly say. But I am told that nowadays country society is quite honeycombed（使……千疮百孔） with them. I think it most irreligious. And then the eldest son has quarrelled with his father, and it is said that when they meet at the club Lord Brancaster always hides himself behind the money article in *The Times*. However, I believe that is quite a common occurrence nowadays and that they have to take in（订阅） extra copies of *The Times* at all the clubs in St. James's Street; there are so many sons who won't have anything to do with their fathers, and so many fathers who won't speak to their sons. I think myself, it is very much to be regretted.

MRS. CHEVELEY: So do I. Fathers have so much to learn from their sons nowadays.

LADY MARKBY: Really, dear? What?

MRS. CHEVELEY: The art of living. The only really Fine Art we have produced in modern times.

LADY MARKBY *[shaking her head]*: Ah! I am afraid Lord Brancaster knew a good deal about that. More than his poor wife ever did. *[Turning to LADY CHILTERN.]* You know Lady Brancaster, don't you, dear?

LADY CHILTERN: Just slightly. She was staying at Langton last autumn, when we were there.

LADY MARKBY: Well, like all stout women, she looks the very picture of happiness, as no doubt you noticed. But there are many tragedies in her family, besides this affair of the curate. Her own sister, Mrs. Jekyll, had a most unhappy life; through no fault of her own, I am sorry to say. She ultimately was so broken-hearted that she went into a convent（女修道院）, or on to the operatic（歌剧的） stage, I forget which. No; I think it was decorative art-needlework she took up. I know she had lost all sense of pleasure in life. *[Rising.]* And now, Gertrude, if you will allow me, I shall leave Mrs. Cheveley in your charge and call back for her in a quarter of an hour. Or perhaps, dear Mrs. Cheveley, you wouldn't mind waiting in the carriage while I am with Lady Brancaster. As I intend it to be a visit of condolence（慰问）, I shan't stay long.

MRS. CHEVELEY *[rising]*: I don't mind waiting in the carriage at all, provided there is somebody to look at one.

LADY MARKBY: Well, I hear the curate is always prowling（徘徊） about the house.

MRS. CHEVELEY: I am afraid I am not fond of girl friends.

LADY CHILTERN *[rising]*: Oh, I hope Mrs. Cheveley will stay here a little. I should like to have a few minutes' conversation with her.

MRS. CHEVELEY: How very kind of you, Lady Chiltern! Believe me, nothing would give me greater pleasure.

LADY MARKBY: Ah! no doubt you both have many pleasant reminiscences（回忆） of your schooldays to talk over together. Good-bye, dear Gertrude! Shall I see you at Lady Bonar's tonight? She has discovered a wonderful new genius. He does… nothing at all, I believe. That is a great comfort, is it not?

LADY CHILTERN: Robert and I are dining at home by ourselves tonight, and I don't think I shall go anywhere afterwards. Robert, of course, will have to be in the House. But there is nothing interesting on.

LADY MARKBY: Dining at home by yourselves? Is that quite prudent（审慎的）? Ah, I forgot, your husband is an exception. Mine is the general rule, and nothing ages a woman so rapidly as having married the general rule.

[Exit LADY MARKBY.]

MRS. CHEVELEY: Wonderful woman, Lady Markby, isn't she? Talks more and says less than anybody I ever met. She is made to be a public speaker. Much more so than her husband, though he is a typical Englishman, always dull and usually violent.

LADY CHILTERN [makes no answer, but remains standing. There is a pause. Then the eyes of the two women meet. LADY CHILTERN looks stern and pale. MRS. CHEVELEY seems rather amused]: Mrs. Cheveley, I think it is right to tell you quite frankly that, had I known who you really were, I should not have invited you to my house last night.

MRS. CHEVELEY [with an impertinent（无礼的） smile]: Really?

LADY CHILTERN: I could not have done so.

MRS. CHEVELEY: I see that after all these years you have not changed a bit, Gertrude.

LADY CHILTERN: I never change.

MRS. CHEVELEY [elevating her eyebrows]: Then life has taught you nothing?

LADY CHILTERN: It has taught me that a person who has once been guilty of a dishonest and dishonourable action may be guilty of it a second time, and should be shunned.

MRS. CHEVELEY: Would you apply that rule to every one?

LADY CHILTERN: Yes, to every one, without exception.

MRS. CHEVELEY: Then I am sorry for you, Gertrude, very sorry for you.

LADY CHILTERN: You see now, I was sure, that for many reasons any further acquaintance between us during your stay in London is quite impossible?

MRS. CHEVELEY [leaning back in her chair]: Do you know, Gertrude, I don't mind your talking morality a bit. Morality is simply the attitude we adopt towards people whom we personally dislike. You dislike me. I am quite aware of that. And I have always detested you. And yet I have come here to do you a service.

LADY CHILTERN [contemptuously]: Like the service you wished to render my husband last night, I suppose. Thank heaven, I saved him from that.

MRS. CHEVELEY [starting to her feet]: It was you who made him write that insolent （傲慢的） letter to me? It was you who made him break his promise?

LADY CHILTERN: Yes.

MRS. CHEVELEY: Then you must make him keep it. I give you till tomorrow morning—no more. If by that time your husband does not solemnly bind himself to（承诺） help me in this great scheme in which I am interested—

LADY CHILTERN: This fraudulent（欺诈性的） speculation—

MRS. CHEVELEY: Call it what you choose. I hold your husband in the hollow of my hand, and if you are wise you will make him do what I tell him.

LADY CHILTERN [*rising and going towards her*]: You are impertinent. What has my husband to do with you? With a woman like you?

MRS. CHEVELEY [*with a bitter laugh*]: In this world like meets like（物以类聚）. It is because your husband is himself fraudulent and dishonest that we pair so well together. Between you and him there are chasms（鸿沟）. He and I are closer than friends. We are enemies linked together. The same sin binds us.

LADY CHILTERN: How dare you class my husband with yourself? How dare you threaten him or me? Leave my house. You are unfit to enter it.

> [*SIR ROBERT CHILTERN enters from behind. He hears his wife's last words, and sees to whom they are addressed. He grows deadly pale.*]

MRS. CHEVELEY: Your house! A house bought with the price of dishonour. A house, everything in which has been paid for by fraud. [*Turns round and sees SIR ROBERT CHILTERN.*] Ask him what the origin of his fortune is! Get him to tell you how he sold to a stockbroker（股票经纪人） a Cabinet secret. Learn from him to what you owe your position.

LADY CHILTERN: It is not true! Robert! It is not true!

MRS. CHEVELEY [*pointing at him with outstretched finger*]: Look at him! Can he deny it? Does he dare to?

SIR ROBERT CHILTERN: Go! Go at once. You have done your worst now.

MRS. CHEVELEY: My worst? I have not yet finished with you, with either of you. I give you both till tomorrow at noon. If by then you don't do what I bid you to do, the whole world shall know the origin of Robert Chiltern.

> [*SIR ROBERT CHILTERN strikes the bell. Enter MASON.*]

SIR ROBERT CHILTERN: Show Mrs. Cheveley out.

> [*MRS. CHEVELEY starts; then bows with somewhat exaggerated politeness to LADY CHILTERN, who makes no sign of response. As she passes by SIR ROBERT CHILTERN, who is standing close to the door, she pauses for a moment and looks him straight in the face. She then goes out, followed by the servant, who closes the door after him. The husband and wife are left alone. LADY CHILTERN stands like someone in a dreadful dream. Then she turns round and looks at her husband. She looks at him with strange eyes, as though she was seeing him for the first time.*]

LADY CHILTERN: You sold a Cabinet secret for money! You began your life with fraud! You built up your career on dishonour! Oh, tell me it is not true! Lie to me! Lie to me! Tell me it is not true!

SIR ROBERT CHILTERN: What this woman said is quite true. But, Gertrude, listen to me. You don't realise how I was tempted. Let me tell you the whole thing.

[Goes towards her.]

LADY CHILTERN: Don't come near me. Don't touch me. I feel as if you had soiled me for ever. Oh! what a mask you have been wearing all these years! A horrible painted mask! You sold yourself for money. Oh! a common thief were better. You put yourself up to sale to the highest bidder! You were bought in the market. You lie to the whole world. And yet you will not lie to me.

SIR ROBERT CHILTERN *[rushing towards her]*: Gertrude! Gertrude!

LADY CHILTERN *[thrusting him back with outstretched hands]*: No, don't speak! Say nothing! Your voice wakes terrible memories—memories of things that made me love you—memories of words that made me love you—memories that now are horrible to me. And how I worshipped you! You were to me something apart from common life, a thing pure, noble, honest, without stain. The world seemed to me finer because you were in it, and goodness more real because you lived. And now—oh, when I think that I made of a man like you my ideal! the ideal of my life!

SIR ROBERT CHILTERN: There was your mistake. There was your error. The error all women commit. Why can't you women love us, faults and all? Why do you place us on monstrous <u>pedestal</u>s（基座）? We have all feet of <u>clay</u>（黏土）, women as well as men; but when we men love women, we love them knowing their weaknesses, their follies, their imperfections, love them all the more, it may be, for that reason. It is not the perfect, but the imperfect, who have need of love. It is when we are wounded by our own hands, or by the hands of others, that love should come to cure us—else what use is love at all? All sins, except a sin against itself, Love should forgive. All lives, save loveless lives, true Love should pardon. A man's love is like that. It is wider, larger, more human than a woman's. Women think that they are making ideals of men. What they are making of us are false idols merely. You made your false idol of me, and I had not the courage to come down, show you my wounds, tell you my weaknesses. I was afraid that I might lose your love, as I have lost it now. And so, last night you ruined my life for me—yes, ruined it! What this woman asked of me was nothing compared to what she offered to me. She offered security, peace, stability. The sin of my youth, that I had thought was buried, rose up in front of me, <u>hideous</u>（令人憎恶的）, horrible, with its hands at my throat. I could have killed it for ever, sent it back into its tomb, destroyed its record, burned the one witness against me. You prevented me. No one but you, you know it. And now what is there before me but public disgrace, ruin, terrible shame, the mockery（嘲笑） of the world, a lonely dishonoured life, a lonely dishonoured death, it may be, some day? Let women make no more ideals of men! let them not put them on altars（圣坛） and bow before them, or they may ruin other lives as completely as you—you whom I have so wildly loved—have ruined mine!

> *[He passes from the room. LADY CHILTERN rushes towards him, but the door is closed when she reaches it. Pale with anguish, bewildered, helpless, she sways（摇摆） like a plant in the water. Her hands, outstretched, seem to tremble in the air like blossoms in the wind. Then she flings herself down beside a sofa and buries her face. Her sobs are like the sobs of a child.]*

Excerpt 6 (from Act 3)

Act 3 takes place in Lord Goring's house, in the library, which is connected to a number of other rooms. Lord Goring is preparing to go out for the evening. However, he has to cancel his plan due to a number of unexpected visitors who have come in quick succession, each with a different purpose.

> *[Enter LORD GORING in evening dress with a buttonhole（襟花）. He is wearing a silk hat and Inverness cape（圆领披风）. White-gloved, he carries a Louis Seize（路易十六风格的） cane. His are all the delicate fopperies（纨绔子弟的打扮） of Fashion. One sees that he stands in immediate relation to modern life, makes it indeed, and so masters it. He is the first well-dressed philosopher in the history of thought.]*

LORD GORING: Got my second buttonhole for me, Phipps?

PHIPPS: Yes, my lord.

> *[Takes his hat, cane, and cape, and presents new buttonhole on salver（托盘）.]*

LORD GORING: Rather distinguished thing, Phipps. I am the only person of the smallest importance in London at present who wears a buttonhole.

PHIPPS: Yes, my lord. I have observed that.

LORD GORING *[taking out old buttonhole]*: You see, Phipps, Fashion is what one wears oneself. What is unfashionable is what other people wear.

PHIPPS: Yes, my lord.

LORD GORING: Just as vulgarity is simply the conduct of other people.

PHIPPS: Yes, my lord.

LORD GORING *[putting in a new buttonhole]*: And falsehoods the truths of other people.

Unit 2
Oscar Wilde and *An Ideal Husband*

PHIPPS: Yes, my lord.

LORD GORING: Other people are quite dreadful. The only possible society（陪伴）is oneself.

PHIPPS: Yes, my lord.

LORD GORING: To love oneself is the beginning of a lifelong romance, Phipps.

PHIPPS: Yes, my lord.

LORD GORING *[looking at himself in the glass]*: Don't think I quite like this buttonhole, Phipps. Makes me look a little too old. Makes me almost in the prime（全盛时期）of life, eh, Phipps?

PHIPPS: I don't observe any alteration in your lordship's appearance.

LORD GORING: You don't, Phipps?

PHIPPS: No, my lord.

LORD GORING: I am not quite sure. For the future a more trivial（普通的）buttonhole, Phipps, on Thursday evenings.

PHIPPS: I will speak to the florist, my lord. She has had a loss in her family lately, which perhaps accounts for the lack of triviality（浅薄）your lordship complains of in the buttonhole.

LORD GORING: Extraordinary thing about the lower class in England—they are always losing their relations.

PHIPPS: Yes, my lord! They are extremely fortunate in that respect.

LORD GORING *[turns round and looks at him. PHIPPS remains impassive（冷漠的）]*: Hum! Any letters, Phipps?

PHIPPS: Three, my lord.

[Hands letters on a salver.]

LORD GORING *[takes letters]*: Want my cab round in twenty minutes.

PHIPPS: Yes, my lord.

[Goes towards door.]

LORD GORING *[holds up letter in pink envelope]*: Ahem! Phipps, when did this letter arrive?

PHIPPS: It was brought by hand just after your lordship went to the club.

LORD GORING: That will do. *[Exit PHIPPS]* Lady Chiltern's handwriting on Lady Chiltern's pink notepaper. That is rather curious. I thought Robert was to write. Wonder what Lady Chiltern has got to say to me? *[Sits at bureau, opens letter, and reads it.]* "I want you. I trust you. I am coming to you. Gertrude." *[Puts down the letter with a puzzled look. Then takes it up, and reads it again slowly.]* "I want you. I trust you. I am coming to you." So she has found out everything! Poor woman! Poor woman! *[Pulls out watch and looks at it.]* But what an hour to call! Ten o'clock! I shall have to give up going to the Berkshires. However, it is always nice to be expected, and not to arrive. I am not expected at the Bachelors', so I shall certainly go there. Well, I will make her stand by her husband. That is the only thing for her to do. That is the only thing for any woman to do. It is the growth of the moral sense in women that makes marriage such a hopeless, one-sided institution. Ten o'clock. She should be here soon. I must tell Phipps I am not in to any one else.

 [Goes towards bell.]

 [Enter PHIPPS]

PHIPPS: Lord Caversham.

LORD GORING: Oh, why will parents always appear at the wrong time? Some extraordinary mistake in nature, I suppose. *[Enter LORD CAVERSHAM.]* Delighted to see you, my dear father.

 [Goes to meet him.]

LORD CAVERSHAM: Take my cloak off.

LORD GORING: Is it worth while, father?

LORD CAVERSHAM: Of course it is worth while, sir. Which is the most comfortable chair?

LORD GORING: This one, father. It is the chair I use myself, when I have visitors.

LORD CAVERSHAM: Thank ye. No draught（穿堂风）, I hope, in this room?

LORD GORING: No, father.

LORD CAVERSHAM *[sitting down]*: Glad to hear it. Can't stand draughts. No draughts at home.

LORD GORING: Good many breezes（微风）, father.

LORD CAVERSHAM: Eh? Eh? Don't understand what you mean. Want to have a serious conversation with you, sir.

LORD GORING: My dear father! At this hour?

LORD CAVERSHAM: Well, sir, it is only ten o'clock. What is your objection to the hour? I think the hour is an admirable hour!

LORD GORING: Well, the fact is, father, this is not my day for talking seriously. I am very sorry, but it is not my day.

LORD CAVERSHAM: What do you mean, sir?

LORD GORING: During the Season, father, I only talk seriously on the first Tuesday in every month, from four to seven.

LORD CAVERSHAM: Well, make it Tuesday, sir, make it Tuesday.

LORD GORING: But it is after seven, father, and my doctor says I must not have any serious conversation after seven. It makes me talk in my sleep.

LORD CAVERSHAM: Talk in your sleep, sir? What does that matter? You are not married.

LORD GORING: No, father, I am not married.

LORD CAVERSHAM: Hum! That is what I have come to talk to you about, sir. You have got to get married, and at once. Why, when I was your age, sir, I had been an inconsolable（伤心欲绝的） widower for three months, and was already paying my addresses to your admirable mother. Damme, sir, it is your duty to get married. You can't be always living for pleasure. Every man of position is married nowadays. Bachelors are not fashionable any more. They are a damaged lot（一类人）. Too much is known about them. You must get a wife, sir. Look where your friend Robert Chiltern has got to by probity（正直廉洁）, hard work, and a sensible marriage with a good woman. Why don't you imitate him, sir? Why don't you take him for your model?

LORD GORING: I think I shall, father.

LORD CAVERSHAM: I wish you would, sir. Then I should be happy. At present I make your mother's life miserable on your account. You are heartless, sir, quite heartless.

LORD GORING: I hope not, father.

LORD CAVERSHAM: And it is high time for you to get married. You are thirty-four years of age, sir.

LORD GORING: Yes, father, but I only admit to thirty-two—thirty-one and a half when I have a really good buttonhole. This buttonhole is not... trivial enough.

LORD CAVERSHAM: I tell you you are thirty-four, sir. And there is a draught in your room, besides, which makes your conduct worse. Why did you tell me there was no draught, sir? I feel a draught, sir, I feel it distinctly.

LORD GORING: So do I, father. It is a dreadful draught. I will come and see you tomorrow, father. We can talk over anything you like. Let me help you on with your cloak, father.

LORD CAVERSHAM: No, sir; I have called this evening for a definite purpose, and I am going to see it through at all costs to my health or yours. Put down my cloak, sir.

LORD GORING: Certainly, father. But let us go into another room. *[Rings bell.]* There is a dreadful draught here. *[Enter PHIPPS.]* Phipps, is there a good fire in the smoking-room?

PHIPPS: Yes, my lord.

LORD GORING: Come in there, father. Your sneezes（喷嚏） are quite heartrending（令人心碎的）.

LORD CAVERSHAM: Well, sir, I suppose I have a right to sneeze when I choose?

LORD GORING *[apologetically]*: Quite so, father. I was merely expressing sympathy.

LORD CAVERSHAM: Oh, damn sympathy. There is a great deal too much of that sort of thing going on nowadays.

LORD GORING: I quite agree with you, father. If there was less sympathy in the world there would be less trouble in the world.

LORD CAVERSHAM *[going towards the smoking-room]*: That is a paradox（悖论，

自相矛盾的说法), sir. I hate paradoxes.

LORD GORING: So do I, father. Everybody one meets is a paradox nowadays. It is a great bore. It makes society so obvious.

LORD CAVERSHAM [*turning round, and looking at his son beneath his bushy eyebrows*]: Do you always really understand what you say, sir?

LORD GORING [*after some hesitation*]: Yes, father, if I listen attentively.

LORD CAVERSHAM [*indignantly*]: If you listen attentively! ... Conceited(自以为是的) young puppy!

[*Goes off grumbling into the smoking-room. PHIPPS enters.*]

LORD GORING: Phipps, there is a lady coming to see me this evening on particular business. Show her into the drawing-room when she arrives. You understand?

PHIPPS: Yes, my lord.

LORD GORING: It is a matter of the gravest importance, Phipps.

PHIPPS: I understand, my lord.

LORD GORING: No one else is to be admitted, under any circumstances.

PHIPPS: I understand, my lord.

[*Bell rings.*]

LORD GORING: Ah! that is probably the lady. I shall see her myself.

[*Just as he is going towards the door LORD CAVERSHAM enters from the smoking-room.*]

LORD CAVERSHAM: Well, sir? am I to wait attendance(伺候) on you?

LORD GORING [*considerably perplexed*]: In a moment, father. Do excuse me. [*LORD CAVERSHAM goes back.*] Well, remember my instructions, Phipps—into that room.

PHIPPS: Yes, my lord.

[*LORD GORING goes into the smoking-room. HAROLD, the footman shows MRS. CHEVELEY in. Lamia-like*①, *she is in green and silver. She has a cloak of black satin, lined with dead rose-leaf silk.*]

HAROLD: What name, madam?

MRS. CHEVELEY [*to PHIPPS, who advances towards her*]: Is Lord Goring not here? I was told he was at home?

PHIPPS: His lordship is engaged at present with Lord Caversham, madam.

[*Turns a cold, glassy eye on HAROLD, who at once retires.*]

MRS. CHEVELEY [*To herself*]: How very filial(孝顺的)!

PHIPPS: His lordship told me to ask you, madam, to be kind enough to wait in the drawing-room for him. His lordship will come to you there.

MRS. CHEVELEY [*with a look of surprise*]: Lord Goring expects me?

---

① Lamia-like: Lamia is a monster in classical mythology, commonly represented with the head and breast of a woman and the body of a serpent, said to allure youths and children in order to suck their blood.

Unit 2

Oscar Wilde and *An Ideal Husband*

PHIPPS: Yes, madam.

MRS. CHEVELEY: Are you quite sure?

PHIPPS: His lordship told me that if a lady called I was to ask her to wait in the drawing-room. *[Goes to the door of the drawing-room and opens it.]* His lordship's directions on the subject were very precise.

MRS. CHEVELEY *[to herself]*: How thoughtful of him! To expect the unexpected shows a thoroughly modern intellect. *[Goes towards the drawing-room and looks in.]* Ugh! How dreary a bachelor's drawing-room always looks. I shall have to alter all this. *[PHIPPS brings the lamp from the writing-table.]* No, I don't care for that lamp. It is far too glaring. Light some candles.

PHIPPS *[replaces lamp]*: Certainly, madam.

MRS. CHEVELEY: I hope the candles have very becoming shades.

PHIPPS: We have had no complaints about them, madam, as yet.

[Passes into the drawing-room and begins to light the candles.]

MRS. CHEVELEY *[to herself]*: I wonder what woman he is waiting for tonight. It will be delightful to catch him. Men always look so silly when they are caught. And they are always being caught. *[Looks about room and approaches the writing-table.]* What a very interesting room! What a very interesting picture! Wonder what his correspondence is like. *[Takes up letters.]* Oh, what a very uninteresting correspondence! Bills and cards, debts and dowagers (贵妇)! Who on earth writes to him on pink paper? How silly to write on pink paper! It looks like the beginning of a middle-class romance. Romance should never begin with sentiment. It should begin with science and end with a settlement (财产转让). *[Puts letter down, then takes it up again.]* I know that handwriting. That is Gertrude Chiltern's. I remember it perfectly. The ten commandments[①] in every stroke of the pen, and the moral law all over the page. Wonder what Gertrude is writing to him about? Something horrid about me, I suppose. How I detest that woman! *[Reads it.]* I trust you. I want you. I am coming to you. Gertrude. I trust you. I want you. I am coming to you.

[A look of triumph comes over her face. She is just about to steal the letter, when PHIPPS comes in.]

PHIPPS: The candles in the drawing-room are lit, madam, as you directed.

MRS. CHEVELEY: Thank you.

[Rises hastily and slips the letter under a large silver-cased blotting (吸墨纸) -book that is lying on the table.]

PHIPPS: I trust the shades will be to your liking, madam. They are the most becoming we have. They are the same as his lordship uses himself when he is dressing for dinner.

---

① ten commandments: the precepts spoken by God to Israel, delivered to Moses on Mount Sinai.

MRS. CHEVELEY [*with a smile*]: Then I am sure they will be perfectly right.

PHIPPS [*gravely*]: Thank you, madam.

> [*MRS. CHEVELEY goes into the drawing-room. PHIPPS closes the door and retires. The door is then slowly opened, and MRS. CHEVELEY comes out and creeps stealthily towards the writing-table. Suddenly voices are heard from the smoking-room. MRS. CHEVELEY grows pale, and stops. The voices grow louder, and she goes back into the drawing-room, biting her lip.*]
>
> [*Enter LORD GORING and LORD CAVERSHAM.*]

LORD GORING [*expostulating（规劝）*]: My dear father, if I am to get married, surely you will allow me to choose the time, place, and person? Particularly the person.

LORD CAVERSHAM [*testily（暴躁地）*]: That is a matter for me, sir. You would probably make a very poor choice. It is I who should be consulted, not you. There is property at stake（有风险）. It is not a matter for affection. Affection comes later on in married life.

LORD GORING: Yes. In married life affection comes when people thoroughly dislike each other, father, doesn't it?

> [*Puts on LORD CAVERSHAM'S cloak for him.*]

LORD CAVERSHAM: Certainly, sir. I mean certainly not, sir. You are talking very foolishly tonight. What I say is that marriage is a matter for common sense（常识）.

LORD GORING: But women who have common sense are so curiously plain, father, aren't they? Of course I only speak from hearsay（道听途说）.

LORD CAVERSHAM: No woman, plain or pretty, has any common sense at all, sir. Common sense is the privilege of our sex.

LORD GORING: Quite so. And we men are so self-sacrificing that we never use it, do we, father?

LORD CAVERSHAM: I use it, sir. I use nothing else.

LORD GORING: So my mother tells me.

LORD CAVERSHAM: It is the secret of your mother's happiness. You are very heartless, sir, very heartless.

LORD GORING: I hope not, father.

> [*Goes out for a moment. Then returns, looking rather put out, with SIR ROBERT CHILTERN.*]

SIR ROBERT CHILTERN: My dear Arthur, what a piece of good luck meeting you on the doorstep! Your servant had just told me you were not at home. How extraordinary!

LORD GORING: The fact is, I am horribly busy tonight, Robert, and I gave orders I was not at home to any one. Even my father had a comparatively cold reception

（接待）. He complained of a draught the whole time.

SIR ROBERT CHILTERN: Ah! you must be at home to me, Arthur. You are my best friend. Perhaps by tomorrow you will be my only friend. My wife has discovered everything.

LORD GORING: Ah! I guessed as much!

SIR ROBERT CHILTERN [looking at him]: Really! How?

LORD GORING [after some hesitation]: Oh, merely by something in the expression of your face as you came in. Who told her?

SIR ROBERT CHILTERN: Mrs. Cheveley herself. And the woman I love knows that I began my career with an act of low dishonesty, that I built up my life upon sands of shame—that I sold, like a common huckster（叫卖的小贩）, the secret that had been intrusted（托付） to me as a man of honour. I thank heaven poor Lord Radley died without knowing that I betrayed him. I would to God I had died before I had been so horribly tempted, or had fallen so low.

[Burying his face in his hands.]

LORD GORING [after a pause]: You have heard nothing from Vienna yet, in answer to your wire?

SIR ROBERT CHILTERN [looking up]: Yes; I got a telegram from the first secretary at eight o'clock tonight.

LORD GORING: Well?

SIR ROBERT CHILTERN: Nothing is absolutely known against her. On the contrary, she occupies a rather high position in society. It is a sort of open secret that Baron Arnheim left her the greater portion of his immense fortune. Beyond that I can learn nothing.

LORD GORING: She doesn't turn out to be a spy, then?

SIR ROBERT CHILTERN: Oh! spies are of no use nowadays. Their profession is over. The newspapers do their work instead.

LORD GORING: And thunderingly（异乎寻常） well they do it.

SIR ROBERT CHILTERN: Arthur, I am parched（口干舌燥） with thirst. May I ring for something? Some hock（霍克酒） and seltzer（赛尔脱兹矿泉水）?

LORD GORING: Certainly. Let me.

[Rings the bell.]

SIR ROBERT CHILTERN: Thanks! I don't know what to do, Arthur, I don't know what to do, and you are my only friend. But what a friend you are—the one friend I can trust. I can trust you absolutely, can't I?

[Enter PHIPPS.]

LORD GORING: My dear Robert, of course. Oh! [To PHIPPS.] Bring some hock and seltzer.

PHIPPS: Yes, my lord.

LORD GORING: And Phipps!

PHIPPS: Yes, my lord.

LORD GORING: Will you excuse me for a moment, Robert? I want to give some directions to my servant.

SIR ROBERT CHILTERN: Certainly.

LORD GORING: When that lady calls, tell her that I am not expected home this evening. Tell her that I have been suddenly called out of town. You understand?

PHIPPS: The lady is in that room, my lord. You told me to show her into that room, my lord.

LORD GORING: You did perfectly right. *[Exit PHIPPS.]* What a mess I am in. No; I think I shall get through it. I'll give her a lecture through the door. Awkward thing to manage, though.

SIR ROBERT CHILTERN: Arthur, tell me what I should do. My life seems to have crumbled about me. I am a ship without a rudder（船舵）in a night without a star.

LORD GORING: Robert, you love your wife, don't you?

SIR ROBERT CHILTERN: I love her more than anything in the world. I used to think ambition the great thing. It is not. Love is the great thing in the world. There is nothing but love, and I love her. But I am defamed（名誉败坏）in her eyes. I am ignoble（卑劣）in her eyes. There is a wide gulf between us now. She has found me out, Arthur, she has found me out.

LORD GORING: Has she never in her life done some folly—some indiscretion—that she should not forgive your sin?

SIR ROBERT CHILTERN: My wife! Never! She does not know what weakness or temptation is. I am of clay like other men. She stands apart as good women do—pitiless in her perfection—cold and stern and without mercy. But I love her, Arthur. We are childless, and I have no one else to love, no one else to love me. Perhaps if God had sent us children she might have been kinder to me. But God has given us a lonely house. And she has cut my heart in two. Don't let us talk of it. I was brutal to her this evening. But I suppose when sinners talk to saints they are brutal always. I said to her things that were hideously true, on my side, from my standpoint, from the standpoint of men. But don't let us talk of that.

LORD GORING: Your wife will forgive you. Perhaps at this moment she is forgiving you. She loves you, Robert. Why should she not forgive?

SIR ROBERT CHILTERN: God grant it! God grant it! *[Buries his face in his hands.]* But there is something more I have to tell you, Arthur.

[Enter PHIPPS with drinks.]

PHIPPS *[hands hock and seltzer to SIR ROBERT CHILTERN]*: Hock and seltzer, sir.

SIR ROBERT CHILTERN: Thank you.

LORD GORING: Is your carriage here, Robert?

SIR ROBERT CHILTERN: No; I walked from the club.

LORD GORING: Sir Robert will take my cab, Phipps.

PHIPPS: Yes, my lord.

    [Exit.]

LORD GORING: Robert, you don't mind my sending you away?

SIR ROBERT CHILTERN: Arthur, you must let me stay for five minutes. I have made up my mind what I am going to do tonight in the House. The debate on the Argentine Canal is to begin at eleven. *[A chair falls in the drawing-room.]* What is that?

LORD GORING: Nothing.

SIR ROBERT CHILTERN: I heard a chair fall in the next room. Some one has been listening.

LORD GORING: No, no; there is no one there.

SIR ROBERT CHILTERN: There is someone. There are lights in the room, and the door is ajar（微开的）. Some one has been listening to every secret of my life. Arthur, what does this mean?

LORD GORING: Robert, you are excited, unnerved（心慌意乱）. I tell you there is no one in that room. Sit down, Robert.

SIR ROBERT CHILTERN: Do you give me your word that there is no one there?

LORD GORING: Yes.

SIR ROBERT CHILTERN: Your word of honour?

    [Sits down.]

LORD GORING: Yes.

SIR ROBERT CHILTERN *[rises]*: Arthur, let me see for myself.

LORD GORING: No, no.

SIR ROBERT CHILTERN: If there is no one there why should I not look in that room? Arthur, you must let me go into that room and satisfy myself. Let me know that no eavesdropper（窃听者）has heard my life's secret. Arthur, you don't realise what I am going through.

LORD GORING: Robert, this must stop. I have told you that there is no one in that room—that is enough.

SIR ROBERT CHILTERN *[rushes to the door of the room]*: It is not enough. I insist on going into this room. You have told me there is no one there, so what reason can you have for refusing me?

LORD GORING: For God's sake, don't! There is someone there. Someone whom you must not see.

SIR ROBERT CHILTERN: Ah, I thought so!

LORD GORING: I forbid you to enter that room.

SIR ROBERT CHILTERN: Stand back. My life is at stake. And I don't care who is there. I will know who it is to whom I have told my secret and my shame.
 [Enters room.]
LORD GORING: Great heavens! his own wife!
 [SIR ROBERT CHILTERN comes back, with a look of scorn（蔑视） and anger on his face.]
SIR ROBERT CHILTERN: What explanation have you to give me for the presence of that woman here?
LORD GORING: Robert, I swear to you on my honour that that lady is stainless（纯洁无瑕的） and guiltless of all offence（罪过） towards you.
SIR ROBERT CHILTERN: She is a vile（邪恶的）, an infamous thing!
LORD GORING: Don't say that, Robert! It was for your sake she came here. It was to try and save you she came here. She loves you and no one else.
SIR ROBERT CHILTERN: You are mad. What have I to do with her intrigues（阴谋诡计） with you? Let her remain your mistress! You are well suited to each other. She, corrupt and shameful—you, false as a friend, treacherous（奸诈的） as an enemy even—
LORD GORING: It is not true, Robert. Before heaven, it is not true. In her presence and in yours I will explain all.
SIR ROBERT CHILTERN: Let me pass, sir. You have lied enough upon your word of honour.
 [SIR ROBERT CHILTERN goes out. LORD GORING rushes to the door of the drawing-room, when MRS. CHEVELEY comes out, looking radiant and much amused.]

Excerpt 7 (from Act 3, continued)

After Sir Robert Chiltern leaves angrily, Mrs. Cheveley tries to make a deal with Lord Goring. This excerpt shows the confrontation between the two most sophisticated characters in the story. At the end of it, a crisis is resolved but a new one is created.

MRS. CHEVELEY *[with a mock（佯装的） curtsey（屈膝礼）]*: Good evening, Lord Goring!
LORD GORING: Mrs. Cheveley! Great heavens! ... May I ask what you were doing in my drawing-room?
MRS. CHEVELEY: Merely listening. I have a perfect passion for listening through keyholes. One always hears such wonderful things through them.
LORD GORING: Doesn't that sound rather like tempting Providence（招惹天谴）?

MRS. CHEVELEY: Oh! surely Providence can resist temptation by this time.
   [Makes a sign to him to take her cloak off, which he does.]
LORD GORING: I am glad you have called. I am going to give you some good advice.
MRS. CHEVELEY: Oh! pray don't. One should never give a woman anything that she can't wear in the evening.
LORD GORING: I see you are quite as wilful（任性） as you used to be.
MRS. CHEVELEY: Far more! I have greatly improved. I have had more experience.
LORD GORING: Too much experience is a dangerous thing. Pray have a cigarette. Half the pretty women in London smoke cigarettes. Personally I prefer the other half.
MRS. CHEVELEY: Thanks. I never smoke. My dressmaker wouldn't like it, and a woman's first duty in life is to her dressmaker, isn't it? What the second duty is, no one has as yet discovered.
LORD GORING: You have come here to sell me Robert Chiltern's letter, haven't you?
MRS. CHEVELEY: To offer it to you on conditions. How did you guess that?
LORD GORING: Because you haven't mentioned the subject. Have you got it with you?
MRS. CHEVELEY: *[Sitting down.]* Oh, no! A well-made dress has no pockets.
LORD GORING: What is your price for it?
MRS. CHEVELEY: How absurdly English you are! The English think that a cheque-book can solve every problem in life. Why, my dear Arthur, I have very much more money than you have, and quite as much as Robert Chiltern has got hold of. Money is not what I want.
LORD GORING: What do you want then, Mrs. Cheveley?
MRS. CHEVELEY: Why don't you call me Laura?
LORD GORING: I don't like the name.
MRS. CHEVELEY: You used to adore it.
LORD GORING: Yes: that's why.
   [MRS. CHEVELEY motions to him to sit down beside her. He smiles, and does so.]
MRS. CHEVELEY: Arthur, you loved me once.
LORD GORING: Yes.
MRS. CHEVELEY: And you asked me to be your wife.
LORD GORING: That was the natural result of my loving you.
MRS. CHEVELEY: And you threw me over because you saw, or said you saw, poor old Lord Mortlake trying to have a violent flirtation with me in the conservatory（温室） at Tenby.
LORD GORING: I am under the impression that my lawyer settled that matter with you on certain terms... dictated by yourself.
MRS. CHEVELEY: At that time I was poor; you were rich.

LORD GORING: Quite so. That is why you pretended to love me.

MRS. CHEVELEY *[shrugging her shoulders]*: Poor old Lord Mortlake, who had only two topics of conversation, his gout（痛风） and his wife! I never could quite make out which of the two he was talking about. He used the most horrible language about them both. Well, you were silly, Arthur. Why, Lord Mortlake was never anything more to me than an amusement. One of those utterly tedious amusements one only finds at an English country house on an English country Sunday. I don't think anyone at all morally responsible for what he or she does at an English country house.

LORD GORING: Yes. I know lots of people think that.

MRS. CHEVELEY: I loved you, Arthur.

LORD GORING: My dear Mrs. Cheveley, you have always been far too clever to know anything about love.

MRS. CHEVELEY: I did love you. And you loved me. You know you loved me; and love is a very wonderful thing. I suppose that when a man has once loved a woman, he will do anything for her, except continue to love her?

[Puts her hand on his.]

LORD GORING *[taking his hand away quietly]*: Yes: except that.

MRS. CHEVELEY *[after a pause]*: I am tired of living abroad. I want to come back to London. I want to have a charming house here. I want to have a salon. If one could only teach the English how to talk, and the Irish how to listen, society here would be quite civilised. Besides, I have arrived at the romantic stage. When I saw you last night at the Chilterns', I knew you were the only person I had ever cared for, if I ever have cared for anybody, Arthur. And so, on the morning of the day you marry me, I will give you Robert Chiltern's letter. That is my offer. I will give it to you now, if you promise to marry me.

LORD GORING: Now?

MRS. CHEVELEY *[smiling]*: Tomorrow.

LORD GORING: Are you really serious?

MRS. CHEVELEY: Yes, quite serious.

LORD GORING: I should make you a very bad husband.

MRS. CHEVELEY: I don't mind bad husbands. I have had two. They amused me immensely.

LORD GORING: You mean that you amused yourself immensely, don't you?

MRS. CHEVELEY: What do you know about my married life?

LORD GORING: Nothing: but I can read it like a book.

MRS. CHEVELEY: What book?

Unit 2

Oscar Wilde and *An Ideal Husband*

LORD GORING [*rising*]: The Book of Numbers①.

MRS. CHEVELEY: Do you think it is quite charming of you to be so rude to a woman in your own house?

LORD GORING: In the case of very fascinating women, sex is a challenge, not a defence.

MRS. CHEVELEY: I suppose that is meant for a compliment. My dear Arthur, women are never disarmed by compliments. Men always are. That is the difference between the two sexes.

LORD GORING: Women are never disarmed by anything, as far as I know them.

MRS. CHEVELEY [*after a pause*]: Then you are going to allow your greatest friend, Robert Chiltern, to be ruined, rather than marry some one who really has considerable attractions left. I thought you would have risen to some great height of self-sacrifice, Arthur. I think you should. And the rest of your life you could spend in contemplating your own perfections.

LORD GORING: Oh! I do that as it is. And self-sacrifice is a thing that should be <u>put down</u>（取缔） by law. It is so <u>demoralising</u>（使人道德败坏或灰心丧气） to the people for whom one sacrifices oneself. They always go to the bad.

MRS. CHEVELEY: As if anything could demoralise Robert Chiltern! You seem to forget that I know his real character.

LORD GORING: What you know about him is not his real character. It was an act of folly done in his youth, dishonourable, I admit, shameful, I admit, unworthy of him, I admit, and therefore... not his true character.

MRS. CHEVELEY: How you men stand up for each other!

LORD GORING: How you women war against each other!

MRS. CHEVELEY [*bitterly*]: I only war against one woman, against Gertrude Chiltern. I hate her. I hate her now more than ever.

LORD GORING: Because you have brought a real tragedy into her life, I suppose?

MRS. CHEVELEY [*with a sneer*]: Oh, there is only one real tragedy in a woman's life. The fact that her past is always her lover, and her future invariably her husband.

LORD GORING: Lady Chiltern knows nothing of the kind of life to which you are alluding.

MRS. CHEVELEY: A woman whose size in gloves is seven and three-quarters② never knows much about anything. You know Gertrude has always worn seven and three-quarters? That is one of the reasons why there was never any moral sympathy between us.... Well, Arthur, I suppose this romantic interview may be regarded as at an end. You admit it was romantic, don't you? For the privilege of

---

① Book of Numbers: the fourth book of the Old Testament that documents Israel's 40-year wanderings in the desert, its name coming from the two censuses taken of the people.

② size ... three-quarters: the big size of gloves implies inelegant hands.

being your wife I was ready to surrender a great prize, the climax of my diplomatic career. You decline. Very well. If Sir Robert doesn't uphold my Argentine scheme, I expose him. *Voilà tout*①.

LORD GORING: You mustn't do that. It would be vile, horrible, infamous.

MRS. CHEVELEY [*shrugging her shoulders*]: Oh! Don't use big words. They mean so little. It is a commercial transaction. That is all. There is no good mixing <u>sentimentality</u>（多愁善感） in it. I offered to sell Robert Chiltern a certain thing. If he won't pay me my price, he will have to pay the world a greater price. There is no more to be said. I must go. Good-bye. Won't you shake hands?

LORD GORING: With you? No. Your transaction with Robert Chiltern may pass as a loathsome commercial transaction of a loathsome commercial age; but you seem to have forgotten that you came here tonight to talk of love, you whose lips <u>desecrated</u>（亵渎） the word love, you to whom the thing is a book closely sealed, went this afternoon to the house of one of the most noble and gentle women in the world to <u>degrade</u>（贬低、侮辱） her husband in her eyes, to try and kill her love for him, to put poison in her heart, and bitterness in her life, to break her idol, and, it may be, spoil her soul. That I cannot forgive you. That was horrible. For that there can be no forgiveness.

MRS. CHEVELEY: Arthur, you are unjust to me. Believe me, you are quite unjust to me. I didn't go to taunt Gertrude at all. I had no idea of doing anything of the kind when I entered. I called with Lady Markby simply to ask whether an ornament, a jewel, that I lost somewhere last night, had been found at the Chilterns'. If you don't believe me, you can ask Lady Markby. She will tell you it is true. The scene that occurred happened after Lady Markby had left, and was really forced on me by Gertrude's rudeness and sneers. I called, oh!—a little out of <u>malice</u>（怨恨） if you like—but really to ask if a diamond brooch of mine had been found. That was the origin of the whole thing.

LORD GORING: A diamond snake-brooch with a ruby?

MRS. CHEVELEY: Yes. How do you know?

LORD GORING: Because it is found. In point of fact, I found it myself, and stupidly forgot to tell the butler anything about it as I was leaving. *[Goes over to the writing-table and pulls out the drawers.]* It is in this drawer. No, that one. This is the brooch, isn't it?

[*Holds up the brooch.*]

MRS. CHEVELEY: Yes. I am so glad to get it back. It was... a present.

LORD GORING: Won't you wear it?

MRS. CHEVELEY: Certainly, if you pin it in. *[LORD GORING suddenly <u>clasps</u>（扣紧） it on her arm.]* Why do you put it on as a <u>bracelet</u>（手镯）? I never knew it

---

① *Voilà tout*: (French) That's all.

could be worn as a bracelet.

LORD GORING: Really?

MRS. CHEVELEY [*holding out her handsome arm*]: No; but it looks very well on me as a bracelet, doesn't it?

LORD GORING: Yes; much better than when I saw it last.

MRS. CHEVELEY: When did you see it last?

LORD GORING: [*calmly*] Oh, ten years ago, on Lady Berkshire, from whom you stole it.

MRS. CHEVELEY: [*starting*] What do you mean?

LORD GORING: I mean that you stole that ornament from my cousin, Mary Berkshire, to whom I gave it when she was married. Suspicion fell on a wretched servant, who was sent away in disgrace. I recognised it last night. I determined to say nothing about it till I had found the thief. I have found the thief now, and I have heard her own confession.

MRS. CHEVELEY [*tossing her head*]: It is not true.

LORD GORING: You know it is true. Why, thief is written across your face at this moment.

MRS. CHEVELEY: I will deny the whole affair from beginning to end. I will say that I have never seen this wretched thing, that it was never in my possession.

   [*MRS. CHEVELEY tries to get the bracelet off her arm, but fails. LORD GORING looks on amused. Her thin fingers tear at the jewel to no purpose. A curse breaks from her.*]

LORD GORING: The drawback of stealing a thing, Mrs. Cheveley, is that one never knows how wonderful the thing that one steals is. You can't get that bracelet off, unless you know where the spring（弹簧） is. And I see you don't know where the spring is. It is rather difficult to find.

MRS. CHEVELEY: You brute（野兽）! You coward（懦夫）!

   [*She tries again to unclasp the bracelet, but fails.*]

LORD GORING: Oh! don't use big words. They mean so little.

MRS. CHEVELEY [*again tears at the bracelet in a paroxysm（发作） of rage, with inarticulate sounds. Then stops, and looks at LORD GORING*]: What are you going to do?

LORD GORING: I am going to ring for my servant. He is an admirable servant. Always comes in the moment one rings for him. When he comes I will tell him to fetch the police.

MRS. CHEVELEY [*trembling*]: The police? What for?

LORD GORING: Tomorrow the Berkshires will prosecute（起诉） you. That is what the police are for.

MRS. CHEVELEY [*is now in an agony of physical terror. Her face is distorted. Her mouth awry. A mask has fallen from her. She is, for the moment, dreadful to look at]*: Don't do that. I will do anything you want. Anything in the world you want.

LORD GORING: Give me Robert Chiltern's letter.

MRS. CHEVELEY: Stop! Stop! Let me have time to think.

LORD GORING: Give me Robert Chiltern's letter.

MRS. CHEVELEY: I have not got it with me. I will give it to you tomorrow.

LORD GORING: You know you are lying. Give it to me at once. *[MRS. CHEVELEY pulls the letter out, and hands it to him. She is horribly pale.]* This is it?

MRS. CHEVELEY *[in a hoarse voice]*: Yes.

LORD GORING *[takes the letter, examines it, sighs, and burns it with the lamp]*: For so well-dressed a woman, Mrs. Cheveley, you have moments of admirable common sense. I congratulate you.

MRS. CHEVELEY *[catches sight of LADY CHILTERN'S letter, the cover of which is just showing from under the blotting-book.]*: Please get me a glass of water.

LORD GORING: Certainly.

[Goes to the corner of the room and pours out a glass of water. While his back is turned MRS. CHEVELEY steals LADY CHILTERN'S letter. When LORD GORING returns the glass she refuses it with a gesture.]

MRS. CHEVELEY: Thank you. Will you help me on with my cloak?

LORD GORING: With pleasure.

[Puts her cloak on.]

MRS. CHEVELEY: Thanks. I am never going to try to harm Robert Chiltern again.

LORD GORING: Fortunately you have not the chance, Mrs. Cheveley.

MRS. CHEVELEY: Well, even if I had the chance, I wouldn't. On the contrary, I am going to render him a great service.

LORD GORING: I am charmed to hear it. It is a reformation（革新）.

MRS. CHEVELEY: Yes. I can't bear so upright a gentleman, so honourable an English gentleman, being so shamefully deceived, and so—

LORD GORING: Well?

MRS. CHEVELEY: I find that somehow Gertrude Chiltern's dying speech and confession has strayed（误入歧途） into my pocket.

LORD GORING: What do you mean?

MRS. CHEVELEY *[with a bitter note of triumph in her voice]*: I mean that I am going to send Robert Chiltern the love-letter his wife wrote to you tonight.

LORD GORING: Love-letter?

MRS. CHEVELEY *[laughing]*: "I want you. I trust you. I am coming to you. Gertrude."

[LORD GORING rushes to the bureau and takes up the envelope, finds it is empty, and turns round.]

Unit 2

Oscar Wilde and *An Ideal Husband*

LORD GORING: You wretched woman, must you always be thieving（偷窃）? Give me back that letter. I'll take it from you by force. You shall not leave my room till I have got it.

> [*He rushes towards her, but MRS. CHEVELEY at once puts her hand on the electric bell that is on the table. The bell sounds with shrill reverberations（回响）, and PHIPPS enters.*]

MRS. CHEVELEY [*after a pause*]: Lord Goring merely rang that you should show me out. Good night, Lord Goring!

> [*Goes out followed by PHIPPS. Her face is illumined with evil triumph. There is joy in her eyes. Youth seems to have come back to her. Her last glance is like a swift arrow. LORD GORING bites his lip, and lights a cigarette.*]

✣ Excerpt 8 (from Act 4)

The next morning witnesses many happy events. Lord Goring finally makes a proposal to Mabel, who joyously accepts it; Mrs. Cheveley's scheme regarding Lady Chiltern's pink letter fails to work; and Sir Robert has made such a successful speech in the House of Commons he is offered a seat in the cabinet. However, he declines it in deference to Lady Chiltern, who has forgiven Sir Robert but still believes he must give up public life. Seeing this, Goring tries to change her mind.

LORD GORING: Lady Chiltern, why are you playing Mrs. Cheveley's cards?

LADY CHILTERN [*startled*]: I don't understand you.

LORD GORING: Mrs. Cheveley made an attempt to ruin your husband. Either to drive him from public life, or to make him adopt a dishonourable position. From the latter tragedy you saved him. The former you are now thrusting（强迫接受）on him. Why should you do him the wrong Mrs. Cheveley tried to do and failed?

LADY CHILTERN: Lord Goring?

LORD GORING [*pulling himself together for a great effort, and showing the philosopher that underlies（位于……之下）the dandy*]: Lady Chiltern, allow me. You wrote me a letter last night in which you said you trusted me and wanted my help. Now is the moment when you really want my help, now is the time when you have got to trust me, to trust in my counsel（建议）and judgment. You love Robert. Do you want to kill his love for you? What sort of existence will he have if you rob him of the fruits of his ambition, if you take him from the splendour of a great political career, if you close the doors of public life against him, if you condemn him to sterile（枯燥乏味的）failure, he who was made for triumph and success? Women are not meant to judge us, but to forgive us when we need forgiveness. Pardon, not punishment, is their mission. Why should you scourge（鞭打）him with rods（鞭杖）for a sin done in his youth, before he knew you, before he knew himself? A man's life is of more value than a woman's. It has larger issues, wider scope（范围）, greater ambitions. A woman's life revolves（旋转）in curves of emotions. It is upon lines of intellect that a man's life progresses. Don't make any terrible mistake, Lady Chiltern. A woman who can keep a man's love, and love him in return, has done all the world wants of women, or should want of them.

LADY CHILTERN [*troubled and hesitating*]: But it is my husband himself who wishes to retire from public life. He feels it is his duty. It was he who first said so.

LORD GORING: Rather than lose your love, Robert would do anything, wreck his whole career, as he is on the brink of（即将，濒临）doing now. He is making for you a terrible sacrifice. Take my advice, Lady Chiltern, and do not accept a sacrifice so great. If you do you will live to repent（后悔）it bitterly. We men and women are not made to accept such sacrifices from each other. We are not worthy of them. Besides, Robert has been punished enough.

LADY CHILTERN: We have both been punished. I set him up too high.

LORD GORING [*with deep feeling in his voice*]: Do not for that reason set him down now too low. If he has fallen from his altar, do not thrust him into the mire（泥潭）. Failure to Robert would be the very mire of shame. Power is his passion. He would lose everything, even his power to feel love. Your husband's life is at this moment in your hands, your husband's love is in your hands. Don't mar（损坏）both for him.

[*Enter SIR ROBERT CHILTERN.*]

SIR ROBERT CHILTERN: Gertrude, here is the draft of my letter. Shall I read it to you?

LADY CHILTERN: Let me see it.

[*SIR ROBERT hands her the letter. She reads it, and then, with a gesture of passion, tears it up.*]

SIR ROBERT CHILTERN: What are you doing?

LADY CHILTERN: A man's life is of more value than a woman's. It has larger issues, wider scope, greater ambitions. Our lives revolve in curves of emotions. It is upon lines of intellect that a man's life progresses. I have just learnt this, and much else with it, from Lord Goring. And I will not spoil your life for you, nor see you spoil it as a sacrifice to me, a useless sacrifice!

SIR ROBERT CHILTERN: Gertrude! Gertrude!

LADY CHILTERN: You can forget. Men easily forget. And I forgive. That is how women help the world. I see that now.

SIR ROBERT CHILTERN [*deeply overcome by emotion, embraces her*]: My wife! my wife! *[To LORD GORING.]* Arthur, it seems that I am always to be <u>in your debt</u>（欠人情）.

LORD GORING: Oh dear no, Robert. Your debt is to Lady Chiltern, not to me!

SIR ROBERT CHILTERN: I owe you much. And now tell me what you were going to ask me just now as Lord Caversham came in.

LORD GORING: Robert, you are your sister's guardian, and I want your consent to my marriage with her. That is all.

LADY CHILTERN: Oh, I am so glad! I am so glad!

    [Shakes hands with LORD GORING.]

LORD GORING: Thank you, Lady Chiltern.

SIR ROBERT CHILTERN *[with a troubled look]*: My sister to be your wife?

LORD GORING: Yes.

SIR ROBERT CHILTERN *[speaking with great firmness]*: Arthur, I am very sorry, but the thing is quite <u>out of the question</u>（不可能）. I have to think of Mabel's future happiness. And I don't think her happiness would be safe in your hands. And I cannot have her sacrificed!

LORD GORING: Sacrificed!

SIR ROBERT CHILTERN: Yes, utterly sacrificed. Loveless marriages are horrible. But there is one thing worse than an absolutely loveless marriage. A marriage in which there is love, but on one side only; faith, but on one side only; devotion, but on one side only, and in which of the two hearts one is sure to be broken.

LORD GORING: But I love Mabel. No other woman has any place in my life.

LADY CHILTERN: Robert, if they love each other, why should they not be married?

SIR ROBERT CHILTERN: Arthur cannot bring Mabel the love that she deserves.

LORD GORING: What reason have you for saying that?

SIR ROBERT CHILTERN *[after a pause]*: Do you really require me to tell you?

LORD GORING: Certainly I do.

SIR ROBERT CHILTERN: As you choose. When I called on you yesterday evening I found Mrs. Cheveley concealed in your rooms. It was between ten and eleven o'clock at night. I do not wish to say anything more. Your relations with Mrs. Cheveley have, as I said to you last night, nothing whatsoever to do with me. I know you were engaged to be married to her once. The <u>fascination</u>（魅力） she exercised over you then seems to have returned. You spoke to me last night of her as of a woman pure and stainless, a woman whom you respected and honoured. That may be so. But I cannot give my sister's life into your hands. It would be wrong of me. It would be unjust, infamously unjust to her.

LORD GORING: I have nothing more to say.

LADY CHILTERN: Robert, it was not Mrs. Cheveley whom Lord Goring expected last night.

SIR ROBERT CHILTERN: Not Mrs. Cheveley! Who was it then?
LORD GORING: Lady Chiltern!
LADY CHILTERN: It was your own wife. Robert, yesterday afternoon Lord Goring told me that if ever I was in trouble I could come to him for help, as he was our oldest and best friend. Later on, after that terrible scene in this room, I wrote to him telling him that I trusted him, that I had need of him, that I was coming to him for help and advice. *[SIR ROBERT CHILTERN takes the letter out of his pocket.]* Yes, that letter. I didn't go to Lord Goring's, after all. I felt that it is from ourselves alone that help can come. Pride made me think that. Mrs. Cheveley went. She stole my letter and sent it <u>anonymously</u>（匿名地） to you this morning, that you should think... Oh! Robert, I cannot tell you what she wished you to think....
SIR ROBERT CHILTERN: What! Had I fallen so low in your eyes that you thought that even for a moment I could have doubted your goodness? Gertrude, Gertrude, you are to me the white image of all good things, and sin can never touch you. Arthur, you can go to Mabel, and you have my best wishes! Oh! stop a moment. There is no name at the beginning of this letter. The brilliant Mrs. Cheveley does not seem to have noticed that. There should be a name.
LADY CHILTERN: Let me write yours. It is you I trust and need. You and none else.
LORD GORING: Well, really, Lady Chiltern, I think I should have back my own letter.
LADY CHILTERN *[smiling]*: No; you shall have Mabel.
　　[Takes the letter and writes her husband's name on it.]
LORD GORING: Well, I hope she hasn't changed her mind. It's nearly twenty minutes since I saw her last.
　　[Enter MABEL CHILTERN and LORD CAVERSHAM.]
MABEL CHILTERN: Lord Goring, I think your father's conversation much more <u>improving</u>（有教育意义） than yours. I am only going to talk to Lord Caversham in the future, and always under the usual palm tree.
LORD GORING: Darling!
　　[Kisses her.]
LORD CAVERSHAM *[considerably taken aback]*: What does this mean, sir? You don't mean to say that this charming, clever young lady has been so foolish as to accept you?
LORD GORING: Certainly, father! And Chiltern's been wise enough to accept the seat in the Cabinet.
LORD CAVERSHAM: I am very glad to hear that, Chiltern... I congratulate you, sir. If the country doesn't go to the dogs or the Radicals, we shall have you Prime Minister, some day.
　　[Enter MASON.]
MASON: <u>Luncheon</u>（午宴） is on the table, my Lady!

Unit 2

Oscar Wilde and *An Ideal Husband*

[MASON goes out.]

MABEL CHILTERN: You'll stop to luncheon, Lord Caversham, won't you?

LORD CAVERSHAM: With pleasure, and I'll drive you down to Downing Street[①] afterwards, Chiltern. You have a great future before you, a great future. *[To LORD GORING.]* Wish I could say the same for you, sir. But your career will have to be entirely domestic.

LORD GORING: Yes, father, I prefer it domestic.

LORD CAVERSHAM: And if you don't make this young lady an ideal husband, I'll cut you off with a shilling（剥夺继承权）.

MABEL CHILTERN: An ideal husband! Oh, I don't think I should like that. It sounds like something in the next world.

LORD CAVERSHAM: What do you want him to be then, dear?

MABEL CHILTERN: He can be what he chooses. All I want is to be... to be... oh! a real wife to him.

LORD CAVERSHAM: Upon my word, there is a good deal of common sense in that, Lady Chiltern.

[They all go out except SIR ROBERT CHILTERN. He sinks into a chair, wrapt in thought（陷入沉思）. After a little time LADY CHILTERN returns to look for him.]

LADY CHILTERN *[leaning over the back of the chair]*: Aren't you coming in, Robert?

SIR ROBERT CHILTERN *[taking her hand]*: Gertrude, is it love you feel for me, or is it pity merely?

LADY CHILTERN *[kisses him]*: It is love, Robert. Love, and only love. For both of us a new life is beginning.

2.2.4 Exercises

❶ Give a brief answer to each of the following questions.

Act 1

1) What are the characteristics of Lord Goring?
2) Why does Mrs. Cheveley come to visit Sir Robert Chiltern? What does Mrs. Cheveley threaten to do if Sir Robert rejects her proposition?
3) How does Lady Chiltern know Mrs. Cheveley? What's her impression of Mrs. Cheveley's past behavior?
4) How does Sir Robert account for his change of mind to his wife regarding the canal scheme?

---

① Downing Street: a street in west central London, known for housing the official residences and offices of the Prime Minister and the Chancellor of the Exchequer.

5) How, in Lady Chiltern's opinion, do men and women differ in love?
6) What does Lady Chiltern make Sir Robert do to Mrs. Cheveley?

Act 2

7) What is Baron Arnheim's philosophy of power, and gospel of gold?
8) Why was Sir Robert so easily influenced by Arnheim's doctrines? Does he say he ever felt remorse for what he did in the past?
9) What was the relationship between Lord Goring and Mrs. Cheveley in the past? What happened next?
10) Why does Mrs. Cheveley visit Lady Chiltern the second day?
11) Why doesn't Mabel love Tommy Trafford? What does this show about her character?
12) What is Sir Robert's response after his wife learns about his past secret?

Act 3

13) What does Lord Caversham continually urge his son to do? What kind of person does he expect his son to be?
14) How do Lord Caversham and Lord Goring differ on the subject of marriage?
15) Why does Lord Goring swear to Robert on his honour that "that lady is stainless and guiltless of all offence towards you"?
16) What is Mrs. Cheveley willing to trade Sir Robert's letter for?
17) What is the ultimate fate of Sir Robert's letter to Baron Arnheim?

Act 4

18) What does Sir Robert say about the Argentine Canal in his address to the House of Commons?
19) What happens after Lady Chiltern's pink letter is posted to Sir Robert?
20) What appointment is Sir Robert offered near the end of the play? Why does he decline it at first?

❷ Identify the following characters.

1) _____ is confronted by his disreputable past and blackmailed. He capitulates to his blackmailer's demands at first but changes his mind under the influence of his wife. Thanks to his friend, he is finally saved from any public scandal.

2) _____ is firmly opposed to the excesses of his dandified son. He spends his time chastising his son and lecturing him about what he should do with his time. Despite his exasperation, he is fond of his lazy son.

3) _____ has her eye on Lord Goring as a husband, but she does not expect perfection from him or any other human being. She matches Lord Goring's wit throughout the play.

4) _____ is able to prevent Mrs. Cheveley from carrying out her threat because he acquires proof that she is a thief. If it were not for his father's importunities, he

would undoubtedly continue in his life of perfect leisure and self-absorption.

5) _____ embodies the Victorian new woman. Until she learns the truth about her husband's past, she is certain that he is indeed her ideal. She must learn a stern lesson in the play: nobody is perfect.

6) _____ plays an important role in the play even though he does not appear on stage. It is he who convinced the young Sir Robert to sell him confidential state information many years ago.

7) _____ is a quiet man. His job is not to assert himself or his own personality in any way. Yet, he shows subtle humor in conversation with his master.

8) _____ introduces Mrs. Cheveley to persons whom she does not yet know in London and chaperones her around town. She is an established older member of the aristocratic society.

9) _____ adores all things English but his speech is comically awkward. Apparently, his purpose in the play is to give the English audiences of the time something French to snicker at.

10) _____ knows Sir Robert Chiltern's terrible, scandalous secret and has concrete evidence of his transgression. She is determined either to get her own way or to destroy those who will not help her achieve her ends.

3 Plot review

Sir Robert Chiltern is a top government official with a promising future. However, his life is suddenly disturbed by the arrival of Mrs. Cheveley, who wants to 1) _____ him into supporting a 2) _____ Argentine Canal scheme in which she has invested heavily. She has in her possession a 3) _____ which Sir Robert wrote many years ago to Baron Arnheim, a stockbroker, in which he revealed a cabinet 4) _____ that enabled the latter to buy Suez Canal 5) _____ shortly before the British government announced its purchase. In fact, Sir Robert owes his current power and wealth largely to this dishonorable act. Consequently, he has to 6) _____ with Mrs. Cheveley's demand. However, when his morally inflexible wife Lady Chiltern, who has always loved and worshipped him as an 7) _____ husband, questions him over this sudden change of mind, he is obliged to withdraw his promise to Mrs. Cheveley while knowing disgrace is in store for him.

Desperate, he tries to seek help from his best friend, Lord Goring, who is a typical 8) _____ that is dressed fashionably, talks wittily, and 9) _____ with life. Sir Robert confesses the cause of his youthful folly: he was well-born and ambitious, but unfortunately he was 10) _____, so he was easily seduced by the teachings of Baron Arnheim, and came to view 11) _____ as the most important weapon of the modern age to get 12) _____. Anyway, the two friends decide to fight Mrs. Cheveley by all means.

Soon Mrs. Cheveley pays a second visit to Lady Chiltern, claiming that she lost a 13) _____ at the party the previous night, which, in fact, has been found and taken away by Lord Goring. During their conversation, Mrs. Cheveley exposes to Lady Chiltern the secret of her husband. As a result, Lady Chiltern feels that she has been 14) _____ by Sir Robert, and the couple have a quarrel.

Later that night, Lord Goring receives a pink note from Lady Chiltern stating that she will come to him for advice. However, other unexpected guests arrive one after another. The first one is his father Lord Caversham, who urges him to 15) _____ and adopt a serious 16) _____. Then Mrs. Cheveley, who is mistaken for Lady Chiltern by the butler and led into one of the rooms, discovers Lady Chiltern's note and mistakes it for a 17) _____ letter. Sir Robert Chiltern also comes to talk with Lord Goring, and when he discovers Mrs. Cheveley in the adjacent room, he misconstrues the 18) _____ between his friend and his enemy. After he leaves in a rage, Mrs. Cheveley proposes to trade Sir Robert's letter for 19) _____ with Lord Goring. Then Lord Goring reveals that the object Mrs. Cheveley has been looking for was actually a gift he gave his cousin years ago, and he accuses Mrs. Cheveley of having 20)_____ it. Fearing 21) _____, Mrs. Cheveley has to surrender Sir Robert's letter, but she manages to steal Lady Chiltern's pink note before leaving. She intends to mail it to Sir Robert so as to destroy his marriage.

However, as no 22) _____ is mentioned on the note, Sir Robert Chiltern mistakes it for his wife's letter of 23) _____ written for him. Also, because he has made a successful speech in parliament in which he 24) _____ the Argentine scheme, he is offered a seat in the 25) _____. But he 26) _____ it in deference to his wife's wishes. Seeing this, Lord Goring talks with Lady Chiltern about the 27) _____ of women in a marriage, and persuades her to change her husband's decision. When Lord Goring proposes to Mabel, Sir Robert 28) _____ on the ground that Lord Goring and Mrs. Cheveley are lovers. At this moment, Lady Chiltern steps out and clears the 29) _____ even though this might mean a blemish on her 30) _____. Finally, Lord Goring is allowed to marry Mabel, and the Chilterns confirm their love.

4 **Identify the speakers of the following lines, briefly tell the situation in which each of them is uttered, and explain its significance.**

1) —I will give you any sum of money you want.
   —Even you are not rich enough to buy back your past, Sir Robert. No man is.
2) —I don't know how you stand society. A lot of damned nobodies talking about nothing.
   —I love talking about nothing, Father. It's the only thing I know anything about.

Unit 2

Oscar Wilde and *An Ideal Husband*

3) Nowadays, with our modern mania for morality, every one has to pose as a paragon of purity, incorruptibility, and all the other seven deadly virtues — and what is the result? You all go over like ninepins — one after the other.

4) —No one should be entirely judged by their past.
   —One's past is what one is. It is the only way by which people should be judged.

5) —I am not changed. But circumstances alter things.
   —Circumstances should never alter principles!

6) And money that comes from a tainted source is a degradation. Power? But power is nothing in itself. It is power to do good that is fine — that, and the only.

7) —Private information is practically the source of every large modern fortune.
   —And public scandal invariably the result.

8) Every man of ambition has to fight his century with its own weapons. What this century worships is wealth. The god of this century is wealth. To succeed one must have wealth. At all costs one must have wealth.

9) I would to God that I had been able to tell the truth... to live the truth. Ah! that is the great thing in life, to live the truth.

10) All I do know is that life cannot be understood without much charity, cannot be lived without much charity. It is love, and not German philosophy, that is the true explanation of this world, whatever may be the explanation of the next.

11) Do you know, Gertrude, I don't mind your talking morality a bit. Morality is simply the attitude we adopt towards people whom we personally dislike.

12) It is not the perfect, but rather the imperfect who have need of love. It is when we are wounded by our own hands, or by the hands of others, that love should come to cure us—else what use is love at all? All sins, except a sin against itself, Love should forgive. All lives, save loveless lives, true Love should pardon.

13) To love oneself is the beginning of a lifelong romance.

14) —Do you always understand everything you say?
    —Yes... if I listen attentively.

15) I used to think ambition the great thing. It is not. Love is the great thing in the world.

16) Certainly, and you well deserve it too. You have got what we want so much in political life nowadays—high character, high moral tone, high principles. [*To LORD GORING.*] Everything that you have not got, sir, and never will have.

17) A man's life is of more value than a woman's. It has larger issues, wider scope, greater ambitions.

18) —We have both been punished. I set him up too high.
    —Do not for that reason set him down now too low.

19) Gertrude, Gertrude, you are to me the white image of all good things, and sin can never touch you.

20) An ideal husband! Oh, I don't think I should like that. It sounds like something in the next world.

5 Questions for essay or discussion

1) What do you think are the themes of the play?
2) Not only is Robert Chiltern's secret concealed in the end, but he is offered a seat in the cabinet even. In your opinion, should he take up the post? Why or why not?
3) Compare the qualities and personalities of Lady Chiltern, Mabel Chiltern and Mrs. Cheveley.
4) Take from the play a few examples of Wildean banter that interest you and explain why you like them.
5) What aspects of the play do you still find relevant today? What are irrelevant?

Unit 3

George Bernard Shaw and *Pygmalion*

3.1 George Bernard Shaw: Life and Works

3.1.1 About the Playwright

George Bernard Shaw (1856—1950) was an Irish comic dramatist, literary critic, and socialist propagandist. He was the winner of the Nobel Prize for Literature in 1925. Shaw was astonishing not only for the range of his writing but for the length and vigor of his life. He was a public figure for most of his days, with an especially keen ability to catch public attention and make his presence felt. His early work was devoted to criticism in newspapers, then to a series of fairly successful novels. He began writing plays in his late thirties; once he began, he realized that he had discovered his vocation, and he continued to write more than fifty. Some of them are among the most performed plays by any English language writer of his time.

George Bernard Shaw was born on July 26, 1856, in Dublin, Ireland, the third and youngest child (and only son) of unhappily married and inattentive parents. Shaw grew up in an atmosphere of genteel poverty, which to him was more humiliating than being merely poor. His education was irregular, due to his dislike of any organized training. After working in an estate agent's office for a while he moved to London as a young man (1876), where he established himself as a leading music and theatre critic in the eighties and nineties and became a prominent member of the Fabian Society—a middle-class socialist group that aimed at the transformation of English society not through revolution but through "permeation" (in Sidney Webb's term) of the country's intellectual and political life, for which Shaw composed many pamphlets. Shaw was a freethinker, a supporter of women's rights, and an advocate of equality of income, the abolition of private property, and a radical change in the voting system. He also campaigned for the simplification of spelling and punctuation and the reform of English alphabet.

Shaw turned to playwriting in 1892. His earliest dramas were called appropriately *Plays Pleasant and Unpleasant*. Shaw called these first plays "unpleasant," because "their dramatic power is used to force the spectator to face unpleasant facts." He followed them with four "pleasant" plays in an effort to find the producers and audiences that his mordant comedies had offended. Both groups of plays were revised and published in *Plays Pleasant and Unpleasant* (1898). Among these, *Widowers' Houses* and *Mrs. Warren's Profession* savagely attack social hypocrisy, while in plays such as *Arms and the Man* and *The Man of Destiny* the criticism is less fierce. Shaw's radical rationalism, his utter disregard of conventions, his keen dialectic interest and verbal wit often turn the stage into a forum of ideas.

His first commercial success was *The Devil's Disciple* (1897), a satire on courtship as well as nineteenth-century romantic drama. In the opening years of the twentieth century Shaw's "revolutionary imagination" began to realize its ambition to create a "New Drama" on the stage of the Royal Court Theatre in London. In the seasons organized between 1904 and 1907 the Royal Court performed *John Bull's Other Island* (one of Shaw's rare direct treatments of Ireland and the Irish), *Man and Superman*, and *Major Barbara*. The 1905 production of *Man and Superman* daringly introduced an on-stage motor car. *Major Barbara*, which explores the conflict and the ultimate mutual assent of a strong-willed father and his equally strong-minded daughter, disturbed many of Shaw's socialist friends with its quizzical espousal of the idea of the future reconstruction of society by an energetic, highly-motivated, power-manipulating minority. Manipulation of a different order figures in *Pygmalion* (1913), ostensibly a withdrawal from politics and philosophy, but in fact a carefully worked study of the developing relationship between a "creator" and his "creation."

Shaw was not merely the best comic dramatist of his time but also one of the most significant playwrights in the English language since the 17th century. Some of his greatest works for the stage—*Caesar and Cleopatra*, the "Don Juan in Hell" episode of *Man and Superman*, *Major Barbara*, *Heartbreak House*, and *Saint Joan*—have a high seriousness and prose beauty that were unmatched by his stage contemporaries. His development of a drama of moral passion and of intellectual conflict and debate, his revivifying of the comedy of manners, and his ventures into symbolic farce and into a theatre of disbelief helped shape the theatre of his time and after. A visionary and mystic whose philosophy of moral passion permeates his plays, Shaw was also the most trenchant pamphleteer since Jonathan Swift, the most readable music critic in English, the best theatre critic of his generation, a prodigious lecturer and essayist on politics, economics, and sociological subjects, and one of the most prolific letter writers in literature. By bringing a bold critical intelligence to his many other areas of interest, he helped mold the political, economic, and sociological thought of three generations.

In 1898 Shaw married Charlotte Payne-Townshend. It seems to have been a marriage of companionship, and they lived together until her death in 1943, in the midst of World War II. Shaw, frail and feeling the effects of wartime privations, made permanent his retreat from his London apartment to his country home at Ayot St. Lawrence, a Hertfordshire village in which he had lived since 1906. Shaw was a strict vegetarian and never drank spirits, coffee, or tea. He died at the age of 94, on November 2, 1950, as independent as ever and still writing for the theatre.

3.1.2 George Bernard Shaw's Major Plays

Widowers' Houses (1892/1893)《鳏夫的房产》
Arms and the Man (1894)《武器与人》
Candida (1897)《康蒂妲》
Mrs. Warren's Profession (1894/1898)《华伦夫人的职业》
The Devil's Disciple (1897)《魔鬼的门徒》
Man and Superman (1901—1903)《人与超人》
Major Barbara (1905)《巴巴拉少校》
Pygmalion (1913)《皮格马利翁》(《卖花女》)
Heartbreak House (1919)《伤心之家》
Saint Joan (1923)《圣女贞德》
The Apple Cart (1929/1930)《苹果车》
Too True to be Good (1931)《真相毕露》

3.2 *Pygmalion*

3.2.1 About the Play

Pygmalion (1913) is possibly Shaw's comedic masterpiece, and certainly his funniest and most popular play. It has been both filmed (1938), winning an Academy

Award for Shaw for his screenplay, and adapted into an immensely popular musical, *My Fair Lady* (1956; motion-picture version, 1964).

Pygmalion describes the transformation of a cockney flower-seller, Eliza Doolittle, into a passable imitation of a duchess by the phonetician Professor Henry Higgins, who undertakes this task in order to win a bet and to prove his own points about English speech and the class system: he teaches her to speak standard English and introduces her successfully to social life, thus winning his bet, but she rebels against his dictatorial and thoughtless behavior, and "bolts" from his tyranny. The play ends with a truce between the two of them, as Higgins acknowledges that she has achieved freedom and independence, and emerged from his treatment as a "tower of strength: a consort battleship." In his postscript Shaw tells us that she marries the docile and devoted Freddy Eynsford Hill. *My Fair Lady*, the musical version, makes the relationship between Eliza and Higgins significantly more romantic.

Pygmalion derives its name from the famous story in Ovid's *Metamorphoses*, in which Pygmalion, King of Cyprus, a sculptor and a misogynist, creates a beautiful ivory statue of a girl more perfect than any living woman. The more he looks upon her, the more deeply he falls in love with her, until he wishes that she were more than a statue. Lovesick, Pygmalion goes to the temple of the goddess Venus and prays that she give him a lover like his statue; Venus is touched by his love and endows the statue with life and transforms it into the flesh-and-blood of Galatea. When Pygmalion returns from Venus' temple and kisses his statue, he is delighted to find that she is warm and soft to the touch — "The maiden felt the kisses, blushed and, lifting her timid eyes up to the light, saw the sky and her lover at the same time." The work of his own hands becomes his wife.

3.2.2 Characters

Eliza (or Liza) Doolittle, a poor girl below twenty who makes a living by selling flowers in the streets of London. She has a strong desire to better her position in life.

Alfred Doolittle, Eliza's father, a dustman. He pursues a carefree life and loathes responsibility.

Henry Higgins, a professor of phonetics. A forty-year-old bachelor, he is harmless at heart but can be haughty and egotistical.

Unit 3

George Bernard Shaw and *Pygmalion*

Colonel Pickering, Henry Higgins's friend, an Englishman who has served in India. He shares Higgins's passion for phonetics, but is, unlike him, courteous and considerate.

Mrs Higgins, Henry Higgins's mother. She is kind and elegant.

Mrs Pearce, Henry Higgins's housekeeper. She is outspoken and is not afraid of pointing out Higgins's bad manners.

Freddy Eynsford Hill, a poor but well-bred young gentleman. He is infatuated with Eliza after she is transformed by Higgins.

Clara Eynsford Hill, Freddy's sister. She is pampered and irritable.

Mrs Eynsford Hill, Freddy's mother. She is reduced to poverty but still tries to cling to her gentility.

Nepommuck (or named Aristid Karpathy in the 1938 film version), Henry Higgins's former student. He is a flattering, boastful man.

3.2.3 Selected Readings from the Play

Excerpt 1 (from Act 1)

It is 11.15 pm in Covent Garden, a marketplace in London. A thunderstorm brings people from different social classes running for shelter in front of the church. Freddy, a young gentleman, is asked by his demanding sister and mother to go into the rain and find a taxi. In his hurry, he collides into Eliza, a flower girl, and scatters her flowers. After he departs, Eliza convinces his mother to pay for the damaged flowers. Then she tries to sell flowers to Pickering, an elderly military gentleman.

> *An elderly gentleman of the <u>amiable</u>（和蔼的） military type rushes into the shelter, and closes a dripping umbrella. He is in the same <u>plight</u>（困境） as Freddy, very wet about the ankles. He is in evening dress, with a light overcoat. He takes the place left vacant by the daughter.*

THE GENTLEMAN. Phew!

THE MOTHER *[to the gentleman]* Oh, sir, is there any sign of its stopping?

THE GENTLEMAN. I'm afraid not. It started worse than ever about two minutes ago.

> *[He goes to the <u>plinth</u>（柱基） beside the flower girl; puts up his foot on it; and stoops to turn down his trouser ends.]*

THE MOTHER. Oh, dear! *[She retires sadly and joins her daughter.]*

THE FLOWER GIRL *[taking advantage of the military gentleman's <u>proximity</u>（邻近） to establish friendly relations with him]* If it's worse, it's a sign it's nearly over. So cheer up, Captain; and buy a flower off a poor girl.

THE GENTLEMAN. I'm sorry, I haven't any change.

THE FLOWER GIRL. I can give you change, Captain.

THE GENTLEMEN. For a sovereign（一英镑金币）? I've nothing less.

THE FLOWER GIRL. Garn（瞎说）! Oh do buy a flower off me, Captain. I can change half-a-crown（半克朗硬币）. Take this for tuppence（两便士）.

THE GENTLEMAN. Now don't be troublesome: there's a good girl. *[Trying his pockets]* I really haven't any change—Stop: here's three hapence（=halfpence 半便士）, if that's any use to you *[he retreats to the other pillar]*.

THE FLOWER GIRL *[disappointed, but thinking three halfpence better than nothing]* Thank you, sir.

THE BYSTANDER *[to the girl]* You be careful: give him a flower for it. There's a bloke（家伙）here behind taking down every blessed word you're saying. *[All turn to the man who is taking notes.]*

THE FLOWER GIRL *[springing up terrified]* I ain't done nothing wrong by speaking to the gentleman. I've a right to sell flowers if I keep off the kerb（路缘石）. *[Hysterically（歇斯底里地）]* I'm a respectable girl: so help me, I never spoke to him except to ask him to buy a flower off me.

General hubbub（喧哗）, mostly sympathetic to the flower girl, but deprecating（反对）her excessive sensibility. Cries of Don't start hollerin（叫喊）. Who's hurting you? Nobody's going to touch you. What's the good of fussing? Steady on（冷静）. Easy easy, etc., *come from the elderly* staid（沉着的）*spectators, who pat her comfortingly. Less patient ones bid her* shut her head（闭嘴）, *or ask her roughly what is wrong with her. A remoter group, not knowing what the matter is, crowd in and increase the noise with question and answer:* What's the row（争吵）? What she do? Where is he? A tec（侦探）taking her down. What! him? Yes: him over there: Took money off the gentleman, etc.

THE FLOWER GIRL *[breaking through them to the gentleman, crying wildly]* Oh, sir, don't let him charge me. You dunno what it means to me. They'll take away my character and drive me on the streets for speaking to gentlemen. They—

THE NOTE TAKER *[coming forward on her right, the rest crowding after him]* There! there! there! there! Who's hurting you, you silly girl? What do you take me for?

THE BYSTANDER. It's aw rawt: e's a gentleman: look at his bə-oots. *[Explaining to the note taker]* She thought you was a copper's（警察）nark（密探）, sir.

THE NOTE TAKER *[with quick interest]* What's a copper's nark?

THE BYSTANDER *[inept（笨拙的）at definition]* It's a—well, it's a copper's nark, as you might say. What else would you call it? A sort of informer（告密者）.

THE FLOWER GIRL *[still hysterical]* I take my Bible oath I never said a word—

THE NOTE TAKER *[overbearing（专横的）but good-humored]* Oh, shut up, shut up. Do I look like a policeman?

THE FLOWER GIRL *[far from reassured（安心的）]* Then what did you take down

Unit 3

George Bernard Shaw and *Pygmalion*

my words for? How do I know whether you took me down right? You just show me what you've wrote about me. *[The note taker opens his book and holds it steadily under her nose, though the pressure of the mob trying to read it over his shoulders would upset a weaker man.]* What's that? That ain't proper writing. I can't read that.

THE NOTE TAKER. I can. *[Reads, reproducing her pronunciation exactly]* "Cheer ap, Keptin; n' baw ya flahr orf a pore gel."

THE FLOWER GIRL *[much distressed（忧虑的）]* It's because I called him Captain. I meant no harm. *[To the gentleman]* Oh, sir, don't let him lay a charge agen me for a word like that. You —

THE GENTLEMAN. Charge! I make no charge. *[To the note taker]* Really, sir, if you are a detective, you need not begin protecting me against molestation（骚扰） by young women until I ask you. Anybody could see that the girl meant no harm.

THE BYSTANDERS GENERALLY *[demonstrating against police espionage（间谍活动）]* Course they could. What business is it of yours? You mind your own affairs. He wants promotion, he does. Taking down people's words! Girl never said a word to him. What harm if she did? Nice thing a girl can't shelter from the rain without being insulted, etc., etc., etc. *[She is conducted by the more sympathetic demonstrators back to her plinth, where she resumes her seat and struggles with her emotion.]*

THE BYSTANDER. He ain't a tec. He's a blooming（该死的） busybody（管闲事的人）: that's what he is. I tell you, look at his bə-oots.

THE NOTE TAKER *[turning on him genially（和气地）]* And how are all your people down at Selsey?

THE BYSTANDER *[suspiciously]* Who told you my people come from Selsey?

THE NOTE TAKER. Never you mind. They did. *[To the girl]* How do you come to be up so far east? You were born in Lisson Grove.

THE FLOWER GIRL *[appalled（惊骇地）]* Oh, what harm is there in my leaving Lisson Grove? It wasn't fit for a pig to live in; and I had to pay four-and-six a week. *[In tears]* Oh, boo—hoo—oo—

THE NOTE TAKER. Live where you like; but stop that noise.

THE GENTLEMAN *[to the girl]* Come, come! He can't touch you: you have a right to live where you please.

A SARCASTIC BYSTANDER *[thrusting himself between the note taker and the gentleman]* Park Lane①, for instance. I'd like to go into（谈论） the Housing Question with you, I would.

THE FLOWER GIRL *[subsiding（平息） into a brooding（沉思的） melancholy over her basket, and talking very low-spiritedly to herself]* I'm a good girl, I am.

---

① Park Lane: one of the most fashionable roads in London.

THE SARCASTIC BYSTANDER [*not attending to her*] Do you know where *I* come from?

THE NOTE TAKER [*promptly（立即地）*] Hoxton.

    Titterings（傻笑）. Popular interest in the note taker's performance increases.

THE SARCASTIC ONE [*amazed*] Well, who said I didn't? Bly me（天哪）! You know everything, you do.

THE FLOWER GIRL [*still nursing her sense of injury*] Ain't no call（理由） to meddle with me, he ain't.

THE BYSTANDER [*to her*] Of course he ain't. Don't you stand it from him. [*To the note taker*] See here: what call have you to know about people what never offered to meddle with you?

THE FLOWER GIRL. Let him say what he likes. I don't want to have no truck（打交道） with him.

THE BYSTANDER. You take us for dirt under your feet, don't you? Catch you（你绝不会） taking liberties with（失礼于） a gentleman!

THE SARCASTIC BYSTANDER. Yes: tell him where he come from if you want to go fortune-telling.

THE NOTE TAKER. Cheltenham, Harrow, Cambridge, and India.

THE GENTLEMAN. Quite right.

Great laughter. Reaction in the note taker's favor. Exclamations of He knows all about it. Told him proper. Hear him tell the toff（有钱人） where he come from? etc.

THE GENTLEMAN. May I ask, sir, do you do this for your living at a music hall?

THE NOTE TAKER. I've thought of that. Perhaps I shall some day.

    The rain has stopped; and the persons on the outside of the crowd begin to drop off（逐个走开）.

THE FLOWER GIRL [*resenting the reaction*] He's no gentleman, he ain't, to interfere with a poor girl.

THE DAUGHTER [*out of patience, pushing her way rudely to the front and displacing the gentleman, who politely retires to the other side of the pillar*] What on earth is Freddy doing? I shall get pneumownia if I stay in this draught any longer.

THE NOTE TAKER [*to himself, hastily making a note of her pronunciation of* "monia"] Earlscourt.

THE DAUGHTER [*violently*] Will you please keep your impertinent remarks to yourself?

THE NOTE TAKER. Did I say that out loud? I didn't mean to. I beg your pardon. Your mother's Epsom, unmistakeably.

THE MOTHER [*advancing between her daughter and the note taker*] How very curious! I was brought up in Largelady Park, near Epsom.

THE NOTE TAKER [*uproariously（喧闹地） amused*] Ha! ha! What a devil of a

Unit 3

George Bernard Shaw and *Pygmalion*

name! Excuse me. *[To the daughter]* You want a cab, do you?

THE DAUGHTER. Don't dare speak to me.

THE MOTHER. Oh, please, please, Clara. *[Her daughter repudiates（拒绝）her with an angry shrug and retires haughtily.]* We should be so grateful to you, sir, if you found us a cab. *[The note taker produces a whistle.]* Oh, thank you. *[She joins her daughter]*.

The note taker blows a piercing blast（轰鸣声）.

THE SARCASTIC BYSTANDER. There! I knowed he was a plain-clothes copper.

THE BYSTANDER. That ain't a police whistle: that's a sporting whistle.

THE FLOWER GIRL *[still preoccupied with her wounded feelings]* He's no right to take away my character. My character is the same to me as any lady's.

THE NOTE TAKER. I don't know whether you've noticed it; but the rain stopped about two minutes ago.

THE BYSTANDER. So it has. Why didn't you say so before? and us losing our time listening to your silliness. *[He walks off towards the Strand.[1]]*

THE SARCASTIC BYSTANDER. I can tell where you come from. You come from Anwell. Go back there.

THE NOTE TAKER *[helpfully]* Hanwell[2].

THE SARCASTIC BYSTANDER *[affecting great distinction of speech]* Thenk you, teacher. Haw haw! So long *[he touches his hat with mock（假装的）respect and strolls off]*.

THE FLOWER GIRL. Frightening people like that! How would he like it himself.

THE MOTHER. It's quite fine now, Clara. We can walk to a motor bus. Come. *[She gathers her skirts above her ankles and hurries off towards the Strand]*.

THE DAUGHTER. But the cab—*[her mother is out of hearing]*. Oh, how tiresome（烦人的）! *[She follows angrily.]*

All the rest have gone except the note taker, the gentleman, and the flower girl, who sits arranging her basket, and still pitying herself in murmurs.

THE FLOWER GIRL. Poor girl! Hard enough for her to live without being worrited（使……担忧）and chivied（困扰）.

THE GENTLEMAN *[returning to his former place on the note taker's left]* How do you do it, if I may ask?

THE NOTE TAKER. Simply phonetics（语音学）. The science of speech. That's my profession; also my hobby. Happy is the man who can make a living by his hobby! You can spot an Irishman or a Yorkshireman by his brogue（土腔）. I can place any man within six miles. I can place him within two miles in London. Sometimes within two streets.

---

[1] the Strand: a major thoroughfare in Central London, well-known for hotels and theatres.

[2] Hanwell: Hanwell Insane Asylum, which opened in 1831, was a public asylum built for the pauper insane.

THE FLOWER GIRL. Ought to be ashamed of himself, unmanly coward!

THE GENTLEMAN. But is there a living in that?

THE NOTE TAKER. Oh yes. Quite a fat one. This is an age of upstarts(暴发户). Men begin in Kentish Town① with 80 pounds a year, and end in Park Lane with a hundred thousand. They want to drop Kentish Town; but they give themselves away(暴露) every time they open their mouths. Now I can teach them—

THE FLOWER GIRL. Let him mind his own business and leave a poor girl—

THE NOTE TAKER [explosively] Woman: cease this detestable(可恶的) boohooing(哭闹) instantly; or else seek the shelter of some other place of worship.

THE FLOWER GIRL [with feeble defiance(反抗)] I've a right to be here if I like, same as you.

THE NOTE TAKER. A woman who utters such depressing and disgusting sounds has no right to be anywhere—no right to live. Remember that you are a human being with a soul and the divine gift of articulate(发音清晰的) speech: that your native language is the language of Shakespeare② and Milton③ and The Bible; and don't sit there crooning(低吟) like a bilious(乖僻的) pigeon.

THE FLOWER GIRL [quite overwhelmed, and looking up at him in mingled wonder and deprecation without daring to raise her head] Ah-ah-ah-ow-ow-oo!

THE NOTE TAKER [whipping(快速拿取) out his book] Heavens! what a sound! [He writes; then holds out the book and reads, reproducing her vowels exactly] Ah-ah-ah-ow-ow-ow-oo!

THE FLOWER GIRL [tickled(逗乐) by the performance, and laughing in spite of herself(不由自主地)] Garn!

THE NOTE TAKER. You see this creature with her kerbstone(路缘石) English: the English that will keep her in the gutter(贫民区) to the end of her days. Well, sir, in three months I could pass that girl off as a duchess(女公爵) at an ambassador's garden party. I could even get her a place as lady's maid or shop assistant, which requires better English.

THE FLOWER GIRL. What's that you say?

THE NOTE TAKER. Yes, you squashed(压烂的) cabbage leaf, you disgrace to the noble architecture of these columns, you incarnate(化身了的) insult to the English language: I could pass you off as the Queen of Sheba④. [To the Gentleman] Can you believe that?

THE GENTLEMAN. Of course I can. I am myself a student of Indian dialects(方言); and—

---

① Kentish Town: an area of northwest London.
② Shakespeare: William Shakespeare (1564—1616), the greatest English dramatist.
③ Milton: John Milton (1606—1674), an English poet famous for his epic *Paradise Lost* (1667).
④ Queen of Sheba: in the Bible, a queen who visited Solomon to test his wisdom. (I Kings 10:1–13)

Unit 3

George Bernard Shaw and *Pygmalion*

THE NOTE TAKER [*eagerly*] Are you? Do you know Colonel（陆军上校）Pickering, the author of Spoken Sanscrit（梵语）?

THE GENTLEMAN. I am Colonel Pickering. Who are you?

THE NOTE TAKER. Henry Higgins, author of Higgins's Universal Alphabet.

PICKERING [*with enthusiasm*] I came from India to meet you.

HIGGINS. I was going to India to meet you.

PICKERING. Where do you live?

HIGGINS. 27A Wimpole Street. Come and see me tomorrow.

PICKERING. I'm at the Carlton①. Come with me now and let's have a jaw（闲谈）over some supper.

HIGGINS. Right you are.

THE FLOWER GIRL [*to Pickering, as he passes her*] Buy a flower, kind gentleman. I'm short for my lodging.

PICKERING. I really haven't any change. I'm sorry [*he goes away*].

HIGGINS [*shocked at girl's mendacity（谎言）*] Liar. You said you could change half-a-crown.

THE FLOWER GIRL [*rising in desperation*] You ought to be stuffed with nails, you ought. [*Flinging（抛）the basket at his feet*] Take the whole blooming basket for sixpence.

The church clock strikes the second quarter.

HIGGINS [*hearing in it the voice of God, rebuking（谴责）him for his Pharisaic（形式上遵守教义的，伪善的）want（缺乏）of charity to the poor girl*] A reminder. [*He raises his hat solemnly; then throws a handful of money into the basket and follows Pickering.*]

THE FLOWER GIRL [*picking up a half-crown*] Ah-ow-ooh! [*Picking up a couple of florins（弗罗林银币）*] Aaah-ow-ooh! [*Picking up several coins*] Aaaaah-ow-ooh! [*Picking up a half-sovereign*] Aaaaaaaaaaaah—ow—ooh!!!

FREDDY [*springing out of a taxicab*] Got one at last. Hallo! [*To the girl*] Where are the two ladies that were here?

THE FLOWER GIRL. They walked to the bus when the rain stopped.

FREDDY. And left me with a cab on my hands. Damnation（该死）!

THE FLOWER GIRL [*with grandeur（庄严）*] Never you mind, young man. I'm going home in a taxi. [*She sails off to the cab. The driver puts his hand behind him and holds the door firmly shut against her. Quite understanding his mistrust, she shows him her handful of money*]. A taxi fare ain't no object（不在话下）to me, Charlie. [*He grins and opens the door*]. Here. What about the basket?

THE TAXIMAN. Give it here. Tuppence extra.

LIZA. No: I don't want nobody to see it. [*She crushes it into the cab and gets in,*

---

① Carlton: a luxury hotel in London that operated from 1899 to 1940.

continuing the conversation through the window] Goodbye, Freddy.

FREDDY *[dazedly raising his hat]* Goodbye.

TAXIMAN. Where to?

LIZA. Bucknam Pellis *[Buckingham Palace[1]].*

TAXIMAN. What d'ye mean—Bucknam Pellis?

LIZA. Don't you know where it is? In the Green Park, where the King lives. Goodbye, Freddy. Don't let me keep you standing there. Goodbye.

FREDDY. Goodbye. *[He goes.]*

TAXIMAN. Here? What's this about Bucknam Pellis? What business have you at Bucknam Pellis?

LIZA. Of course I havn't none. But I wasn't going to let him know that. You drive me home.

TAXIMAN. And where's home?

LIZA. Angel Court, Drury Lane, next Meiklejohn's oil shop.

TAXIMAN. That sounds more like it, Judy. *[He drives off.]*

✂ Excerpt 2 (from Act 2)

Next day at 11 a.m., Higgins is discussing phonetics with Pickering at his laboratory in Wimpole Street, when Mrs Pearce, the housekeeper, announces that a common girl with a dreadful accent has come to visit him. Excitedly expecting a new subject for his phonetic research, Higgins asks Mrs Pearce to let the girl in.

The flower girl enters <u>in state</u>（庄严地）. She has a hat with three ostrich feathers, orange, sky-blue, and red. She has a nearly clean apron, and the <u>shoddy</u>（冒牌的） coat has been tidied a little. The <u>pathos</u>（可怜劲儿） of this <u>deplorable</u>（可悲的） figure, with its innocent vanity and <u>consequential</u>（自大的） air, touches Pickering, who has already straightened himself in the presence of Mrs Pearce. But as to Higgins, the only distinction he makes between men and women is that when he is neither <u>bullying</u>（恃强凌弱） nor exclaiming to the heavens against some feather-weight <u>cross</u>（烦恼）, he <u>coaxes</u>（哄骗） women as a child coaxes its nurse when it wants to get anything out of her.

HIGGINS *[<u>brusquely</u>（唐突地）, recognizing her with unconcealed disappointment, and at once, baby-like, making an intolerable <u>grievance</u>（抱怨） of it]* Why, this is the girl I jotted down last night. She's no use: I've got all the records I want of the Lisson Grove <u>lingo</u>（行话）; and I'm not going to waste another <u>cylinder</u>（圆

---

[1] Buckingham Palace: a residence of the British sovereigns since 1837, in London.

柱唱片） on it. *[To the girl]* Be off with you: I don't want you.

THE FLOWER GIRL. Don't you be so saucy（无礼）. You ain't heard what I come for yet. *[To Mrs Pearce, who is waiting at the door for further instructions]* Did you tell him I come in a taxi?

MRS PEARCE. Nonsense, girl! what do you think a gentleman like Mr Higgins cares what you came in?

THE FLOWER GIRL. Oh, we are proud! He ain't above（不屑于） giving lessons, not him: I heard him say so. Well, I ain't come here to ask for any compliment（恭维）; and if my money's not good enough I can go elsewhere.

HIGGINS. Good enough for what?

THE FLOWER GIRL. Good enough for yə-oo. Now you know, don't you? I'm come to have lessons, I am. And to pay for em tə-oo: make no mistake.

HIGGINS *[stupent（惊愕）]* WELL!!! *[Recovering his breath with a gasp]* What do you expect me to say to you?

THE FLOWER GIRL. Well, if you was a gentleman, you might ask me to sit down, I think. Don't I tell you I'm bringing you business?

HIGGINS. Pickering: shall we ask this baggage（邋遢女人） to sit down or shall we throw her out of the window?

THE FLOWER GIRL *[running away in terror to the piano, where she turns at bay（转身顽抗）]* Ah-ah-oh-ow-ow ow-oo! *[Wounded and whimpering（呜咽）]* I won't be called a baggage when I've offered to pay like any lady.

Motionless, the two men stare at her from the other side of the room, amazed.

PICKERING *[gently]* But what is it you want?

THE FLOWER GIRL. I want to be a lady in a flower shop stead of selling at the corner of Tottenham Court Road. But they won't take me unless I can talk more genteel（文雅的）. He said he could teach me. Well, here I am ready to pay him—not asking any favor—and he treats me zif I was dirt.

MRS PEARCE. How can you be such a foolish ignorant girl as to think you could afford to pay Mr Higgins?

THE FLOWER GIRL. Why shouldn't I? I know what lessons cost as well as you do; and I'm ready to pay.

HIGGINS. How much?

THE FLOWER GIRL *[coming back to him, triumphant]* Now you're talking! I thought you'd come off it（停止胡扯） when you saw a chance of getting back a bit of what you chucked（抛） at me last night. *[Confidentially]* You'd had a drop（一点酒） in, hadn't you?

HIGGINS *[peremptorily（蛮横地）]* Sit down.

THE FLOWER GIRL. Oh, if you're going to make a compliment of it—

HIGGINS *[thundering at her]* Sit down.

MRS PEARCE [severely] Sit down, girl. Do as you're told.

THE FLOWER GIRL. Ah-ah-ah-ow-ow-oo! [She stands, half rebellious, half bewildered.]

PICKERING [very courteous] Won't you sit down? [He places the stray（散置一旁的）chair near the hearthrug between himself and Higgins.]

LIZA [coyly（忸怩作态地）] Don't mind if I do. [She sits down. Pickering returns to the hearthrug.]

HIGGINS. What's your name?

THE FLOWER GIRL. Liza Doolittle.

HIGGINS [declaiming（朗诵）gravely]

Eliza, Elizabeth, Betsy and Bess,

They went to the woods to get a bird's nes':

PICKERING. They found a nest with four eggs in it:

HIGGINS. They took one apiece（每人）, and left three in it.

      They laugh heartily at their own fun.

LIZA. Oh, don't be silly.

MRS PEARCE [placing herself behind Eliza's chair] You mustn't speak to the gentleman like that.

LIZA. Well, why won't he speak sensible to me?

HIGGINS. Come back to business. How much do you propose to pay me for the lessons?

LIZA. Oh, I know what's right. A lady friend of mine gets French lessons for eighteenpence an hour from a real French gentleman. Well, you wouldn't have the face to ask me the same for teaching me my own language as you would for French; so I won't give more than a shilling（先令）. Take it or leave it.

HIGGINS [walking up and down the room, rattling his keys and his cash in his pockets] You know, Pickering, if you consider a shilling, not as a simple shilling, but as a percentage of this girl's income, it works out as fully equivalent to sixty or seventy guineas（基尼）from a millionaire.

PICKERING. How so?

HIGGINS. Figure it out. A millionaire has about £150 a day. She earns about half-a-crown.

LIZA [haughtily（傲慢地）] Who told you I only—

HIGGINS [continuing] She offers me two-fifths of her day's income for a lesson. Two-fifths of a millionaire's income for a day would be somewhere about £60. It's handsome. By George, it's enormous! it's the biggest offer I ever had.

LIZA [rising, terrified] Sixty pounds! What are you talking about? I never offered you sixty pounds. Where would I get—

HIGGINS. Hold your tongue.

Unit 3

George Bernard Shaw and *Pygmalion*

LIZA *[weeping]* But I ain't got sixty pounds. Oh—

MRS PEARCE. Don't cry, you silly girl. Sit down. Nobody is going to touch your money.

HIGGINS. Somebody is going to touch you, with a broomstick（扫帚把）, if you don't stop sniveling（哭哭啼啼）. Sit down.

LIZA *[obeying slowly]* Ah-ah-ah-ow-oo-o! One would think you was my father.

HIGGINS. If I decide to teach you, I'll be worse than two fathers to you. Here *[he offers her his silk handkerchief]*!

LIZA. What's this for?

HIGGINS. To wipe your eyes. To wipe any part of your face that feels moist（湿润的）. Remember: that's your handkerchief; and that's your sleeve. Don't mistake the one for the other if you wish to become a lady in a shop.

Liza, utterly bewildered, stares helplessly at him.

MRS PEARCE. It's no use talking to her like that, Mr Higgins: she doesn't understand you. Besides, you're quite wrong: she doesn't do it that way at all *[she takes the handkerchief]*.

LIZA *[snatching it]* Here! You give me that handkerchief. He give it to me, not to you.

PICKERING *[laughing]* He did. I think it must be regarded as her property, Mrs Pearce.

MRS PEARCE *[resigning herself（屈从）]* Serve you right, Mr Higgins.

PICKERING. Higgins: I'm interested. What about the ambassador's garden party? I'll say you're the greatest teacher alive if you make that good. I'll bet you all the expenses of the experiment you can't do it. And I'll pay for the lessons.

LIZA. Oh, you are real good. Thank you, Captain.

HIGGINS *[tempted, looking at her]* It's almost irresistible. She's so deliciously low—so horribly dirty—

LIZA *[protesting extremely]* Ah-ah-ah-ah-ow-ow-oo-oo!!! I ain't dirty: I washed my face and hands afore I come, I did.

PICKERING. You're certainly not going to turn her head（使……神魂颠倒） with flattery, Higgins.

MRS PEARCE *[uneasy]* Oh, don't say that, sir: there's more ways than one of turning a girl's head; and nobody can do it better than Mr Higgins, though he may not always mean it. I do hope, sir, you won't encourage him to do anything foolish.

HIGGINS *[becoming excited as the idea grows on him]* What is life but a series of inspired follies? The difficulty is to find them to do. Never lose a chance: it doesn't come every day. I shall make a duchess of this draggletailed（邋遢的） guttersnipe（贫民窟的流浪儿）.

LIZA *[strongly deprecating this view of her]* Ah-ah-ah-ow-ow-oo!

HIGGINS *[carried away（忘乎所以）]* Yes: in six months—in three if she has a good ear and a quick tongue—I'll take her anywhere and pass her off as（把……冒充成）anything. We'll start today: now! this moment! Take her away and clean her, Mrs Pearce. Monkey Brand[①], if it won't come off（洗掉）any other way. Is there a good fire in the kitchen?

MRS PEARCE *[protesting]* Yes; but—

HIGGINS *[storming on]* Take all her clothes off and burn them. Ring up Whiteley or somebody for new ones. Wrap her up in brown paper（牛皮纸）till they come.

LIZA. You're no gentleman, you're not, to talk of such things. I'm a good girl, I am; and I know what the like of you are, I do.

HIGGINS. We want none of your Lisson Grove prudery（假正经）here, young woman. You've got to learn to behave like a duchess. Take her away, Mrs Pearce. If she gives you any trouble, wallop（揍）her.

LIZA *[springing up and running between Pickering and Mrs Pearce for protection]* No! I'll call the police, I will.

MRS PEARCE. But I've no place to put her.

HIGGINS. Put her in the dustbin.

LIZA. Ah-ah-ah-ow-ow-oo!

PICKERING. Oh come, Higgins! be reasonable.

MRS PEARCE *[resolutely]* You must be reasonable, Mr Higgins: really you must. You can't walk over（欺负）everybody like this.

Higgins, thus scolded, subsides. The hurricane is succeeded by a zephyr（和风）of amiable surprise.

HIGGINS *[with professional exquisiteness of modulation（语调）]* I walk over everybody! My dear Mrs Pearce, my dear Pickering, I never had the slightest intention of walking over anyone. All I propose is that we should be kind to this poor girl. We must help her to prepare and fit herself for her new station in life. If I did not express myself clearly it was because I did not wish to hurt her delicacy（敏感情绪）, or yours.

Liza, reassured, steals back to her chair.

MRS PEARCE *[to Pickering]* Well, did you ever hear anything like that, sir?

PICKERING *[laughing heartily]* Never, Mrs Pearce: never.

HIGGINS *[patiently]* What's the matter?

MRS PEARCE. Well, the matter is, sir, that you can't take a girl up like that as if you were picking up a pebble（卵石）on the beach.

HIGGINS. Why not?

MRS PEARCE. Why not! But you don't know anything about her. What about her parents? She may be married.

LIZA. Garn!

---

① Monkey Brand: a brand of soap.

HIGGINS. There! As the girl very properly says, Garn! Married indeed! Don't you know that a woman of that class looks a worn out drudge（苦工）of fifty a year after she's married.

LIZA. Whood marry me?

HIGGINS [*suddenly resorting to the most thrillingly beautiful low tones in his best elocutionary（演说术的） style*] By George, Eliza, the streets will be strewn with（撒满） the bodies of men shooting themselves for your sake before I've done with you.

MRS PEARCE. Nonsense, sir. You mustn't talk like that to her.

LIZA [*rising and squaring herself（挺直腰身） determinedly*] I'm going away. He's off his chump（疯了）, he is. I don't want no balmies（疯子） teaching me.

HIGGINS [*wounded in his tenderest point by her insensibility to his elocution*] Oh, indeed! I'm mad, am I? Very well, Mrs Pearce: you needn't order the new clothes for her. Throw her out.

LIZA [*whimpering*] Nah-ow. You got no right to touch me.

MRS PEARCE. You see now what comes of being saucy. [*Indicating the door*] This way, please.

LIZA [*almost in tears*] I didn't want no clothes. I wouldn't have taken them [*she throws away the handkerchief*]. I can buy my own clothes.

HIGGINS [*deftly retrieving（接住） the handkerchief and intercepting（拦截） her on her reluctant way to the door*] You're an ungrateful wicked girl. This is my return for offering to take you out of the gutter and dress you beautifully and make a lady of you.

MRS PEARCE. Stop, Mr Higgins. I won't allow it. It's you that are wicked. Go home to your parents, girl; and tell them to take better care of you.

LIZA. I ain't got no parents. They told me I was big enough to earn my own living and turned me out.

MRS PEARCE. Where's your mother?

LIZA. I ain't got no mother. Her that turned me out was my sixth stepmother. But I done without them. And I'm a good girl, I am.

HIGGINS. Very well, then, what on earth is all this fuss about? The girl doesn't belong to anybody—is no use to anybody but me. [*He goes to Mrs Pearce and begins coaxing.*] You can adopt her, Mrs Pearce: I'm sure a daughter would be a great amusement to you. Now don't make any more fuss. Take her downstairs; and—

MRS PEARCE. But what's to become of her? Is she to be paid anything? Do be sensible, sir.

HIGGINS. Oh, pay her whatever is necessary: put it down in the housekeeping book. [*Impatiently*] What on earth will she want with money? She'll have her food and her clothes. She'll only drink if you give her money.

LIZA *[turning on him]* Oh you are a brute（野兽）. It's a lie: nobody ever saw the sign of liquor on me. *[To Pickering]* Oh, sir: you're a gentleman: don't let him speak to me like that.

PICKERING *[in good-humored remonstrance（告诫）]* Does it occur to you, Higgins, that the girl has some feelings?

HIGGINS *[looking critically at her]* Oh no, I don't think so. Not any feelings that we need bother about. *[Cheerily]* Have you, Eliza?

LIZA. I got my feelings same as anyone else.

HIGGINS *[to Pickering, reflectively]* You see the difficulty?

PICKERING. Eh? What difficulty?

HIGGINS. To get her to talk grammar. The mere pronunciation is easy enough.

LIZA. I don't want to talk grammar. I want to talk like a lady in a flower-shop.

MRS PEARCE. Will you please keep to the point, Mr Higgins. I want to know on what terms the girl is to be here. Is she to have any wages? And what is to become of her when you've finished your teaching? You must look ahead a little.

HIGGINS *[impatiently]* What's to become of her if I leave her in the gutter? Tell me that, Mrs Pearce.

MRS PEARCE. That's her own business, not yours, Mr Higgins.

HIGGINS. Well, when I've done with her, we can throw her back into the gutter; and then it will be her own business again; so that's all right.

LIZA. Oh, you've no feeling heart in you: you don't care for nothing but yourself. *[She rises and takes the floor（起立发言） resolutely.]* Here! I've had enough of this. I'm going *[making for the door]*. You ought to be ashamed of yourself, you ought.

HIGGINS *[snatching a chocolate cream from the piano, his eyes suddenly beginning to twinkle with mischief]* Have some chocolates, Eliza.

LIZA *[halting, tempted]* How do I know what might be in them? I've heard of girls being drugged by the like of you.

> *Higgins whips out his penknife; cuts a chocolate in two; puts one half into his mouth and bolts（囫囵吞下） it; and offers her the other half.*

HIGGINS. Pledge（誓约） of good faith, Eliza. I eat one half: you eat the other. *[Liza opens her mouth to retort（反驳）: he pops the half chocolate into it.]* You shall have boxes of them, barrels of them, every day. You shall live on them. Eh?

LIZA *[who has disposed of（解决掉） the chocolate after being nearly choked by it]* I wouldn't have ate it, only I'm too ladylike to take it out of my mouth.

HIGGINS. Listen, Eliza. I think you said you came in a taxi.

LIZA. Well, what if I did? I've as good a right to take a taxi as anyone else.

HIGGINS. You have, Eliza; and in future you shall have as many taxis as you want. You shall go up and down and round the town in a taxi every day. Think of that, Eliza.

Unit 3

George Bernard Shaw and *Pygmalion*

MRS PEARCE. Mr Higgins: you're tempting the girl. It's not right. She should think of the future.

HIGGINS. At her age! Nonsense! Time enough to think of the future when you haven't any future to think of. No, Eliza: do as this lady does: think of other people's futures; but never think of your own. Think of chocolates, and taxis, and gold, and diamonds.

LIZA. No: I don't want no gold and no diamonds. I'm a good girl, I am. *[She sits down again, with an attempt at dignity.]*

HIGGINS. You shall remain so, Eliza, under the care of Mrs Pearce. And you shall marry an officer in the Guards（近卫团）, with a beautiful moustache: the son of a marquis（侯爵）, who will disinherit（剥夺……的继承权）him for marrying you, but will relent（发慈悲）when he sees your beauty and goodness—

PICKERING. Excuse me, Higgins; but I really must interfere. Mrs Pearce is quite right. If this girl is to put herself in your hands for six months for an experiment in teaching, she must understand thoroughly what she's doing.

HIGGINS. How can she? She's incapable of understanding anything. Besides, do any of us understand what we are doing? If we did, would we ever do it?

PICKERING. Very clever, Higgins; but not to the present point. *[To Eliza]* Miss Doolittle—

LIZA *[overwhelmed]* Ah-ah-ow-oo!

HIGGINS. There! That's all you get out of Eliza. Ah-ah-ow-oo! No use explaining. As a military man you ought to know that. Give her her orders: that's enough for her. Eliza: you are to live here for the next six months, learning how to speak beautifully, like a lady in a florist's shop. If you're good and do whatever you're told, you shall sleep in a proper bedroom, and have lots to eat, and money to buy chocolates and take rides in taxis. If you're naughty and idle you will sleep in the back kitchen among the black beetles, and be walloped by Mrs Pearce with a broomstick. At the end of six months you shall go to Buckingham Palace in a carriage, beautifully dressed. If the King finds out you're not a lady, you will be taken by the police to the Tower of London[①], where your head will be cut off as a warning to other presumptuous（胆大妄为的）flower girls. If you are not found out, you shall have a present of seven-and-sixpence to start life with as a lady in a shop. If you refuse this offer you will be a most ungrateful and wicked girl; and the angels will weep for you. *[To Pickering]* Now are you satisfied, Pickering? *[To Mrs Pearce]* Can I put it more plainly and fairly, Mrs Pearce?

MRS PEARCE *[patiently]* I think you'd better let me speak to the girl properly in private. I don't know that I can take charge of her or consent to the arrangement

---

① Tower of London: a historic fortress in London; originally a royal palace, later a prison, now an arsenal and museum.

at all. Of course I know you don't mean her any harm; but when you get what you call interested in people's accents, you never think or care what may happen to them or you. Come with me, Eliza.

HIGGINS. That's all right. Thank you, Mrs Pearce. <u>Bundle</u>（撵走） her off to the bathroom.

LIZA *[rising reluctantly and suspiciously]* You're a great bully, you are. I won't stay here if I don't like. I won't let nobody wallop me. I never asked to go to Bucknam Palace, I didn't. I was never in trouble with the police, not me. I'm a good girl—

MRS PEARCE. Don't answer back, girl. You don't understand the gentleman. Come with me. *[She leads the way to the door, and holds it open for Eliza.]*

LIZA *[as she goes out]* Well, what I say is right. I won't go near the king, not if I'm going to have my head cut off. If I'd known what I was letting myself in for, I wouldn't have come here. I always been a good girl; and I never offered to say a word to him; and I don't owe him nothing; and I don't care; and I won't be <u>put upon</u>（利用，欺骗）; and I have my feelings the same as anyone else—

Mrs Pearce shuts the door; and Eliza's <u>plaints</u>（抱怨） are no longer audible.

✂ Excerpt 3 (from Act 2)

After Eliza is sent upstairs to bathe, Pickering wants to make sure that Higgins's intentions towards the girl are honorable, and Mrs. Pearce asks Higgins to be more careful of his manners now that a young girl is with them. Soon Alfred Doolittle, Eliza's father, arrives.

MRS PEARCE. If you please, sir, the trouble's beginning already. There's a dustman downstairs, Alfred Doolittle, wants to see you. He says you have his daughter here.

PICKERING *[rising]* <u>Phew</u>（啨）! I say!

HIGGINS *[promptly]* Send the <u>blackguard</u>（无赖） up.

MRS PEARCE. Oh, very well, sir. *[She goes out.]*

PICKERING. He may not be a blackguard, Higgins.

HIGGINS. Nonsense. Of course he's a blackguard.

PICKERING. Whether he is or not, I'm afraid we shall have some trouble with him.

HIGGINS *[confidently]* Oh no: I think not. If there's any trouble he shall have it with me, not I with him. And we are sure to get something interesting out of him.

PICKERING. About the girl?

HIGGINS. No. I mean his dialect.

PICKERING. Oh!

MRS PEARCE *[at the door]* Doolittle, sir. *[She admits Doolittle and retires.]*

Unit 3

George Bernard Shaw and *Pygmalion*

Alfred is an elderly but vigorous dustman, <u>clad</u>（穿着） in the costume of his profession, including a hat with a back <u>brim</u>（帽檐） covering his neck and shoulders. He has well marked and rather interesting features, and seems equally free from fear and conscience. He has a remarkably expressive voice, the result of a habit of <u>giving vent to</u>（发泄） his feelings without reserve. His present <u>pose</u>（佯装的姿态） is that of wounded honor and <u>stern</u>（坚定的） resolution.

DOOLITTLE *[at the door, uncertain which of the two gentlemen is his man]* Professor Iggins?

HIGGINS. Here. Good morning. Sit down.

DOOLITTLE. Morning, <u>Governor</u>（先生）. *[He sits down <u>magisterially</u>（威严地）]* I come about a very serious matter, Governor.

HIGGINS *[to Pickering]* Brought up in Hounslow. Mother Welsh, I should think. *[Doolittle opens his mouth, amazed. Higgins continues.]* What do you want, Doolittle?

DOOLITTLE *[<u>menacingly</u>（胁迫地）]* I want my daughter: that's what I want. See?

HIGGINS. Of course you do. You're her father, aren't you? You don't suppose anyone else wants her, do you? I'm glad to see you have some spark of family feeling left. She's upstairs. Take her away at once.

DOOLITTLE *[rising, fearfully <u>taken aback</u>（惊讶）]* What!

HIGGINS. Take her away. Do you suppose I'm going to keep your daughter for you?

DOOLITTLE *[remonstrating]* Now, now, look here, Governor. Is this reasonable? Is it fairity to take advantage of a man like this? The girl belongs to me. You got her. Where do I <u>come in</u>（得好处）? *[He sits down again.]*

HIGGINS. Your daughter had the <u>audacity</u>（大胆） to come to my house and ask me to teach her how to speak properly so that she could get a place in a flower-shop. This gentleman and my housekeeper have been here all the time. *[Bullying him]* How dare you come here and attempt to blackmail me? You sent her here on purpose.

DOOLITTLE *[protesting]* No, Governor.

HIGGINS. You must have. How else could you possibly know that she is here?

DOOLITTLE. Don't <u>take a man up</u>（斥责） like that, Governor.

HIGGINS. The police shall <u>take you up</u>（拘捕）. This is a <u>plant</u>（栽赃）—a <u>plot</u>（阴谋） to <u>extort</u>（敲诈） money by threats. I shall telephone for the police *[he goes resolutely to the telephone and opens the directory]*.

DOOLITTLE. Have I asked you for <u>a brass farthing</u>（一丁点儿钱）? I leave it to the gentleman here: have I said a word about money?

HIGGINS *[throwing the book aside and marching down on Doolittle with a <u>poser</u>（难题）]* What else did you come for?

DOOLITTLE *[sweetly]* Well, what would a man come for? Be human, governor.

HIGGINS *[disarmed（消了气）]* Alfred: did you put her up（教唆） to it?

DOOLITTLE. So help me（上天作证）, Governor, I never did. I take my Bible oath I ain't seen the girl these two months past.

HIGGINS. Then how did you know she was here?

DOOLITTLE *["most musical, most melancholy"]* I'll tell you, Governor, if you'll only let me get a word in. I'm willing to tell you. I'm wanting to tell you. I'm waiting to tell you.

HIGGINS. Pickering: this chap has a certain natural gift of rhetoric（修辞学）. Observe the rhythm of his native（朴素自然的） woodnotes（林中鸟鸣声） wild. "I'm willing to tell you: I'm wanting to tell you: I'm waiting to tell you." Sentimental rhetoric! That's the Welsh strain（个性特质） in him. It also accounts for his mendacity and dishonesty.

PICKERING. Oh, please, Higgins: I'm west country myself. *[To Doolittle]* How did you know the girl was here if you didn't send her?

DOOLITTLE. It was like this, Governor. The girl took a boy in the taxi to give him a jaunt（短途旅行）. Son of her landlady, he is. He hung about（闲荡） on the chance of her giving him another ride home. Well, she sent him back for her luggage when she heard you was willing for her to stop here. I met the boy at the corner of Long Acre and Endell Street.

HIGGINS. Public house（酒吧）. Yes?

DOOLITTLE. The poor man's club, Governor: why shouldn't I?

PICKERING. Do let him tell his story, Higgins.

DOOLITTLE. He told me what was up. And I ask you, what was my feelings and my duty as a father? I says to the boy, "You bring me the luggage," I says—

PICKERING. Why didn't you go for it yourself?

DOOLITTLE. Landlady wouldn't have trusted me with it, Governor. She's that kind of woman: you know. I had to give the boy a penny afore he trusted me with it, the little swine（猪猡）. I brought it to her just to oblige（为……效劳） you like, and make myself agreeable. That's all.

HIGGINS. How much luggage?

DOOLITTLE. Musical instrument, Governor. A few pictures, a trifle of（一点儿） jewelry, and a bird-cage. She said she didn't want no clothes. What was I to think from that, Governor? I ask you as a parent what was I to think?

HIGGINS. So you came to rescue her from worse than death, eh?

DOOLITTLE *[appreciatively: relieved at being understood]* Just so, Governor. That's right.

PICKERING. But why did you bring her luggage if you intended to take her away?

DOOLITTLE. Have I said a word about taking her away? Have I now?

HIGGINS *[determinedly]* You're going to take her away, double quick. *[He crosses to*

Unit 3

George Bernard Shaw and *Pygmalion*

the hearth and rings the bell.]

DOOLITTLE *[rising]* No, Governor. Don't say that. I'm not the man to <u>stand in my girl's light</u>（妨害……的利益）. Here's a career <u>opening</u>（机会） for her, as you might say; and—

Mrs Pearce opens the door and awaits orders.

HIGGINS. Mrs Pearce: this is Eliza's father. He has come to take her away. Give her to him. *[He goes back to the piano, with an air of <u>washing his hands of</u>（洗清与……的关系） the whole affair.]*

DOOLITTLE. No. This is a misunderstanding. Listen here—

MRS PEARCE. He can't take her away, Mr Higgins: how can he? You told me to burn her clothes.

DOOLITTLE. That's right. I can't carry the girl through the streets like a blooming monkey, can I? I put it to you.

HIGGINS. You have put it to me that you want your daughter. Take your daughter. If she has no clothes go out and buy her some.

DOOLITTLE *[desperate]* Where's the clothes she come in? Did I burn them or did your <u>missus</u>（夫人） here?

MRS PEARCE. I am the housekeeper, <u>if you please</u>（请注意）. I have sent for some clothes for your girl. When they come you can take her away. You can wait in the kitchen. This way, please.

Doolittle, much troubled, accompanies her to the door; then hesitates; finally turns confidentially to Higgins.

DOOLITTLE. Listen here, Governor. You and me is men of the world, ain't we?

HIGGINS. Oh! Men of the world, are we? You'd better go, Mrs Pearce.

MRS PEARCE. I think so, indeed, sir. *[She goes, with dignity.]*

PICKERING. <u>The floor is yours</u>（请说）, Mr Doolittle.

DOOLITTLE *[to Pickering]* I thank you, Governor. *[To Higgins, who takes refuge on the piano bench, a little overwhelmed by the proximity of his visitor; for Doolittle has a professional flavor of dust about him.]* Well, the truth is, I've taken a sort of fancy to you, Governor; and if you want the girl, I'm not so set on having her back home again but what I might be open to an arrangement. Regarded <u>in the light of</u>（看作） a young woman, she's a fine handsome girl. As a daughter she's not worth her <u>keep</u>（抚养）; and so I tell you straight. All I ask is my rights as a father; and you're the last man alive to expect me to let her go for nothing; for I can see you're one of the straight sort, Governor. Well, what's a five-pound note to you? And what's Eliza to me? *[He returns to his chair and sits down <u>judicially</u>（法官似的，公正明断的）.]*

PICKERING. I think you ought to know, Doolittle, that Mr Higgins's intentions are entirely honorable.

DOOLITTLE. Course they are, Governor. If I thought they wasn't, I'd ask fifty.

HIGGINS [_revolted（厌恶的）_] Do you mean to say that you would sell your daughter for £50?

DOOLITTLE. Not in a general way I would; but to oblige a gentleman like you I'd do a good deal, I do assure you.

PICKERING. Have you no morals（道德原则）, man?

DOOLITTLE [_unabashed（恬不知耻地）_] Can't afford them, Governor. Neither could you if you was as poor as me. Not that I mean any harm, you know. But if Liza is going to have a bit out of this, why not me too?

HIGGINS [_troubled_] I don't know what to do, Pickering. There can be no question that as a matter of morals it's a positive crime to give this chap a farthing. And yet I feel a sort of rough justice in his claim.

DOOLITTLE. That's it, Governor. That's all I say. A father's heart, as it were.

PICKERING. Well, I know the feeling; but really it seems hardly right—

DOOLITTLE. Don't say that, Governor. Don't look at it that way. What am I, Governors both? I ask you, what am I? I'm one of the undeserving poor[①]: that's what I am. Think of what that means to a man. It means that he's up agen middle class morality（中产阶级道德观） all the time. If there's anything going, and I put in（提出） for a bit of it, it's always the same story: "You're undeserving; so you can't have it." But my needs is as great as the most deserving widow's that ever got money out of six different charities in one week for the death of the same husband. I don't need less than a deserving man: I need more. I don't eat less hearty than him; and I drink a lot more. I want a bit of amusement, cause I'm a thinking man. I want cheerfulness and a song and a band（乐队） when I feel low. Well, they charge me just the same for everything as they charge the deserving. What is middle class morality? Just an excuse for never giving me anything. Therefore, I ask you, as two gentlemen, not to play that game on me. I'm playing straight with you. I ain't pretending to be deserving. I'm undeserving; and I mean to go on being undeserving. I like it; and that's the truth. Will you take advantage of a man's nature to do him out of（骗取，剥夺） the price of his own daughter what he's brought up and fed and clothed by the sweat of his brow until she's growed big enough to be interesting to you two gentlemen? Is five pounds unreasonable? I put it to you; and I leave it to you.

HIGGINS [_rising, and going over to Pickering_] Pickering: if we were to take this man in hand for three months, he could choose between a seat in the Cabinet（内阁） and a popular pulpit（布道坛） in Wales.

PICKERING. What do you say to that, Doolittle?

DOOLITTLE. Not me, Governor, thank you kindly. I've heard all the preachers（布道

---

① undeserving poor: poor people who are thought to have bad moral character and do not deserve to be helped.

者) and all the prime ministers—for I'm a thinking man and game for (敢于从事) politics or religion or social reform same as all the other amusements — and I tell you it's a dog's life any way you look at it. Undeserving poverty is my line (行当). Taking one station in society with another, it's—it's—well, it's the only one that has any ginger (刺激) in it, to my taste.

HIGGINS. I suppose we must give him a fiver.

PICKERING. He'll make a bad use of it, I'm afraid.

DOOLITTLE. Not me, Governor, so help me I won't. Don't you be afraid that I'll save it and spare (吝惜) it and live idle on it. There won't be a penny of it left by Monday: I'll have to go to work same as if I'd never had it. It won't pauperize (使……贫穷) me, you bet. Just one good spree (狂欢) for myself and the missus, giving pleasure to ourselves and employment to others, and satisfaction to you to think it's not been throwed away. You couldn't spend it better.

HIGGINS *[taking out his pocket book and coming between Doolittle and the piano]* This is irresistible. Let's give him ten. *[He offers two notes to the dustman.]*

DOOLITTLE. No, Governor. She wouldn't have the heart to spend ten; and perhaps I shouldn't neither. Ten pounds is a lot of money: it makes a man feel prudent (谨慎) like; and then goodbye to happiness. You give me what I ask you, Governor: not a penny more, and not a penny less.

PICKERING. Why don't you marry that missus of yours? I rather draw the line at (反对) encouraging that sort of immorality.

DOOLITTLE. Tell her so, Governor: tell her so. I'm willing. It's me that suffers by it. I've no hold on her. I got to be agreeable to her. I got to give her presents. I got to buy her clothes something sinful. I'm a slave to that woman, Governor, just because I'm not her lawful husband. And she knows it too. Catch her marrying me! Take my advice, Governor: marry Eliza while she's young and don't know no better. If you don't you'll be sorry for it after. If you do, she'll be sorry for it after; but better her than you, because you're a man, and she's only a woman and don't know how to be happy anyhow.

HIGGINS. Pickering: if we listen to this man another minute, we shall have no convictions (信仰) left. *[To Doolittle]* Five pounds I think you said.

DOOLITTLE. Thank you kindly, Governor.

HIGGINS. You're sure you won't take ten?

DOOLITTLE. Not now. Another time, Governor.

HIGGINS *[handing him a five-pound note]* Here you are.

DOOLITTLE. Thank you, Governor. Good morning. *[He hurries to the door, anxious to get away with his booty (战利品). When he opens it he is confronted with a dainty (俊俏的) and exquisitely clean young Japanese lady in a simple blue cotton kimono (和服) printed cunningly with small white jasmine (茉莉)*

blossoms. Mrs Pearce is with her. He gets out of her way deferentially（恭敬地） and apologizes.] Beg pardon, miss.

THE JAPANESE LADY. Garn! Don't you know your own daughter?

[Doolittle, Higgins and Pickering exclaiming simultaneously:]

DOOLITTLE. Bly me! It's Eliza!

HIGGINS. What's that! This!

PICKERING. By Jove（天啊）!

LIZA. Don't I look silly?

HIGGINS. Silly?

MRS PEARCE [at the door] Now, Mr Higgins, please don't say anything to make the girl conceited（自负的） about herself.

HIGGINS [conscientiously] Oh! Quite right, Mrs Pearce. [To Eliza] Yes: damned silly.

MRS PEARCE. Please, sir.

HIGGINS [correcting himself] I mean extremely silly.

LIZA. I should look all right with my hat on. [She takes up her hat; puts it on; and walks across the room to the fireplace with a fashionable air.]

HIGGINS. A new fashion, by George（确实）! And it ought to look horrible!

DOOLITTLE [with fatherly pride] Well, I never thought she'd clean up as good looking as that, Governor. She's a credit to（为……增光添彩的人） me, ain't she?

LIZA. I tell you, it's easy to clean up here. Hot and cold water on tap（可随时使用）, just as much as you like, there is. Woolly towels, there is; and a towel horse（毛巾架） so hot, it burns your fingers. Soft brushes to scrub yourself, and a wooden bowl of soap smelling like primroses（报春花）. Now I know why ladies is so clean. Washing's a treat（乐事） for them. Wish they could see what it is for the like of me!

HIGGINS. I'm glad the bathroom met with your approval.

LIZA. It didn't: not all of it; and I don't care who hears me say it. Mrs Pearce knows.

HIGGINS. What was wrong, Mrs Pearce?

MRS PEARCE [blandly（无动于衷地）] Oh, nothing, sir. It doesn't matter.

LIZA. I had a good mind to break it. I didn't know which way to look. But I hung a towel over it, I did.

HIGGINS. Over what?

MRS PEARCE. Over the looking-glass, sir.

HIGGINS. Doolittle: you have brought your daughter up too strictly.

DOOLITTLE. Me! I never brought her up at all, except to give her a lick of a strap（鞭打） now and again. Don't put it on me, Governor. She ain't accustomed to it, you see: that's all. But she'll soon pick up your free-and-easy ways.

LIZA. I'm a good girl, I am; and I won't pick up no free-and-easy ways.

Unit 3

George Bernard Shaw and *Pygmalion*

HIGGINS. Eliza: if you say again that you're a good girl, your father shall take you home.

LIZA. Not him. You don't know my father. All he come here for was to touch（骗取） you for some money to get drunk on.

DOOLITTLE. Well, what else would I want money for? To put into the plate（捐款盘） in church, I suppose. *[She puts out her tongue at him. He is so incensed（激怒） by this that Pickering presently（立即） finds it necessary to step between them.]* Don't you give me none of your lip; and don't let me hear you giving this gentleman any of it neither, or you'll hear from me about it. See?

HIGGINS. Have you any further advice to give her before you go, Doolittle? Your blessing, for instance.

DOOLITTLE. No, Governor: I ain't such a mug（傻瓜） as to put up my children to all I know myself. Hard enough to hold them in（约束） without that. If you want Eliza's mind improved, Governor, you do it yourself with a strap. So long, gentlemen. *[He turns to go.]*

HIGGINS *[impressively（威严地）]* Stop. You'll come regularly to see your daughter. It's your duty, you know. My brother is a clergyman; and he could help you in your talks with her.

DOOLITTLE *[evasively（推诿地）]* Certainly. I'll come, Governor. Not just this week, because I have a job at a distance. But later on you may depend on me. Afternoon, gentlemen. Afternoon, ma'am. *[He touches his hat to Mrs Pearce, who disdains（鄙视） the salutation and goes out. He winks（使眼色） at Higgins, thinking him probably a fellow-sufferer from Mrs Pearce's difficult disposition, and follows her.]*

✣ Excerpt 4 (from Act 3)

It is Mrs Higgins's at-home day. Much to her displeasure, Henry Higgins tells her he is bringing a common flower girl to her party. Soon Pickering and other guests arrive. Higgins is about to embarrass his mother in front of her guests when Eliza is announced.

Eliza, who is exquisitely dressed, produces an impression of such remarkable distinction（卓越） and beauty as she enters that they all rise, quite fluttered（激动不安的）. Guided by Higgins's signals, she comes to Mrs Higgins with studied（做作的） grace.

LIZA *[speaking with pedantic（学究式的） correctness of pronunciation and great beauty of tone]* How do you do, Mrs Higgins? *[She gasps（喘气） slightly in making sure of the H in Higgins, but is quite successful.]* Mr Higgins told me I might come.

MRS HIGGINS [cordially（诚挚地）] Quite right: I'm very glad indeed to see you.

PICKERING. How do you do, Miss Doolittle?

LIZA [shaking hands with him] Colonel Pickering, is it not?

MRS EYNSFORD HILL. I feel sure we have met before, Miss Doolittle. I remember your eyes.

LIZA. How do you do? [She sits down on the ottoman（软垫椅） gracefully in the place just left vacant by Higgins.]

MRS EYNSFORD HILL [introducing] My daughter Clara.

LIZA. How do you do?

CLARA [impulsively] How do you do? [She sits down on the ottoman beside Eliza, devouring（热切地盯着） her with her eyes.]

FREDDY [coming to their side of the ottoman] I've certainly had the pleasure.

MRS EYNSFORD HILL [introducing] My son Freddy.

LIZA. How do you do?

    Freddy bows and sits down in the Elizabethan chair, infatuated（迷恋的）.

HIGGINS [suddenly] By George, yes: it all comes back to me! [They stare at him]. Covent Garden! [Lamentably（哀叹地）] What a damned thing!

MRS HIGGINS. Henry, please! [He is about to sit on the edge of the table]. Don't sit on my writing-table: you'll break it.

HIGGINS [sulkily（闷闷不乐地）] Sorry.

    He goes to the divan（长沙发椅）, stumbling into the fender（炉围） and over the fire-irons（火钳） on his way; extricating（使……解脱） himself with muttered imprecations（诅咒）; and finishing his disastrous journey by throwing himself so impatiently on the divan that he almost breaks it. Mrs Higgins looks at him, but controls herself and says nothing.

    A long and painful pause ensues（紧随）.

MRS HIGGINS [at last, conversationally（寒暄地）] Will it rain, do you think?

LIZA. The shallow depression（低气压） in the west of these islands is likely to move slowly in an easterly direction. There are no indications of any great change in the barometrical（气压的） situation.

FREDDY. Ha! ha! how awfully funny!

LIZA. What is wrong with that, young man? I bet I got it right.

FREDDY. Killing!

MRS EYNSFORD HILL. I'm sure I hope it won't turn cold. There's so much influenza about. It runs right through our whole family regularly every spring.

LIZA [darkly] My aunt died of influenza: so they said.

MRS EYNSFORD HILL [clicks her tongue（舌头作啧啧声） sympathetically]!!!

LIZA [in the same tragic tone] But it's my belief they done the old woman in.

Unit 3

George Bernard Shaw and *Pygmalion*

MRS HIGGINS *[puzzled]* Done her in?

LIZA. Y-e-e-e-es, Lord love you! Why should she die of influenza? She come through diphtheria（白喉） right enough the year before. I saw her with my own eyes. Fairly blue（沮丧） with it, she was. They all thought she was dead; but my father he kept ladling（用勺灌） gin（杜松子酒） down her throat til she came to（苏醒） so sudden that she bit the bowl off the spoon.

MRS EYNSFORD HILL *[startled]* Dear me!

LIZA *[piling up the indictment（指控）]* What call would a woman with that strength in her have to die of influenza? What become of her new straw hat that should have come to mc? Somebody pinched（偷） it; and what I say is, them as pinched it done her in.

MRS EYNSFORD HILL. What does doing her in mean?

HIGGINS *[hastily]* Oh, that's the new small talk（闲谈）. To do a person in means to kill them.

MRS EYNSFORD HILL *[to Eliza, horrified]* You surely don't believe that your aunt was killed?

LIZA. Do I not! Them she lived with would have killed her for a hat-pin, let alone a hat.

MRS EYNSFORD HILL. But it can't have been right for your father to pour spirits（烈酒） down her throat like that. It might have killed her.

LIZA. Not her. Gin was mother's milk to her. Besides, he'd poured so much down his own throat that he knew the good of it.

MRS EYNSFORD HILL. Do you mean that he drank?

LIZA. Drank! My word! Something chronic（积习难改的）.

MRS EYNSFORD HILL. How dreadful for you!

LIZA. Not a bit. It never did him no harm what I could see. But then he did not keep it up regular. *[Cheerfully]* On the burst（爆发式的）, as you might say, from time to time. And always more agreeable when he had a drop in. When he was out of work, my mother used to give him fourpence and tell him to go out and not come back until he'd drunk himself cheerful and loving-like. There's lots of women has to make their husbands drunk to make them fit to live with. *[Now quite at her ease]* You see, it's like this. If a man has a bit of a conscience, it always takes him when he's sober; and then it makes him low-spirited. A drop of booze（酒） just takes that off and makes him happy. *[To Freddy, who is in convulsions（抽搐） of suppressed laughter]* Here! what are you sniggering（窃笑） at?

FREDDY. The new small talk. You do it so awfully well.

LIZA. If I was doing it proper, what was you laughing at? *[To Higgins]* Have I said anything I oughtn't?

MRS HIGGINS *[interposing（插话）]* Not at all, Miss Doolittle.

147

LIZA. Well, that's a mercy（幸运）, anyhow. *[Expansively]* What I always say is—
HIGGINS *[rising and looking at his watch]* Ahem!
LIZA *[looking round at him; taking the hint; and rising]* Well: I must go. *[They all rise. Freddy goes to the door.]* So pleased to have met you. Goodbye. *[She shakes hands with Mrs Higgins.]*
MRS HIGGINS. Goodbye.
LIZA. Goodbye, Colonel Pickering.
PICKERING. Goodbye, Miss Doolittle. *[They shake hands.]*
LIZA *[nodding to the others]* Goodbye, all.
FREDDY *[opening the door for her]* Are you walking across the Park, Miss Doolittle? If so—
LIZA *[with perfectly elegant diction]* Walk! Not bloody（该死）likely. *[Sensation（震惊四座）]* I am going in a taxi. *[She goes out.]*

  Pickering gasps and sits down. Freddy goes out on the balcony to catch another glimpse of Eliza.

MRS EYNSFORD HILL *[suffering from shock]* Well, I really can't get used to the new ways.
CLARA *[throwing herself discontentedly into the Elizabethan chair]* Oh, it's all right, mamma, quite right. People will think we never go anywhere or see anybody if you are so old-fashioned.
MRS EYNSFORD HILL. I daresay I am very old-fashioned; but I do hope you won't begin using that expression, Clara. I have got accustomed to hear you talking about men as rotters（无赖）, and calling everything filthy and beastly（可恶的，糟糕的）; though I do think it horrible and unladylike. But this last is really too much. Don't you think so, Colonel Pickering?
PICKERING. Don't ask me. I've been away in India for several years; and manners have changed so much that I sometimes don't know whether I'm at a respectable dinnertable or in a ship's forecastle（前甲板）.
CLARA. It's all a matter of habit. There's no right or wrong in it. Nobody means anything by it. And it's so quaint（奇特有趣的）, and gives such a smart emphasis to things that are not in themselves very witty. I find the new small talk delightful and quite innocent.
MRS EYNSFORD HILL *[rising]* Well, after that, I think it's time for us to go.
  Pickering and Higgins rise.
CLARA *[rising]* Oh yes: we have three at-homes（家庭招待会）to go to still. Goodbye, Mrs Higgins. Goodbye, Colonel Pickering. Goodbye, Professor Higgins.
HIGGINS *[coming grimly at her from the divan, and accompanying her to the door]* Goodbye. Be sure you try on that small talk at the three at-homes. Don't be nervous about it. Pitch it in strong.

Unit 3

George Bernard Shaw and *Pygmalion*

CLARA *[all smiles]* I will. Goodbye. Such nonsense, all this early Victorian（维多利亚时代的） prudery!

HIGGINS *[tempting her]* Such damned nonsense!

CLARA. Such bloody nonsense!

MRS EYNSFORD HILL *[convulsively]* Clara!

CLARA. Ha! ha! *[She goes out radiant, conscious of being thoroughly up to date, and is heard descending the stairs in a stream of* silvery（银铃般的） *laughter.]*

FREDDY *[to the heavens at large]* Well, I ask you— *[He gives it up, and comes to Mrs Higgins]*. Goodbye.

MRS HIGGINS *[shaking hands]* Goodbye. Would you like to meet Miss Doolittle again?

FREDDY *[eagerly]* Yes, I should, most awfully.

MRS HIGGINS. Well, you know my days.

FREDDY. Yes. Thanks awfully. Goodbye. *[He goes out.]*

MRS EYNSFORD HILL. Goodbye, Mr Higgins.

HIGGINS. Goodbye. Goodbye.

MRS EYNSFORD HILL *[to Pickering]* It's no use. I shall never be able to bring myself to use that word.

PICKERING. Don't. It's not compulsory, you know. You'll get on quite well without it.

MRS EYNSFORD HILL. Only, Clara is so down on（埋怨） me if I am not positively reeking with（满口） the latest slang. Goodbye.

PICKERING. Goodbye *[They shake hands]*.

MRS EYNSFORD HILL *[to Mrs Higgins]* You mustn't mind Clara. *[Pickering, catching from her lowered tone that this is not meant for him to hear, discreetly joins Higgins at the window.]* We're so poor! and she gets so few parties, poor child! She doesn't quite know. *[Mrs Higgins, seeing that her eyes are moist, takes her hand sympathetically and goes with her to the door.]* But the boy is nice. Don't you think so?

MRS HIGGINS. Oh, quite nice. I shall always be delighted to see him.

MRS EYNSFORD HILL. Thank you, dear. Goodbye. *[She goes out]*.

HIGGINS *[eagerly]* Well? Is Eliza presentable（像样的，体面的）? *[He swoops（猛扑） on his mother and drags her to the ottoman, where she sits down in Eliza's place with her son on her left.]*

    Pickering returns to his chair on her right.

MRS HIGGINS. You silly boy, of course she's not presentable. She's a triumph of your art and of her dressmaker's; but if you suppose for a moment that she doesn't give herself away in every sentence she utters, you must be perfectly cracked（疯狂的，热恋的） about her.

PICKERING. But don't you think something might be done? I mean something to eliminate the sanguinary（言语污秽的） element from her conversation.

MRS HIGGINS. Not as long as she is in Henry's hands.

HIGGINS [aggrieved] Do you mean that my language is improper?

MRS HIGGINS. No, dearest: it would be quite proper—say on a canal barge（驳船）; but it would not be proper for her at a garden party.

HIGGINS [deeply injured] Well I must say—

PICKERING [interrupting him] Come, Higgins: you must learn to know yourself. I haven't heard such language as yours since we used to review（检阅）the volunteers（志愿兵）in Hyde Park[①] twenty years ago.

HIGGINS [sulkily] Oh, well, if you say so, I suppose I don't always talk like a bishop（主教）.

MRS HIGGINS [quieting Henry with a touch] Colonel Pickering: will you tell me what is the exact state of things in Wimpole Street?

PICKERING [cheerfully: as if this completely changed the subject] Well, I have come to live there with Henry. We work together at my Indian Dialects; and we think it more convenient—

MRS HIGGINS. Quite so. I know all about that: it's an excellent arrangement. But where does this girl live?

HIGGINS. With us, of course. Where should she live?

MRS HIGGINS. But on what terms? Is she a servant? If not, what is she?

PICKERING [slowly] I think I know what you mean, Mrs Higgins.

HIGGINS. Well, dash me if I do! I've had to work at the girl every day for months to get her to her present pitch（程度）. Besides, she's useful. She knows where my things are, and remembers my appointments and so forth.

MRS HIGGINS. How does your housekeeper get on with her?

HIGGINS. Mrs Pearce? Oh, she's jolly glad to get so much taken off her hands; for before Eliza came, she used to have to find things and remind me of my appointments. But she's got some silly bee in her bonnet about（想……入了迷）Eliza. She keeps saying "You don't think, sir": doesn't she, Pick?

PICKERING. Yes: that's the formula. "You don't think, sir." That's the end of every conversation about Eliza.

HIGGINS. As if I ever stop thinking about the girl and her confounded（该死的）vowels and consonants. I'm worn out, thinking about her, and watching her lips and her teeth and her tongue, not to mention her soul, which is the quaintest of the lot.

MRS HIGGINS. You certainly are a pretty pair of babies, playing with your live doll.

HIGGINS. Playing! The hardest job I ever tackled: make no mistake about that, mother. But you have no idea how frightfully interesting it is to take a human being and

---

① Hyde Park: a major park in Central London that was established by Henry VIII in 1536 as a hunting ground, and has been well-known for free speech and demonstrations since the 19th century.

change her into a quite different human being by creating a new speech for her. It's filling up the deepest gulf（鸿沟） that separates class from class and soul from soul.

PICKERING [*drawing his chair closer to Mrs Higgins and bending over to her eagerly*] Yes: it's enormously interesting. I assure you, Mrs Higgins, we take Eliza very seriously. Every week— every day almost—there is some new change. [*Closer again*] We keep records of every stage—dozens of gramophone（留声机） disks and photographs—

HIGGINS [*assailing her at the other ear*] Yes, by George: it's the most absorbing experiment I ever tackled. She regularly fills our lives up: doesn't she, Pick?

PICKERING. We're always talking Eliza.

HIGGINS. Teaching Eliza.

PICKERING. Dressing Eliza.

MRS HIGGINS. What!

HIGGINS. Inventing new Elizas.

[*Higgins and Pickering, speaking together:*]

HIGGINS. You know, she has the most extraordinary quickness of ear:

PICKERING. I assure you, my dear Mrs Higgins, that girl

HIGGINS. just like a parrot. I've tried her with every

PICKERING. is a genius. She can play the piano quite beautifully.

HIGGINS. possible sort of sound that a human being can make—

PICKERING. We have taken her to classical concerts and to music

HIGGINS. Continental dialects, African dialects, Hottentot[①]

PICKERING. halls; and it's all the same to her: she plays everything

HIGGINS. clicks（吸气音）, things it took me years to get hold of; and

PICKERING. she hears right off when she comes home, whether it's

HIGGINS. she picks them up like a shot, right away, as if she had

PICKERING. Beethoven and Brahms or Lehar[②] and Lionel Morickton;

HIGGINS. been at it all her life.

PICKERING. though six months ago, she'd never as much as touched a piano—

MRS HIGGINS [*putting her fingers in her ears, as they are by this time shouting one another down with an intolerable noise*] Sh-sh-sh—sh! [*They stop.*]

PICKERING. I beg your pardon. [*He draws his chair back apologetically.*]

HIGGINS. Sorry. When Pickering starts shouting nobody can get a word in（插话） edgeways（从旁边）.

MRS HIGGINS. Be quiet, Henry. Colonel Pickering: don't you realize that when Eliza walked into Wimpole Street, something walked in with her?

---

① Hottentot: any of the Khoisan languages of the Khoikhoi peoples in southern Africa.
② Beethoven ... Lehar: all of these are musicians.

PICKERING. Her father did. But Henry soon got rid of him.

MRS HIGGINS. It would have been more to the point if her mother had. But as her mother didn't something else did.

PICKERING. But what?

MRS HIGGINS [unconsciously dating（显示出……的年龄） herself by the word] A problem.

PICKERING. Oh, I see. The problem of how to pass her off as a lady.

HIGGINS. I'll solve that problem. I've half solved it already.

MRS HIGGINS. No, you two infinitely stupid male creatures: the problem of what is to be done with her afterwards.

HIGGINS. I don't see anything in that. She can go her own way, with all the advantages I have given her.

MRS HIGGINS. The advantages of that poor woman who was here just now! The manners and habits that disqualify a fine lady from earning her own living without giving her a fine lady's income! Is that what you mean?

PICKERING [indulgently（放任地）, being rather bored] Oh, that will be all right, Mrs Higgins. [He rises to go].

HIGGINS [rising also] We'll find her some light employment.

PICKERING. She's happy enough. Don't you worry about her. Goodbye. [He shakes hands as if he were consoling（安慰） a frightened child, and makes for the door.]

HIGGINS. Anyhow, there's no good bothering now. The thing's done. Goodbye, mother. [He kisses her, and follows Pickering.]

PICKERING [turning for a final consolation] There are plenty of openings. We'll do what's right. Goodbye.

HIGGINS [to Pickering as they go out together] Let's take her to the Shakespeare exhibition at Earls Court.

PICKERING. Yes: let's. Her remarks will be delicious.

HIGGINS. She'll mimic all the people for us when we get home.

PICKERING. Ripping（好极了）. [Both are heard laughing as they go downstairs].

MRS HIGGINS [rises with an impatient bounce, and returns to her work at the writing-table. She sweeps a litter of disarranged papers out of her way; snatches a sheet of paper from her stationery case; and tries resolutely to write. At the third line she gives it up; flings down her pen; grips the table angrily and exclaims] Oh, men! men!! men!!!

Unit 3

George Bernard Shaw and *Pygmalion*

Excerpt 5 (from Act 4)

It is a summer midnight at Higgins's laboratory. Higgins, Pickering and Eliza have just returned from the ambassador's dinner party. Something is wrong with Eliza, but the two men fail to notice it.

HIGGINS [*calling down to Pickering*] I say, Pick: lock up, will you? I shan't be going out again.

PICKERING. Right. Can Mrs Pearce go to bed? We don't want anything more, do we?

HIGGINS. Lord, no!

>*Eliza opens the door and is seen on the lighted <u>landing</u>（楼梯平台） in all the <u>finery</u>（华丽的服饰） in which she has just won Higgins's bet for him. She comes to the hearth, and switches on the electric lights there. She is tired: her <u>pallor</u>（苍白的面色） contrasts strongly with her dark eyes and hair; and her expression is almost tragic. She takes off her cloak; puts her fan and gloves on the piano; and sits down on the bench, brooding and silent. Higgins, in evening dress, with overcoat and hat, comes in, carrying a <u>smoking jacket</u>（男式晚便服） which he has picked up downstairs. He takes off the hat and overcoat; throws them carelessly on the newspaper stand; disposes of his coat in the same way; puts on the smoking jacket; and throws himself wearily into the easy-chair at the hearth. Pickering, similarly <u>attired</u>（穿着，打扮）, comes in. He also takes off his hat and overcoat, and is about to throw them on Higgins's when he hesitates.*

PICKERING. I say: Mrs Pearce will row if we leave these things lying about in the drawing-room.

HIGGINS. Oh, chuck them over the <u>bannisters</u>（栏杆） into the hall. She'll find them there in the morning and put them away all right. She'll think we were drunk.

PICKERING. We are, slightly. Are there any letters?

HIGGINS. I didn't look. [*Pickering takes the overcoats and hats and goes downstairs. Higgins begins half singing half <u>yawn</u>ing（打哈欠） an <u>air</u>（曲调） from La Fanciulla del Golden West[①]. Suddenly he stops and exclaims*] I wonder where the devil my slippers are!

>*Eliza looks at him darkly; then leaves the room.*
>
>*Higgins yawns again, and resumes his song.*
>
>*Pickering returns, with the contents of the letter-box in his hand.*

PICKERING. Only <u>circulars</u>（传单）, and this <u>coroneted</u>（印着冠冕图案的） <u>billet-</u>

---

① La ... West: or "The Girl of the West", is an opera in three acts by Giacomo Puccini, based on the play *The Girl of the Golden West* by the American author David Belasco.

doux（情书） for you. *[He throws the circulars into the fender, and posts himself on the hearthrug, with his back to the grate（炉子的格栅）.]*

HIGGINS *[glancing at the billet-doux]* Money-lender. *[He throws the letter after the circulars].*

  Eliza returns with a pair of large down-at-heel（破后跟的） slippers. She places them on the carpet before Higgins, and sits as before without a word.

HIGGINS *[yawning again]* Oh Lord! What an evening! What a crew! What a silly tomfoollery（蠢事）! *[He raises his shoe to unlace（解开带子） it, and catches sight of the slippers. He stops unlacing and looks at them as if they had appeared there of their own accord（自发地）.]* Oh! They're there, are they?

PICKERING *[stretching himself]* Well, I feel a bit tired. It's been a long day. The garden party, a dinner party, and the reception! Rather too much of a good thing. But you've won your bet, Higgins. Eliza did the trick（成功）, and something to spare（剩余）, eh?

HIGGINS *[fervently]* Thank God it's over!

  Eliza flinches（畏缩） violently; but they take no notice of her; and she recovers herself and sits stonily as before.

PICKERING. Were you nervous at the garden party? I was. Eliza didn't seem a bit nervous.

HIGGINS. Oh, she wasn't nervous. I knew she'd be all right. No: it's the strain of putting the job through all these months that has told on（使……疲乏） me. It was interesting enough at first, while we were at the phonetics; but after that I got deadly sick of it. If I hadn't backed（下赌注于） myself to do it I should have chucked the whole thing up two months ago. It was a silly notion: the whole thing has been a bore.

PICKERING. Oh come! the garden party was frightfully exciting. My heart began beating like anything.

HIGGINS. Yes, for the first three minutes. But when I saw we were going to win hands down（易如反掌）, I felt like a bear in a cage, hanging about doing nothing. The dinner was worse: sitting gorging（狼吞虎咽） there for over an hour, with nobody but a damned fool of a fashionable woman to talk to! I tell you, Pickering, never again for me. No more artificial（假冒的） duchesses. The whole thing has been simple purgatory（炼狱）.

PICKERING. You've never been broken in（逐渐适应、习惯） properly to the social routine. *[Strolling over to the piano]* I rather enjoy dipping into（涉猎） it occasionally myself: it makes me feel young again. Anyhow, it was a great success: an immense success. I was quite frightened once or twice because Eliza was doing it so well. You see, lots of the real people can't do it at all: they're such fools that they think style（风度） comes by nature to people in their position; and so they never learn. There's always something professional about doing a thing superlatively（至高无上地）well.

HIGGINS. Yes: that's what drives me mad: the silly people don't know their own silly business. *[Rising]* However, it's over and done with（完毕）; and now I can go to bed at last without dreading tomorrow.

Eliza's beauty becomes murderous.

PICKERING. I think I shall turn in（上床睡觉）too. Still, it's been a great occasion: a triumph for you. Goodnight. *[He goes.]*

HIGGINS *[following him]* Goodnight. *[Over his shoulder, at the door]* Put out the lights, Eliza; and tell Mrs Pearce not to make coffee for me in the morning: I'll take tea. *[He goes out.]*

Eliza tries to control herself and feel indifferent as she rises and walks across to the hearth to switch off the lights. By the time she gets there she is on the point of screaming. She sits down in Higgins's chair and holds on hard to the arms. Finally she gives way（失控） and flings herself furiously on the floor raging（发怒）.

HIGGINS *[in despairing wrath（愤怒） outside]* What the devil have I done with my slippers? *[He appears at the door.]*

LIZA *[snatching up the slippers, and hurling them at him one after the other with all her force]* There are your slippers. And there. Take your slippers; and may you never have a day's luck with them!

HIGGINS *[astounded（惊愕的）]* What on earth—! *[He comes to her.]* What's the matter? Get up. *[He pulls her up.]* Anything wrong?

LIZA *[breathless]* Nothing wrong—with you. I've won your bet for you, haven't I? That's enough for you. *I* don't matter, I suppose.

HIGGINS. You won my bet! You! Presumptuous insect! *I* won it. What did you throw those slippers at me for?

LIZA. Because I wanted to smash（打破）your face. I'd like to kill you, you selfish brute. Why didn't you leave me where you picked me out of—in the gutter? You thank God it's all over, and that now you can throw me back again there, do you? *[She crisps her fingers（扳扭手指）frantically.]*

HIGGINS *[looking at her in cool wonder]* The creature is nervous, after all.

LIZA *[gives a suffocated scream of fury, and instinctively darts her nails at his face]*!!

HIGGINS *[catching her wrists]* Ah! would you? Claws in, you cat. How dare you show your temper to me? Sit down and be quiet. *[He throws her roughly into the easy-chair.]*

LIZA *[crushed by superior strength and weight]* What's to become of me? What's to become of me?

HIGGINS. How the devil do I know what's to become of you? What does it matter what becomes of you?

LIZA. You don't care. I know you don't care. You wouldn't care if I was dead. I'm nothing to you—not so much as them slippers.

HIGGINS [*thundering*] Those slippers.

LIZA [*with bitter submission（服从）*] Those slippers. I didn't think it made any difference now.

    A pause. Eliza hopeless and crushed. Higgins a little uneasy.

HIGGINS [*in his loftiest manner*] Why have you begun going on like this? May I ask whether you complain of your treatment here?

LIZA. No.

HIGGINS. Has anybody behaved badly to you? Colonel Pickering? Mrs Pearce? Any of the servants?

LIZA. No.

HIGGINS. I presume you don't pretend that I have treated you badly.

LIZA. No.

HIGGINS. I am glad to hear it. [*He moderates（缓和） his tone*]. Perhaps you're tired after the strain of the day. Will you have a glass of champagne? [*He moves towards the door*].

LIZA. No. [*Recollecting（回想起） her manners*] Thank you.

HIGGINS [*good-humored again*] This has been coming on you for some days. I suppose it was natural for you to be anxious about the garden party. But that's all over now. [*He pats her kindly on the shoulder. She writhes（因痛苦而扭动）.*] There's nothing more to worry about.

LIZA. No. Nothing more for you to worry about. [*She suddenly rises and gets away from him by going to the piano bench, where she sits and hides her face*]. Oh God! I wish I was dead.

HIGGINS [*staring after her in sincere surprise*] Why? in heaven's name, why? [*Reasonably, going to her*] Listen to me, Eliza. All this irritation is purely subjective（主观的）.

LIZA. I don't understand. I'm too ignorant.

HIGGINS. It's only imagination. Low spirits and nothing else. Nobody's hurting you. Nothing's wrong. You go to bed like a good girl and sleep it off. Have a little cry and say your prayers: that will make you comfortable.

LIZA. I heard your prayers. "Thank God it's all over!"

HIGGINS [*impatiently*] Well, don't you thank God it's all over? Now you are free and can do what you like.

LIZA [*pulling herself together（振作） in desperation*] What am I fit for? What have you left me fit for? Where am I to go? What am I to do? What's to become of me?

HIGGINS [*enlightened（恍然大悟）, but not at all impressed*] Oh, that's what's worrying you, is it? [*He thrusts his hands into his pockets, and walks about in his usual manner, rattling the contents of his pockets, as if condescending（屈

Unit 3

George Bernard Shaw and *Pygmalion*

尊俯就） to a <u>trivial</u>（微不足道的） subject out of pure kindness.] I shouldn't bother about it if I were you. I should imagine you won't have much difficulty in settling yourself somewhere or other, though I hadn't quite realized that you were going away. *[She looks quickly at him: he does not look at her, but examines the <u>dessert stand</u>（甜食架） on the piano and decides that he will eat an apple.]* You might marry, you know. *[He bites a large piece out of the apple, and <u>munches</u>（大声咀嚼） it noisily.]* You see, Eliza, all men are not <u>confirmed</u>（坚定的） old bachelors like me and the Colonel. Most men are the marrying sort (poor devils!); and you're not bad-looking; it's quite a pleasure to look at you sometimes—not now, of course, because you're crying and looking as ugly as the very devil; but when you're all right and quite yourself, you're what I should call attractive. That is, to the people in the marrying <u>line</u>（类别）, you understand. You go to bed and have a good nice rest; and then get up and look at yourself in the glass; and you won't feel so cheap.

Eliza again looks at him, speechless, and does not stir.

The look is quite lost on him: he eats his apple with a dreamy expression of happiness, as it is quite a good one.

HIGGINS *[a <u>genial</u>（天才的） afterthought occurring to him]* I daresay my mother could find some <u>chap</u>（小伙子） or other who would do very well.

LIZA. We were above that at the corner of Tottenham Court Road.

HIGGINS *[waking up]* What do you mean?

LIZA. I sold flowers. I didn't sell myself. Now you've made a lady of me I'm not fit to sell anything else. I wish you'd left me where you found me.

HIGGINS *[slinging the core of the apple decisively into the grate]* <u>Tosh</u>（胡说）, Eliza. Don't you insult human relations by dragging all this <u>cant</u>（伪善之语） about buying and selling into it. You needn't marry the fellow if you don't like him.

LIZA. What else am I to do?

HIGGINS. Oh, lots of things. What about your old idea of a florist's shop? Pickering could set you up in one: he has lots of money. *[Chuckling]* He'll have to pay for all those <u>togs</u>（衣服） you have been wearing today; and that, with the hire of the jewellery, will make a big hole in two hundred pounds. Why, six months ago you would have thought it the <u>millennium</u>（理想中的黄金时代） to have a flower shop of your own. Come! You'll be all right. I must clear off to bed: I'm devilish sleepy. By the way, I came down for something: I forget what it was.

LIZA. Your slippers.

HIGGINS. Oh yes, of course. You <u>shied</u>（投掷） them at me. *[He picks them up, and is going out when she rises and speaks to him.]*

LIZA. Before you go, sir—

HIGGINS [*dropping the slippers in his surprise at her calling him sir*] Eh?

LIZA. Do my clothes belong to me or to Colonel Pickering?

HIGGINS [*coming back into the room as if her question were the very climax of unreason*] What the devil use would they be to Pickering?

LIZA. He might want them for the next girl you pick up to experiment on.

HIGGINS [*shocked and hurt*] Is that the way you feel towards us?

LIZA. I don't want to hear anything more about that. All I want to know is whether anything belongs to me. My own clothes were burnt.

HIGGINS. But what does it matter? Why need you start bothering about that in the middle of the night?

LIZA. I want to know what I may take away with me. I don't want to be accused of stealing.

HIGGINS [*now deeply wounded*] Stealing! You shouldn't have said that, Eliza. That shows a want of feeling.

LIZA. I'm sorry. I'm only a common ignorant girl; and in my station I have to be careful. There can't be any feelings between the like of you and the like of me. Please will you tell me what belongs to me and what doesn't?

HIGGINS [*very sulky*] You may take the whole damned houseful if you like. Except the jewels. They're hired. Will that satisfy you? [*He <u>turns on his heel</u>（急转身） and is about to go in extreme <u>dudgeon</u>（愤怒）.*]

LIZA [*drinking in his emotion like <u>nectar</u>（琼浆）, and <u>nagging</u>（纠缠） him to provoke a further supply*] Stop, please. [*She takes off her jewels.*] Will you take these to your room and keep them safe? I don't want to run the risk of their being missing.

HIGGINS [*furious*] Hand them over. [*She puts them into his hands.*] If these belonged to me instead of to the jeweler, I'd <u>ram</u>（塞） them down your ungrateful throat. [*He <u>perfunctorily</u>（胡乱地） thrusts them into his pockets, unconsciously decorating himself with the <u>protruding</u>（突出的） ends of the chains.*]

LIZA [*taking a ring off*] This ring isn't the jeweler's: it's the one you bought me in Brighton. I don't want it now. [*Higgins dashes the ring violently into the fireplace, and turns on her so threateningly that she <u>crouches</u>（蹲伏） over the piano with her hands over her face, and exclaims.*] Don't you hit me.

HIGGINS. Hit you! You <u>infamous</u>（无耻的） creature, how dare you accuse me of such a thing? It is you who have hit me. You have wounded me to the heart.

LIZA [*thrilling with hidden joy*] I'm glad. I've got a little of my own back, anyhow.

HIGGINS [*with dignity, in his finest professional style*] You have caused me to lose my temper: a thing that has hardly ever happened to me before. I prefer to say nothing more tonight. I am going to bed.

LIZA [*<u>pertly</u>（傲慢无礼地）*] You'd better leave a note for Mrs Pearce about the coffee; for she won't be told by me.

HIGGINS [*formally*] Damn Mrs Pearce; and damn the coffee; and damn you; and damn my own folly in having lavished（挥霍）my hard-earned knowledge and the treasure of my regard and intimacy on a heartless guttersnipe. [*He goes out with impressive decorum（礼仪）, and spoils it by slamming the door savagely.*]

Eliza goes down on her knees on the hearthrug to look for the ring. When she finds it she considers for a moment what to do with it. Finally she flings it down on the dessert stand and goes upstairs in a tearing rage.

Excerpt 6 (from Act 5)

The next day, Henry Higgins and Pickering arrive at Mrs Higgins's home and complain about the disappearance of Eliza. They have even telephoned the police, but Mrs Higgins reproaches them for being so childish. Just then, Alfred Doolittle arrives.

Doolittle enters. He is brilliantly dressed as for a fashionable wedding, and might, in fact, be the bridegroom. A flower in his buttonhole（纽扣眼）, a dazzling silk hat, and patent leather（漆革）shoes complete the effect. He is too concerned with the business he has come on to notice Mrs Higgins. He walks straight to Higgins, and accosts（走近和……说话）him with vehement reproach（斥责）.

DOOLITTLE [*indicating his own person*] See here! Do you see this? You done this.

HIGGINS. Done what, man?

DOOLITTLE. This, I tell you. Look at it. Look at this hat. Look at this coat.

PICKERING. Has Eliza been buying you clothes?

DOOLITTLE. Eliza! not she. Why would she buy me clothes?

MRS HIGGINS. Good morning, Mr Doolittle. Won't you sit down?

DOOLITTLE [*taken aback as he becomes conscious that he has forgotten his hostess*] Asking your pardon, ma'am. [*He approaches her and shakes her proffered（主动伸出）hand.*] Thank you. [*He sits down on the ottoman, on Pickering's right.*] I am that full of what has happened to me that I can't think of anything else.

HIGGINS. What the dickens（究竟）has happened to you?

DOOLITTLE. I shouldn't mind if it had only happened to me: anything might happen to anybody and nobody to blame but Providence（上帝）, as you might say. But this is something that you done to me: yes, you, Enry Iggins.

HIGGINS. Have you found Eliza?

DOOLITTLE. Have you lost her?

HIGGINS. Yes.

DOOLITTLE. You have all the luck, you have. I ain't found her; but she'll find me quick enough now after what you done to me.

MRS HIGGINS. But what has my son done to you, Mr Doolittle?

DOOLITTLE. Done to me! Ruined me. Destroyed my happiness. Tied me up and delivered me into the hands of middle class morality.

HIGGINS [*rising intolerantly and standing over Doolittle*] You're raving（胡言乱语）. You're drunk. You're mad. I gave you five pounds. After that I had two conversations with you, at half-a-crown an hour. I've never seen you since.

DOOLITTLE. Oh! Drunk am I? Mad am I? Tell me this. Did you or did you not write a letter to an old blighter（家伙） in America that was giving five millions to found Moral Reform Societies all over the world, and that wanted you to invent a universal language for him?

HIGGINS. What! Ezra D. Wannafeller! He's dead. *[He sits down again carelessly.]*

DOOLITTLE. Yes: he's dead; and I'm done for（完蛋了）. Now did you or did you not write a letter to him to say that the most original（有独到见解的） moralist（道德家） at present in England, to the best of your knowledge, was Alfred Doolittle, a common dustman.

HIGGINS. Oh, after your last visit I remember making some silly joke of the kind.

DOOLITTLE. Ah! you may well call it a silly joke. It put the lid on（是对……的致命一击） me right enough. Just give him the chance he wanted to show that Americans is not like us: that they recognize and respect merit（优点） in every class of life, however humble. Them words is in his blooming will, in which, Henry Higgins, thanks to your silly joking, he leaves me a share in his Pre-digested Cheese Trust（托拉斯） worth three thousand a year on condition that I lecture for his Wannafeller Moral Reform World League as often as they ask me up to six times a year.

HIGGINS. The devil he does! Whew! *[Brightening suddenly]* What a lark（玩笑）!

PICKERING. A safe thing for you, Doolittle. They won't ask you twice.

DOOLITTLE. It ain't the lecturing I mind. I'll lecture them blue in the face（因精疲力竭而脸色发青）, I will, and not turn a hair（毫不畏惧）. It's making a gentleman of me that I object to. Who asked him to make a gentleman of me? I was happy. I was free. I touched pretty nigh（几乎） everybody for money when I wanted it, same as I touched you, Enry Iggins. Now I am worried; tied neck and heels（彻头彻尾地）; and everybody touches me for money. It's a fine thing for you, says my solicitor（律师）. Is it? says I. You mean it's a good thing for you, I says. When I was a poor man and had a solicitor once when they found a pram（婴儿车） in the dust cart, he got me off（使……逃脱惩罚）, and got shut of（摆脱掉） me and got me shut of him as quick as he could. Same with the doctors: used to shove（推挤） me out of the hospital before I could hardly stand on my legs, and nothing to pay. Now they finds out that I'm not a healthy man and can't live unless they looks after me twice a day. In the house I'm not let do a hand's turn（零星杂务） for myself: somebody else must do it and touch me for it. A year ago I hadn't a relative in the world except two or three that wouldn't speak to me. Now I've fifty, and not a decent week's wages among the lot of them. I have to live for others and not for myself: that's middle class morality. You talk of losing Eliza. Don't you be anxious: I bet she's on my doorstep by this: she that could support herself easy by selling flowers if I wasn't respectable. And the next one to touch me will be you, Enry Iggins. I'll have to learn to speak middle class language from you, instead of speaking proper English. That's where you'll come in; and I daresay that's what you done it for.

MRS HIGGINS. But, my dear Mr Doolittle, you need not suffer all this if you are really in earnest. Nobody can force you to accept this bequest（遗产）. You can repudiate（拒绝） it. Isn't that so, Colonel Pickering?

PICKERING. I believe so.

DOOLITTLE *[softening his manner in deference to（鉴于） her sex]* That's the tragedy of it, ma'am. It's easy to say chuck it; but I haven't the nerve. Which one of us has? We're all intimidated（恐吓）. Intimidated, ma'am: that's what we are. What is there for me if I chuck it but the workhouse[①] in my old age? I have to dye my hair already to keep my job as a dustman. If I was one of the deserving poor, and had put by（储蓄） a bit, I could chuck it; but then why should I, acause（因为） the deserving poor might as well be millionaires for all the happiness they ever has. They don't know what happiness is. But I, as one of the undeserving poor, have nothing between me and the pauper's uniform but this here blasted four thousand a year that shoves me into the middle class. (Excuse the expression, ma'am: you'd use it yourself if you had my provocation（惹人恼火的事）. They've got you every way you turn: it's a choice between the Skilly of the workhouse and the Char Bydis of the middle class[②]; and I haven't the nerve for the workhouse. Intimidated: that's what I am. Broke. Bought up. Happier men than me will call for my dust（垃圾）, and touch me for their tip; and I'll look on helpless, and envy them. And that's what your son has brought me to. *[He is overcome by emotion.]*

MRS HIGGINS. Well, I'm very glad you're not going to do anything foolish, Mr Doolittle. For this solves the problem of Eliza's future. You can provide for（供养） her now.

DOOLITTLE *[with melancholy resignation（无可奈何）]* Yes, ma'am; I'm expected

---

[①] workhouse: a place where those unable to support themselves were offered accommodation and employment. Life in a workhouse was intended to be harsh, to deter the able-bodied poor and to ensure that only the truly destitute would apply.

[②] between...class: between Scylla and Charybdis, a phrase that means between two equally hazardous alternatives.

to provide for everyone now, out of four thousand a year.

HIGGINS [*jumping up*] Nonsense! he can't provide for her. He shan't provide for her. She doesn't belong to him. I paid him five pounds for her. Doolittle: either you're an honest man or a rogue（流氓）.

DOOLITTLE [*tolerantly*] A little of both, Henry, like the rest of us: a little of both.

HIGGINS. Well, you took that money for the girl; and you have no right to take her as well.

MRS HIGGINS. Henry: don't be absurd. If you really want to know where Eliza is, she is upstairs.

HIGGINS [*amazed*] Upstairs!!! Then I shall jolly（非常） soon fetch her downstairs. [*He makes resolutely for the door.*]

MRS HIGGINS [*rising and following him*] Be quiet, Henry. Sit down.

HIGGINS. I—

MRS HIGGINS. Sit down, dear; and listen to me.

HIGGINS. Oh very well, very well, very well. [*He throws himself ungraciously on the ottoman, with his face towards the windows.*] But I think you might have told me this half an hour ago.

Excerpt 7 (from Act 5)

Mrs Higgins blames Henry Higgins and Pickering for their inconsiderate treatment of Eliza after the ambassador's party. Pickering feels a bit guilty but Higgins remains proud and angry. After a few moments, Eliza shows up.

Eliza enters, sunny, self-possessed（镇定的）, and giving a staggeringly （惊人地） convincing exhibition of ease of manner. She carries a little work-basket（针线筐）, and is very much at home（自在）. Pickering is too much taken aback to rise.

LIZA. How do you do, Professor Higgins? Are you quite well?

HIGGINS [*choking*] Am I— [*He can say no more.*]

LIZA. But of course you are: you are never ill. So glad to see you again, Colonel Pickering. [*He rises hastily; and they shake hands.*] Quite chilly this morning, isn't it? [*She sits down on his left. He sits beside her.*]

HIGGINS. Don't you dare try this game on me. I taught it to you; and it doesn't take me in（欺骗）. Get up and come home; and don't be a fool.

Eliza takes a piece of needlework（针线活） from her basket, and begins to stitch（缝补） at it, without taking the least notice of this outburst.

MRS HIGGINS. Very nicely put, indeed, Henry. No woman could resist such an invitation.

HIGGINS. You let her alone, mother. Let her speak for herself. You will jolly soon see whether she has an idea that I haven't put into her head or a word that I haven't put into her mouth. I tell you I have created this thing out of the squashed cabbage leaves of Covent Garden; and now she pretends to play the fine lady with me.

MRS HIGGINS [*placidly*（平静地）] Yes, dear; but you'll sit down, won't you?

  Higgins sits down again, savagely.

LIZA [*to Pickering, taking no apparent notice of Higgins, and working away deftly（熟练地）*] Will you drop me altogether now that the experiment is over, Colonel Pickering?

PICKERING. Oh don't. You mustn't think of it as an experiment. It shocks me, somehow.

LIZA. Oh, I'm only a squashed cabbage leaf.

PICKERING [*impulsively*] No.

LIZA [*continuing quietly*]—but I owe so much to you that I should be very unhappy if you forgot me.

PICKERING. It's very kind of you to say so, Miss Doolittle.

LIZA. It's not because you paid for my dresses. I know you are generous to everybody with money. But it was from you that I learnt really nice manners; and that is what makes one a lady, isn't it? You see it was so very difficult for me with the example of Professor Higgins always before me. I was brought up to be just like him, unable to control myself, and using bad language on the slightest provocation. And I should never have known that ladies and gentlemen didn't behave like that if you hadn't been there.

HIGGINS. Well!!

PICKERING. Oh, that's only his way, you know. He doesn't mean it.

LIZA. Oh, *I* didn't mean it either, when I was a flower girl. It was only my way. But you see I did it; and that's what makes the difference after all.

PICKERING. No doubt. Still, he taught you to speak; and I couldn't have done that, you know.

LIZA [*trivially*] Of course: that is his profession.

HIGGINS. Damnation!

LIZA [*continuing*] It was just like learning to dance in the fashionable way: there was nothing more than that in it. But do you know what began my real education?

PICKERING. What?

LIZA [*stopping her work for a moment*] Your calling me Miss Doolittle that day when I first came to Wimpole Street. That was the beginning of self-respect for me. [*She resumes her stitching.*] And there were a hundred little things you never noticed, because they came naturally to you. Things about standing up and taking off your hat and opening doors—

PICKERING. Oh, that was nothing.

LIZA. Yes: things that showed you thought and felt about me as if I were something better than a scullery-maid（洗碗女工）; though of course I know you would have been just the same to a scullery-maid if she had been let into the drawing-room. You never took off your boots in the dining room when I was there.

PICKERING. You mustn't mind that. Higgins takes off his boots all over the place.

LIZA. I know. I am not blaming him. It is his way, isn't it? But it made such a difference to me that you didn't do it. You see, really and truly, apart from the things anyone can pick up（学会）(the dressing and the proper way of speaking, and so on), the difference between a lady and a flower girl is not how she behaves, but how she's treated. I shall always be a flower girl to Professor Higgins, because he always treats me as a flower girl, and always will; but I know I can be a lady to you, because you always treat me as a lady, and always will.

MRS HIGGINS. Please don't grind your teeth, Henry.

PICKERING. Well, this is really very nice of you, Miss Doolittle.

LIZA. I should like you to call me Eliza, now, if you would.

PICKERING. Thank you. Eliza, of course.

LIZA. And I should like Professor Higgins to call me Miss Doolittle.

HIGGINS. I'll see you damned first.

MRS HIGGINS. Henry! Henry!

PICKERING *[laughing]* Why don't you slang（辱骂） back at him? Don't stand it. It would do him a lot of good.

LIZA. I can't. I could have done it once; but now I can't go back to it. You told me, you know, that when a child is brought to a foreign country, it picks up the language in a few weeks, and forgets its own. Well, I am a child in your country. I have forgotten my own language, and can speak nothing but yours. That's the real break-off（脱离） with the corner of Tottenham Court Road. Leaving Wimpole Street finishes it.

PICKERING *[much alarmed]* Oh! but you're coming back to Wimpole Street, aren't you? You'll forgive Higgins?

HIGGINS *[rising]* Forgive! Will she, by George! Let her go. Let her find out how she can get on without us. She will relapse（重新陷入） into the gutter in three weeks without me at her elbow（在……身边）.

> Doolittle appears at the centre window. With a look of dignified reproach at Higgins, he comes slowly and silently to his daughter, who, with her back to the window, is unconscious of his approach.

PICKERING. He's incorrigible（积习难改的）, Eliza. You won't relapse, will you?

LIZA. No: Not now. Never again. I have learnt my lesson. I don't believe I could utter one of the old sounds if I tried. *[Doolittle touches her on her left shoulder. She drops her work, losing her self-possession utterly at the spectacle（景象）of her father's splendor.]* A-a-a-a-ah-ow-ooh!

HIGGINS *[with a crow（啼叫；欢呼）of triumph]* Aha! Just so. A-a-a-a-ahowooh! A-a-a-a-ahowooh! A-a-a-a-ahowooh! Victory! Victory! *[He throws himself on the divan, folding his arms, and spraddling（叉开腿）arrogantly.]*

DOOLITTLE. Can you blame the girl? Don't look at me like that, Eliza. It ain't my fault. I've come into money.

LIZA. You must have touched a millionaire this time, dad.

DOOLITTLE. I have. But I'm dressed something special today. I'm going to St. George's, Hanover Square. Your stepmother is going to marry me.

LIZA *[angrily]* You're going to let yourself down to marry that low common woman!

PICKERING *[quietly]* He ought to, Eliza. *[To Doolittle]* Why has she changed her mind?

DOOLITTLE *[sadly]* Intimidated, Governor. Intimidated. Middle class morality claims its victim. Won't you put on your hat, Liza, and come and see me turned off?

LIZA. If the Colonel says I must, I—I'll *[almost sobbing]* I'll demean（降低……的身份）myself. And get insulted for my pains, like enough.

DOOLITTLE. Don't be afraid: she never comes to words（争论）with anyone now, poor woman! respectability has broke all the spirit out of her.

PICKERING *[squeezing Eliza's elbow gently]* Be kind to them, Eliza. Make the best of it（勉为其难）.

LIZA *[forcing a little smile for him through her vexation]* Oh well, just to show there's no ill feeling. I'll be back in a moment. *[She goes out.]*

DOOLITTLE *[sitting down beside Pickering]* I feel uncommon nervous about the ceremony, Colonel. I wish you'd come and see me through it.

PICKERING. But you've been through it before, man. You were married to Eliza's mother.

DOOLITTLE. Who told you that, Colonel?

PICKERING. Well, nobody told me. But I concluded—naturally—

DOOLITTLE. No: that ain't the natural way, Colonel: it's only the middle class way. My way was always the undeserving way. But don't say nothing to Eliza. She don't know: I always had a delicacy about telling her.

PICKERING. Quite right. We'll leave it so, if you don't mind.

DOOLITTLE. And you'll come to the church, Colonel, and put me through straight?

PICKERING. With pleasure. As far as a bachelor can.

MRS HIGGINS. May I come, Mr Doolittle? I should be very sorry to miss your wedding.

DOOLITTLE. I should indeed be honored by your condescension, ma'am; and my poor old woman would take it as a tremendous compliment. She's been very low, thinking of the happy days that are no more.

MRS HIGGINS *[rising]* I'll order the carriage and get ready. *[The men rise, except Higgins.]* I shan't be more than fifteen minutes. *[As she goes to the door Eliza comes in, hatted and buttoning her gloves.]* I'm going to the church to see your father married, Eliza. You had better come in the brougham（有篷马车） with me. Colonel Pickering can go on with the bridegroom.

> *Mrs Higgins goes out. Eliza comes to the middle of the room between the centre window and the ottoman. Pickering joins her.*

DOOLITTLE. Bridegroom! What a word! It makes a man realize his position, somehow. *[He takes up his hat and goes towards the door.]*

PICKERING. Before I go, Eliza, do forgive Higgins and come back to us.

LIZA. I don't think dad would allow me. Would you, dad?

DOOLITTLE *[sad but magnanimous（宽宏大量的）]* They played you off（对付） very cunning, Eliza, them two sportsmen. If it had been only one of them, you could have nailed（抓住） him. But you see, there was two; and one of them chaperoned（监护） the other, as you might say. *[To Pickering]* It was artful（狡猾的） of you, Colonel; but I bear no malice: I should have done the same myself. I been the victim of one woman after another all my life; and I don't grudge（怨恨） you two getting the better of（战胜） Liza. I shan't interfere. It's time for us to go, Colonel. So long, Henry. See you in St. George's, Eliza. *[He goes out.]*

PICKERING *[coaxing]* Do stay with us, Eliza. *[He follows Doolittle.]*

Excerpt 8 (from Act 5)

While the others are getting ready to attend Alfred Doolittle's wedding, Eliza and Higgins are left alone. In this excerpt, both make clear what they expect from each other, and Eliza finally succeeds in asserting herself.

> *Eliza goes out on the balcony to avoid being alone with Higgins. He rises and joins her there. She immediately comes back into the room and makes for the door; but he goes along the balcony quickly and gets his back to the door before she reaches it.*

HIGGINS. Well, Eliza, you've had a bit of your own back, as you call it. Have you had enough? and are you going to be reasonable? Or do you want any more?

LIZA. You want me back only to pick up your slippers and put up with your tempers and fetch and carry for you.

HIGGINS. I haven't said I wanted you back at all.

LIZA. Oh, indeed. Then what are we talking about?

HIGGINS. About you, not about me. If you come back I shall treat you just as I have always treated you. I can't change my nature; and I don't intend to change my manners. My manners are exactly the same as Colonel Pickering's.

LIZA. That's not true. He treats a flower girl as if she was a duchess.

HIGGINS. And I treat a duchess as if she was a flower girl.

LIZA. I see. *[She turns away composedly, and sits on the ottoman, facing the window.]* The same to everybody.

HIGGINS. Just so.

LIZA. Like father.

HIGGINS *[grinning, a little taken down（煞了气焰）]* Without accepting the comparison at all points（完全地）, Eliza, it's quite true that your father is not a snob（势利眼）, and that he will be quite at home in any station of life to which his eccentric（古怪的） destiny may call him. *[Seriously]* The great secret, Eliza, is not having bad manners or good manners or any other particular sort of manners, but having the same manner for all human souls: in short, behaving as if you were in Heaven, where there are no third-class carriages, and one soul is as good as another.

LIZA. Amen. You are a born preacher（说教者）.

HIGGINS *[irritated]* The question is not whether I treat you rudely, but whether you ever heard me treat anyone else better.

LIZA *[with sudden sincerity]* I don't care how you treat me. I don't mind your swearing at me. I don't mind a black eye: I've had one before this. But *[standing up and facing him]* I won't be passed over（忽略）.

HIGGINS. Then get out of my way; for I won't stop for you. You talk about me as if I were a motor bus.

LIZA. So you are a motor bus: all bounce（猛闯） and go, and no consideration for anyone. But I can do without you: don't think I can't.

HIGGINS. I know you can. I told you you could.

LIZA *[wounded, getting away from him to the other side of the ottoman with her face to the hearth]* I know you did, you brute. You wanted to get rid of me.

HIGGINS. Liar.

LIZA. Thank you. *[She sits down with dignity.]*

HIGGINS. You never asked yourself, I suppose, whether I could do without YOU.

LIZA *[earnestly]* Don't you try to get round（用哄骗的手法说服） me. You'll have to do without me.

HIGGINS *[arrogant]* I can do without anybody. I have my own soul: my own spark of divine fire. But *[with sudden humility]* I shall miss you, Eliza. *[He sits down near her on the ottoman.]* I have learnt something from your idiotic notions: I confess that humbly and gratefully. And I have grown accustomed to your voice and appearance. I like them, rather.

LIZA. Well, you have both of them on your gramophone and in your book of photographs. When you feel lonely without me, you can turn the machine on. It's got no feelings to hurt.

HIGGINS. I can't turn your soul on. Leave me those feelings; and you can take away the voice and the face. They are not you.

LIZA. Oh, you are a devil. You can twist the heart in a girl as easy as some could twist her arms to hurt her. Mrs Pearce warned me. Time and again she has wanted to leave you; and you always got round her at the last minute. And you don't care a bit for her. And you don't care a bit for me.

HIGGINS. I care for life, for humanity; and you are a part of it that has come my way and been built into my house. What more can you or anyone ask?

LIZA. I won't care for anybody that doesn't care for me.

HIGGINS. Commercial principles, Eliza. Like *[reproducing her Covent Garden pronunciation with professional exactness]* s'yollin voylets [selling violets], isn't it?

LIZA. Don't sneer（讥笑）at me. It's mean to sneer at me.

HIGGINS. I have never sneered in my life. Sneering doesn't become（适合）either the human face or the human soul. I am expressing my righteous contempt for Commercialism（商业主义）. I don't and won't trade in affection. You call me a brute because you couldn't buy a claim on me by fetching my slippers and finding my spectacles. You were a fool: I think a woman fetching a man's slippers is a disgusting sight: did I ever fetch your slippers? I think a good deal more of you for throwing them in my face. No use slaving for me and then saying you want to be cared for: who cares for a slave? If you come back, come back for the sake of good fellowship; for you'll get nothing else. You've had a thousand times as much out of me as I have out of you; and if you dare to set up your little dog's tricks of fetching and carrying slippers against my creation of a Duchess Eliza, I'll slam the door in your silly face.

LIZA. What did you do it for if you didn't care for me?

HIGGINS *[heartily]* Why, because it was my job.

LIZA. You never thought of the trouble it would make for me.

HIGGINS. Would the world ever have been made if its maker had been afraid of making trouble? Making life means making trouble. There's only one way of escaping trouble; and that's killing things. Cowards, you notice, are always shrieking to have troublesome people killed.

LIZA. I'm no preacher: I don't notice things like that. I notice that you don't notice me.

HIGGINS *[jumping up and walking about intolerantly]* Eliza: you're an idiot. I waste the treasures of my Miltonic（弥尔顿式的，庄严的） mind by spreading them before you. Once for all（最后说一次）, understand that I go my way and do my work without caring twopence（一丁点儿） what happens to either of us. I am not intimidated, like your father and your stepmother. So you can come back or go to the devil: which you please.

LIZA. What am I to come back for?

HIGGINS *[bouncing up on his knees on the ottoman and leaning over it to her]* For the fun of it. That's why I took you on.

LIZA *[with averted（移开） face]* And you may throw me out tomorrow if I don't do everything you want me to?

HIGGINS. Yes; and you may walk out tomorrow if I don't do everything you want me to.

LIZA. And live with my stepmother?

HIGGINS. Yes, or sell flowers.

LIZA. Oh! if I only could go back to my flower basket! I should be independent of both you and father and all the world! Why did you take my independence from me? Why did I give it up? I'm a slave now, for all my fine clothes.

HIGGINS. Not a bit. I'll adopt you as my daughter and settle money on you if you like. Or would you rather marry Pickering?

LIZA *[looking fiercely round at him]* I wouldn't marry you if you asked me; and you're nearer my age than what he is.

HIGGINS *[gently]* Than he is: not "than what he is."

LIZA *[losing her temper and rising]* I'll talk as I like. You're not my teacher now.

HIGGINS *[reflectively]* I don't suppose Pickering would, though. He's as confirmed an old bachelor as I am.

LIZA. That's not what I want; and don't you think it. I've always had chaps enough wanting me that way. Freddy Hill writes to me twice and three times a day, sheets and sheets.

HIGGINS *[disagreeably surprised]* Damn his impudence（厚颜无耻）! *[He recoils（退缩） and finds himself sitting on his heels.]*

LIZA. He has a right to if he likes, poor lad. And he does love me.

HIGGINS *[getting off the ottoman]* You have no right to encourage him.

LIZA. Every girl has a right to be loved.

HIGGINS. What! By fools like that?

LIZA. Freddy's not a fool. And if he's weak and poor and wants me, maybe he'd make me happier than my betters that bully me and don't want me.

HIGGINS. Can he make anything of you? That's the point.

LIZA. Perhaps I could make something of him. But I never thought of us making anything of one another; and you never think of anything else. I only want to be natural.

HIGGINS. In short, you want me to be as infatuated about you as Freddy? Is that it?

LIZA. No I don't. That's not the sort of feeling I want from you. And don't you be too sure of yourself or of me. I could have been a bad girl if I'd liked. I've seen more of some things than you, for all your learning. Girls like me can drag gentlemen down to make love to them easy enough. And they wish each other dead the next minute.

HIGGINS. Of course they do. Then what in thunder（到底） are we quarrelling about?

LIZA [much troubled] I want a little kindness. I know I'm a common ignorant girl, and you a book-learned gentleman; but I'm not dirt under your feet. What I done [correcting herself] what I did was not for the dresses and the taxis: I did it because we were pleasant together and I come—came—to care for you; not to want you to make love to me, and not forgetting the difference between us, but more friendly like.

HIGGINS. Well, of course. That's just how I feel. And how Pickering feels. Eliza: you're a fool.

LIZA. That's not a proper answer to give me [she sinks on the chair at the writing-table in tears].

HIGGINS. It's all you'll get until you stop being a common idiot. If you're going to be a lady, you'll have to give up feeling neglected if the men you know don't spend half their time snivelling over you and the other half giving you black eyes. If you can't stand the coldness of my sort of life, and the strain of it, go back to the gutter. Work til you are more a brute than a human being; and then cuddle（搂抱） and squabble（争吵） and drink til you fall asleep. Oh, it's a fine life, the life of the gutter. It's real: it's warm: it's violent: you can feel it through the thickest skin: you can taste it and smell it without any training or any work. Not like Science and Literature and Classical Music and Philosophy and Art. You find me cold, unfeeling, selfish, don't you? Very well: be off with you to the sort of people you like. Marry some sentimental hog（猪猡） or other with lots of money, and a thick pair of lips to kiss you with and a thick pair of boots to kick you with. If you can't appreciate what you've got, you'd better get what you can appreciate.

LIZA [desperate] Oh, you are a cruel tyrant. I can't talk to you: you turn everything against me: I'm always in the wrong. But you know very well all the time that you're nothing but a bully. You know I can't go back to the gutter, as you call it, and that I have no real friends in the world but you and the Colonel. You know well I couldn't bear to live with a low common man after you two; and it's wicked and cruel of you to insult me by pretending I could. You think I must go back to Wimpole Street because I have nowhere else to go but father's. But don't you be too sure that you have me under your feet to be trampled on and talked down. I'll marry Freddy, I will, as soon as I'm able to support him.

HIGGINS. *[thunderstruck]* Freddy!!! That young fool! That poor devil who couldn't get a job as an errand boy even if he had the guts to try for it! Woman: do you not understand that I have made you a consort（配偶） for a king?

LIZA. Freddy loves me: that makes him king enough for me. I don't want him to work: he wasn't brought up to it as I was. I'll go and be a teacher.

HIGGINS. What'll you teach, in heaven's name?

LIZA. What you taught me. I'll teach phonetics.

HIGGINS. Ha! Ha! Ha!

LIZA. I'll offer myself as an assistant to that hairyfaced Hungarian[①].

HIGGINS *[rising in a fury]* What! That impostor（冒牌货）! that humbug（骗子）! that toadying（谄媚的） ignoramus（不学无术的人）! Teach him my methods! my discoveries! You take one step in his direction and I'll wring（拧） your neck. *[He lays hands on her.]* Do you hear?

LIZA *[defiantly（蔑视地） non-resistant]* Wring away. What do I care? I knew you'd strike me some day. *[He lets her go, stamping（跺脚） with rage at having forgotten himself（失态）, and recoils so hastily that he stumbles back into his seat on the ottoman.]* Aha! Now I know how to deal with you. What a fool I was not to think of it before! You can't take away the knowledge you gave me. You said I had a finer ear than you. And I can be civil and kind to people, which is more than you can. Aha! *[Purposely dropping her aitches（H音） to annoy him]* That's done you, Henry Higgins, it az. Now I don't care that *[snapping her fingers（打榧子）]* for your bullying and your big talk. I'll advertize it in the papers that your duchess is only a flower girl that you taught, and that she'll teach anybody to be a duchess just the same in six months for a thousand guineas. Oh, when I think of myself crawling under your feet and being trampled on and called names, when all the time I had only to lift up my finger to be as good as you, I could just kick myself.

HIGGINS *[wondering at her]* You damned impudent slut, you! But it's better than snivelling; better than fetching slippers and finding spectacles, isn't it? *[Rising]* By George, Eliza, I said I'd make a woman of you; and I have. I like you like this.

LIZA. Yes: you turn round and make up to me now that I'm not afraid of you, and can do without you.

HIGGINS. Of course I do, you little fool. Five minutes ago you were like a millstone（磨盘） round my neck. Now you're a tower of strength: a consort battleship（护航舰）. You and I and Pickering will be three old bachelors together instead of

---

① that … Hungarian: Nepommuck, who appears at the ambassador's dinner party in Act Three in some versions of the play. He is the former student and current rival of Professor Higgins.

only two men and a silly girl.

Mrs Higgins returns, dressed for the wedding. Eliza instantly becomes cool and elegant.

MRS HIGGINS. The carriage is waiting, Eliza. Are you ready?

LIZA. Quite. Is the Professor coming?

MRS HIGGINS. Certainly not. He can't behave himself in church. He makes remarks out loud all the time on the clergyman's pronunciation.

LIZA. Then I shall not see you again, Professor. Goodbye. *[She goes to the door.]*

MRS HIGGINS *[coming to Higgins]* Goodbye, dear.

HIGGINS. Goodbye, mother. *[He is about to kiss her, when he recollects something.]* Oh, by the way, Eliza, order a ham and a Stilton cheese(斯提尔顿干酪), will you? And buy me a pair of reindeer gloves, number eights, and a tie to match that new suit of mine. You can choose the color. *[His cheerful, careless, vigorous voice shows that he is incorrigible.]*

LIZA *[disdainfully]* Number eights are too small for you if you want them lined with lamb's wool. You have three new ties that you have forgotten in the drawer of your washstand. Colonel Pickering prefers double Gloucester(双料格洛斯特硬干酪) to Stilton; and you don't notice the difference. I telephoned Mrs Pearce this morning not to forget the ham. What you are to do without me I cannot imagine. *[She sweeps(昂首阔步地走) out.]*

MRS HIGGINS. I'm afraid you've spoiled that girl, Henry. I should be uneasy about you and her if she were less fond of Colonel Pickering.

HIGGINS. Pickering! Nonsense: she's going to marry Freddy. Ha ha! Freddy! Freddy!! Ha ha ha ha!!!!! *[He roars with laughter as the play ends.]*

3.2.4 Exercises

❶ Give a brief answer to each of the following questions.

Act 1
1) Why does the flower girl protest, "I am a good girl, I am!"?

Act 2
2) Why does Eliza think it important that Higgins know she came in a cab?
3) What is the bet between Pickering and Higgins?
4) Why does Alfred Doolittle come to see Professor Higgins?
5) What does Eliza's father assume about the relationship between Higgins and his daughter?

Act 3
6) Where does Henry Higgins decide to take Eliza to test her skills? Is Mrs. Higgins pleased to see Higgins show up? Why or why not?

Unit 3

George Bernard Shaw and *Pygmalion*

7) What subjects is Eliza asked to talk about?
8) How does Eliza's behavior and conversation cause an uproar?
9) How do Freddy, Clara and Mrs. Eynsford Hill interpret Eliza's performance?
10) How does Mrs. Higgins view her son's scientific experiment with Eliza?
11) What does Mrs. Higgins understand that the men don't see?

Act 4

12) What do Higgins and Pickering say after the ambassador's party?
13) Why is Eliza so distraught after the party?
14) Why does Eliza throw Higgins's slippers at him?
15) What is Higgins's advice to Eliza when he realizes she is upset (although he cannot understand why she is upset)?
16) Why does Eliza wish Higgins had left her where he had found her?

Act 5

17) Why do both Henry Higgins and Eliza Doolittle choose to go to Mrs. Higgins for guidance after the conflict between them?
18) How does Alfred Doolittle get the new job? Why does he say he's ruined by Higgins?
19) Why does Eliza believe Colonel Pickering helps her to become a lady?
20) When does Eliza rise in Higgins's estimation? When does he admit that he likes her?

❷ Identify the following characters.

1) _____ gives Higgins the idea for the bet involving Eliza. He treats Eliza kindly and considers her feelings. At the end of the play, he apologizes to Eliza for treating her like the subject of an experiment.

2) _____ leads an idle, carefree life without the burden of being responsible to anybody. When he gets rich, however, he claims that his new, middle-class lifestyle destroys his happiness.

3) _____ is so focused on his academic interest that he lacks empathy and fails to consider other people's feelings. However, he sees through the hypocrisy and fallacies of the Victorian social hierarchy, and relishes the opportunity to beat high society at its own game by making Eliza pass as a lady.

4) _____ comes from a family that used to be rich but has now declined. He is a nice, harmless fellow and becomes infatuated with Eliza. He is somewhat a foil to Henry Higgins in terms of his tender affection.

5) _____ shows a good taste in art. She always appears self-composed and understanding, and is able to give guidance and suggestion when other characters turn to her for help.

6) _____ is familiar with her employer's bad manners and is not at all afraid of pointing them out in his face. She is the first character in the play to sense possible trouble in Higgins's experiment.

7) _____ learns to act like a lady and pass as a member of the upper class. She desires independence and is generally unafraid to stand up for herself. At the end of the play, she stands up to Higgins and leaves him.

8) _____ takes her children to different social occasions in the hope of giving them a better life than they can afford. Hers is the poor life of a lady without sufficient economic backup.

9) _____ tries to appear very cool and modern but is actually a bit impertinent. She disappoints her mother, who wants to see more lady-like manners in her.

10) _____ boasts about his expertise on language, but is regarded by Higgins as a fool. At the ambassador's party, he is completely fooled by Eliza's performance.

❸ Plot review

On a rainy evening in London, Henry Higgins, a professor of 1) _____, is wandering among the crowd in a marketplace, taking notes of people's 2) _____. There he meets Eliza Doolittle, a poor 3) _____ girl speaking cockney, and Colonel Pickering, a retired officer who, like Higgins, is interested in language. Higgins 4) _____ Eliza for her poor English, and boasts that in a matter of months he can turn her into an elegant lady by transforming her language.

Eliza, who has taken Higgins's words 5) _____, makes a visit to his house on Wimpole Street. She wants to take language 6) _____ from Professor Higgins, so that she can speak more genteelly and be able to work in a flower 7) _____. Goaded by Pickering, the two men make a 8) _____, i.e., if Higgins can successfully pass Eliza off as a 9) _____, then Pickering will pay for the 10) _____ of the training. Before long, Alfred Doolittle comes to visit Higgins. He claims that he intends to save the 11) _____ of his daughter, but his real purpose is to take advantage of the situation and extort some 12) _____. Higgins, at first disgusted by this amoral man, comes to be impressed by his ability in 13) _____, so he gives Doolittle five pounds as requested.

After three months of intense training in basic pronunciation, Higgins takes Eliza to his mother's at-home for a 14) _____ of her progress. She has been asked to talk only about the 15) _____ and 16) _____. Eliza, proud of her newly acquired capacity to pronounce accurately, soon forgets herself and begins to wander into other very 17) _____ subject matters like her aunt's suspected murder and her father's alcoholism. In her excitement she even slips back into her cockney accent. Her performance 18) _____ most of the guests, but Freddy Eynsford Hill, a young gentleman, is amused by Eliza's speech and is attracted to her.

The failure of Eliza's performance prompts her to work even harder, and she works not only on pronunciation but also on etiquette. As a result, she gives a brilliant show at an 19) _____'s dinner party, where she is believed to be a duchess by the

Unit 3

George Bernard Shaw and *Pygmalion*

guests because of her elegant demeanor. However, Eliza feels 20) _____ after the party because Higgins and Pickering only focus on their own achievement. She also feels 21) _____ about her future, not sure what she can do. Higgins does not quite understand her feelings. The two quarrel and Eliza leaves Higgin the same night.

After an unsuccessful attempt to find the runaway Eliza, Higgins and Pickering turn to Mrs. Higgins for 22) _____. They are followed by another visitor, Alfred Doolittle, who has transformed into a well-dressed 23) _____ after he gets an unexpected large sum of money every year from an American millionaire, all due to an unintentional 24) _____ Higgins has made in a letter to the American. But Alfred says he is not as happy as before, as with money comes 25) _____, and he has to get 26) _____ with his woman, which he has never done before.

Then Mrs. Higgins reveals that Eliza has actually been in her house all the while. In their last conversation, Eliza tells Higgins that she wants more 27) _____ from him if he wants her back to his house, and she claims that she can 28) _____ herself by teaching what she has learned from him, and that she will marry Freddy because he loves and respects her. Finally, Higgins is shaken by the 29) _____ Eliza demonstrates and says he has made a 30) "_____" of her. However, his manners do not seem to be changing, and he asks Eliza to run a few errands for him on her way back from her father's wedding, but Eliza leaves without a clear word whether she will return to him or not.

4 Identify the speakers of the following lines, briefly tell the situation in which each of them is uttered, and explain its significance.

1) Yes, you squashed cabbage leaf, you disgrace to the noble architecture of these columns, you incarnate insult to the English language, I could pass you off as the Queen of Sheba!
2) What is life but a series of inspired follies? The difficulty is to find them to do. Never lose a chance: it doesn't come every day. I shall make a duchess of this draggletailed guttersnipe.
3) The matter is, sir, that you can't take a girl up like that as if you were picking up a pebble on the beach.
4) I suppose the woman wants to live her own life; and the man wants to live his; and each tries to drag the other on to the wrong track. One wants to go north and the other south; and the result is that both have to go east, though they both hate the east wind.
5) — Have you no morals, man?
   — Can't afford them, Governor. Neither could you if you was as poor as me.
6) I'm one of the undeserving poor: that's what I am. Think of what that means to a man. It means that he's up agen middle class morality all the time.

7) You silly boy, of course she's not presentable. She's a triumph of your art and of her dressmaker's; but if you suppose for a moment that she doesn't give herself away in every sentence she utters, you must be perfectly cracked about her.

8) But you have no idea how frightfully interesting it is to take a human being and change her into a quite different human being by creating a new speech for her. It's filling up the deepest gulf that separates class from class and soul from soul.

9) The advantages of that poor woman who was here just now! The manners and habits that disqualify a fine lady from earning her own living without giving her a fine lady's income!

10) I was quite frightened once or twice because Eliza was doing it so well. You see, lots of the real people can't do it at all: they're such fools that they think style comes by nature to people in their position; and so they never learn.

11) I sold flowers. I didn't sell myself. Now you've made a lady of me I'm not fit to sell anything else.

12) Done to me! Ruined me. Destroyed my happiness. Tied me up and delivered me into the hands of middle class morality.

13) And then you were surprised because she threw your slippers at you! I should have thrown the fire-irons at you.

14) You see, really and truly, apart from the things anyone can pick up (the dressing and the proper way of speaking, and so on), the difference between a lady and a flower girl is not how she behaves, but how she's treated.

15) The great secret, Eliza, is not having bad manners or good manners or any other particular sort of manners, but having the same manner for all human souls: in short, behaving as if you were in Heaven, where there are no third-class carriages, and one soul is as good as another.

16) I can't turn your soul on. Leave me those feelings; and you can take away the voice and the face. They are not you.

17) I think a woman fetching a man's slippers is a disgusting sight: did I ever fetch your slippers? I think a good deal more of you for throwing them in my face.

18) Every girl has a right to be loved.

19) I want a little kindness. I know I'm a common ignorant girl, and you a book-learned gentleman; but I'm not dirt under your feet.

20) You find me cold, unfeeling, selfish, don't you? Very well: be off with you to the sort of people you like. Marry some sentimental hog or other with lots of money, and a thick pair of lips to kiss you with and a thick pair of boots to kick you with. If you can't appreciate what you've got, you'd better get what you can appreciate.

❺ Questions for essay or discussion

1) How is the ending in the original play different from that in the film (1938 version)?

Which one do you like better, why?
2) This play has a subtitle: A Romance in Five Acts. Is the play, first and foremost, a romantic love story? How do you understand the word "romance" in the subtitle?
3) How is Henry Higgins different from Pygmalion in the Greek myth? How is Eliza Doolittle different from Galatea in the same myth, or from Cinderella in the famous fairytale?
4) The Chinese translation of the play's title shifts the focus from the male "Pygmalion" to the female "flower girl" (《卖花女》). How do you like it?
5) Shaw says in his Preface to the play that good art is always didactic. What is the ultimate "lesson" he probably wanted us to take away from this play?

Volume Two

American Drama and Film

Unit 4

Tennessee Williams and *A Streetcar Named Desire*

4.1 Tennessee Williams: Life and Works

4.1.1 About the Playwright

Tennessee Williams (1911—1983) is considered one of the greatest American playwrights of the twentieth century to achieve an international reputation. Although invariably ranked second (just behind Eugene O'Neill) among American dramatists, Williams is indisputably the most important southern playwright. He is a prolific author, a two-time winner of the Pulitzer Prize for Drama and a four-time recipient of the New York Drama Critics' Circle Award. Starting with the debut of *The Glass Menagerie* and through his subsequent works, Williams transforms the American stage by introducing innovative dramatic forms and styles, creating a collection of realistic and memorable characters and producing scripts which, according to many critics, lift stage dialogue to the level of poetry.

Born Thomas Lanier Williams on March 26, 1911 in Columbus, Mississippi, where his much loved maternal grandfather was an Episcopalian minister, he absorbed a tradition many years older than the world of his peers. By 1919 he had been transplanted with his family to St. Louis, Missouri. The contrast between these two cultures—an agrarian South that looked back nostalgically to a partly mythical past of refinement and gentility, and a forward-looking urban North that valued pragmatism and practicality over civility and beauty—would haunt Williams throughout his life, providing one of the enduring tensions in his plays.

Williams's father was a traveling shoe salesman who visited the family periodically but when he was seven, his father was promoted to sales manager of a St. Louis shoe company and wanted to establish a home. That home, however, was filled with violence and drinking. His elder sister Rose, the model for many of Williams's later fragile female characters, suffered not only the terror of her father's rage but the fear that her mother, constantly ill, would die. Both as a brother and an artist, Williams was preoccupied with Rose. Over the years her mental state deteriorated; she was one of the first Americans to undergo a frontal lobotomy.

Many of Williams's characters whose brutal masculinity menaces the gentler characters around them may have been created in memory of the father Williams openly "hated." Frail and overly protected by his mother, especially after a near-fatal bout of diphtheria when five, Williams was a target for school bullies. His weakness and lack of physical prowess disappointed his father, who called him "Miss Nancy." As an adolescent, Williams, finding himself in a society that was all too ready to adopt his father's scorn, took to the solitary pursuits of reading and writing. He attended, but dropped out of, the University of Missouri and Washington University in St. Louis, and spent three years working in a shoe factory. He then returned to college and earned a bachelor's degree in playwriting at the State University of Iowa. While in college Williams began writing plays and won prizes for fiction. He experimented with different forms, but his short stories were his first works to be published, in "little" magazines.

After college Williams spent brief periods in numerous cities, doing menial jobs and writing. It was then that he gave himself the romanticized name "Tennessee." In 1940 the Theater Guild produced his *Battle of Angels* in Boston. It was such a distinct failure that he feared his career was stunted from the beginning. But he kept writing and managed to live for a few years on foundation grants. His first success was *The Glass Menagerie* (1944), a New York Drama Critics' Circle Award winner. *The Glass Menagerie* ran on Broadway for 561 performances. The play introduced themes that would become apparent in later plays: illusion vs. reality; fear of isolation; need for understanding of the dispossessed; as well as clashes between sensitive and worldly people, Southern and Northern lifestyles, and the practical against the ideal. In 1947 his second success, *A Streetcar Named Desire*, was an even bigger box-office smash. It won another Drama Critics' Circle Award and his first Pulitzer Prize in 1948. By the time Williams was thirty-six, he was thought of as one of the most important playwrights in America.

Williams followed these successes with a number of plays that were not all as well received as his first works. *Summer and Smoke* (1948), *The Rose Tattoo* (1951), and *Camino Real* (1953) were met with measured enthusiasm from the public, although the critics thought highly of them. These plays were followed by the saga of a southern family, *Cat on a Hot Tin Roof*, which won all the major drama prizes in 1955, including the Pulitzer, but by this time Williams's physical health was deteriorating and he was relying increasingly on alcohol and drugs. *The Night of the Iguana* (1961), which is considered Williams's last great work for the theater, was written and produced while Williams was suffering from complications due to drug addiction. The play received immediate attention and won the New York Drama Critics' Circle Award.

Williams continued to compose for the theater, but his worsening physical and mental health is clear in the first-draft title page of *The Two-Character Play* (1969), written "from the state of lunacy… It is the story of the last six to seven years of the 1960s. The play is about disorientation—these people are lost as I am. They are two sides of one person."

Through the last few years of his life, Tennessee Williams wrote continually. He completed such plays as *Small Craft Warnings* (1972) and numerous nondramatic works, including the novel *Noise and the World of Reason* (1975), in which a homosexual writer recalls his youth and his search for love, the poetry collection *Androgyne, Mon Armour* (1977), and *Memoirs* (1975). His recovery from seizures suffered during drug withdrawal was miraculous, though his continuing alcoholism crippled his strength. His accidental death by choking in 1983 shocked the theater community. In his long career he wrote twenty-five full-length plays (five made into movies), five screenplays, over seventy one-act plays, hundreds of short stories, two novels, poetry, and a memoir. The mark he left on the tradition of realism in American drama is indelible.

4.1.2 Tennessee Williams's Major Plays

The Glass Menagerie (1944) 《玻璃动物园》
A Streetcar Named Desire (1947) 《欲望号街车》
Summer and Smoke (1948) 《夏与烟》
Cat on a Hot Tin Roof (1955) 《热铁皮屋顶上的猫》
Suddenly, Last Summer (1958) 《去夏骤至》
The Night of the Iguana (1961) 《鬣蜥之夜》

Unit 4

Tennessee Williams and *A Streetcar Named Desire*

4.2 *A Streetcar Named Desire*

4.2.1 About the Play

A Streetcar Named Desire is one of the most remarkable plays of the twentieth century. When it opened in New York on December 3, 1947, at the Barrymore Theatre, at the final curtain the audience cheered for 30 minutes. It ran for 855 performances and became the first play ever to win all three of the Pulitzer, Donaldson, and New York Drama Critics' Circle Awards.

The play exists, however, in the American memory as a film, and even those who know little of the theater are likely to know Marlon Brando's Stanley Kowalski character. His "Stella!" echoes down from 1951 to the present, bringing with it the powerful contrast between fame in American theater and the more lucrative, widespread fame in Hollywood.

Back and forth across a dilapidated street in the New Orleans French Quarter run two streetcars, one named Desire, the other Cemeteries. As the characters appear, weaving in and out to the sounds of a blues piano, lovers shouting, and air moving audibly through the languor of humid speech, the story shapes itself into an atmospheric tale of heat and mistrust. What ease and passion there is between Stella and Stanley Kowalski is a tale that has been told before the play begins. Their connection is one of powerful attraction and learned acceptance: Stella's past as a genteel southern girl seems gratefully relinquished for the vitality of Stanley's physical presence. Their Eden is interrupted as the play opens with the arrival of Blanche DuBois, Stella's sister, an affected, girlish schoolteacher whose disbelief at the poverty into which Stella has married immediately begins to erode the Kowalskis' ease. Social strictures are evoked subtly, the sense that some presence of authority has arrived and the couple must now curtail their energy, must now behave in their small, cramped apartment. Williams clearly represents the struggles of class inherent in this seemingly classless society.

In some ways Blanche represents the world of imagination. With paper lanterns to soften the effects of harsh light, coy slips into French or German, and educated conversation, Blanche stands in contrast to Stanley's blunt sensuality and uncultured manners. She sadly mirrors the position of the artist in the everyday world. While Blanche upholds the code for a woman, particularly a southern woman, of soft lies and supposed purity, her vitality, mirrored in Stanley's passion, is suppressed. Williams accurately portrays a society uncomfortable with its own imagination, which seems to hold unbearable secrets. Speaking of Blanche DuBois, Williams once said, "She was a demonic creature; the size of her feeling was too great for her to contain." And Williams said in an interview, "Desire is rooted in a longing for companionship, a release from the loneliness that haunts every individual." Loneliness and desire propel his characters into extreme behavior, no doubt, but such behavior literally dramatizes the plight that Williams saw as universal.

The most striking feature of *Streetcar*'s dramatic structure is its division into scenes rather than acts. Each of the eleven scenes that make up the play ends in a dramatic climax, and the tension of each individual scene builds up to the tension of the final climax. This structure allows the audience to focus on the emotions and actions of Blanche— the only character to appear in every scene.

4.2.2 Characters

Blanche DuBois, a member of the fading southern aristocracy. She has lost her home, her reputation and her job. She is fragile, sensitive and vain.

Stella Kowalski, Blanche's younger sister who has willingly given up her genteel upbringing in order to live with Stanley. She is calm, soothing and reasonable.

Stanley Kowalski, Stella's husband, a working-class man with an immigrant background. He is virile, coarse and violent.

Harold "Mitch" Mitchell, Stanley's friend, who temporarily considers marrying Blanche. He is gentle and well-mannered.

Eunice, the Kowalskis' landlady and upstairs neighbor. She is earthy and practical. She often quarrels with her husband Steve.

Steve, Eunice's husband and Stanley's poker buddy.

Pablo, Stanley's poker buddy.

A Doctor, who takes Blanche to the mental hospital at the end of the play. He is professional and gentlemanlike.

A Nurse, also called the "Matron," who comes with the doctor. She possesses a severe, unfeminine manner.

A Young Collector, a young man who comes to collect newspaper subscription fee when Blanche is alone in the flat.

A Negro Woman, a neighbor of the Kowalskis' who is talking with Eunice when Blanche first arrives.

A Mexican Woman, a street vendor who comes to sell Mexican funeral flowers, frightening Blanche.

Allan Grey, Blanche's dead young husband. He does not appear onstage.

Unit 4
Tennessee Williams and *A Streetcar Named Desire*

Shep Huntleigh, a former admirer of Blanche's. He does not appear onstage.

4.2.3 Selected Readings from the Play

> ### Excerpt 1 (from Scene 1)
> It is an evening early in May. Eunice and a Negro woman are relaxing on the steps of the apartment building when Stanley and his buddy Mitch show up. Stanley hollers for Stella and tells her that he and Mitch are going to the bowling alley. They depart, and Stella soon follows to watch them. Soon after Stella leaves, her sister, Blanche, arrives.

[Blanche comes around the corner, carrying a <u>valise</u>（手提箱）. She looks at a slip of paper, then at the building, then again at the slip and again at the building. Her expression is one of shocked disbelief. Her appearance is <u>incongruous to</u>（与……不协调）this setting. She is <u>daintily</u>（讲究地）dressed in a white suit with a <u>fluffy</u>（毛茸茸的）<u>bodice</u>（紧身胸衣）, necklace and earrings of pearl, white gloves and hat, looking as if she were arriving at a summer tea or cocktail party in the garden district. She is about five years older than Stella. Her <u>delicate</u>（娇弱的） beauty must avoid a strong light. There is something about her uncertain manner, as well as her white clothes, that suggests a <u>moth</u>（飞蛾）.]

EUNICE *[finally]*: What's the matter, honey? Are you lost?

BLANCHE *[with faintly hysterical humor]*: They told me to take a street-car named Desire, and then transfer to one called Cemeteries and ride six blocks and get off at—Elysian Fields[①]!

EUNICE: That's where you are now.

BLANCHE: At Elysian Fields?

EUNICE: This here is Elysian Fields.

BLANCHE: They mustn't have—understood—what number I wanted...

EUNICE: What number you lookin' for?

[Blanche wearily refers to the slip of paper.]

BLANCHE: Six thirty-two.

EUNICE: You don't have to look no further.

BLANCHE *[<u>uncomprehendingly</u>（不解地）]*: I'm looking for my sister, Stella DuBois. I mean—Mrs. Stanley Kowalski.

EUNICE: That's the <u>party</u>（当事人）.—You just did miss her, though.

BLANCHE: This—can this be—her home?

EUNICE: She's got the downstairs here and I got the up.

---

① Elysian Fields: also called Elysium. In classical mythology, it is the abode of the blessed after death.

BLANCHE: Oh. She's—out?
EUNICE: You noticed that bowling alley（保龄球馆）around the corner?
BLANCHE: I'm—not sure I did.
EUNICE: Well, that's where she's at, watchin' her husband bowl.
[There is a pause] You want to leave your suitcase here an' go find her?
BLANCHE: No.
NEGRO WOMAN: I'll go tell her you come.
BLANCHE: Thanks.
NEGRO WOMAN: You welcome. *[She goes out.]*
EUNICE: She wasn't expecting you?
BLANCHE: No. No, not tonight.
EUNICE: Well, why don't you just go in and make yourself at home till they get back.
BLANCHE: How could I—do that?
EUNICE: We own this place so I can let you in.

> *[She gets up and opens the downstairs door. A light goes on behind the blind（遮帘）, turning it light blue. Blanche slowly follows her into the downstairs flat. The surrounding areas dim out as the interior is lighted.]*
>
> *[Two rooms can be seen, not too clearly defined（划定界限）. The one first entered is primarily a kitchen but contains a folding bed to be used by Blanche. The room beyond this is a bedroom. Off this room is a narrow door to a bathroom.]*

EUNICE *[defensively（辩解地）, noticing Blanche's look]*: It's sort of messed up right now but when it's clean it's real sweet.
BLANCHE: Is it?
EUNICE: Uh-huh, I think so. So you're Stella's sister?
BLANCHE: Yes. *[Wanting to get rid of her]* Thanks for letting me in.
EUNICE: *Por nada*[①], as the Mexicans say, *por nada!* Stella spoke of you.
BLANCHE: Yes?
EUNICE: I think she said you taught school.
BLANCHE: Yes.
EUNICE: And you're from Mississippi, huh?
BLANCHE: Yes.
EUNICE: She showed me a picture of your home-place, the plantation（种植园）.
BLANCHE: Belle Reve[②]?
EUNICE: A great big place with white columns.
BLANCHE: Yes...
EUNICE: A place like that must be awful hard to keep up（保养）.

---

① *Por nada*: (Spanish) It's nothing.
② Belle Reve: (French) beautiful dream.

Unit 4

Tennessee Williams and *A Streetcar Named Desire*

BLANCHE: If you will excuse me, I'm just about to drop.

EUNICE: Sure, honey. Why don't you set down?

BLANCHE: What I meant was I'd like to be left alone.

EUNICE: Aw. I'll make myself scarce（走了）, in that case.

BLANCHE: I didn't mean to be rude, but—

EUNICE: I'll drop by the bowling alley an' hustle（催促） her up. *[She goes out the door.]*

[Blanche sits in a chair very stiffly with her shoulders slightly hunched（耸起，弓起） and her legs pressed close together and her hands tightly clutching her purse as if she were quite cold. After a while the blind look goes out of her eyes and she begins to look slowly around. A cat screeches（尖叫）. She catches her breath with a startled gesture. Suddenly she notices something in a half-opened closet. She springs up and crosses to it, and removes a whiskey bottle. She pours a half tumbler（平底酒杯） of whiskey and tosses it down（一饮而尽）. She carefully replaces the bottle and washes out the tumbler at the sink. Then she resumes her seat in front of the table.]

BLANCHE *[faintly to herself]*: I've got to keep hold of myself!

[Stella comes quickly around the corner of the building and runs to the door of the downstairs flat.]

STELLA *[calling out joyfully]*: Blanche!

[For a moment they stare at each other. Then Blanche springs up and runs to her with a wild cry.]

BLANCHE: Stella, oh, Stella, Stella! Stella for Star[①]!

[She begins to speak with feverish vivacity（快活） as if she feared for either of them to stop and think. They catch each other in a spasmodic（间歇性的） embrace.]

BLANCHE: Now, then, let me look at you. But don't you look at me, Stella, no, no, no, not till later, not till I've bathed and rested! And turn that over-light off! Turn that off! I won't be looked at in this merciless glare! *[Stella laughs and complies（依从）]* Come back here now! Oh, my baby! Stella! Stella for Star! *[She embraces her again]* I thought you would never come back to this horrible place! What am I saying? I didn't mean to say that. I meant to be nice about it and say—Oh, what a convenient location and such—Ha-a-ha! Precious lamb! You haven't said a *word* to me.

STELLA: You haven't given me a chance to, honey! *[She laughs, but her glance at Blanche is a little anxious.]*

BLANCHE: Well, now you talk. Open your pretty mouth and talk while I look around

---

[①] Stella for Star: The name "Stella" originally means star.

for some liquor! I know you must have some liquor on the place! Where could it be, I wonder? Oh, I spy（仔细查看）, I spy!

> [She rushes to the closet and removes the bottle; she is shaking all over and panting（喘息）for breath as she tries to laugh. The bottle nearly slips from her grasp.]

STELLA [noticing]: Blanche, you sit down and let me pour the drinks. I don't know what we've got to mix with. Maybe a coke's in the icebox（冰箱）. Look'n see, honey, while I'm—

BLANCHE: No coke, honey, not with my nerves（神经紧张）tonight! Where—where—where is—?

STELLA: Stanley? Bowling! He loves it. They're having a—found some soda!—tournament（比赛）...

BLANCHE: Just water, baby, to chase it! Now don't get worried, your sister hasn't turned into a drunkard, she's just all shaken up（心烦意乱）and hot and tired and dirty! You sit down, now, and explain this place to me! What are you doing in a place like this?

STELLA: Now, Blanche—

BLANCHE: Oh, I'm not going to be hypocritical（虚伪的）, I'm going to be honestly critical（批评的）about it! Never, never, never in my worst dreams could I picture—Only Poe! Only Mr. Edgar Allan Poe[①]!—could do it justice（恰当描写）! Out there I suppose is the ghoul-haunted（食尸鬼出没的）woodland of Weir[②]! [She laughs.]

STELLA: No, honey, those are the L & N tracks（轨道）.

BLANCHE: No, now seriously, putting joking aside. Why didn't you tell me, why didn't you write me, honey, why didn't you let me know?

STELLA [carefully, pouring herself a drink]: Tell you what, Blanche?

BLANCHE: Why, that you had to live in these conditions!

STELLA: Aren't you being a little intense about it? It's not that bad at all! New Orleans isn't like other cities.

BLANCHE: This has got nothing to do with New Orleans. You might as well say—forgive me, blessed baby! [She suddenly stops short] The subject is closed!

STELLA [a little drily]: Thanks.

> [During the pause, Blanche stares at her. She smiles at Blanche.]

BLANCHE [looking down at her glass, which shakes in her hand]: You're all I've got in the world, and you're not glad to see me!

STELLA [sincerely]: Why, Blanche, you know that's not true.

---

① Edgar Allen Poe: an American writer (1809—1849) best known for his poetry and short stories, particularly his tales of mystery and horror.
② ghoul-haunted woodland of Weir: a reference to Poe's poem "Ulalume," which tells a gloomy story set in the region of Weir.

BLANCHE: No? —I'd forgotten how quiet you were.

STELLA: You never did give me a chance to say much, Blanche. So I just got in the habit of being quiet around you.

BLANCHE [*vaguely*]: A good habit to get into ... [*then, abruptly*] You haven't asked me how I happened to get away from the school before the spring term ended.

STELLA: Well, I thought you'd volunteer that information—if you wanted to tell me.

BLANCHE: You thought I'd been fired?

STELLA: No, I—thought you might have—resigned...

BLANCHE: I was so exhausted by all I'd been through my—nerves broke. [*Nervously tamping cigarette*（把烟丝卷成烟）] I was on the verge of—lunacy（疯癫）, almost! So Mr. Graves—Mr. Graves is the high school superintendent（监管人）—he suggested I take a leave of absence（休假）. I couldn't put all of those details into the wire（电报）... [*She drinks quickly*] Oh, this buzzes（吡吡作响）right through me and feels so *good!*

STELLA: Won't you have another?

BLANCHE: No, one's my limit.

STELLA: Sure?

BLANCHE: You haven't said a word about my appearance.

STELLA: You look just fine.

BLANCHE: God love you for a liar! Daylight never exposed so total a ruin! But you—you've put on some weight, yes, you're just as plump as a little partridge（鹧鸪）! And it's so becoming（合适）to you!

STELLA: Now, Blanche—

BLANCHE: Yes, it is, it is or I wouldn't say it! You just have to watch around the hips a little. Stand up.

STELLA: Not now.

BLANCHE: You hear me? I said stand up! [*Stella complies reluctantly*] You messy child, you, you've spilt something on the pretty white lace collar! About your hair—you ought to have it cut in a feather bob（羽式短发）with your dainty features. Stella, you have a maid（女仆）, don't you?

STELLA: No. With only two rooms it's—

BLANCHE: What? *Two* rooms, did you say?

STELLA: This one and—[*She is embarrassed.*]

BLANCHE: The other one? [*She laughs sharply. There is an embarrassed silence.*]

BLANCHE: I am going to take just one little tiny nip（一小口）more, sort of to put the stopper（塞子）on, so to speak.... Then put the bottle away so I won't be tempted. [*She rises*] I want you to look at *my* figure! [*She turns around*] You know I haven't put on one ounce（盎司）in ten years, Stella? I weigh what I weighed the summer you left Belle Reve. The summer Dad died and you left us...

STELLA [*a little wearily*]: It's just incredible, Blanche, how well you're looking.

BLANCHE: [*They both laugh uncomfortably*] But, Stella, there's only two rooms, I don't see where you're going to put me!

STELLA: We're going to put you in here.

BLANCHE: What kind of bed's this—one of those collapsible（可折叠的） things? [*She sits on it.*]

STELLA: Does it feel all right?

BLANCHE [*dubiously（含糊地）*]: Wonderful, honey. I don't like a bed that gives（有弹性） much. But there's no door between the two rooms, and Stanley—will it be decent?

STELLA: Stanley is Polish, you know.

BLANCHE: Oh, yes. They're something like Irish, aren't they?

STELLA: Well—

BLANCHE: Only not so—highbrow（趣味高雅的）? [*They both laugh again in the same way*] I brought some nice clothes to meet all your lovely friends in.

STELLA: I'm afraid you won't think they are lovely.

BLANCHE: What are they like?

STELLA: They're Stanley's friends.

BLANCHE: Polacks（波兰佬）?

STELLA: They're a mixed lot, Blanche.

BLANCHE: Heterogeneous（异类混杂的）—types?

STELLA: Oh, yes. Yes, types is right!

BLANCHE: Well—anyhow—I brought nice clothes and I'll wear them. I guess you're hoping I'll say I'll put up at a hotel, but I'm not going to put up at a hotel. I want to be *near* you, got to be *with* somebody, I *can't* be *alone!* Because—as you must have noticed—I'm—not very *well*... [*Her voice drops and her look is frightened.*]

STELLA: You seem a little bit nervous or overwrought（过度激动） or something.

BLANCHE: Will Stanley like me, or will I be just a visiting in-law, Stella? I couldn't stand that.

STELLA: You'll get along fine together, if you'll just try not to—well—compare him with men that we went out with at home.

BLANCHE: Is he so—different?

STELLA: Yes. A different species.

BLANCHE: In what way; what's he like?

STELLA: Oh, you can't describe someone you're in love with! Here's a picture of him! [*She hands a photograph to Blanche.*]

BLANCHE: An officer?

STELLA: A Master Sergeant（军士长） in the Engineers' Corps（工兵团）. Those are decorations（奖章）!

BLANCHE: He had those on when you met him?

STELLA: I assure you I wasn't just blinded by all the brass（黄铜；勋章）.

BLANCHE: That's not what I—

STELLA: But of course there were things to adjust myself to later on.

BLANCHE: Such as his civilian（平民的） background! *[Stella laughs uncertainly]* How did he take it when you said I was coming?

STELLA: Oh, Stanley doesn't know yet.

BLANCHE *[frightened]*: You—haven't told him?

STELLA: He's on the road（旅行推销，出差） a good deal.

BLANCHE: Oh. Travels?

STELLA: Yes.

BLANCHE: Good. I mean—isn't it?

STELLA *[half to herself]*: I can hardly stand it when he is away for a night …

BLANCHE: Why, Stella!

STELLA: When he's away for a week I nearly go wild!

BLANCHE: Gracious（天啊）!

STELLA: And when he comes back I cry on his lap like a baby...

[She smiles to herself.]

BLANCHE: I guess that is what is meant by being in love… *[Stella looks up with a radiant smile.]* Stella—

STELLA: What?

BLANCHE *[in an uneasy rush]*: I haven't asked you the things you probably thought I was going to ask. And so I'll expect you to be understanding about what *I* have to tell *you*.

STELLA: What, Blanche? *[Her face turns anxious.]*

BLANCHE: Well, Stella—you're going to reproach me, I know that you're bound to reproach me—but before you do—take into consideration—you left! I stayed and struggled! You came to New Orleans and looked out for yourself! *I* stayed at *Belle Reve* and tried to hold it together! I'm not meaning this in any reproachful way, but *all* the burden descended（降落） on *my* shoulders.

STELLA: The best I could do was make my own living, Blanche.

[Blanche begins to shake again with intensity.]

BLANCHE: I know, I know. But you are the one that abandoned Belle Reve, not I! I stayed and fought for it, bled for it, almost died for it!

STELLA: Stop this hysterical outburst and tell me what's happened? What do you mean fought and bled? What kind of—

BLANCHE: I knew you would, Stella. I knew you would take this attitude about it!

STELLA: About—what?—please!

BLANCHE *[slowly]*: The loss—the loss...

STELLA: Belle Reve? Lost, is it? No!

BLANCHE: Yes, Stella.

> [They stare at each other across the yellow-checked（格子花纹的）linoleum（油布）of the table. Blanche slowly nods her head and Stella looks slowly down at her hands folded on the table. The music of the "blue piano" grows louder. Blanche touches her handkerchief to her forehead.]

STELLA: But how did it go? What happened?

BLANCHE [springing up]: You're a fine one to ask me how it went!

STELLA: Blanche!

BLANCHE: You're a fine one to sit there *accusing me* of it!

STELLA: *Blanche!*

BLANCHE: I, I, *I* took the blows in my face and my body! All of those deaths! The long parade（游行队伍）to the graveyard! Father, mother! Margaret, that dreadful way! So big with it, it couldn't be put in a coffin! But had to be burned like rubbish! You just came home in time for the funerals, Stella. And funerals are pretty compared to deaths. Funerals are quiet, but deaths—not always. Sometimes their breathing is hoarse（沙哑的）, and sometimes it rattles（咯咯作响）, and sometimes they even cry out to you, "Don't let me go!" Even the old, sometimes, say, "Don't let me go." As if you were able to stop them! But funerals are quiet, with pretty flowers. And, oh, what gorgeous boxes they pack them away in! Unless you were there at the bed when they cried out, "Hold me!" you'd never suspect there was the struggle for breath and bleeding. You didn't dream, but I saw! *Saw! Saw!* And now you sit there telling me with your eyes that I let the place go! How in hell do you think all that sickness and dying was paid for? Death is expensive, Miss Stella! And old Cousin Jessie's right after Margaret's, hers! Why, the Grim Reaper[①] had put up his tent on our doorstep! ... Stella. Belle Reve was his headquarters! Honey—that's how it slipped through my fingers! Which of them left us a fortune? Which of them left a cent of insurance even? Only poor Jessie—one hundred to pay for her coffin. That was all, Stella! And I with my pitiful salary at the school. Yes, accuse me! Sit there and stare at me, thinking I let the place go! *I* let the place go? Where were *you!* In bed with your—Polack!

STELLA [springing]: Blanche! You be still! That's enough! [She starts out.]

BLANCHE: Where are you going?

STELLA: I'm going into the bathroom to wash my face.

BLANCHE: Oh, Stella, Stella, you're crying!

STELLA: Does that surprise you?

BLANCHE: Forgive me—I didn't mean to—

> [The sound of men's voices is heard. Stella goes into the bathroom, closing

---

① Grim Reaper: the personification of death as a man or cloaked skeleton holding a scythe.

Unit 4

Tennessee Williams and *A Streetcar Named Desire*

the door behind her. When the men appear, and Blanche realizes it must be Stanley returning, she moves uncertainly from the bathroom door to the dressing table, looking <u>apprehensively</u>（担忧地） toward the front door. Stanley enters, followed by Steve and Mitch. Stanley pauses near his door, Steve by the foot of the <u>spiral</u>（螺旋形的） stair, and Mitch is slightly above and to the right of them, about to go out. As the men enter, we hear some of the following dialogue.]

STANLEY: Is that how he got it?
STEVE: Sure that's how he got it. He hit the old weather-bird for 300 bucks on a six-number-ticket.
MITCH: Don't tell him those things; he'll believe it.
  [Mitch starts out.]
STANLEY *[<u>restraining</u>（叫住） Mitch]*: Hey, Mitch—come back here.
  [Blanche, at the sound of voices, retires in the bedroom. She picks up Stanley's photo from dressing table, looks at it, puts it down. When Stanley enters the apartment, she <u>darts</u>（飞奔） and hides behind the screen at the head of bed.]
STEVE *[to Stanley and Mitch]*: Hey, are we playin' poker tomorrow?
STANLEY: Sure—at Mitch's.
MITCH *[hearing this, returns quickly to the stair <u>rail</u>（扶栏）]*: No—not at my place. My mother's still sick!
STANLEY: Okay, at my place ... *[Mitch starts out again]* But you bring the beer!
  [Mitch pretends not to hear,—calls out "Goodnight all," and goes out, singing. Eunice's voice is heard, above]
EUNICE: Break it up down there! I made the spaghetti dish and ate it myself.
STEVE *[going upstairs]*: I told you and phoned you we was playing. *[To the men]* Jax beer!
EUNICE: You never phoned me once.
STEVE: I told you at breakfast—and phoned you at lunch...
EUNICE: Well, never mind about that. You just get yourself home here once in a while.
STEVE: You want it in the papers?
  [More laughter and shouts of parting come from the men. Stanley throws the screen door of the kitchen open and comes in. He is of medium height, about five feet eight or nine, and strongly, compactly built. Animal joy in his being is <u>implicit</u>（暗含的） in all his movements and attitudes. Since earliest manhood the center of his life has been pleasure with women, the giving and taking of it, not with weak <u>indulgence</u>（沉迷）, dependently, but with the power and pride of a richly feathered male bird among hens. Branching out from this complete and satisfying center are all the <u>auxiliary</u>（辅助性的） channels of his life, such as his <u>heartiness</u>（热诚） with men, his

appreciation of <u>rough</u>（粗俗的） humor, his love of good drink and food and games, his car, his radio, everything that is his, that bears his <u>emblem</u>（标记） of the <u>gaudy</u>（艳俗的） seed-bearer. He sizes women up at a glance, with sexual classifications, <u>crude</u>（粗俗的） images flashing into his mind and determining the way he smiles at them.]

BLANCHE [drawing <u>involuntarily</u>（不由自主地） back from his stare]: You must be Stanley. I'm Blanche.

STANLEY: Stella's sister?

BLANCHE: Yes.

STANLEY: H'lo. Where's the little woman?

BLANCHE: In the bathroom.

STANLEY: Oh. Didn't know you were coming in town.

BLANCHE: I—uh—

STANLEY: Where you from, Blanche?

BLANCHE: Why, I—live in Laurel.

[He has crossed to the closet and removed the whiskey bottle.]

STANLEY: In Laurel, huh? Oh, yeah. Yeah, in Laurel, that's right. Not in my <u>territory</u>（推销区）. Liquor goes fast in hot weather.

[He holds the bottle to the light to observe its <u>depletion</u>（消耗）.]

Have a <u>shot</u>（一小杯）?

BLANCHE: No, I—rarely touch it.

STANLEY: Some people rarely touch it, but it touches them often.

BLANCHE [faintly]: Ha-ha.

STANLEY: My clothes're stickin' to me. Do you mind if I make myself comfortable?

[He starts to remove his shirt.]

BLANCHE: Please, please do.

STANLEY: Be comfortable is my motto.

BLANCHE: It's mine, too. It's hard to stay looking fresh. I haven't washed or even powdered my face and—here you are!

STANLEY: You know you can catch cold sitting around in damp things, especially when you been exercising hard like bowling is. You're a teacher, aren't you?

BLANCHE: Yes.

STANLEY: What do you teach, Blanche?

BLANCHE: English.

STANLEY: I never was a very good English student. How long you here for, Blanche?

BLANCHE: I—don't know yet.

STANLEY: You going to <u>shack up</u>（暂住） here?

BLANCHE: I thought I would if it's not inconvenient for you all.

STANLEY: Good.

BLANCHE: Traveling wears me out.

STANLEY: Well, take it easy.

    [A cat screeches near the window. Blanche springs up.]

BLANCHE: What's that?

STANLEY: Cats ... Hey, Stella!

STELLA *[faintly, from the bathroom]*: Yes, Stanley.

STANLEY: Haven't <u>fallen in</u>（累垮）, have you? *[He grins at Blanche. She tries unsuccessfully to smile back. There is a silence]* I'm afraid I'll strike you as being the <u>unrefined</u>（不文雅的） type. Stella's spoke of you a good deal. You were married once, weren't you?

    [The music of the <u>polka</u>（波尔卡舞曲） rises up, faint in the distance.]

BLANCHE: Yes. When I was quite young.

STANLEY: What happened?

BLANCHE: The boy—the boy died. *[She sinks back down]* I'm afraid I'm—going to be sick!

    [Her head falls on her arms.]

⚜ Excerpt 2 (from Scene 2)

The following evening, Stanley is going to host a poker party with his friends, so Stella decides to take Blanche out for dinner. While Blanche is offstage, taking a bath to soothe her nerves, Stella explains Blanche's ordeal of losing Belle Reve and asks that Stanley be kind to Blanche. However, Stanley thinks Blanche has swindled Stella out of her rightful share of the estate. Looking for a bill of sale, Stanley angrily pulls all of Blanche's belongings out of her trunk. Enraged at Stanley's actions and ignorance, Stella storms out onto the porch. Then Blanche finishes her bath and appears before Stanley.

    [Stella goes out to the porch. Blanche comes out of the bathroom in a red <u>satin</u>（绸缎） robe.]

BLANCHE *[<u>airily</u>（轻快地）]*: Hello, Stanley! Here I am, all freshly bathed and <u>scented</u>（有香味的）, and feeling like a brand new human being!

    [He lights a cigarette.]

STANLEY: That's good.

BLANCHE *[drawing the curtains at the windows]*: Excuse me while I <u>slip</u>（快速穿上） on my pretty new dress!

STANLEY: Go right ahead, Blanche.

    [She closes the <u>drapes</u>（帘子） between the rooms.]

BLANCHE: I understand there's to be a little card party to which we ladies are <u>cordially</u>（诚挚地） *not* invited!

STANLEY *[<u>ominously</u>（恶意地）]*: Yeah?

[Blanche throws off her robe and slips into a flowered print dress.]

BLANCHE: Where's Stella?

STANLEY: Out on the porch.

BLANCHE: I'm going to ask a favor of you in a moment.

STANLEY: What could that be, I wonder?

BLANCHE: Some buttons in back! You may enter!

[He crosses through drapes with a smoldering（愠怒的）look.]

How do I look?

STANLEY: You look all right.

BLANCHE: Many thanks! Now the buttons!

STANLEY: I can't do nothing with them.

BLANCHE: You men with your big clumsy fingers. May I have a drag（吸烟）on your cig?

STANLEY: Have one for yourself.

BLANCHE: Why, thanks! ... It looks like my trunk has exploded.

STANLEY: Me an' Stella were helping you unpack.

BLANCHE: Well, you certainly did a fast and thorough job of it!

STANLEY: It looks like you raided（抢劫）some stylish shops in Paris.

BLANCHE: Ha-ha! Yes—clothes are my passion!

STANLEY: What does it cost for a string of fur-pieces（皮货）like that?

BLANCHE: Why, those were a tribute（礼物）from an admirer of mine!

STANLEY: He must have had a lot of—admiration!

BLANCHE: Oh, in my youth I excited some admiration. But look at me now! *[She smiles at him radiantly]* Would you think it possible that I was once considered to be—attractive?

STANLEY: Your looks are okay.

BLANCHE: I was fishing for（捞取）a compliment, Stanley.

STANLEY: I don't go in for（喜欢）that stuff.

BLANCHE: What—stuff?

STANLEY: Compliments to women about their looks. I never met a woman that didn't know if she was good-looking or not without being told, and some of them give themselves credit（称赞）for more than they've got. I once went out with a doll（无头脑的漂亮女郎）who said to me, "I am the glamorous（有魅力的）type, I am the glamorous type!" I said, "So what?"

BLANCHE: And what did she say then?

STANLEY: She didn't say nothing. That shut her up like a clam（蛤蜊）.

BLANCHE: Did it end the romance?

STANLEY: It ended the conversation—that was all. Some men are took in（受骗）by this Hollywood glamor stuff and some men are not.

BLANCHE: I'm sure you belong in the second category.

STANLEY: That's right.

BLANCHE: I cannot imagine any witch of a woman casting a spell（魔咒） over you.

STANLEY: That's—right.

BLANCHE: You're simple, straightforward and honest, a little bit on the primitive side I should think. To interest you a woman would have to—*[She pauses with an indefinite gesture.]*

STANLEY *[slowly]*: Lay ... her cards on the table.

BLANCHE *[smiling]*: Well, I never cared for wishy-washy（软弱、无决断力的）people. That was why, when you walked in here last night, I said to myself—"My sister has married a man!"—Of course that was all that I could tell about you.

STANLEY *[booming（雷鸣般的）]*: Now let's cut the re-bop（胡说八道）!

BLANCHE *[pressing hands to her ears]*: Ouuuuu!

STELLA *[calling from the steps]*: Stanley! You come out here and let Blanche finish dressing!

BLANCHE: I'm through dressing, honey.

STELLA: Well, you come out, then.

STANLEY: Your sister and I are having a little talk.

BLANCHE *[lightly]*: Honey, do me a favor. Run to the drug-store and get me a lemon-coke with plenty of chipped ice（碎冰） in it!—Will you do that for me, Sweetie?

STELLA *[uncertainly]*: Yes. *[She goes around the corner of the building.]*

BLANCHE: The poor little thing was out there listening to us, and I have an idea she doesn't understand you as well as I do. ... All right; now, Mr. Kowalski, let us proceed without any more double-talk（含糊其辞的话）. I'm ready to answer all questions. I've nothing to hide. What is it?

STANLEY: There is such a thing in this State of Louisiana as the Napoleonic code[①], according to which whatever belongs to my wife is also mine—and vice versa（反之亦然）.

BLANCHE: My, but you have an impressive judicial（法官似的） air（派头）!

[She sprays herself with her atomizer（香水喷雾器）; then playfully sprays him with it. He seizes the atomizer and slams it down on the dresser（梳妆台）. She throws back her head and laughs.]

STANLEY: If I didn't know that you was my wife's sister I'd get ideas about you!

BLANCHE: Such as what!

STANLEY: Don't play so dumb. You know what!

BLANCHE *[she puts the atomizer on the table]*: All right. Cards on the table. That suits me *[She turns to Stanley.]* I know I fib（撒小谎） a good deal. After all, a

---

① Napoleonic code: the civil code of France, enacted in 1804 and officially designated in 1807. It was recognized in New Orleans from the days of French rule.

woman's charm is fifty per cent illusion, but when a thing is important I tell the truth, and this is the truth: I haven't cheated my sister or you or anyone else as long as I have lived.

STANLEY: Where's the papers? In the trunk?

BLANCHE: Everything that I own is in that trunk.

> [Stanley crosses to the trunk, shoves（猛推） it roughly open and begins to open compartments（隔层）.]

BLANCHE: What in the name of heaven are you thinking of! What's in the back of that little boy's mind of yours? That I am absconding（逃匿） with something, attempting some kind of treachery（背信行为） on my sister?—Let me do that! It will be faster and simpler... [She crosses to the trunk and takes out a box] I keep my papers mostly in this tin box. [She opens it.]

STANLEY: What's them underneath? [He indicates another sheaf（捆，束） of papers.]

BLANCHE: These are love-letters, yellowing with antiquity（古旧）, all from one boy. [He snatches them up. She speaks fiercely] Give those back to me!

STANLEY: I'll have a look at them first!

BLANCHE: The touch of your hands insults them!

STANLEY: Don't pull that stuff（耍花招）!

> [He rips off the ribbon and starts to examine them. Blanche snatches them from him, and they cascade（撒落） to the floor.]

BLANCHE: Now that you've touched them I'll burn them!

STANLEY [staring, baffled（困惑的）]: What in hell are they?

BLANCHE [on the floor gathering them up]: Poems a dead boy wrote. I hurt him the way that you would like to hurt me, but you can't! I'm not young and vulnerable any more. But my young husband was and I—never mind about that! Just give them back to me!

STANLEY: What do you mean by saying you'll have to burn them?

BLANCHE: I'm sorry, I must have lost my head for a moment. Everyone has something he won't let others touch because of their—intimate nature...

> [She now seems faint with exhaustion and she sits down with the strong box and puts on a pair of glasses and goes methodically（有条不紊地） through a large stack of papers.]

Ambler & Ambler. Hmmmmm.... Crabtree.... More Ambler & Ambler.

STANLEY: What is Ambler & Ambler?

BLANCHE: A firm that made loans on the place.

STANLEY: Then it *was* lost on a mortgage（贷款抵押）?

BLANCHE [touching her forehead]: That must've been what happened.

STANLEY: I don't want no ifs, ands or buts! What's all the rest of them papers?

[She hands him the entire box. He carries it to the table and starts to examine the papers.]

BLANCHE *[picking up a large envelope containing more papers]*: There are thousands of papers, stretching back over hundreds of years, affecting Belle Reve as, piece by piece, our improvident（无远见的；挥霍的） grandfathers and father and uncles and brothers exchanged the land for their epic（史诗一般的） fornications（私通）—to put it plainly! *[She removes her glasses with an exhausted laugh]* The four-letter word deprived us of our plantation, till finally all that was left—and Stella can verify（核实） that!—was the house itself and about twenty acres of ground, including a graveyard, to which now all but Stella and I have retreated. *[She pours the contents of the envelope on the table]* Here all of them are, all papers! I hereby（特此） endow（赋予） you with them! Take them, peruse（审阅） them—commit them to memory, even! I think it's wonderfully fitting that Belle Reve should finally be this bunch of old papers in your big, capable hands! ... I wonder if Stella's come back with my lemon-coke... *[She leans back and closes her eyes.]*

STANLEY: I have a lawyer acquaintance who will study these out.

BLANCHE: Present them to him with a box of aspirin tablets（阿司匹林药片）.

STANLEY *[becoming somewhat sheepish（懦弱的）]*: You see, under the Napoleonic code—a man has to take an interest in his wife's affairs—especially now that she's going to have a baby.

[Blanche opens her eyes. The "blue piano" sounds louder.]

BLANCHE: Stella? Stella going to have a baby? *[dreamily]* I didn't know she was going to have a baby!

[She gets up and crosses to the outside door. Stella appears around the corner with a carton from the drug-store.

[Stanley goes into the bedroom with the envelope and the box.

[The inner rooms fade to darkness and the outside wall of the house is visible. Blanche meets Stella at the foot of the steps to the sidewalk（人行道）.]

BLANCHE: Stella, Stella for star! How lovely to have a baby! It's all right. Everything's all right.

STELLA: I'm sorry he did that to you.

BLANCHE: Oh, I guess he's just not the type that goes for jasmine（茉莉花） perfume, but maybe he's what we need to mix with our blood now that we've lost Belle Reve. We thrashed it out（通过讨论解决问题）. I feel a bit shaky, but I think I handled it nicely, I laughed and treated it all as a joke. *[Steve and Pablo appear, carrying a case of beer.]* I called him a little boy and laughed and flirted. Yes, I was flirting with your husband! *[as the men approach]* The guests are gathering for the poker party.

[The two men pass between them, and enter the house.]
    Which way do we go now, Stella—this way?
STELLA: No, this way. *[She leads Blanche away.]*
BLANCHE *[laughing]*: The blind are leading the blind[①]!
    [A tamale（墨西哥玉米粉蒸肉） vendor is heard calling.]
VENDOR'S VOICE: Red-hot!

Excerpt 3 (from Scene 3)

It is around 2:30 A.M. Stanley and his friends are still playing poker in the kitchen when Stella and Blanche return. Mitch is sheepish and awkward upon meeting Blanche, indicating that he is attracted to her. When Stella and Blanche begin their sisterly chat in the bedroom, Stanley, drunk, hollers at them to be quiet. Later, Blanche turns on the radio, further angering Stanley, who springs up and rudely shuts off the radio. The poker party continues, but Mitch skips the next hand to accost Blanche.

    [Mitch laughs uncomfortably and continues through the portieres（门帘）. He stops just inside.]
BLANCHE *[softly]*: Hello! The Little Boys' Room is busy right now.
MITCH: We've—been drinking beer.
BLANCHE: I hate beer.
MITCH: It's—a hot weather drink.
BLANCHE: Oh, I don't think so; it always makes me warmer. Have you got any cigs?
    [She has slipped on the dark red satin wrapper（浴袍）.]
MITCH: Sure.
BLANCHE: What kind are they?
MITCH: Luckies.
BLANCHE: Oh, good. What a pretty case. Silver?
MITCH: Yes. Yes; read the inscription（铭文）.
BLANCHE: Oh, is there an inscription? I can't make it out. *[He strikes a match and moves closer]* Oh! *[reading with feigned（假装） difficulty]*:
    "And if God choose,
    I shall but love thee better—after—death!"

---

① The ... blind: a quote from the Bible: "And if the blind lead the blind, both shall fall into the ditch." (Matthew 15:14). It has become a proverb which means that those people without knowledge or experience should not try to guide or advise others in a similar position.

Why, that's from my favorite sonnet by Mrs. Browning①!

MITCH: You know it?

BLANCHE: Certainly I do!

MITCH: There's a story connected with that inscription.

BLANCHE: It sounds like a romance.

MITCH: A pretty sad one.

BLANCHE: Oh?

MITCH: The girl's dead now.

BLANCHE [*in a tone of deep sympathy*]: Oh!

MITCH: She knew she was dying when she give me this. A very strange girl, very sweet—very!

BLANCHE: She must have been fond of you. Sick people have such deep, sincere attachments（依恋）.

MITCH: That's right, they certainly do.

BLANCHE: Sorrow makes for（导致）sincerity, I think.

MITCH: It sure brings it out in people.

BLANCHE: The little there is belongs to people who have experienced some sorrow.

MITCH: I believe you are right about that.

BLANCHE: I'm positive that I am. Show me a person who hasn't known any sorrow and I'll show you a shuperficial②—Listen to me! My tongue is a little—thick（口齿不清）! You boys are responsible for it. The show let out（散场）at eleven and we couldn't come home on account of the poker game so we had to go somewhere and drink. I'm not accustomed to having more than one drink. Two is the limit—and *three!* [*She laughs*] Tonight I had three.

STANLEY: Mitch!

MITCH: Deal me out（不把……算在里面）. I'm talking to Miss—

BLANCHE: DuBois.

MITCH: Miss DuBois?

BLANCHE: It's a French name. It means woods and Blanche means white, so the two together mean white woods. Like an orchard in spring! You can remember it by that.

MITCH: You're French?

BLANCHE: We are French by extraction（出身）. Our first American ancestors were French Huguenots③.

MITCH: You are Stella's sister, are you not?

---

① Mrs. Browning: Elizabeth Barrett Browning (1806–1861), a popular English poetess of the Victorian era who wrote many love poems.
② shuperficial: superficial.
③ Huguenots: members of a French Protestant denomination with origins in the 16th or 17th centuries. They were inspired by the writings of John Calvin.

BLANCHE: Yes, Stella is my precious little sister. I call her little in spite of the fact she's somewhat older than I. Just slightly. Less than a year. Will you do something for me?

MITCH: Sure. What?

BLANCHE: I bought this adorable little colored paper lantern at a Chinese shop on Bourbon[①]. Put it over the light bulb（灯泡）! Will you, please?

MITCH: Be glad to.

BLANCHE: I can't stand a naked light bulb, any more than I can a rude remark or a vulgar action.

MITCH [adjusting the lantern]: I guess we strike you as being a pretty rough bunch.

BLANCHE: I'm very adaptable—to circumstances.

MITCH: Well, that's a good thing to be. You are visiting Stanley and Stella?

BLANCHE: Stella hasn't been so well lately, and I came down to help her for a while. She's very run down（疲乏的）.

MITCH: You're not—?

BLANCHE: Married? No, no. I'm an old maid schoolteacher!

MITCH: You may teach school but you're certainly not an old maid.

BLANCHE: Thank you, sir! I appreciate your gallantry（绅士风度）!

MITCH: So you are in the teaching profession?

BLANCHE: Yes. Ah, yes...

MITCH: Grade school（小学）or high school or—

STANLEY [bellowing（吼叫）]: Mitch!

MITCH: Coming!

BLANCHE: Gracious, what lung-power! ... I teach high school. In Laurel.

MITCH: What do you teach? What subject?

BLANCHE: Guess!

MITCH: I bet you teach art or music? [Blanche laughs delicately（雅致地）] Of course I could be wrong. You might teach arithmetic（算数）.

BLANCHE: Never arithmetic, sir; never arithmetic! [with a laugh] I don't even know my multiplication tables（乘法表）! No, I have the misfortune of being an English instructor. I attempt to instill（灌输）a bunch of bobby-soxers[②] and drug-store Romeos[③] with reverence（尊敬）for Hawthorne and Whitman and Poe[④]!

MITCH: I guess that some of them are more interested in other things.

BLANCHE: How very right you are! Their literary heritage is not what most of them

---

① Bourbon: a famous bar street in the French Quarter of New Orleans.
② bobby-soxers: teenage girls who wear bobby sox/socks.
③ drug-store Romeos: boys who bought their hair gel and cheap cologne from drugstores.
④ Hawthorne ... Poe: famous 19th-century American writers or poets.

treasure above all else! But they're sweet things! And in the spring, it's touching to notice them making their first discovery of love! As if nobody had ever known it before!

[The bathroom door opens and Stella comes out. Blanche continues talking to Mitch.]

Oh! Have you finished? Wait—I'll turn on the radio.

[She turns the knobs（旋钮） on the radio and it begins to play "Wien, Wien, nur du allein."① Blanche waltzes（跳华尔兹舞） to the music with romantic gestures. Mitch is delighted and moves in awkward imitation like a dancing bear.

[Stanley stalks（昂首阔步地走） fiercely through the portieres into the bedroom. He crosses to the small white radio and snatches it off the table. With a shouted oath, he tosses the instrument out the window.]

STELLA: *Drunk—drunk—animal thing, you! [She rushes through to the poker table]*
All of you—please go home! If any of you have one spark of decency in you—

BLANCHE *[wildly]*: Stella, watch out, he's—

[Stanley charges after Stella.]

MEN *[feebly]*: Take it easy, Stanley. Easy, fellow.—Let's all—

STELLA: You lay your hands on me and I'll—

[She backs out of sight. He advances and disappears. There is the sound of a blow. Stella cries out. Blanche screams and runs into the kitchen. The men rush forward and there is grappling（扭打） and cursing. Something is overturned with a crash.]

BLANCHE *[shrilly]*: My sister is going to have a baby!

MITCH: This is terrible.

BLANCHE: Lunacy, absolute lunacy!

MITCH: Get him in here, men.

[Stanley is forced, pinioned（束缚） by the two men, into the bedroom. He nearly throws them off. Then all at once he subsides and is limp（软弱无力的） in their grasp.

[They speak quietly and lovingly to him and he leans his face on one of their shoulders.]

STELLA *[in a high, unnatural voice, out of sight]*: I want to go away, I want to go away!

MITCH: Poker shouldn't be played in a house with women.

[Blanche rushes into the bedroom]

BLANCHE: I want my sister's clothes! We'll go to that woman's upstairs!

MITCH: Where is the clothes?

---

① "Wien ... allein": (German) "Vienna, Vienna, you alone."

BLANCHE *[opening the closet]*: I've got them! *[She rushes through to Stella]* Stella, Stella, precious! Dear, dear little sister, don't be afraid!

  [With her arms around Stella, Blanche guides her to the outside door and upstairs.]

STANLEY *[dully]*: What's the matter; what's happened?

MITCH: You just <u>blew your top</u>（暴怒）, Stan.

PABLO: He's okay, now.

STEVE: Sure, my boy's okay!

MITCH: Put him on the bed and get a wet towel.

PABLO: I think coffee would do him a world of good, now.

STANLEY *[thickly]*: I want water.

MITCH: Put him under the shower!

  [The men talk quietly as they lead him to the bathroom.]

STANLEY: Let the rut go of me, you sons of bitches!

  [Sounds of blows are heard. The water goes on <u>full tilt</u>（全速地）.]

STEVE: Let's get quick out of here!

  [They rush to the poker table and sweep up their winnings on their way out.]

MITCH *[sadly but firmly]*: Poker should not be played in a house with women.

  [The door closes on them and the place is still. The Negro entertainers in the bar around the corner play "Paper Doll" slow and blue. After a moment Stanley comes out of the bathroom dripping water and still in his clinging wet <u>polka dot</u>（圆点花纹） <u>drawers</u>（底裤）.]

STANLEY: Stella! *[There is a pause]* My baby doll's left me!

  [He breaks into sobs. Then he goes to the phone and dials, still shuddering with sobs.]

 Eunice? I want my baby. *[He waits a moment; then he hangs up and dials again]* Eunice! I'll keep on ringin' until I talk with my baby!

  [An <u>indistinguishable</u>（听不清的） shrill voice is heard. He <u>hurls</u>（猛掷） phone to floor. <u>Dissonant</u>（刺耳的） <u>brass</u>（铜管乐器） and piano sounds as the rooms dim out to darkness and the outer walls appear in the night light. The "blue piano" plays for a brief <u>interval</u>（间歇）.

  [Finally, Stanley <u>stumbles</u>（跌跌撞撞地走） half-dressed out to the porch and down the wooden steps to the pavement before the building. There he throws back his head like a <u>baying</u>（吠叫） <u>hound</u>（猎犬） and bellows his wife's name: "Stella! Stella, sweetheart! Stella!"]

STANLEY: Stell-*lahhhhh!*

EUNICE *[calling down from the door of her upper apartment]*: Quit that howling out there an' go back to bed!

STANLEY: I want my baby down here. Stella, Stella!

EUNICE: She ain't comin' down so you quit! Or you'll git th' law on you!

Unit 4

Tennessee Williams and *A Streetcar Named Desire*

STANLEY: Stella!

EUNICE: You can't beat on a woman an' then call 'er back! She won't come! And her goin' t' have a baby! ... You stinker! You whelp（狗崽）of a Polack, you! I hope they do haul you in and turn the fire hose（消防水龙带）on you, same as the last time!

STANLEY [*humbly*]: Eunice, I want my girl to come down with me!

EUNICE: Hah! [*She slams her door.*]

STANLEY [*with heaven-splitting（劈开）violence*]: STELL-LAHHHHH!

> [*The low-tone clarinet（低音单簧管）moans（沉吟）. The door upstairs opens again. Stella slips down the rickety（摇晃不稳的）stairs in her robe. Her eyes are glistening with tears and her hair loose about her throat and shoulders. They stare at each other. Then they come together with low, animal moans. He falls to his knees on the steps and presses his face to her belly, curving a little with maternity（怀孕）. Her eyes go blind with tenderness as she catches his head and raises him level with her. He snatches the screen door（纱门）open and lifts her off her feet and bears her into the dark flat.*
> *Blanche comes out on the upper landing in her robe and slips fearfully down the steps.*]

BLANCHE: Where is my little sister? Stella? Stella?

> [*She stops before the dark entrance of her sister's flat. Then catches her breath as if struck. She rushes down to the walk before the house. She looks right and left as if for a sanctuary（避难所）.*
> *The music fades away. Mitch appears from around the corner.*]

MITCH: Miss DuBois?

BLANCHE: Oh!

MITCH: All quiet on the Potomac[①] now?

BLANCHE: She ran downstairs and went back in there with him.

MITCH: Sure she did.

BLANCHE: I'm terrified!

MITCH: Ho-ho! There's nothing to be scared of. They're crazy about each other.

BLANCHE: I'm not used to such—

MITCH: Naw[②], it's a shame this had to happen when you just got here. But don't take it serious.

BLANCHE: Violence! Is so—

MITCH: Set down on the steps and have a cigarette with me.

BLANCHE: I'm not properly dressed.

---

① All ... Potomac: Nothing is happening right now. "All Quiet Along the Potomac Tonight" is a poem by the American writer Ethel Lynn Beers during the US Civil War and refers to the Potomac River.

② Naw: (dialect) no.

MITCH: That don't make no difference in the Quarter[①].

BLANCHE: Such a pretty silver case.

MITCH: I showed you the inscription, didn't I?

BLANCHE: Yes. *[During the pause, she looks up at the sky]* There's so much—so much confusion in the world ... *[He coughs diffidently（羞怯地）]* Thank you for being so kind! I need kindness now.

> ### ✂ Excerpt 4 (from Scene 4)
> *The morning after the poker party, Blanche timidly goes into Stella's apartment and finds her alone in her bedroom. She asks how Stella could go back and spend the night with Stanley after he has beaten her. Stella explains that violence is just one of Stanley's bad habits and she doesn't think too much of it. As Stella begins to clean the apartment, Blanche says they need to get out of their situation.*

BLANCHE: Oh, let me think, if only my mind would function! We've got to get hold of some money, that's the way out!

STELLA: I guess that money is always nice to get hold of.

BLANCHE: Listen to me. I have an idea of some kind. *[Shakily she twists a cigarette into her holder（烟嘴）]* Do you remember Shep Huntleigh? *[Stella shakes her head]* Of course you remember Shep Huntleigh. I went out with him at college and wore his pin（徽章）for a while. Well—

STELLA: Well?

BLANCHE: I ran into him last winter. You know I went to Miami during the Christmas holidays?

STELLA: No.

BLANCHE: Well, I did. I took the trip as an investment, thinking I'd meet someone with a million dollars.

STELLA: Did you?

BLANCHE: Yes. I ran into Shep Huntleigh—I ran into him on Biscayne Boulevard, on Christmas Eve, about dusk ... getting into his car—Cadillac convertible（敞篷车）; must have been a block long!

STELLA: I should think it would have been—inconvenient in traffic!

BLANCHE: You've heard of oil-wells?

STELLA: Yes—remotely.

BLANCHE: He has them, all over Texas. Texas is literally spouting（喷射）gold in

---

① the Quarter: the French Quarter, the oldest neighborhood in the city of New Orleans.

his pockets.

STELLA: My, my.

BLANCHE: Y'know how indifferent I am to money. I think of money in terms of what it does for you. But he could do it, he could certainly do it!

STELLA: Do what, Blanche?

BLANCHE: Why—set us up in a—shop!

STELLA: What kind of a shop?

BLANCHE: Oh, a—shop of some kind! He could do it with half what his wife throws away at the races.

STELLA: He's married?

BLANCHE: Honey, would I be here if the man weren't married? *[Stella laughs a little. Blanche suddenly springs up and crosses to phone. She speaks shrilly]* How do I get Western Union[①]?—Operator! Western Union!

STELLA: That's a dial phone（拨盘式电话）, honey.

BLANCHE: I can't dial, I'm too—

STELLA: Just dial O.

BLANCHE: O?

STELLA: Yes, "O" for Operator! *[Blanche considers a moment; then she puts the phone down.]*

BLANCHE: Give me a pencil. Where is a slip of paper? I've got to write it down first—the message, I mean...

[She goes to the dressing table, and grabs up a sheet of Kleenex[②] and an eyebrow pencil for writing equipment.]

Let me see now ... *[She bites the pencil]* "Darling Shep. Sister and I in desperate situation."

STELLA: I beg your pardon!

BLANCHE: "Sister and I in desperate situation. Will explain details later. Would you be interested in—?" *[She bites the pencil again]* "Would you be—interested—in..." *[She smashes（猛摔）the pencil on the table and springs up]* You never get anywhere with direct appeals!

STELLA *[with a laugh]*: Don't be so ridiculous, darling!

BLANCHE: But I'll think of something, I've *got* to think of—*some*thing! Don't, don't laugh at me, Stella! Please, please don't—I—I want you to look at the contents of my purse! Here's what's in it! *[She snatches her purse open]* Sixty-five measly（极少的） cents in coin of the realm（法定货币）!

STELLA *[crossing to bureau]*: Stanley doesn't give me a regular allowance（零用钱）, he likes to pay bills himself, but this morning he gave me ten dollars to smooth

---

① Western Union: name of a telegraph company.
② Kleenex: a brand name of tissues.

things over. You take five of it, Blanche, and I'll keep the rest.

BLANCHE: Oh, no. No, Stella.

STELLA [insisting]: I know how it helps your morale（士气）just having a little pocket-money on you.

BLANCHE: No, thank you—I'll take to the streets!

STELLA: Talk sense! How did you happen to get so low on funds?

BLANCHE: Money just goes—it goes places. [She rubs her forehead] Sometime today I've got to get hold of a bromo（止头痛药）!

STELLA: I'll fix you one now.

BLANCHE: Not yet—I've got to keep thinking!

STELLA: I wish you'd just let things go, at least for a—while...

BLANCHE: Stella, I can't live with him! You can, he's your husband. But how could I stay here with him, after last night, with just those curtains between us?

STELLA: Blanche, you saw him at his worst last night.

BLANCHE: On the contrary, I saw him at his best! What such a man has to offer is animal force and he gave a wonderful exhibition of that! But the only way to live with such a man is to—go to bed with him! And that's your job—not mine!

STELLA: After you've rested a little, you'll see it's going to work out. You don't have to worry about anything while you're here. I mean—expenses...

BLANCHE: I have to plan for us both, to get us both—out!

STELLA: You take it for granted that I am in something that I want to get out of.

BLANCHE: I take it for granted that you still have sufficient memory of Belle Reve to find this place and these poker players impossible to live with.

STELLA: Well, you're taking entirely too much for granted.

BLANCHE: I can't believe you're in earnest.

STELLA: No?

BLANCHE: I understand how it happened—a little. You saw him in uniform, an officer, not here but—

STELLA: I'm not sure it would have made any difference where I saw him.

BLANCHE: Now don't say it was one of those mysterious electric things between people! If you do I'll laugh in your face.

STELLA: I am not going to say anything more at all about it!

BLANCHE: All right, then, don't!

STELLA: But there are things that happen between a man and a woman in the dark—that sort of make everything else seem—unimportant. [Pause.]

BLANCHE: What you are talking about is brutal desire（兽欲）—just Desire!—the name of that rattle-trap（破车）street-car that bangs through the Quarter, up one old narrow street and down another...

STELLA: Haven't you ever ridden on that street-car?

BLANCHE: It brought me here.—Where I'm not wanted and where I'm ashamed to be...

STELLA: Then don't you think your superior attitude is a bit <u>out of place</u>（不合适）?

BLANCHE: I am not being or feeling at all superior, Stella. Believe me I'm not! It's just this. This is how I look at it. A man like that is someone to go out with—once—twice—three times when the devil is in you. But live with? Have a child by?

STELLA: I have told you I love him.

BLANCHE: Then I *tremble* for you! I just—*tremble* for you....

STELLA: I can't help your trembling if you insist on trembling!

   [*There is a pause.*]

BLANCHE: May I—speak—*plainly?*

STELLA: Yes, do. Go ahead. As plainly as you want to.

   [*Outside, a train approaches. They are silent till the noise subsides. They are both in the bedroom.*]

   [*Under cover of the train's noise Stanley enters from outside. He stands unseen by the women, holding some packages in his arms, and <u>overhears</u>（无意中听到） their following conversation. He wears an undershirt and <u>grease-stained</u>（沾满油污的） <u>seersucker</u>（绉布） pants.*]

BLANCHE: Well—if you'll forgive me—he's *common!*

STELLA: Why, yes, I suppose he is.

BLANCHE: Suppose! You can't have forgotten that much of our <u>bringing up</u>（教养）, Stella, that you just *suppose* that any part of a gentleman's in his nature! *Not one <u>particle</u>*（丁点）, *no!* Oh, if he was just—*ordinary!* Just *plain*—but good and wholesome, but—*no.* There's something downright—<u>bestial</u>（兽性的）—about him! You're hating me saying this, aren't you?

STELLA [*coldly*]: Go on and say it all, Blanche.

BLANCHE: He acts like an animal, has an animal's habits! Eats like one, moves like one, talks like one! There's even something—<u>sub-human</u>（低于人类的）—something not quite to the stage of humanity yet! Yes, something—<u>ape-like</u>（类似猿猴的） about him, like one of those pictures I've seen in—<u>anthropological</u>（人类学的） studies! Thousands and thousands of years have passed him right by, and there he is—Stanley Kowalski—survivor of the stone age! Bearing the <u>raw meat</u>（生肉） home from the kill in the jungle! And you—*you* here—*waiting* for him! Maybe he'll strike you or maybe <u>grunt</u>（发出咕哝声） and kiss you! That is, if kisses have been discovered yet! Night falls and the other apes gather! There in the front of the cave, all grunting like him, and <u>swilling</u>（大口喝） and <u>gnawing</u>（啃） and <u>hulking</u>（笨重地行走）! His poker night!—you call it—this party of apes! Somebody <u>growls</u>（咆哮）—some creature snatches at something—the fight is on! *God!* Maybe we are a long way from being made in

God's image, but Stella—my sister—there has been *some* progress since then! Such things as art—as poetry and music—such kinds of new light have come into the world since then! In some kinds of people some tenderer feelings have had some little beginning! That we have got to make *grow*! And cling to（紧抓不放）, and hold as our flag! In this dark march toward whatever it is we're approaching.... Don't—don't hang back（畏缩不前） with the brutes!

> [Another train passes outside. Stanley hesitates, licking his lips. Then suddenly he turns stealthily（偷偷地） about and withdraws through front door. The women are still unaware of his presence. When the train has passed he calls through the closed front door.]

STANLEY: Hey! Hey, Stella!

STELLA [who has listened gravely to Blanche]: Stanley!

BLANCHE: Stella, I—

> [But Stella has gone to the front door. Stanley enters casually（漫不经心地） with his packages.]

STANLEY: Hiyuh①, Stella. Blanche back?

STELLA: Yes, she's back.

STANLEY: Hiyuh, Blanche. [He grins at her.]

STELLA: You must've got under the car.

STANLEY: Them darn（该死的） mechanics at Fritz's don't know their ass fr'm②— Hey!

> [Stella has embraced him with both arms, fiercely, and full in the view of Blanche. He laughs and clasps（搂住） her head to him. Over her head he grins through the curtains at Blanche.
> [As the lights fade away, with a lingering brightness on their embrace, the music of the "blue piano" and trumpet and drums is heard.]

✂ Excerpt 5 (from Scene 6)

Late one night, Blanche and Mitch return to the Kowalski flat after their date. They are both low-spirited. Blanche is upset because Stanley has found out something about her past. Mitch is discouraged because Blanche has responded negatively to his attempts for a bit more "familiarity." Then Blanche invites him in for a drink.

> [Blanche precedes（走在……之前） him into the kitchen. The outer wall

---

① Hiyuh: or hiya, shortened form of "how are you."
② don't ... fr'm: "not knowing one's ass from a hole in the ground" is a phrase that means not having an adequate level of knowledge or skill; not understanding what one is doing or talking about.

of the building disappears and the interiors of the two rooms can be dimly seen.]

BLANCHE *[remaining in the first room]*: The other room's more comfortable—go on in. This crashing around in the dark is my search for some liquor.

MITCH: You want a drink?

BLANCHE: I want *you* to have a drink! You have been so anxious and solemn all evening, and so have I; we have both been anxious and solemn and now for these few last remaining moments of our lives together—I want to create—*joie de vivre*①*!* I'm lighting a candle.

MITCH: That's good.

BLANCHE: We are going to be very Bohemian（放荡不羁的）. We are going to pretend that we are sitting in a little artists' cafe on the Left Bank② in Paris! *[She lights a candle stub（蜡烛头） and puts it in a bottle.] Je suis la Dame aux Camellias! Vous êtes Armand!*③ Understand French?

MITCH *[heavily]*: Naw. Naw, I—

BLANCHE: *Voulez-vous coucher avec moi ce soir? Vous ne comprenez pas? Ah, quelle dommage!*④—I mean it's a damned good thing.... I've found some liquor! Just enough for two shots without any dividends（附赠品）, honey...

MITCH *[heavily]*: That's—good.

[She enters the bedroom with the drinks and the candle.]

BLANCHE: Sit down! Why don't you take off your coat and loosen your collar?

MITCH: I better leave it on.

BLANCHE: No. I want you to be comfortable.

MITCH: I am ashamed of the way I perspire（出汗）. My shirt is sticking to me.

BLANCHE: Perspiration is healthy. If people didn't perspire they would die in five minutes. *[She takes his coat from him]* This is a nice coat. What kind of material is it?

MITCH: They call that stuff alpaca⑤.

BLANCHE: Oh. Alpaca.

MITCH: It's very light weight alpaca.

BLANCHE: Oh. Light weight alpaca.

MITCH: I don't like to wear a wash-coat even in summer because I sweat through it.

BLANCHE: Oh.

---

① joie de vivre: (French) joy of living.
② Left Bank: or "la Rive Gauche" in French, is the southern bank of the river Seine in Paris. It generally refers to the Paris of an earlier era: the Paris of artists, writers, and philosophers.
③ Je ... Armand: (French) "I am the Lady of the Camellias! You are Armand!" These two are characters in the French novel *La Dame aux Camélias*, commonly known in English as *Camille*, written by Alexandre Dumas, fils; she is a courtesan who gives up her true love, Armand.
④ Voulez-vous ... dommage: (French) "Would you like to sleep with me tonight? You don't understand? Ah, what a pity!"
⑤ alpaca: a soft, luxurious fiber, and naturally water-repellent.

MITCH: And it don't look neat on me. A man with a heavy build has got to be careful of what he puts on him so he don't look too clumsy.

BLANCHE: You are not too heavy.

MITCH: You don't think I am?

BLANCHE: You are not the delicate type. You have a massive（魁梧的） bone-structure and a very imposing physique（体格）.

MITCH: Thank you. Last Christmas I was given a membership to the New Orleans Athletic Club.

BLANCHE: Oh, good.

MITCH: It was the finest present I ever was given. I work out there with the weights and I swim and I keep myself fit. When I started there, I was getting soft in the belly but now my belly is hard. It is so hard now that a man can punch（重击） me in the belly and it don't hurt me. Punch me! Go on! See? *[She pokes（戳） lightly at him.]*

BLANCHE: Gracious. *[Her hand touches her chest.]*

MITCH: Guess how much I weigh, Blanche?

BLANCHE: Oh, I'd say in the vicinity（邻近） of—one hundred and eighty?

MITCH: Guess again.

BLANCHE: Not that much?

MITCH: No. More.

BLANCHE: Well, you're a tall man and you can carry a good deal of weight without looking awkward.

MITCH: I weigh two hundred and seven pounds and I'm six feet one and one-half inches tall in my bare feet—without shoes on. And that is what I weigh stripped（脱去衣服）.

BLANCHE: Oh, my goodness, me! It's awe-inspiring（令人敬畏的）.

MITCH *[embarrassed]*: My weight is not a very interesting subject to talk about. *[He hesitates for a moment.]* What's yours?

BLANCHE: My weight?

MITCH: Yes.

BLANCHE: Guess!

MITCH: Let me lift you.

BLANCHE: Samson①! Go on, lift me. *[He comes behind her and puts his hands on her waist and raises her lightly off the ground]* Well?

MITCH: You are light as a feather.

BLANCHE: Ha-ha! *[He lowers her but keeps his hands on her waist. Blanche speaks with an affection（假装） of demureness（矜持）]* You may release me now.

MITCH: Huh?

---

① Samson: legendary strong man in the Old Testament.

Unit 4

Tennessee Williams and *A Streetcar Named Desire*

BLANCHE [*gaily*（高兴地）]: I said unhand me, sir. [*He fumblingly*（笨手笨脚地）*embraces her. Her voice sounds gently reproving*（责备的）] Now, Mitch. Just because Stanley and Stella aren't at home is no reason why you shouldn't behave like a gentleman.

MITCH: Just give me a slap（耳光） whenever I step out of bounds（界限）.

BLANCHE: That won't be necessary. You're a natural gentleman, one of the very few that are left in the world. I don't want you to think that I am severe and old maid schoolteacherish or anything like that. It's just—well—

MITCH: Huh?

BLANCHE: I guess it is just that I have—old-fashioned（守旧的） ideals! [*She rolls her eyes, knowing he cannot see her face. Mitch goes to the front door. There is a considerable silence between them. Blanche sighs and Mitch coughs selfconsciously*（局促地）.]

MITCH [*finally*]: Where's Stanley and Stella tonight?

BLANCHE: They have gone out. With Mr. and Mrs. Hubbell upstairs.

MITCH: Where did they go?

BLANCHE: I think they were planning to go to a midnight prevue（预演） at Loew's State[①].

MITCH: We should all go out together some night.

BLANCHE: No. That wouldn't be a good plan.

MITCH: Why not?

BLANCHE: You are an old friend of Stanley's?

MITCH: We was together in the Two-forty-first[②].

BLANCHE: I guess he talks to you frankly?

MITCH: Sure.

BLANCHE: Has he talked to you about me?

MITCH: Oh—not very much.

BLANCHE: The way you say that, I suspect that he has.

MITCH: No, he hasn't said much.

BLANCHE: But what he *has* said. What would you say his attitude toward me was?

MITCH: Why do you want to ask that?

BLANCHE: Well—

MITCH: Don't you get along with him?

BLANCHE: What do you think?

MITCH: I don't think he understands you.

BLANCHE: That is putting it mildly（说得委婉）. If it weren't for Stella about to have a baby, I wouldn't be able to endure things here.

---

① Loew's State: a theatre in New Orleans, opened in April 1926.
② Two-forty-first: battalion of engineers in World War II.

MITCH: He isn't—nice to you?

BLANCHE: He is insufferably（不可忍受地） rude. Goes out of his way to offend me.

MITCH: In what way, Blanche?

BLANCHE: Why, in every conceivable（能想到的） way.

MITCH: I'm surprised to hear that.

BLANCHE: Are you?

MITCH: Well, I—don't see how anybody could be rude to you.

BLANCHE: It's really a pretty frightful situation. You see, there's no privacy here. There's just these portieres between the two rooms at night. He stalks through the rooms in his underwear at night. And I have to ask him to close the bathroom door. That sort of commonness（粗俗） isn't necessary. You probably wonder why I don't move out. Well, I'll tell you frankly. A teacher's salary is barely sufficient for her living-expenses. I didn't save a penny last year and so I had to come here for the summer. That's why I have to put up with（容忍） my sister's husband. And he has to put up with me, apparently so much against his wishes…. Surely he must have told you how much he hates me!

MITCH: I don't think he hates you.

BLANCHE: He hates me. Or why would he insult me? The first time I laid eyes on him I thought to myself, that man is my executioner（刽子手）! That man will destroy me, unless—

MITCH: Blanche—

BLANCHE: Yes, honey?

MITCH: Can I ask you a question?

BLANCHE: Yes. What?

MITCH: How old are you?

   [She makes a nervous gesture.]

BLANCHE: Why do you want to know?

MITCH: I talked to my mother about you and she said, "How old is Blanche?" And I wasn't able to tell her. *[There is another pause.]*

BLANCHE: You talked to your mother about me?

MITCH: Yes.

BLANCHE: Why?

MITCH: I told my mother how nice you were, and I liked you.

BLANCHE: Were you sincere about that?

MITCH: You know I was.

BLANCHE: Why did your mother want to know my age?

MITCH: Mother is sick.

BLANCHE: I'm sorry to hear it. Badly?

MITCH: She won't live long. Maybe just a few months.

BLANCHE: Oh.

MITCH: She worries because I'm not settled.

BLANCHE: Oh.

MITCH: She wants me to be settled down before she—*[His voice is hoarse and he clears his throat twice, <u>shuffling</u>（走来走去） nervously around with his hands in and out of his pockets.]*

BLANCHE: You love her very much, don't you?

MITCH: Yes.

BLANCHE: I think you have a great capacity for <u>devotion</u>（深情）. You will be lonely when she <u>passes on</u>（去世）, won't you? *[Mitch clears his throat and nods.]* I understand what that is.

MITCH: To be lonely?

BLANCHE: I loved someone, too, and the person I loved I lost.

MITCH: Dead? *[She crosses to the window and sits on the <u>sill</u>（窗台）, looking out. She pours herself another drink.]* A man?

BLANCHE: He was a boy, just a boy, when I was a very young girl. When I was sixteen, I made the discovery—love. All at once and much, much too completely. It was like you suddenly turned a blinding light on something that had always been half in shadow, that's how it struck the world for me. But I was unlucky. <u>Deluded</u>（欺骗）. There was something different about the boy, a nervousness, a softness and tenderness which wasn't like a man's, although he wasn't the least bit <u>effeminate</u>（女人气） looking—still—that thing was there.... He came to me for help. I didn't know that. I didn't find out anything till after our marriage when we'd run away and come back and all I knew was I'd failed him in some mysterious way and wasn't able to give the help he needed but couldn't speak of! He was in the <u>quicksands</u>（危难） and <u>clutching at</u>（企图抓住） me—but I wasn't holding him out, I was slipping in with him! I didn't know that. I didn't know anything except I loved him <u>unendurably</u>（难以忍受地） but without being able to help him or help myself. Then I found out. In the worst of all possible ways. By coming suddenly into a room that I thought was empty—which wasn't empty, but had two people in it ... the boy I had married and an older man who had been his friend for years...

> *[A <u>locomotive</u>（火车头） is heard approaching outside. She claps her hands to her ears and crouches over. The headlight of the locomotive glares into the room as it thunders past. As the noise <u>recedes</u>（消退） she straightens slowly and continues speaking.]*

Afterwards we pretended that nothing had been discovered. Yes, the three of us drove out to Moon Lake <u>Casino</u>（游乐场）, very drunk and laughing all the way.

[*Polka music sounds, in a <u>minor key</u>（小调）faint with distance.*]
We danced the Varsouviana①! Suddenly in the middle of the dance the boy I had married broke away from me and ran out of the casino. A few moments later—a shot!

[*The Polka stops abruptly.*]

[*Blanche rises stiffly. Then, the Polka resumes in a <u>major key</u>（大调）.*]
I ran out—all did!—all ran and gathered about the terrible thing at the edge of the lake! I couldn't get near for the crowding. Then somebody caught my arm. "Don't go any closer! Come back! You don't want to see!" See? See what! Then I heard voices say—Allan! Allan! The Grey boy! He'd stuck the <u>revolver</u>（左轮手枪） into his mouth, and fired—so that the back of his head had been—blown away!

[*She <u>sways</u>（摇晃） and covers her face.*]
It was because—on the dance-floor—unable to stop myself—I'd suddenly said—"I saw! I know! You disgust me..." And then the <u>searchlight</u>（探照灯） which had been turned on the world was turned off again and never for one moment since has there been any light that's stronger than this—kitchen—candle...

[*Mitch gets up awkwardly and moves toward her a little. The Polka music increases. Mitch stands beside her.*]

MITCH [*drawing her slowly into his arms*]: You need somebody. And I need somebody, too. Could it be—you and me, Blanche?

[*She stares at him vacantly for a moment. Then with a soft cry <u>huddles</u>（蜷缩） in his embrace. She makes a <u>sobbing</u>（哽咽，啜泣） effort to speak but the words won't come. He kisses her forehead and her eyes and finally her lips. The Polka tune fades out. Her breath is drawn and released in long, grateful sobs.*]

BLANCHE: Sometimes—there's God—so quickly!

✂ Excerpt 6 (from Scene 9)

It is Blanche's birthday, but things have not gone well for her. Mitch does not show up for her birthday party after he has been told by Stanley about her past. Stanley offers her a bus ticket back home as a supposed birthday gift. Stella complains about his cruelty, but then goes into labor and is taken to the hospital. Alone, Blanche gets herself half-drunk to escape the sense of disaster. Then Mitch comes.

BLANCHE: Who is it, please?

---

① Varsouviana: a dance that originated around 1850 in Warsaw, Poland. The name means "from Warsaw." The dance was popular in 19th-century America.

Unit 4

Tennessee Williams and *A Streetcar Named Desire*

MITCH [*hoarsely*]: Me. Mitch.

>[*The polka tune stops.*]

BLANCHE: Mitch!—Just a minute.

>[*She rushes about frantically, hiding the bottle in a closet, crouching at the mirror and <u>dabbing</u>（轻敷） her face with <u>cologne</u>（古龙香水） and powder. She is so excited that her breath is audible as she <u>dashes</u>（猛冲） about. At last she rushes to the door in the kitchen and lets him in.*]

Mitch!—Y'know, I really shouldn't let you in after the treatment I have received from you this evening! So utterly <u>uncavalier</u>（无绅士风度的）! But hello, beautiful!

>[*She offers him her lips. He ignores it and pushes past her into the flat. She looks fearfully after him as he stalks into the bedroom.*]

My, my, what a <u>cold shoulder</u>（冷漠）! And such <u>uncouth</u>（不雅的） <u>apparel</u>（衣着）! Why, you haven't even shaved! The unforgivable insult to a lady! But I forgive you. I forgive you because it's such a relief to see you. You've stopped that polka tune that I had caught in my head. Have you ever had anything caught in your head? No, of course you haven't, you dumb angel-<u>puss</u>（猫咪）[①], you'd never get anything awful caught in your head!

>[*He stares at her while she follows him while she talks. It is obvious that he has had a few drinks on the way over.*]

MITCH: Do we have to have that fan on?

BLANCHE: No!

MITCH: I don't like fans.

BLANCHE: Then let's turn it off, honey. I'm not <u>partial</u>（偏爱） to them!

>[*She presses the switch and the fan nods slowly off. She clears her throat uneasily as Mitch <u>plumps</u>（猛地坐下） himself down on the bed in the bedroom and lights a cigarette.*]

I don't know what there is to drink. I—haven't investigated.

MITCH: I don't want Stan's liquor.

BLANCHE: It isn't Stan's. Everything here isn't Stan's. Some things <u>on the premises</u>（在房屋内） are actually mine! How is your mother? Isn't your mother well?

MITCH: Why?

BLANCHE: Something's the matter tonight, but never mind. I won't <u>cross-examine</u>（盘问） the witness. I'll just—[*She touches her forehead vaguely. The polka tune starts up again.*]—pretend I don't notice anything different about you! That—music again...

MITCH: What music?

---

① angel-puss: *Angel Puss* is a 1944 short animated cartoon about a cat (puss) who pretends to be its own ghost and "haunts" an African-American boy that has been paid to drown it.

BLANCHE: The "Varsouviana"! The polka tune they were playing when Allan—Wait!

[A distant revolver shot is heard. Blanche seems relieved.]

There now, the shot! It always stops after that.

[The polka music dies out again.]

Yes, now it's stopped.

MITCH: Are you boxed out of your mind?

BLANCHE: I'll go and see what I can find in the way of—*[She crosses into the closet, pretending to search for the bottle.]* Oh, by the way, excuse me for not being dressed. But I'd practically（几乎）given you up! Had you forgotten your invitation to supper?

MITCH: I wasn't going to see you any more.

BLANCHE: Wait a minute. I can't hear what you're saying and you talk so little that when you do say something, I don't want to miss a single syllable of it.... What am I looking around here for? Oh, yes—liquor! We've had so much excitement around here this evening that I *am* boxed out of my mind! *[She pretends suddenly to find the bottle. He draws his foot up on the bed and stares at her contemptuously（轻蔑地）.]* Here's something. Southern Comfort①! What is that, I wonder?

MITCH: If you don't know, it must belong to Stan.

BLANCHE: Take your foot off the bed. It has a light cover on it. Of course you boys don't notice things like that. I've done so much with this place since I've been here.

MITCH: I bet you have.

BLANCHE: You saw it before I came. Well, look at it now! This room is almost—dainty（雅致的）! I want to keep it that way. I wonder if this stuff ought to be mixed with something? Ummm, it's sweet, so sweet! It's terribly, terribly sweet! Why, it's a liqueur（烈性甜酒）, I believe! Yes, that's what it *is*, a liqueur! *[Mitch grunts.]* I'm afraid you won't like it, but try it, and maybe you will.

MITCH: I told you already I don't want none of his liquor and I mean it. You ought to lay off his liquor. He says you been lapping（舔舐）it up all summer like a wildcat!

BLANCHE: What a fantastic statement! Fantastic of him to say it, fantastic of you to repeat it! I won't descend to the level of such cheap accusations to answer them, even!

MITCH: Huh.

BLANCHE: What's in your mind? I see something in your eyes!

MITCH *[getting up]*: It's dark in here.

BLANCHE: I like it dark. The dark is comforting to me.

MITCH: I don't think I ever seen you in the light. *[Blanche laughs breathlessly]* That's a fact!

---

① Southern Comfort: a brand name of liqueur.

BLANCHE: Is it?

MITCH: I've never seen you in the afternoon.

BLANCHE: Whose fault is that?

MITCH: You never want to go out in the afternoon.

BLANCHE: Why, Mitch, you're at the plant in the afternoon!

MITCH: Not Sunday afternoon. I've asked you to go out with me sometimes on Sundays but you always make an excuse. You never want to go out till after six and then it's always some place that's not lighted much.

BLANCHE: There is some <u>obscure</u>（隐晦的） meaning in this but I fail to catch it.

MITCH: What it means is I've never had a real good look at you, Blanche. Let's turn the light on here.

BLANCHE [fearfully]: Light? Which light? What for?

MITCH: This one with the paper thing on it. *[He tears the paper lantern off the light bulb. She utters a frightened gasp.]*

BLANCHE: What did you do that for?

MITCH: So I can take a look at you good and plain!

BLANCHE: Of course you don't really mean to be insulting!

MITCH: No, just realistic.

BLANCHE: I don't want realism. I want magic! *[Mitch laughs]* Yes, yes, magic! I try to give that to people. I <u>misrepresent</u>（歪曲） things to them. I don't tell truth, I tell what *ought* to be truth. And if that is sinful, then let me be damned for it!—*Don't turn the light on!*

   [Mitch crosses to the switch. He turns the light on and stares at her. She cries out and covers her face. He turns the light off again.]

MITCH *[slowly and bitterly]*: I don't mind you being older than what I thought. But all the rest of it—Christ! That <u>pitch</u>（鬼话） about your ideals being so old-fashioned and all the <u>malarkey</u>（胡说） that you've <u>dished out</u>（大量供给） all summer. Oh, I knew you weren't sixteen any more. But I was a fool enough to believe you was straight.

BLANCHE: Who told you I wasn't—"straight"? My loving brother-in-law. And you believed him.

MITCH: I called him a liar at first. And then I checked on the story. First I asked our supply-man who travels through Laurel. And then I talked directly over long-distance to this merchant.

BLANCHE: Who is this merchant?

MITCH: Kiefaber.

BLANCHE: The merchant Kiefaber of Laurel! I know the man. He whistled at me. I <u>put him in his place</u>（使之安分）. So now for revenge he makes up stories about me.

MITCH: Three people, Kiefaber, Stanley and Shaw, swore to them!

BLANCHE: Rub-a-dub-dub, three men in a tub! And such a filthy tub!①

MITCH: Didn't you stay at a hotel called The Flamingo（火烈鸟）?

BLANCHE: Flamingo? No! Tarantula（狼蛛） was the name of it! I stayed at a hotel called The Tarantula Arms!

MITCH [stupidly]: Tarantula?

BLANCHE: Yes, a big spider! That's where I brought my victims. [She pours herself another drink] Yes, I had many intimacies（亲昵行为） with strangers. After the death of Allan—intimacies with strangers was all I seemed able to fill my empty heart with.... I think it was panic, just panic, that drove me from one to another, hunting for some protection—here and there, in the most—unlikely places—even, at last, in a seventeen-year-old boy but somebody wrote the superintendent about it—"This woman is morally unfit for her position!"

   [She throws back her head with convulsive（抽搐的）, sobbing laughter. Then she repeats the statement, gasps, and drinks.]

True? Yes, I suppose—unfit somehow—anyway.... So I came here. There was nowhere else I could go. I was played out（穷途末路）. You know what played out is? My youth was suddenly gone up the water-spout（水龙卷）, and—I met you. You said you needed somebody. Well, I needed somebody, too. I thanked God for you, because you seemed to be gentle—a cleft（裂缝） in the rock of the world that I could hide in! But I guess I was asking, hoping—too much! Kiefaber, Stanley and Shaw have tied an old tin can to the tail of the kite.

   [There is a pause. Mitch stares at her dumbly.]

MITCH: You lied to me, Blanche.

BLANCHE: Don't say I lied to you.

MITCH: Lies, lies, inside and out, all lies.

BLANCHE: Never inside, I didn't lie in my heart...

   [A Vendor comes around the corner. She is a blind Mexican woman in a dark shawl（披肩）, carrying bunches of those gaudy tin flowers that lower class Mexicans display at funerals and other festive（节庆的） occasions. She is calling barely audibly. Her figure is only faintly visible outside the building.]

MEXICAN WOMAN: Flores. Flores. Flores para los muertos②. Flores. Flores.

BLANCHE: What? Oh! Somebody outside ... [She goes to the door, opens it and stares at the Mexican Woman.]

MEXICAN WOMAN [she is at the door and offers Blanche some of her flowers]: Flores? Flores para los muertos?

BLANCHE [frightened]: No, no! Not now! Not now!

   [She darts back into the apartment, slamming the door.]

---

① Rub-a-dub-dub ... tub: lyrics from a traditional nursery rhyme.
② Flores ... muertos: (Spanish) Flowers for the dead.

MEXICAN WOMAN [*she turns away and starts to move down the street*]: Flores para los muertos.

    [*The polka tune fades in.*]

BLANCHE [*as if to herself*]: <u>Crumble</u>（崩塌） and fade and—regrets—<u>recriminations</u>（反责）…"If you'd done this, it wouldn't 've cost me that!"

MEXICAN WOMAN: Corones[①] para los muertos. Corones …

BLANCHE: Legacies! Huh…. And other things such as bloodstained <u>pillow-slips</u>（枕套）—"Her linen needs changing"—"Yes Mother. But couldn't we get a colored girl to do it?" No, we couldn't of course. Everything gone but the—

MEXICAN WOMAN: Flores.

BLANCHE: Death—I used to sit here and she used to sit over there and death was as close as you are… We didn't dare even admit we had ever heard of it!

MEXICAN WOMAN: Flores para los muertos, flores—flores…

BLANCHE: The opposite is desire. So do you wonder? How could you possibly wonder! Not far from Belle Reve, before we had lost Belle Reve, was a camp where they trained young soldiers. On Saturday nights they would go in town to get drunk—

MEXICAN WOMAN [*softly*]: Corones…

BLANCHE: —and on the way back they would <u>stagger</u>（蹒跚） onto my lawn and call—"Blanche! Blanche!" The deaf old lady remaining suspected nothing. But sometimes I slipped outside to answer their calls… Later the <u>paddy-wagon</u>（囚车） would gather them up like daisies … the long way home…

    [*The Mexican Woman turns slowly and drifts back off with her soft mournful cries. Blanche goes to the dresser and leans forward on it. After a moment, Mitch rises and follows her purposefully. The polka music fades away. He places his hands on her waist and tries to turn her about.*]

BLANCHE: What do you want?

MITCH [*fumbling to embrace her*]: What I been missing all summer.

BLANCHE: Then marry me, Mitch!

MITCH: I don't think I want to marry you any more.

BLANCHE: No?

MITCH [*dropping his hands from her waist*]: You're not clean enough to bring in the house with my mother.

BLANCHE: Go away, then. [*He stares at her*] Get out of here quick before I start screaming fire! [*Her throat is tightening with hysteria*] Get out of here quick before I start screaming fire. [*He still remains staring. She suddenly rushes to the big window with its pale blue square of the soft summer light and cries wildly.*] Fire! Fire! Fire!

---

① Corones: (Spanish) wreaths.

[With a startled gasp, Mitch turns and goes out the outer door, clatters（跌跌撞撞）awkwardly down the steps and around the corner of the building. Blanche staggers back from the window and falls to her knees. The distant piano is slow and blue.]

✂ Excerpt 7 (from Scene 10)

Scene 10 is the climax of the play. In this excerpt, Blanche and Stanley have their final confrontation. It's a few hours after Mitch's departure, and Blanche sits alone in the bedroom, drunk. She is dressed in a gaudy evening gown and talking to imaginary suitors.

BLANCHE: How about taking a swim, a moonlight swim at the old rock-quarry（采石场）? If anyone's sober（清醒的）enough to drive a car! Ha-ha! Best way in the world to stop your head buzzing（嗡嗡作响）! Only you've got to be careful to dive where the deep pool is—if you hit a rock you don't come up till tomorrow...

　　[Tremblingly she lifts the hand mirror for a closer inspection（细看）. She catches her breath and slams the mirror face down with such violence that the glass cracks. She moans a little and attempts to rise.

　　[Stanley appears around the corner of the building. He still has on the vivid green silk bowling shirt. As he rounds the corner the honky-tonk（低级舞厅或酒吧）music is heard. It continues softly throughout the scene.

　　[He enters the kitchen, slamming the door. As he peers（凝视）in at Blanche, he gives a low whistle. He has had a few drinks on the way and has brought some quart（夸脱）beer bottles home with him.]

BLANCHE: How is my sister?

STANLEY: She is doing okay.

BLANCHE: And how is the baby?

STANLEY [grinning amiably]: The baby won't come before morning so they told me to go home and get a little shut-eye（合眼，睡觉）.

BLANCHE: Does that mean we are to be alone in here?

STANLEY: Yep. Just me and you, Blanche. Unless you got somebody hid under the bed. What've you got on those fine feathers for?

BLANCHE: Oh, that's right. You left before my wire came.

STANLEY: You got a wire?

BLANCHE: I received a telegram from an old admirer of mine.

STANLEY: Anything good?

BLANCHE: I think so. An invitation.

STANLEY: What to? A fireman's ball?

Unit 4

Tennessee Williams and *A Streetcar Named Desire*

BLANCHE *[throwing back her head]*: A cruise of the Caribbean（加勒比海） on a yacht!

STANLEY: Well, well. What do you know?

BLANCHE: I have never been so surprised in my life.

STANLEY: I guess not.

BLANCHE: It came like a bolt from the blue（意外）!

STANLEY: Who did you say it was from?

BLANCHE: An old beau（情郎） of mine.

STANLEY: The one that give you the white fox-pieces?

BLANCHE: Mr. Shep Huntleigh. I wore his ATO[①] pin my last year at college. I hadn't seen him again until last Christmas. I ran into him on Biscayne Boulevard. Then—just now—this wire—inviting me on a cruise of the Caribbean! The problem is clothes. I tore into my trunk to see what I have that's suitable for the tropics!

STANLEY: And come up with that—gorgeous—diamond-tiara（冕状头饰）?

BLANCHE: This old relic（纪念物）? Ha-ha! It's only rhinestones（莱茵石，假钻石）.

STANLEY: Gosh. I thought it was Tiffany[②] diamonds. *[He unbuttons his shirt.]*

BLANCHE: Well, anyhow, I shall be entertained in style（阔气地）.

STANLEY: Uh-huh. It goes to show, you never know what is coming.

BLANCHE: Just when I thought my luck had begun to fail me

STANLEY: Into the picture pops this Miami millionaire.

BLANCHE: This man is not from Miami. This man is from Dallas.

STANLEY: This man is from Dallas?

BLANCHE: Yes, this man is from Dallas where gold spouts out of the ground!

STANLEY: Well, just so he's from somewhere! *[He starts removing his shirt.]*

BLANCHE: Close the curtains before you undress any further.

STANLEY *[amiably]*: This is all I'm going to undress right now. *[He rips the sack（包装袋） off a quart beer bottle]* Seen a bottle-opener?

[She moves slowly toward the dresser, where she stands with her hands knotted（打结） together.]

I used to have a cousin who could open a beer bottle with his teeth. *[Pounding the bottle cap on the corner of table]* That was his only accomplishment, all he could do—he was just a human bottle-opener. And then one time, at a wedding party, he broke his front teeth off! After that he was so ashamed of himself he used t' sneak（溜走） out of the house when company came...

[The bottle cap pops off and a geyser（间歇喷泉） of foam（泡沫） shoots up. Stanley laughs happily, holding up the bottle over his head.] Ha-ha! Rain from

---

① ATO: name of a fraternity.
② Tiffany: a luxury jewelry retailer, headquartered in New York City.

heaven! *[He extends the bottle toward her]* Shall we bury the hatchet（休战，和解） and make it a loving-cup（共饮用的大酒杯）? Huh?

BLANCHE: No, thank you.

STANLEY: Well, it's a red letter（喜庆的） night for us both. You having an oil millionaire and me having a baby.

[He goes to the bureau（衣柜） in the bedroom and crouches to remove something from the bottom drawer.]

BLANCHE *[drawing back]*: What are you doing in here?

STANLEY: Here's something I always break out（取出备用） on special occasions like this. The silk pyjamas I wore on my wedding night!

BLANCHE: Oh.

STANLEY: When the telephone rings and they say, "You've got a son!" I'll tear this off and wave it like a flag! *[He shakes out a brilliant pyjama coat]* I guess we are both entitled（有资格的） to put on the dog（摆架子，炫耀）. *[He goes back to the kitchen with the coat over his arm.]*

BLANCHE: When I think of how divine it is going to be to have such a thing as privacy once more—I could weep with joy!

STANLEY: This millionaire from Dallas is not going to interfere with your privacy any?

BLANCHE: It won't be the sort of thing you have in mind. This man is a gentleman and he respects me. *[Improvising（即兴表演） feverishly]* What he wants is my companionship. Having great wealth sometimes makes people lonely! A cultivated（有修养的） woman, a woman of intelligence and breeding, can enrich a man's life—immeasurably! I have those things to offer, and this doesn't take them away. Physical beauty is passing. A transitory（转瞬即逝的） possession. But beauty of the mind and richness of the spirit and tenderness of the heart—and I have all of those things—aren't taken away, but grow! Increase with the years! How strange that I should be called a destitute（贫困的） woman! When I have all of these treasures locked in my heart. *[A choked sob comes from her]* I think of myself as a very, very rich woman! But I have been foolish—casting my pearls before swine（明珠暗投）!

STANLEY: Swine, huh?

BLANCHE: Yes, swine! Swine! And I'm thinking not only of you but of your friend, Mr. Mitchell. He came to see me tonight. He dared to come here in his work-clothes! And to repeat slander（诽谤） to me, vicious stories that he had gotten from you! I gave him his walking papers（免职书）...

STANLEY: You did, huh?

BLANCHE: But then he came back. He returned with a box of roses to beg my forgiveness! He implored（乞求） my forgiveness. But some things are not forgivable. Deliberate（故意的）cruelty is not forgivable. It is the one unforgivable thing in my opinion and it is the one thing of which I have never, never been guilty. And so I told him, I said to him, "Thank you," but it was foolish of me to think that we could ever adapt ourselves to each other. Our ways of life are too different. Our attitudes and our backgrounds are incompatible（不相容的）. We have to be realistic about such things. So farewell, my friend! And let there be no hard feelings...

STANLEY: Was this before or after the telegram came from the Texas oil millionaire?

BLANCHE: What telegram? No! No, after! As a matter of fact, the wire came just as—

STANLEY: As a matter of fact there wasn't no wire at all!

BLANCHE: Oh, oh!

STANLEY: There isn't no millionaire! And Mitch didn't come back with roses 'cause I know where he is—

BLANCHE: Oh!

STANLEY: There isn't a goddam（他妈的）thing but imagination!

BLANCHE: Oh!

STANLEY: And lies and conceit（妄想）and tricks!

BLANCHE: Oh!

STANLEY: And look at yourself! Take a look at yourself in that worn-out Mardi Gras① outfit（服饰）, rented for fifty cents from some rag-picker（捡破烂的）! And with the crazy crown on! What queen do you think you are?

BLANCHE: Oh—God...

STANLEY: I've been on to（识破）you from the start! Not once did you pull any wool over this boy's eyes（蒙骗某人）! You come in here and sprinkle（撒）the place with powder and spray perfume and cover the light bulb with a paper lantern, and lo and behold the place has turned into Egypt and you are the Queen of the Nile! Sitting on your throne and swilling down my liquor! I say—Ha!—Ha! Do you hear me? Ha—ha—ha! *[He walks into the bedroom.]*

BLANCHE: Don't come in here!

[Lurid（可怕的）reflections appear on the walls around Blanche. The shadows are of a grotesque（奇形怪状的）and menacing form. She catches her breath, crosses to the phone and jiggles（轻摇）the hook. Stanley goes into the bathroom and closes the door.]

Operator, operator! Give me long-distance, please.... I want to get in touch with Mr. Shep Huntleigh of Dallas. He's so well-known he doesn't require any address. Just ask anybody who—Wait!!—No, I couldn't find it right now.... Please understand, I—No! No, wait! ... One moment! Someone is—Nothing! Hold on, please!

---

① Mardi Gras: also called "Fat Tuesday", is a festival of French origin, celebrated in some cities, like New Orleans and Paris, as a day of carnival and merrymaking. A Mardi Gras outfit means it is gaudy and cheap.

[She sets the phone down and crosses warily（警惕地） into the kitchen. The night is filled with inhuman voices like cries in a jungle.
[The shadows and lurid reflections move sinuously（扭曲地，交错地） as flames along the wall spaces.
[Through the back wall of the rooms, which have become transparent, can be seen the sidewalk. A prostitute has rolled（对醉酒或昏睡者行窃） a drunkard. He pursues her along the walk, overtakes her and there is a struggle. A policeman's whistle breaks it up. The figures disappear.
[Some moments later the Negro Woman appears around the corner with a sequined bag which the prostitute had dropped on the walk. She is rooting（翻找） excitedly through it.
[Blanche presses her knuckles（指关节） to her lips and returns slowly to the phone. She speaks in a hoarse whisper.]

BLANCHE: Operator! Operator! Never mind long-distance. Get Western Union. There isn't time to be—Western—Western Union! *[She waits anxiously.]* Western Union? Yes! I—want to—Take down this message! "In desperate, desperate circumstances! Help me! Caught in a trap. Caught in—" Oh!

[The bathroom door is thrown open and Stanley comes out in the brilliant silk pyjamas. He grins at her as he knots the tasseled sash（流苏腰带） about his waist. She gasps and backs away from the phone. He stares at her for a count of ten. Then a clicking becomes audible from the telephone, steady and rasping（发出刺耳声）.]

STANLEY: You left th' phone off th' hook.

[He crosses to it deliberately and sets it back on the hook. After he has replaced it, he stares at her again, his mouth slowly curving into a grin, as he weaves（迂回行进） between Blanche and the outer door.
[The barely audible "blue piano" begins to drum up louder. The sound of it turns into the roar of an approaching locomotive. Blanche crouches, pressing her fists to her ears until it has gone by.]

BLANCHE *[finally straightening]*: Let me—let me get by you!
STANLEY: Get by me? Sure. Go ahead. *[He moves back a pace in the doorway.]*
BLANCHE: You—you stand over there! *[She indicates a further position.]*
STANLEY *[grinning]*: You got plenty of room to walk by me now.
BLANCHE: Not with you there! But I've got to get out somehow!
STANLEY: You think I'll interfere with you? Ha-ha!

[The "blue piano" goes softly. She turns confusedly and makes a faint gesture. The inhuman jungle voices rise up. He takes a step toward her, biting his tongue which protrudes（伸出） between his lips.]

STANLEY *[softly]*: Come to think of it—maybe you wouldn't be bad to interfere with...

   [Blanche moves backward through the door into the bedroom.]
BLANCHE: Stay back! Don't you come toward me another step or I'll—
STANLEY: What?
BLANCHE: Some awful thing will happen! It will!
STANLEY: What are you putting on（上演）now?
   [They are now both inside the bedroom.]
BLANCHE: I warn you, don't, I'm in danger!
   [He takes another step. She smashes a bottle on the table and faces him, clutching the broken top.]
STANLEY: What did you do that for?
BLANCHE: So I could twist the broken end in your face!
STANLEY: I bet you would do that!
BLANCHE: I would! I will if you—
STANLEY: Oh! So you want some rough-house（大闹一场）! All right, let's have some rough-house!
   [He springs toward her, overturning the table. She cries out and strikes at him with the bottle top but he catches her wrist.]
Tiger—tiger! Drop the bottle top! Drop it! We've had this date with each other from the beginning!
   [She moans. The bottle top falls. She sinks to her knees. He picks up her inert（无生气的）figure and carries her to the bed. The hot trumpet and drums from the Four Deuces[①] sound loudly.]

✂ Excerpt 8 (from Scene 11)

It is some weeks later. Stella cries while packing Blanche's belongings. Blanche is taking a bath. Stanley and his buddies are playing poker in the kitchen. Eunice comes downstairs and enters the apartment. Stanley boasts about his own ability to survive and win out against others thanks to his spectacular confidence. Eunice calls the men callous and goes over to Stella to see how the packing is going.

STELLA: How is my baby?
EUNICE: Sleeping like a little angel. Brought you some grapes. *[She puts them on a stool and lowers her voice.]* Blanche?
STELLA: Bathing.

---

① Four Deuces: name of a bar.

EUNICE: How is she?

STELLA: She wouldn't eat anything but asked for a drink.

EUNICE: What did you tell her?

STELLA: I—just told her that—we'd made arrangements for her to rest in the country. She's got it mixed in her mind with Shep Huntleigh.

[Blanche opens the bathroom door slightly.]

BLANCHE: Stella.

STELLA: Yes, Blanche?

BLANCHE: If anyone calls while I'm bathing take the number and tell them I'll call right back.

STELLA: Yes.

BLANCHE: That cool yellow silk—the bouclé（仿羔皮呢）. See if it's crushed（压皱）. If it's not too crushed I'll wear it and on the lapel（西服翻领） that silver and turquoise（绿松石） pin in the shape of a seahorse. You will find them in the heart-shaped box I keep my accessories（首饰） in. And Stella ... Try and locate a bunch of artificial violets in that box, too, to pin with the seahorse on the lapel of the jacket.

[She closes the door. Stella turns to Eunice.]

STELLA: I don't know if I did the right thing.

EUNICE: What else could you do?

STELLA: I couldn't believe her story and go on living with Stanley.

EUNICE: Don't ever believe it. Life has got to go on. No matter what happens, you've got to keep on going.

[The bathroom door opens a little.]

BLANCHE *[looking out]*: Is the coast clear?

STELLA: Yes, Blanche. *[To Eunice]* Tell her how well she's looking.

BLANCHE: Please close the curtains before I come out.

STELLA: They're closed.

STANLEY: —How many for you?

PABLO: —Two.

STEVE: —Three.

[Blanche appears in the amber（琥珀色的） light of the door. She has a tragic radiance（光芒） in her red satin robe following the sculptural（雕塑般的） lines of her body. The "Varsouviana" rises audibly as Blanche enters the bedroom.]

BLANCHE *[with faintly hysterical vivacity]*: I have just washed my hair.

STELLA: Did you?

BLANCHE: I'm not sure I got the soap out.

EUNICE: Such fine hair!

BLANCHE: *[accepting the compliment]*: It's a problem. Didn't I get a call?
STELLA: Who from, Blanche?
BLANCHE: Shep Huntleigh ...
STELLA: Why, not yet, honey!
BLANCHE: How strange! I—
> *[At the sound of Blanche's voice Mitch's arm supporting his cards has <u>sagged</u>（下垂）and his gaze is <u>dissolved</u>（溶解）into space. Stanley slaps him on the shoulder.]*

STANLEY: Hey, Mitch, <u>come to</u>（苏醒）!
> *[The sound of this new voice shocks Blanche. She makes a shocked gesture, forming his name with her lips. Stella nods and looks quickly away. Blanche stands quite still for some moments—the silverbacked mirror in her hand and a look of sorrowful <u>perplexity</u>（困惑）as though all human experience shows on her face. Blanche finally speaks but with sudden hysteria.]*

BLANCHE: What's going on here?
> *[She turns from Stella to Eunice and back to Stella. Her rising voice penetrates the concentration of the game. Mitch <u>ducks</u>（忽然低下）his head lower but Stanley shoves back his chair as if about to rise. Steve places a restraining hand on his arm.]*

BLANCHE *[continuing]*: What's happened here? I want an explanation of what's happened here.
STELLA *[<u>agonizingly</u>（极痛苦地）]*: Hush! Hush!
EUNICE: Hush! Hush! Honey.
STELLA: Please, Blanche.
BLANCHE: Why are you looking at me like that? Is something wrong with me?
EUNICE: You look wonderful, Blanche. Don't she look wonderful?
STELLA: Yes.
EUNICE: I understand you are going on a trip.
STELLA: Yes, Blanche *is*. She's going on a vacation.
EUNICE: I'm green with envy.
BLANCHE: Help me, help me get dressed!
STELLA *[handing her dress]*: Is this what you—
BLANCHE: Yes, it will do! I'm anxious to get out of here—this place is a trap!
EUNICE: What a pretty blue jacket.
STELLA: It's <u>lilac</u>（淡紫色）colored.
BLANCHE: You're both mistaken. It's Della Robbia blue[①]. The blue of the robe in the old <u>Madonna pictures</u>（圣母像）. Are these grapes washed?

---

① Della ... blue: Luca della Robbia (1399/1400–1482) was an Italian sculptor from Florence, noted for his colorful, tin-glazed terracotta statuary.

[*She fingers the bunch of grapes which Eunice had brought in.*]

EUNICE: Huh?

BLANCHE: Washed, I said. Are they washed?

EUNICE: They're from the French Market.

BLANCHE: That doesn't mean they've been washed. [*The cathedral（大教堂）bells chime（钟声鸣响）*] Those cathedral bells—they're the only clean thing in the Quarter. Well, I'm going now. I'm ready to go.

EUNICE [*whispering*]: She's going to walk out before they get here.

STELLA: Wait, Blanche.

BLANCHE: I don't want to pass in front of those men.

EUNICE: Then wait'll the game breaks up.

STELLA: Sit down and...

[*Blanche turns weakly, hesitantly about. She lets them push her into a chair.*]

BLANCHE: I can smell the sea air. The rest of my time I'm going to spend on the sea. And when I die, I'm going to die on the sea. You know what I shall die of? [*She plucks a grape*] I shall die of eating an unwashed grape one day out on the ocean. I will die—with my hand in the hand of some nice-looking ship's doctor, a very young one with a small blond mustache and a big silver watch. "Poor lady," they'll say, "the quinine（奎宁）did her no good. That unwashed grape has transported her soul to heaven." [*The cathedral chimes are heard*] And I'll be buried at sea sewn up in a clean white sack and dropped overboard（向船外）—at noon—in the blaze（强光）of summer—and into an ocean as blue as [*Chimes again*] my first lover's eyes!

[*A Doctor and a Matron（护士长）have appeared around the corner of the building and climbed the steps to the porch. The gravity of their profession is exaggerated—the unmistakable aura（气氛）of the state institution with its cynical（愤世嫉俗的）detachment（冷漠）. The Doctor rings the doorbell. The murmur of the game is interrupted.*]

EUNICE [*whispering to Stella*]: That must be them.

[*Stella presses her fists to her lips.*]

BLANCHE [*rising slowly*]: What is it?

EUNICE [*affectedly casual*]: Excuse me while I see who's at the door.

STELLA: Yes. [*Eunice goes into the kitchen.*]

BLANCHE [*tensely*]: I wonder if it's for me.

[*A whispered colloquy（谈话）takes place at the door.*]

EUNICE [*returning, brightly*]: Someone is calling for Blanche.

BLANCHE: It *is* for me, then! [*She looks fearfully from one to the other and then to the portieres. The "Varsouviana" faintly plays*] Is it the gentleman I was expecting from Dallas?

EUNICE: I think it is, Blanche.

BLANCHE: I'm not quite ready.

STELLA: Ask him to wait outside.

BLANCHE: I...

    [Eunice goes back to the portieres. Drums sound very softly.]

STELLA: Everything packed?

BLANCHE: My silver <u>toilet articles</u>（梳妆用具） are still out.

STELLA: Ah!

EUNICE *[returning]*: They're waiting in front of the house.

BLANCHE: They! Who's "they"?

EUNICE: There's a lady with him.

BLANCHE: I cannot imagine who this "lady" could be! How is she dressed?

EUNICE: Just—just a sort of a—plain-<u>tailored</u>（剪裁） outfit.

BLANCHE: Possibly she's—*[Her voice dies out nervously.]*

STELLA: Shall we go, Blanche?

BLANCHE: Must we go through that room?

STELLA: I will go with you.

BLANCHE: How do I look?

STELLA: Lovely.

EUNICE *[echoing]*: Lovely.

    [Blanche moves fearfully to the portieres. Eunice draws them open for her. Blanche goes into the kitchen.]

BLANCHE *[to the men]*: Please don't get up. I'm only passing through.

    [She crosses quickly to outside door. Stella and Eunice follow. The poker players stand awkwardly at the table—all except Mitch, who remains seated, looking down at the table. Blanche steps out on a small porch at the side of the door. She stops <u>short</u>（唐突地） and catches her breath.]

DOCTOR: How do you do?

BLANCHE: You are not the gentleman I was expecting. *[She suddenly gasps and starts back up the steps. She stops by Stella, who stands just outside the door, and speaks in a frightening whisper]* That man isn't Shep Huntleigh.

    [The "Varsouviana" is playing distantly.]

    [Stella stares back at Blanche. Eunice is holding Stella's arm. There is a moment of silence—no sound but that of Stanley steadily <u>shuffling</u>（洗牌） the cards.

    [Blanche catches her breath again and slips back into the flat with a peculiar smile, her eyes wide and brilliant. As soon as her sister goes past her, Stella closes her eyes and <u>clenches</u>（捏紧） her hands. Eunice throws her arms comfortingly about her. Then she starts up to her flat. Blanche stops just inside the door. Mitch keeps staring down at his hands on the table, but the

other men look at her curiously. At last she starts around the table toward the bedroom. As she does, Stanley suddenly pushes back his chair and rises as if to block her way. The Matron follows her into the flat.]

STANLEY: Did you forget something?

BLANCHE [shrilly]: Yes! Yes, I forgot something!

[She rushes past him into the bedroom. Lurid reflections appear on the walls in odd, sinuous shapes. The "Varsouviana" is <u>filtered</u>（过滤，透出） into a weird <u>distortion</u>（扭曲）, accompanied by the cries and noises of the jungle. Blanche seizes the back of a chair as if to defend herself.]

STANLEY [*sotto voce*（低声）]: Doc, you better go in.

DOCTOR [*sotto voce, motioning to the Matron*]: Nurse, bring her out.

[The Matron advances on one side, Stanley on the other. <u>Divested</u>（使……脱去） of all the softer <u>properties</u>（属性） of womanhood, the Matron is a peculiarly <u>sinister</u>（凶恶的） figure in her <u>severe</u>（肃穆的） dress. Her voice is bold and toneless as a <u>firebell</u>（火警铃）.]

MATRON: Hello, Blanche.

[The greeting is echoed and re-echoed by other mysterious voices behind the walls, as if <u>reverberated</u>（使……回响） through a <u>canyon</u>（峡谷） of rock.]

STANLEY: She says that she forgot something.

[The echo sounds in threatening whispers.]

MATRON: That's all right.

STANLEY: What did you forget, Blanche?

BLANCHE: I—I—

MATRON: It don't matter. We can pick it up later.

STANLEY: Sure. We can send it along with the trunk.

BLANCHE [*retreating in panic*]: I don't know you—I don't know you. I want to be—left alone—please!

MATRON: Now, Blanche!

ECHOES [*rising and falling*]: Now, Blanche—now, Blanche—now, Blanche!

STANLEY: You left nothing here but <u>spilt</u>（散落） <u>talcum</u>（爽身粉） and old empty perfume bottles—unless it's the paper lantern you want to take with you. You want the lantern?

[He crosses to dressing table and seizes the paper lantern, tearing it off the light bulb, and extends it toward her. She cries out as if the lantern was herself. The Matron steps boldly toward her. She screams and tries to break past the Matron. All the men spring to their feet. Stella runs out to the porch, with Eunice following to comfort her, <u>simultaneously with</u>（与……同时） the confused voices of the men in the kitchen. Stella rushes into Eunice's embrace on the porch.]

STELLA: Oh, my God, Eunice help me! Don't let them do that to her, don't let them hurt her! Oh, God, oh, please God, don't hurt her! What are they doing to her? What are they doing? *[She tries to break from Eunice's arms.]*

EUNICE: No, honey, no, no, honey. Stay here. Don't go back in there. Stay with me and don't look.

STELLA: What have I done to my sister? Oh, God, what have I done to my sister?

EUNICE: You done the right thing, the only thing you could do. She couldn't stay here; there wasn't no other place for her to go.

[While Stella and Eunice are speaking on the porch the voices of the men in the kitchen <u>overlap</u>（与……复叠） them. Mitch has started toward the bedroom. Stanley crosses to block him. Stanley pushes him aside. Mitch lunges and strikes at Stanley. Stanley pushes Mitch back. Mitch collapses at the table, sobbing.

During the preceding scenes, the Matron catches hold of Blanche's arm and prevents her <u>flight</u>（逃走）. Blanche turns wildly and scratches at the Matron. The heavy woman pinions her arms. Blanche cries out hoarsely and slips to her knees.]

MATRON: These fingernails have to be <u>trim</u>med（修剪）. *[The Doctor comes into the room and she looks at him.]* <u>Jacket</u>（紧身束缚衣）, Doctor?

DOCTOR: Not unless necessary.

[He takes off his hat and now he becomes personalized. The unhuman quality goes. His voice is gentle and <u>reassuring</u>（让人安心的） as he crosses to Blanche and crouches in front of her. As he speaks her name, her terror subsides a little. The lurid reflections fade from the walls, the inhuman cries and noises die out and her own hoarse crying is calmed.]

DOCTOR: Miss DuBois.

[She turns her face to him and stares at him with desperate pleading. He smiles; then he speaks to the Matron.]

It won't be necessary.

BLANCHE *[faintly]*: Ask her to <u>let go of</u>（松手放开） me.

DOCTOR *[to the Matron]*: Let go.

[The Matron releases her. Blanche extends her hands toward the Doctor. He draws her up gently and supports her with his arm and leads her through the portieres.]

BLANCHE *[holding tight to his arm]*: Whoever you are—I have always depended on the kindness of strangers.

[The poker players stand back as Blanche and the Doctor cross the kitchen to the front door. She allows him to lead her as if she were blind. As they go out on the porch, Stella cries out her sister's name from where she is crouched a few steps up on the stairs.]

STELLA: Blanche! Blanche! Blanche!

[Blanche walks on without turning, followed by the Doctor and the Matron.

They go around the corner of the building.

[Eunice descends to Stella and places the child in her arms. It is wrapped in a pale blue blanket. Stella accepts the child, sobbingly. Eunice continues downstairs and enters the kitchen where the men, except for Stanley, are returning silently to their places about the table. Stanley has gone out on the porch and stands at the foot of the steps looking at Stella.]

STANLEY *[a bit uncertainly]*: Stella?

[She sobs with inhuman abandon（放纵）. There is something luxurious（使人痛快的） in her complete surrender to crying now that her sister is gone.]

STANLEY *[voluptuously（挑逗地）, soothingly（安慰地）]*: Now, honey. Now, love. Now, now, love. *[He kneels beside her and his fingers find the opening of her blouse]* Now, now, love. Now, love....

[The luxurious sobbing, the sensual（性感的） murmur fade away under the swelling（高涨） music of the "blue piano" and the muted trumpet.]

STEVE: This game is seven-card stud①.

CURTAIN

4.2.4 Exercises

❶ Give a brief answer to each of the following questions.

Scene 1
1) What are the symbolic meanings suggested by the names of streetcars or of places (e.g. Desire, Cemeteries, Elysian Fields, Belle Reve)?
2) What are the characteristics of Blanche?

Scene 2
3) In Stanley's opinion, how has Belle Reve been lost? How is it lost according to Blanche?
4) Why does Blanche flirt with Stanley? Why is it dangerous?

Scene 3
5) What do Blanche and Mitch have in common to make them attracted to each other?

Scene 4
6) What does Blanche ask Stella to do the morning after the poker party? How do the two sisters' opinions differ on the matter?

Scene 5
7) What's the significance of the curious episode of Blanche's seduction of a young collector/newspaper boy?

---

① seven-card stud: a very popular variant of stud poker.

Unit 4

Tennessee Williams and *A Streetcar Named Desire*

Scene 6

8) What does Blanche say about her late husband? What role does his death play in her life?

Scene 7

9) What does Stanley reveal to Stella about Blanche's past? How does Stella respond to it?

Scene 8

10) What does Stanley give Blanche for her birthday? How does she feel about it?

11) What do Stanley and Stella quarrel about then?

Scene 9

12) What does Mitch do to Blanche that she later considers cruel?

13) What does Mitch say he cannot tolerate about Blanche?

14) What does Blanche tell Mitch about her past?

Scene 10

15) How does Blanche contrast Shep Huntleigh with Stanley and Mitch?

16) How does Stanley tear down Blanche's fantasy world?

17) What's the significance of the scuffle between a prostitute and a drunkard shown on the transparent wall?

18) What role does Stanley's violation of Blanche play in her tragedy?

Scene 11

19) Where do Stella and Stanley tell Blanche she is going? Where does Blanche think she is going? Where is she really going?

20) How is Blanche different after her ordeal inflicted by Stanley?

❷ Identify the following characters.

1) _____ was recently forced to leave her position as a high school English teacher. She is a fallen woman now, but still clings desperately to the trappings of her fading Southern belle self. Her fragile, insecure personality, combined with her brother-in-law's cruelty, leaves her mentally detached from reality by the play's end.

2) _____ takes Stella in when she is beaten by Stanley. Herself a victim of domestic violence, she advises Stella to go on living with Stanley after he has raped Blanche.

3) _____ wears lurid colors and parades his physicality, stripping off sweaty shirts and smashing objects throughout the play. He is loyal to his friends, passionate to his wife, and heartlessly cruel to Blanche. He is determined to destroy Blanche's social pretensions and shows no remorse.

4) _____ is generally concerned with proper behavior. He is much more courteous than Stanley is, though still a man with physical desires. He develops a relationship with Blanche, but is ultimately driven away when he learns of her sordid past.

5) _____ is a sensitive young man whom Blanche fell in love with and married when she was young. After his homosexuality was discovered, he killed himself with a gun. The memory of his death has haunted Blanche ever since.

6) _____ courted Blanche when she was in college. He is rich now and Blanche hopes to get his financial support so that she can escape from Stanley. In Blanche's fantasy, he is coming to sweep her away.

7) _____ appears briefly in the story to sell flowers for the dead when Blanche is telling her past to Mitch. She is faintly visible in the dark, and her mournful cries scare Blanche.

8) _____ reminds Blanche of her dead husband. Polite and reserved, he feels bewildered by Blanche's unexpected flirtation with him.

9) _____ arrives to take Blanche away to an asylum. He initially seems to be heartless, but, in the end, appears more kindly as he takes off his hat and leads Blanche away.

10) _____ loves Blanche and is hurt when Blanche is hurt. However, unlike Blanche, she has no desire to return to her past: she has chosen her present circumstances willingly. She is drawn into the magnetic pull of her husband's powerful physical presence, and her pregnancy underscores her commitment to him.

❸ Plot Review

Stanley and Stella Kowalski live in a poor section of New Orleans. While Stanley is out bowling with his friends and Stella watching them, Stella's elder sister, Blanche DuBois, arrives. She is disappointed at the shabbiness of their 1) _____. After being let in by the landlady, Eunice, she searches out a supply of 2) _____ to calm her nerves. Soon Stella returns and they greet each other fondly. Evidently nervous, Blanche says that she has been given a leave of 3) _____ from school, and demands compliments about her 4) _____. She also confesses she has 5) _____ their family estate, Belle Reve.

The following evening, while Blanche is bathing, Stanley quarrels with Stella about Belle Reve, claiming that he is 6) _____ to anything his wife owns, and implying that Blanche has 7) _____ the estate. After Stella storms out angrily, he confronts Blanche, who then gives him the estate 8) _____. While examining them, Stanley tells her that Stella is 9) _____. The tension continues later that night after the two sisters return from a dinner outside. Stanley is holding a 10) _____ party. One of his friends, Mitch, takes an 11) _____ in Blanche, who is equally impressed by his 12) _____. Blanche turns on the radio and dances in his presence. In the ensuing quarrel, Stanley 13) _____ Stella, who then retreats briefly to Eunice's apartment but returns to him after he sobers up and screams for her.

The next morning, when questioned by her sister, Stella insists that she loves Stanley and will not 14) _____ him. Blanche then dismisses Stanley as an

Unit 4

Tennessee Williams and *A Streetcar Named Desire*

15) _____, but her words are 16) _____ by him. In revenge, Stanley determines to find out more about her past.

A few months later, Stanley hints that he has known some shameful details about Blanche, who 17) _____ all of them but is clearly terrified. She confesses to Stella that she was not so good in recent years and expresses her hope to settle down by 18) _____ Mitch. Left alone, however, Blanche cannot help 19) _____ with a young newsboy, who has come for subscription fee. Later that evening, Blanche has a date with Mitch, and after they return, Blanche tells him about her dead husband, who committed 20) _____ after she found out his homosexuality. Mitch comforts her compassionately.

On her birthday the next month, Blanche is horrified to learn that Stanley has told Mitch about her past, and Stanley also plans to 21) _____ her away. Stella feels sorry for her sister, and argues with Stanley, but she soon goes into labor and is taken to the hospital. Later, Mitch visits Blanche. He demands to see her in the 22) _____, and accuses her of 23) _____ all the time. Desperate, Blanche reveals how she first began to indulge in sex. After Mitch declares he cannot marry her, she breaks down. Left alone again, she drinks more while packing her trunk, and begins to have 24) _____ of partying with admirers. Just then, Stanley returns from the hospital. Blanche tells him that she has been invited for a cruise and that Mitch has come back to beg for her 25) _____. Stanley mocks her appearance, gives vent to his anger, and in the end, ruthlessly 26) _____ her.

A few weeks later, Stella packs Blanche's trunk before her departure to a 27) _____ hospital. Stella is 28) _____ to believe her sister's story about what Stanley has done; rather, she chooses to agree with Stanley that Blanche has gone 29) _____. A doctor and a matron arrive to pick Blanche up. She tries to escape, but is then charmed by the doctor's 30) _____ and consents to leave with them. For the Kowalskis and their friends, it seems that life, finally, has returned to normal.

❹ Identify the speakers of the following lines, briefly tell the situation in which each of them is uttered, and explain its significance.

1) They told me to take a street-car named Desire, and then transfer to one called Cemeteries and ride six blocks and get off at—Elysian Fields!
2) If I didn't know that you was my wife's sister I'd get ideas about you!
3) I know I fib a good deal. After all, a woman's charm is fifty per cent illusion, but when a thing is important I tell the truth...
4) The blind are leading the blind!
5) I can't stand a naked light bulb, any more than I can a rude remark or a vulgar action.
6) — What you are talking about is brutal desire — just Desire! — the name of that rattle-trap street-car that bangs through the Quarter, up one old narrow street and

down another...

— Haven't you ever ridden on that street-car?

— It brought me here. —Where I'm not wanted and where I'm ashamed to be...

7) I want to *rest*! I want to breathe quietly again! Yes—I *want* Mitch... *very badly*! Just think! If it happens! I can leave here and not be anyone's problem...

8) Don't you just love these long rainy afternoons in New Orleans when an hour isn't just an hour—but a little piece of eternity dropped into your hands—and who knows what to do with it?

9) When I was sixteen, I made the discovery—love. All at once and much, much too completely. It was like you suddenly turned a blinding light on something that had always been half in shadow, that's how it struck the world for me. But I was unlucky. Deluded.

10) Sometimes—there's God—so quickly!

11) You didn't know Blanche as a girl. Nobody, nobody, was tender and trusting as she was. But people like you abused her, and forced her to change.

12) I pulled you down off them columns and how you loved it, having them colored lights going! And wasn't we happy together, wasn't it all okay till she showed here?

13) I don't want realism. I want magic! Yes, yes, magic. I try to give that to people. I misrepresent things to them. I don't tell truth. I tell what *ought* to be truth.

14) Oh, I knew you weren't sixteen any more. But I was a fool enough to believe you was straight.

15) Straight? What's straight? A line can be straight, or a street, but the heart of a human being? (film)

16) Physical beauty is passing. A transitory possession. But beauty of the mind and richness of the spirit and tenderness of the heart—and I have all of those things—aren't taken away, but grow! Increase with the years!

17) But some things are not forgivable. Deliberate cruelty is not forgivable. It is the one unforgivable thing in my opinion and it is the one thing of which I have never, never been guilty.

18) I've been on to you from the start! Not once did you pull any wool over this boy's eyes!

19) — I couldn't believe her story and go on living with Stanley.

— Don't ever believe it. Life has got to go on. No matter what happens, you've got to keep on going.

20) Whoever you are — I have always depended on the kindness of strangers.

5 Questions for essay or discussion

1) What are the causes of Blanche's tragedy? Considering her past life, her deceit, and her artificiality, does she still deserve the audience's sympathy?

2) What are the sources of the hostility between Blanche and Stanley?
3) Compare and contrast Blanche and Stella.
4) How does the play use symbols to strengthen its effect?
5) What do you think are the themes of this play?

Unit 5

Arthur Miller and *The Crucible*

5.1 Arthur Miller: Life and Works

5.1.1 About the Playwright

Arthur Miller (1915—2005) is ranked among the most important and influential American playwrights since World War II. He is also known as an essayist, scriptwriter, short story writer, nonfiction writer, and novelist.

Arthur Miller was born into a German-Jewish family in New York City on October 17, 1915. His father was a ladies-wear manufacturer and shopkeeper. The Millers were a very contented family in the 1920s, wealthy enough to have their own chauffeur and an attractive apartment in Manhattan, overlooking Central Park, just off 5th Avenue. From an early age, Miller admired his mother's artistry and the inquiring mind that had filled their house with books and music. He felt close to his mother and saw her as having had a great influence on the way that he viewed life.

His father's business failed during the Great Depression of the 1920s, and the family, like many others, suffered economic hardship and could not afford to send him to college. Miller worked for two years in an automobile parts warehouse, earning enough money to attend the University of Michigan in 1934, where his talent as a playwright emerged under the tutelage of Kenneth Rowe, his playwriting professor. These were the years of the Spanish Civil War, the rise of Fascism, and the attraction of Marxism as a way out of the depression, and here Miller formed his political views. He began to write plays, which won important university awards and he became noticed by the Theatre Guild, a highly respected theater founded to present excellent plays. Miller graduated in June 1938 and returned to Brooklyn.

Over the next six years, Miller wrote radio plays, screenplays, articles, stories, and a novel. His works covered a wide range of material, much of it growing out of his childhood memories. He also dealt with political issues and problems of anti-Semitism, which was widespread in the 1930s and 1940s. Miller's first play to appear on Broadway was *The Man Who Had All the Luck* (1944), which lasted for only four performances, but it won a Theater Guild award and established Miller as an important young playwright. The play's theme was one that Miller would return to throughout his career: the moral destruction that comes from blind pursuit of material success. His next effort was far more successful: *All My Sons* (1947), a play like most of his major dramas, explores relationships between family members, quite often between fathers, sons, and brothers. It ran on Broadway for 300 performances, a remarkable record for a serious drama. The story centers on a man who knowingly produces defective parts for airplanes and then blames the subsequent crashes on his business partner, who is ruined and imprisoned. When the man's son finds out the truth, he confronts his father and rebukes him. Ultimately, the man realizes not only that he has lost his son because of his deceit but that the dead pilots were also "all my sons." The play won the New York Drama Critics' Circle Award, and with it Miller achieved recognition as an up-and-coming new talent in the American Theater. In 1945 Miller published a novel *Focus*, which deals with discrimination and prejudice. In 1949 his most impressive play *Death of a Salesman* was produced at the Morosco Theater in New York. It ran for 742 performances, and firmly established Miller as a major American playwright. Its concerns were rooted in the American ideal of business success, and its conclusions were a challenge to standard American business values. The play won the Pulitzer Prize, the New York Drama Critics' Circle Award, the Antoinette Perry Award, the Theater Club Award, and the Donaldson Award among many others. It was, and it remains, Miller's greatest play. Translated into all major languages, it is staged throughout the world.

In the 1950s the hysterical search for supposed communist infiltration of American life reaches its height as Senator Joseph McCarthy summoned suspect after suspect to hearings in Washington. Many were accused of communist sympathies and found themselves out of work. In 1950, Miller adapted Ibsen's *An Enemy of the People*, which, according to his introduction, questioned "whether the democratic guarantees protecting political minorities ought to be set aside in time of crisis." Given the climate of the times, the production was not a great success, and Miller was accused by the press of creating anti-American propaganda. Miller's favorite play is *The Crucible* (1953), about the witch trials in Salem Village, Massachusetts, in 1692. The play told of a terror-ridden society, of neighbor forced to testify against neighbor, of innocent people falsely named as disciples of satanic witchcraft. The play so precisely reflected the political atmosphere of 1952 that many reviewers were forced to pretend there was no connection. Later, the hysteria touched Miller personally: he was denied a passport, and in 1957 was convicted of contempt of Congress for refusing to name suspected communists before the House Un-American Activities Committee. The conviction was quickly reversed the following year in the United States Court of Appeals, and during the same period, as if in repudiation of House committee actions, Miller was awarded some of his greatest distinctions: an honorary degree by the University of Michigan, election to the National Institute of Arts and Letters, and the National Institute's Gold Medal for his achievements.

Miller's last play of the 1950s, *A View from the Bridge* (1955, Pulitzer Prize), presents two Italian longshoremen staying illegally in the U.S. It ran for 149 performances. In 1957 Miller published a short story, "The Misfits." He then rewrote it as a screen-play to star his wife, the actress Marilyn Monroe, whom he had married the year before. The movie, filmed in 1958, was a commercial and critical success. But shortly after it was released the two separated. In 1961 they were divorced, and in the following year Marilyn Monroe committed suicide. In 1964 Miller returned to the stage with *After the Fall*, in which the quasi-autobiographical protagonist seeks self-knowledge, a sense of the meaning of his past and its meaning for his future as he reviews his marriage and other major experiences.

Since the 1960s Miller's work has become increasingly wide-ranging in terms of subject and period, and explores Jewish identity much more directly than his earlier works. *Incident at Vichy* (1965) is set in Nazi-occupied France, and *The Price* (1968) in contemporary New York. *The American Clock* (1980) is set during the Depression and is based on testimonies collected by Studs Terkel (b.1912). *The Last Yankee* (1993) is set in a mental hospital, and *Broken Glass* (1994) is set in Germany in 1938 and is concerned with the beginnings of the Holocaust. Despite the wide range of Miller's subjects, these plays share his abiding concern with questions about personal integrity under strain, with the role and limitation of individual responsibility, the human costs of compromise and the relation between private and public morality. His other writings include a short-story collection, *I Don't Need You Any More* (1967), *Theater Essays* (1977), and the autobiography *Timebends* (1987).

Miller's dramatic themes and interests have always been closely related to what's "in the air," which has led the critics to describe him as a "social dramatist." And it is true that Miller has followed the philosophy that the fate of mankind is social; as Miller put it, "society is inside man and man is inside society, and you cannot create a truthfully drawn psychological entity on the stage unless you understand his social relations."

5.1.2 Arthur Miller's Major Plays

All My Sons (1947)《全是我的儿子》
Death of a Salesman (1949)《推销员之死》
An Enemy of the People (1950)《人民公敌》
The Crucible (1953)《萨勒姆的女巫》(《炼狱》)
A View from the Bridge (1955)《桥头眺望》
The Price (1968)《代价》
The American Clock (1980)《美国时钟》

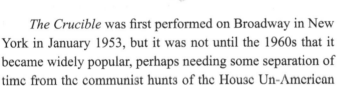

5.2 *The Crucible*

5.2.1 About the Play

The Crucible was first performed on Broadway in New York in January 1953, but it was not until the 1960s that it became widely popular, perhaps needing some separation of time from the communist hunts of the House Un-American Activities Committee (HUAC), against which it so bravely spoke.

Written at the height of Senator McCarthy's campaign against communists and their associates, it was clear to most people that the play draws an analogy between McCarthyism and the witch trials in Salem in 1692. Miller later said that at this time he was reading a book about the Salem witch trials and saw that "the main point of the hearings, precisely

as in seventeenth-century Salem, was that the accused make public confession, damn his confederates as well as his Devil master, and guarantee his sterling new allegiance by breaking disgusting old vows—whereupon he was let loose to rejoin the society of extremely decent people." Miller had spent much of the previous year researching witch trials at the Historical Society in Salem, Massachusetts, to ensure that the play would have an accurate historical basis. With its clear message of resistance against tyranny, *The Crucible* has grown to be Miller's most widely produced work.

The Salem Witch Trials took place in Salem, Massachusetts in 1692, and were based on the accusations of a twelve-year-old girl named Ann Putnam Jr. Putnam claimed that she had witnessed a number of Salem's residents holding back Sabbaths and consorting with Satan. Based on these accusations, an English-American clergyman named Samuel Parris spearheaded the prosecution of dozens of alleged witches in the Massachusetts colony. Nineteen people were hanged and one pressed to death over the following two years.

Miller's play employs these historical events to criticize the moments in human history when reason and fact became clouded by irrational fears and the desire to place the blame for society's problems on others. Dealing with elements such as false accusations, manifestations of mass hysteria, and rumor-mongering, *The Crucible* is seen by many as more of a commentary on "McCarthyism" than the actual Salem trials.

The play's action centers on John Proctor, a farmer whose wife Elizabeth is among those accused of witchcraft by Abigail Williams, a teenaged girl once employed by him and with whom he had an adulterous relationship. In court Proctor confesses to the adultery as a means of exposing Abigail, but he is then himself accused of witchcraft. In the play's climax Proctor is at first willing to confess in order to escape hanging, but he refuses to testify against others. He eventually renounces his confession and allows himself to be executed rather than sign away his name and his children's respect.

Miller himself draws attention to the analogy between the witch-hunts and McCarthysim, but the play has a much wider thematic resonance, exploring issues of self-awareness and integrity, the nature of power and interpretation. *The Crucible* has been produced more often than any of Miller's other plays and remains as a political barometer for unrest in many foreign countries. As a historical, cultural, and political rendition of one of the most terrifying chapters in American history, and as a reminder of how conscience handed over to others can debase the social contract, *The Crucible* remains unique.

5.2.2 Characters

(1) The Parris household

Reverend Samuel Parris, Salem's minister. He is repressive, vain, and very protective of his status.

Betty Parris, Parris's ten-year-old daughter. Her illness and that of Ruth Putnam fuel the first rumors of witchcraft.

Abigail Williams, Parris's seventeen-year-old niece, and once the servant for the Proctors. Manipulative and scheming, she is the leader of the girls who falsely accuse others as witches.

Tituba, Parris's black slave from Barbados. She is among the first to be accused of witchcraft.

Unit 5

Arthur Miller and *The Crucible*

(2) The Proctor household

John Proctor, a local farmer in his mid-thirties who lives just outside town. He is upright and independent-minded, but has a guilty conscience for his affair with Abigail.

Elizabeth Proctor, John Proctor's wife. She is virtuous, but often cold.

Mary Warren, the servant of the Proctors. She is a timid girl easily influenced by others.

(3) The Putnam household

Thomas Putnam, a wealthy landowner. He is greedy and vengeful.

Ann Putnam, Thomas Putnam's wife. She is deeply troubled by the death of her seven babies, and believes a murdering witch is responsible.

Ruth Putnam, the Putnams' only surviving child. Like Betty Parris, she falls ill after the girls are discovered dancing secretly in the woods.

Mercy Lewis, servant of the Putnams. She is sly and merciless.

(4) Other villagers

Francis Nurse, a wealthy landowner, rival of the Putnams. He is well respected by most people in Salem.

Rebecca Nurse, Francis Nurse's wife. She is a gentle, sensible, and upright woman.

Giles Corey, an old farmer. Famous for his tendency to file lawsuits, he is nonetheless a righteous and strong-willed man.

Martha Corey, Giles Corey's wife, one of the accused witches.

Susanna Walcott, Abigail's friend.

Sarah Good, a ragged and crazy woman, one of the first to be accused.

(5) The officials in the court

Reverend John Hale, a young minister from Beverley and an expert on witchcraft. He is an honest man, but is misguided at the beginning of the trials.

Judge Danforth, the Deputy Governor of Massachusetts and the presiding judge at the witch trials. He views his and the court's authority more important than justice.

Judge Hathorne, a "bitter, remorseless Salem Judge" who presides over the trials along with Danforth.

Ezekiel Cheever, a Salem tailor who acts as clerk of the court during the witch trials.

Herrick, the marshal of Salem.

5.2.3 Selected Readings from the Play

🎵 Excerpt 1 (from Act 1)

The play is set in Salem, Massachusetts, 1692. The local residents are Puritans, and their government is a theocracy—rule by God through religious officials. Within the community, there are simmering disputes over land.

As the play opens, Reverend Parris kneels in prayer in front of his daughter's bed. Betty Parris lies in a coma. The rumor that she is the victim of witchcraft is running rampant in Salem, and a crowd has gathered in Parris's parlor. Parris berates his niece, Abigail Williams, because he has discovered her, Betty, and several other girls dancing secretly in the forest in the middle of the night with his slave, Tituba.

ABIGAIL: Uncle, the rumor of witchcraft（巫术） is all about; I think you'd best go down and deny it yourself. The parlor's packed with people, sir. I'll sit with her.

PARRIS, *pressed, turns on her*: And what shall I say to them? That my daughter and my niece I discovered dancing like heathen（异教徒） in the forest?

ABIGAIL: Uncle, we did dance; let you tell them I confessed it—and I'll be whipped if I must be. But they're speakin' of witchcraft. Betty's not witched（中了妖术）.

PARRIS: Abigail, I cannot go before the congregation（教区会众） when I know you have not opened with me. What did you do with her in the forest?

ABIGAIL: We did dance, uncle, and when you leaped out of the bush so suddenly, Betty was frightened and then she fainted. And there's the whole of it.

PARRIS: Child. Sit you down.

ABIGAIL, *quavering, as she sits*: I would never hurt Betty. I love her dearly.

PARRIS: Now look you, child, your punishment will come in its time. But if you trafficked（交易） with spirits in the forest I must know it now, for surely my enemies will, and they will ruin me with it.

ABIGAIL: But we never conjured（念咒召唤） spirits.

PARRIS: Then why can she not move herself since midnight? This child is desperate! *Abigail lowers her eyes.* It must come out—my enemies will bring it out. Let me know what you done there. Abigail, do you understand that I have many enemies?

ABIGAIL: I have heard of it, uncle.

PARRIS: There is a faction（帮派） that is sworn to drive me from my pulpit（讲道台）. Do you understand that?

ABIGAIL: I think so, sir.

PARRIS: Now then, in the midst of such disruption（分裂活动）, my own household is discovered to be the very center of some obscene（淫秽的，可憎的） practice. Abominations（令人厌恶的事） are done in the forest—

Unit 5

Arthur Miller and *The Crucible*

ABIGAIL: It were sport（嬉戏）, uncle!

PARRIS, *pointing at Betty*: You call this sport? *She lowers her eyes. He pleads*: Abigail, if you know something that may help the doctor, for God's sake tell it to me. *She is silent.* I saw Tituba waving her arms over the fire when I came on you. Why was she doing that? And I heard a screeching（尖叫） and gibberish（快而不清的言语） coming from her mouth. She were swaying like a dumb beast over that fire!

ABIGAIL: She always sings her Barbados① songs, and we dance.

PARRIS: I cannot blink（无视） what I saw, Abigail, for my enemies will not blink it. I saw a dress lying on the grass.

ABIGAIL, *innocently*: A dress?

PARRIS—*it is very hard to say*: Aye, a dress. And I thought I saw—someone naked running through the trees!

ABIGAIL, *in terror*: No one was naked! You mistake yourself, uncle!

PARRIS, *with anger*: I saw it! *He moves from her. Then, resolved*: Now tell me true, Abigail. And I pray you feel the weight of truth upon you, for now my ministry's（牧师职位） at stake, my ministry and perhaps your cousin's life. Whatever abomination you have done, give me all of it now, for I dare not be taken unaware when I go before them down there.

ABIGAIL: There is nothin' more. I swear it, uncle.

PARRIS, *studies her, then nods, half convinced*: Abigail, I have sought here three long years to bend these stiff-necked people to me, and now, just now when some good respect is rising for me in the parish（教区）, you compromise（损害） my very character. I have given you a home, child, I have put clothes upon your back—now give me upright answer. Your name in the town—it is entirely white, is it not?

ABIGAIL, *with an edge of resentment*: Why, I am sure it is, sir. There be no blush about my name.

PARRIS, *to the point*: Abigail, is there any other cause than you have told me, for your being discharged（解雇） from Goody② Proctor's service? I have heard it said, and I tell you as I heard it, that she comes so rarely to the church this year for she will not sit so close to something soiled. What signified that remark?

ABIGAIL: She hates me, uncle, she must, for I would not be her slave. It's a bitter woman, a lying, cold, sniveling（哭哭啼啼的） woman, and I will not work for such a woman!

PARRIS: She may be. And yet it has troubled me that you are now seven month out of their house, and in all this time no other family has ever called for your service.

ABIGAIL: They want slaves, not such as I. Let them send to Barbados for that. I will

---

① Barbados: an island in the eastern West Indies constituting an independent state in the Commonwealth of Nations; formerly a British colony.
② Goody: (archaic) a polite term of address for a woman of humble social standing.

not black my face for any of them! *With ill-concealed resentment at him*: Do you begrudge（吝惜）my bed, uncle?

PARRIS: No—no.

ABIGAIL, *in a temper*: My name is good in the village! I will not have it said my name is soiled! Goody Proctor is a gossiping liar!

>   *Enter Mrs. Ann Putnam. She is a twisted soul of forty-five, a death-ridden（受……折磨的）woman, haunted by dreams.*

PARRIS, *as soon as the door begins to open*: No—no, I cannot have anyone. *He sees her, and a certain deference springs into him, although his worry remains.* Why, Goody Putnam, come in.

MRS. PUTNAM, *full of breath, shiny-eyed*: It is a marvel. It is surely a stroke of hell upon you.

PARRIS: No, Goody Putnam, it is—

MRS. PUTNAM, *glancing at Betty*: How high did she fly, how high?

PARRIS: No, no, she never flew—

MRS. PUTNAM, *very pleased with it*: Why, it's sure she did. Mr. Collins saw her goin' over Ingersoll's barn, and come down light as bird, he says!

PARRIS: Now, look you, Goody Putnam, she never... *Enter Thomas Putnam, a well-to-do, hard-handed（手段强硬的）landowner, near fifty.* Oh, good morning, Mr. Putnam.

PUTNAM: It is a providence（天意）the thing is out now! It is a providence. *He goes directly to the bed.*

PARRIS: What's out, sir, what's—?

MRS. PUTNAM *goes to the bed.*

PUTNAM, *looking down at BETTY*: Why, *her* eyes is closed! Look you, Ann.

MRS. PUTNAM: Why, that's strange. *To Parris*: Ours is open.

PARRIS, *shocked*: Your Ruth is sick?

MRS. PUTNAM, *with vicious certainty*: I'd not call it sick; the Devil's touch is heavier than sick. It's death, y'know, it's death drivin' into them, forked（用叉子叉）and hoofed[①]（用蹄子踢）.

PARRIS: Oh, pray not! Why, how does Ruth ail（生病）?

MRS. PUTNAM: She ails as she must—she never waked this morning, but her eyes open and she walks, and hears naught, sees naught, and cannot eat. Her soul is taken, surely.

>   *Parris is struck.*

PUTNAM, *as though for further details*: They say you've sent for Reverend Hale of Beverly?

PARRIS, *with dwindling conviction now*: A precaution（预防措施）only. He has

---

① forked and hoofed: The Devil is often portrayed as carrying a fork and with cloven hoofs.

much experience in all demonic arts（有关魔鬼的学问）, and I—
MRS. PUTNAM: He has indeed; and found a witch in Beverly last year, and let you remember that.
PARRIS: Now, Goody Ann, they only thought that were a witch, and I am certain there be no element of witchcraft here.
PUTNAM: No witchcraft! Now look you, Mr. Parris—
PARRIS: Thomas, Thomas, I pray you, leap not to witchcraft. I know that you—you least of all, Thomas, would ever wish so disastrous a charge laid upon me. We cannot leap to witchcraft. They will howl（轰走） me out of Salem for such corruption（恶行） in my house.

A word about Thomas Putnam. He was a man with many grievances（抱怨）, at least one of which appears justified. Some time before, his wife's brother-in-law, James Bayley, had been turned down as minister of Salem. Bayley had all the qualifications, and a two-thirds vote into the bargain（而且）, but a faction stopped his acceptance, for reasons that are not clear.

Thomas Putnam was the eldest son of the richest man in the village. He had fought the Indians at Narragansett, and was deeply interested in parish affairs. He undoubtedly felt it poor payment that the village should so blatantly（公然） disregard his candidate for one of its more important offices（职务）, especially since he regarded himself as the intellectual superior of most of the people around him.

His vindictive（睚眦必报的） nature was demonstrated long before the witchcraft began. Another former Salem minister, George Burroughs, had had to borrow money to pay for his wife's funeral, and, since the parish was remiss（疏忽的） in his salary, he was soon bankrupt. Thomas and his brother John had Burroughs jailed for debts the man did not owe. The incident is important only in that Burroughs succeeded in becoming minister where Bayley, Thomas Putnam's brother-in-law, had been rejected; the motif of resentment is clear here. Thomas Putnam felt that his own name and the honor of his family had been smirched（玷污） by the village, and he meant to right matters however he could.

Another reason to believe him a deeply embittered man was his attempt to break his father's will, which left a disproportionate amount to a stepbrother. As with every other public cause in which he tried to force his way, he failed in this.

So it is not surprising to find that so many accusations against people are in the handwriting of Thomas Putnam, or that his name is so often found as a witness corroborating（证实） the supernatural testimony（证词）, or that his daughter led the crying-out（呐喊指控） at the most opportune（恰当的） junctures（时机） of the trials, especially when—but we'll speak of that when we come to it.

PUTNAM—*at the moment he is intent upon getting Parris, for whom he has only contempt, to move toward the* abyss（深渊）: Mr. Parris, I have taken your part in all contention（争论） here, and I would continue; but I cannot if you hold back（退缩） in this. There are hurtful, vengeful（报复的） spirits layin' hands on these children.

PARRIS: But, Thomas, you cannot—

PUTNAM: Ann! Tell Mr. Parris what you have done.

MRS. PUTNAM: Reverend Parris, I have laid seven babies unbaptized（未受洗礼的） in the earth. Believe me, sir, you never saw more hearty babies born, And yet, each would wither in my arms the very night of their birth. I have spoke nothin', but my heart has clamored（叫嚷） intimations（暗示）. And now, this year, my Ruth, my only—I see her turning strange. A secret child she has become this year, and shrivels（萎靡） like a sucking mouth were pullin' on her life too. And so I thought to send her to your Tituba—

PARRIS: To Tituba! What may Tituba—?

MRS. PUTNAM: Tituba knows how to speak to the dead, Mr. Parris.

PARRIS: Goody Ann, it is a formidable（极大的） sin to conjure up the dead!

MRS. PUTNAM: I take it on my soul, but who else may surely tell us what person murdered my babies?

PARRIS, *horrified*: Woman!

MRS. PUTNAM: They were murdered, Mr. Parris! And mark this proof! Mark it! Last night my Ruth were ever so close to their little spirits; I know it, sir. For how else is she struck dumb now except some power of darkness would stop her mouth? It is a marvelous sign, Mr. Parris!

PUTNAM: Don't you understand it, sir? There is a murdering witch among us, bound to keep herself in the dark. *Parris turns to Betty, a* frantic（狂乱的） *terror rising in him.* Let your enemies make of it what they will, you cannot blink it more.

PARRIS, *to Abigail*: Then you were conjuring spirits last night.

ABIGAIL, *whispering*: Not I, sir—Tituba and Ruth.

PARRIS *turns now, with new fear, and goes to Betty, looks down at her, and then, gazing off*: Oh, Abigail, what proper payment for my charity! Now I am undone.

PUTNAM: You are not undone! Let you take hold（掌控局势） here. Wait for no one to charge you—declare it yourself. You have discovered witchcraft—

PARRIS: In my house? In my house, Thomas? They will topple（推翻） me with this! They will make of it a—

  Enter Mercy Lewis, the Putnams' servant, a fat, sly, merciless girl of eighteen.

MERCY: Your pardons. I only thought to see how Betty is...

PUTNAM: Why aren't you home? Who's with Ruth?

MERCY: Her grandma come. She's improved a little, I think—she give a powerful sneeze before.

MRS. PUTNAM: Ah, there's a sign of life!

MERCY: I'd fear no more, Goody Putnam. It were a grand sneeze; another like it will shake her wits（神智） together, I'm sure. *She goes to the bed to look.*

PARRIS: Will you leave me now, Thomas? I would pray a while alone.

ABIGAIL: Uncle, you've prayed since midnight. Why do you not go down and—

PARRIS: No—no. *To Putnam*: I have no answer for that crowd. I'll wait till Mr. Hale arrives. *To get Mrs. Putnam to leave*: If you will, Goody Ann...

PUTNAM: Now look you, sir. Let you strike out against the Devil, and the village will bless you for it! Come down, speak to them—pray with them. They're thirsting for your word, Mister! Surely you'll pray with them.

PARRIS, *swayed*: I'll lead them in a psalm（圣歌）, but let you say nothing of witchcraft yet. I will not discuss it. The cause is yet unknown. I have had enough contention since I came; I want no more.

MRS. PUTNAM: Mercy, you go home to Ruth, d'y'hear?

MERCY: Aye, mum.

Mrs. Putnam goes out.

PARRIS, *to Abigail*: If she starts for the window, cry for me at once.

ABIGAIL: I will, uncle.

PARRIS, *to Putnam*: There is a terrible power in her arms today. *He goes out with Putnam.*

✂ Excerpt 2 (from Act 1)

Once they are alone, Abigail updates Mercy on the current situation. Mary Warren, the servant for the Proctor household, enters the room in a breathless, nervous state. She is worried that they will all be labeled witches before long. The three girls begin to argue and Betty wakes. She accuses Abigail of having drunk blood as a charm to kill Elizabeth Proctor, John Proctor's wife. Abigail threatens to kill the girls if they breathe a word about the spell. Betty collapses again in a stupor. Then John Proctor enters.

Enter John Proctor. On seeing him, Mary Warren leaps in fright.

Proctor was a farmer in his middle thirties. He need not have been a partisan（党羽） of any faction in the town, but there is evidence to suggest that he had a sharp and biting（辛辣嘲讽的） way with hypocrites（伪君子）. He was the kind of man—powerful of body, even-tempered, and not easily led—who cannot refuse support to partisans without drawing their deepest resentment. In Proctor's presence a fool felt his foolishness instantly—and a Proctor is always marked for calumny（诽谤） therefore.

But as we shall see, the steady manner he displays does not spring from an untroubled soul. He is a sinner, a sinner not only against the moral fashion of the time, but against his own vision of decent conduct. These people had no ritual for the washing away of sins. It is another trait（特质） we inherited from them, and it has helped to discipline us as well as to breed hypocrisy among us. Proctor, respected and even feared in Salem, has come to regard himself as a kind of fraud. But no hint of this has yet appeared on the surface, and as he enters from the crowded parlor below it is a man in his prime（盛年） we see, with a quiet confidence and an unexpressed, hidden force. Mary Warren, his servant, can barely speak for embarrassment and fear.

MARY WARREN: Oh! I'm just going home, Mr. Proctor.

PROCTOR: Be you foolish, Mary Warren? Be you deaf? I forbid you leave the house, did I not? Why shall I pay you? I am looking for you more often than my cows!

MARY WARREN: I only come to see the great doings in the world.

PROCTOR: I'll show you a great doin' on your arse one of these days. Now get you home; my wife is waitin' with your work! *Trying to retain a shred of dignity, she goes slowly out.*

MERCY LEWIS, *both afraid of him and strangely titillated*（逗引）: I'd best be off. I have my Ruth to watch. Good morning, Mr. Proctor.

Mercy sidles（侧身而行） out. Since Proctor's entrance, Abigail has stood as though on tiptoe, absorbing his presence, wide-eyed. He glances at her, then goes to Betty on the bed.

ABIGAIL: Gad（哼）! I'd almost forgot how strong you are, John Proctor!

PROCTOR, *looking at Abigail now, the faintest suggestion of a knowing smile（会意的微笑） on his face*: What's this mischief here?

ABIGAIL, *with a nervous laugh*: Oh, she's only gone silly somehow.

PROCTOR: The road past my house is a pilgrimage（朝圣之行） to Salem all morning. The town's mumbling witchcraft.

ABIGAIL: Oh, posh（呸）! *Winningly she comes a little closer, with a confidential（私密的）, wicked air.* We were dancin' in the woods last night, and my uncle leaped in on us. She took fright, is all.

PROCTOR, *his smile widening*: Ah, you're wicked yet, aren't y'! *A trill（颤声） of expectant laughter escapes her, and she dares come closer, feverishly looking into his eyes.* you'll be clapped in the stocks（枷具） before you're twenty.

He takes a step to go, and she springs into his path.

ABIGAIL: Give me a word, John. A soft word. *Her concentrated desire destroys his smile.*

PROCTOR: No, no, Abby. That's done with.

ABIGAIL, *tauntingly（讥讽地）*: You come five mile to see a silly girl fly? I know you better.

PROCTOR, *setting her firmly out of his path*: I come to see what mischief your uncle's brewin'（酝酿） now. *With final emphasis*: Put it out of mind, Abby.

ABIGAIL, *grasping his hand before he can release her*: John—I am waitin' for you every night.

PROCTOR: Abby, I never give you hope to wait for me.

ABIGAIL, *now beginning to anger—she can't believe it*: I have something better than hope, I think!

PROCTOR: Abby, you'll put it out of mind. I'll not be comin' for you more.

ABIGAIL: You're surely sportin' with me.

PROCTOR: You know me better.

ABIGAIL: I know how you clutched（紧抓） my back behind your house and sweated like a stallion（种马） whenever I come near! Or did I dream that? It's she put me out, you cannot pretend it were you. I saw your face when she put me out, and you loved me then and you do now!

PROCTOR: Abby, that's a wild thing to say—

ABIGAIL: A wild thing may say wild things. But not so wild, I think. I have seen you since she put me out; I have seen you nights.

PROCTOR: I have hardly stepped off my farm this sevenmonth.

ABIGAIL: I have a sense for heat, John, and yours has drawn me to my window, and I have seen you looking up, burning in your loneliness. Do you tell me you've never looked up at my window?

PROCTOR: I may have looked up.

ABIGAIL, *now softening*: And you must. You are no wintry man. I know you, John. I *know* you. *She is weeping.* I cannot sleep for dreamin'; I cannot dream but I wake and walk about the house as though I'd find you comin' through some door. *She clutches him desperately.*

PROCTOR, *gently pressing her from him, with great sympathy but firmly*: Child—

ABIGAIL, *with a flash of anger*: How do you call me child!

PROCTOR: Abby, I may think of you softly from time to time. But I will cut off my hand before I'll ever reach for you again. Wipe it out of mind. We never touched, Abby.

ABIGAIL: Aye, but we did.

PROCTOR: Aye, but we did not.

ABIGAIL, *with a bitter anger*: Oh, I marvel how such a strong man may let such a sickly wife be—

PROCTOR, *angered—at himself as well*: You'll speak nothin' of Elizabeth!

ABIGAIL: She is blackening my name in the village! She is telling lies about me! She is a cold, sniveling woman, and you bend（屈服） to her! Let her turn you like a—

PROCTOR, *shaking her*: Do you look for whippin'?

 A psalm is heard being sung below.

ABIGAIL, *in tears*: I look for John Proctor that took me from my sleep and put knowledge in my heart! I never knew what pretense(虚伪) Salem was, I never knew the lying lessons I was taught by all these Christian women and their covenanted(立约信仰上帝的) men! And now you bid me tear the light out of my eyes? I will not, I cannot! You loved me, John Proctor, and whatever sin it is, you love me yet! *He turns abruptly to go out. She rushes to him.* John, pity me, pity me!

 The words "going up to Jesus" are heard in the psalm and Betty claps her ears suddenly and whines(哀号) loudly.

ABIGAIL: Betty? *She hurries to Betty, who is now sitting up and screaming. Proctor goes to Betty as Abigail is trying to pull her hands down, calling "Betty!"*

PROCTOR, *growing unnerved*: What's she doing? Girl, what ails you? Stop that wailing(号啕大哭)!

 The singing has stopped in the midst of this, and now Parris rushes in.

PARRIS: What happened? What are you doing to her? Betty! *He rushes to the bed, crying, "Betty, Betty!" Mrs. Putnam enters, feverish with curiosity, and with her Thomas Putnam and Mercy Lewis. Parris, at the bed, keeps lightly slapping Betty's face, while she moans and tries to get up.*

ABIGAIL: She heard you singin' and suddenly she's up and screamin'.

MRS. PUTNAM: The psalm! The psalm! She cannot bear to hear the Lord's name!

PARRIS: No. God forbid. Mercy, run to the doctor! Tell him what's happened here!

 Mercy Lewis rushes out.

MRS. PUTNAM: Mark it for a sign, mark it!

 Rebecca Nurse, seventy-two, enters. She is white-haired, leaning upon her walking-stick.

PUTNAM, *pointing at the whimpering(呜咽) Betty*: That is a notorious(众所周知的) sign of witchcraft afoot, Goody Nurse, a prodigious(异常的) sign!

MRS. PUTNAM: My mother told me that! When they cannot bear to hear the name of—

PARRIS, *trembling*: Rebecca, Rebecca, go to her, we're lost. She suddenly cannot bear to hear the Lord's—

 Giles Corey, eighty-three, enters. He is knotted with muscle, canny(精明的), inquisitive(好寻根问底的), and still powerful.

REBECCA: There is hard sickness here, Giles Corey, so please to keep the quiet.

GILES: I've not said a word. No one here can testify I've said a word. Is she going to fly again? I hear she flies.

PUTNAM: Man, be quiet now!

Unit 5

Arthur Miller and *The Crucible*

Everything is quiet. Rebecca walks across the room to the bed. Gentleness <u>exudes</u>（散发） from her. Betty is quietly whimpering, eyes shut; Rebecca simply stands over the child, who gradually quiets.

And while they are so absorbed, we may put a word in for Rebecca. Rebecca was the wife of Francis Nurse, who, from all accounts, was one of those men for whom both sides of the argument had to have respect. He was called upon to <u>arbitrate</u>（仲裁） disputes as though he were an unofficial judge, and Rebecca also enjoyed the high opinion most people had for him. By the time of the <u>delusion</u>（妄想，错觉）, they had three hundred acres, and their children were settled in separate <u>homesteads</u>（宅地） within the same estate. However, Francis had originally rented the land, and one theory has it that, as he gradually paid for it and raised his social status, there were those who resented his rise.

Another suggestion to explain the systematic campaign against Rebecca, and <u>inferentially</u>（据此推断） against Francis, is the land war he fought with his neighbors, one of whom was a Putnam. This <u>squabble</u>（口角） grew to the proportions of a battle in the woods between partisans of both sides, and it is said to have lasted for two days. As for Rebecca herself, the general opinion of her character was so high that to explain how anyone dared cry her out for a witch—and more, how adults could bring themselves to lay hands on her—we must look to the fields and boundaries of that time.

As we have seen, Thomas Putnam's man for the Salem ministry was Bayley. The Nurse <u>clan</u>（宗族） had been in the faction that prevented Bayley's taking office. In addition, certain families allied to the Nurses by blood or friendship, and whose farms were <u>contiguous with</u>（毗连） the Nurse farm or close to it, combined to break away from the Salem town authority and set up Topsfield, a new and independent <u>entity</u>（实体） whose existence was resented by old Salemites.

That the guiding hand behind the <u>outcry</u>（强烈抗议） was Putnam's is indicated by the fact that, as soon as it began, this Topsfield-Nurse faction <u>absented</u>（使……缺席） themselves from church in protest and disbelief. It was Edward and Jonathan Putnam who signed the first complaint against Rebecca; and Thomas Putnam's little daughter was the one who fell into a <u>fit</u>（发病，晕厥） at the <u>hearing</u>（听讯） and pointed to Rebecca as her attacker. To top it all, Mrs. Putnam—who is now staring at the bewitched child on the bed—soon accused Rebecca's spirit of "tempting her to <u>iniquity</u>（邪恶），" a charge that had more truth in it than Mrs. Putnam could know.

MRS. PUTNAM, *astonished*: What have you done?
    Rebecca, in thought, now leaves the bedside and sits.
PARRIS, *wondrous and relieved*: What do you make of it, Rebecca?
PUTNAM, *eagerly*: Goody Nurse, will you go to my Ruth and see if you can wake

her?

REBECCA, *sitting*: I think she'll wake in time. Pray calm yourselves. I have eleven children, and I am twenty-six times a grandma, and I have seen them all through their silly seasons, and when it come on them they will run the Devil <u>bow-legged</u>（罗圈腿） keeping up with their mischief. I think she'll wake when she tires of it. A child's spirit is like a child, you can never catch it by running after it; you must stand still, and, for love, it will soon itself come back.

PROCTOR: Aye, that's the truth of it, Rebecca.

MRS. PUTNAM: This is no silly season, Rebecca. My Ruth is bewildered, Rebecca; she cannot eat.

REBECCA: Perhaps she is not hungered yet. *To Parris*: I hope you are not decided to go in search of loose spirits, Mr. Parris. I've heard promise of that outside.

PARRIS: A wide opinion's running in the parish that the Devil may be among us, and I would satisfy them that they are wrong.

PROCTOR: Then let you come out and call them wrong. Did you consult the <u>wardens</u>（教区委员） before you called this minister to look for devils?

PARRIS: He is not coming to look for devils!

PROCTOR: Then what's he coming for?

PUTNAM: There be children dyin' in the village, Mister!

PROCTOR: I seen none dyin'. This society will not be a bag to swing around your head, Mr. Putnam. *To Parris*: Did you call a meeting before you—?

PUTNAM: I am sick of meetings; cannot the man turn his head without he have a meeting?

PROCTOR: He may turn his head, but not to Hell!

REBECCA: Pray, John, be calm. *Pause. He <u>defers to</u>（顺从） her.* Mr. Parris, I think you'd best send Reverend Hale back as soon as he come. This will set us all to arguin' again in the society, and we thought to have peace this year; I think we ought rely on the doctor now, and good prayer.

MRS. PUTNAM: Rebecca, the doctor's <u>baffled</u>（困惑的）!

REBECCA: If so he is, then let us go to God for the cause of it. There is prodigious danger in the seeking of loose spirits. I fear it, I fear it. Let us rather blame ourselves and—

PUTNAM: How may we blame ourselves? I am one of nine sons; the Putnam seed have peopled this province. And yet I have but one child left of eight—and now she shrivels!

REBECCA: I cannot <u>fathom</u>（看穿，理解） that.

MRS. PUTNAM, *with a growing edge of sarcasm*: But I must! You think it God's work you should never lose a child, nor grand-child either, and I bury all but one? There are wheels within wheels in this village, and fires within fires!

Unit 5

Arthur Miller and *The Crucible*

PUTNAM, *to Parris*: When Reverend Hale comes, you will proceed to look for signs of witchcraft here.

PROCTOR, *to Putnam*: You cannot command Mr. Parris. We vote by name in this society, not by <u>acreage</u>（田亩数）.

> ### Excerpt 3 (from Act 1)
> *The men begin to argue over a series of issues. Putnam points out that Proctor does not attend church regularly like a good citizen; Proctor criticizes Parris for preaching about money rather than God. Putnam, Proctor, and Giles Corey argue with Parris about his salary and his expectations as the minister of Salem. They are discussing lawsuits and land rights when Reverend Hale arrives at Parris's house. Parris tells Hale that he has found the girls dancing in the forest at night, and Mrs. Putnam admits having sent her daughter to conjure the spirits of her dead children. Then Hale prepares to examine Betty for signs of the Devil.*

GILES: Mr. Hale, I have always wanted to ask a learned man—what signifies the readin' of strange books?

HALE: What books?

GILES: I cannot tell; she hides them.

HALE: Who does this?

GILES: Martha, my wife. I have waked at night many a time and found her in a corner, readin' of a book. Now what do you make of that?

HALE: Why, that's not necessarily—

GILES: It discomfits me! Last night—mark this—I tried and tried and could not say my prayers. And then she close her book and walks out of the house, and suddenly—mark this—I could pray again!

Old Giles must be spoken for, if only because his fate was to be so remarkable and so different from that of all the others. He was in his early eighties at this time, and was the most comical hero in the history. No man has ever been blamed for so much. If a cow was missed, the first thought was to look for her around Corey's house; a fire blazing up at night brought suspicion of <u>arson</u>（纵火罪） to his door. He didn't give a hoot for public opinion, and only in his last years—after he had married Martha—did he bother much with the church. That she stopped his prayer is very probable, but he forgot to say that he'd only recently learned any prayers and it didn't take much to make him stumble over them. He was a <u>crank</u>（怪人） and a nuisance, but <u>withal</u>（仍然） a deeply innocent and brave man. In court once he was asked if it were true that he had been frightened by the strange behavior of a <u>hog</u>（阉猪） and had then said he knew it to be the Devil in an animal's shape. "What frighted you?" he was asked. He forgot everything but the word "frighted," and instantly replied, "I do not know that I ever spoke that word in my life."

HALE: Ah! The stoppage of prayer—that is strange. I'll speak further on that with you.

GILES: I'm not sayin' she's touched the Devil, now, but I'd admire to know what books she reads and why she hides them. She'll not answer me, y' see.

HALE: Aye, we'll discuss it. *To all*: Now mark me, if the Devil is in her you will witness some frightful wonders in this room, so please to keep your wits about you. Mr. Putnam, stand close in case she flies. Now, Betty, dear, will you sit up? *Putnam comes in closer, ready-handed. Hale sits Betty up, but she hangs limp in his hands.* Hmmm. *He observes her carefully. The others watch breathlessly.* Can you hear me? I am John Hale, minister of Beverly. I have come to help you, dear. Do you remember my two little girls in Beverly? *She does not stir in his hands.*

PARRIS, *in fright*: How can it be the Devil? Why would he choose my house to strike? We have all manner of licentious people in the village!

HALE: What victory would the Devil have to win a soul already bad? It is the best the Devil wants, and who is better than the minister?

GILES: That's deep, Mr, Parris, deep, deep!

PARRIS, *with resolution now*: Betty! Answer Mr. Hale! Betty!

HALE: Does someone afflict you, child? It need not be a woman, mind you, or a man. Perhaps some bird invisible to others comes to you—perhaps a pig, a mouse, or any beast at all. Is there some figure bids you fly? *The child remains limp in his hands. In silence he lays her back on the pillow. Now, holding out his hands toward her, he* <u>intones</u>（吟诵）: In nomine Domini Sabaoth sui filiique ite ad infernos. *She does not stir. He turns to Abigail, his eyes narrowing.* Abigail, what sort of dancing were you doing with her in the forest?

ABIGAIL: Why—common dancing is all.

PARRIS: I think I ought to say that I—I saw a kettle in the grass where they were dancing.

ABIGAIL: That were only soup.

HALE: What sort of soup were in this kettle, Abigail?

ABIGAIL: Why, it were beans—and <u>lentils</u>（扁豆）, I think, and—

HALE: Mr. Parris, you did not notice, did you, any living thing in the kettle? A mouse, perhaps, a spider, a frog—?

PARRIS, *fearfully*: I—do believe there were some movement—in the soup.

ABIGAIL: That jumped in, we never put it in!

HALE, *quickly*: What jumped in?

ABIGAIL: Why, a very little frog jumped—

Unit 5

Arthur Miller and *The Crucible*

PARRIS: A frog, Abby!

HALE, *grasping Abigail*: Abigail, it may be your cousin is dying. Did you call the Devil last night?

ABIGAIL: I never called him! Tituba, Tituba...

PARRIS, <u>blanched</u>（面色苍白）: She called the Devil?

HALE: I should like to speak with Tituba.

PARRIS: Goody Ann, will you bring her up? *Mrs. Putnam exits.*

HALE: How did she call him?

ABIGAIL: I know not—she spoke Barbados.

HALE: Did you feel any strangeness when she called him? A sudden cold wind, perhaps? A trembling below the ground?

ABIGAIL: I didn't see no Devil! *Shaking Betty*: Betty, wake up. Betty! Betty!

HALE: You cannot <u>evade</u>（规避） me, Abigail. Did your cousin drink any of the <u>brew</u>（炮制品） in that kettle?

ABIGAIL: She never drank it!

HALE: Did you drink it?

ABIGAIL: No, sir!

HALE: Did Tituba ask you to drink it?

ABIGAIL: She tried, but I refused.

HALE: Why are you concealing? Have you sold yourself to Lucifer[①]?

ABIGAIL: I never sold myself! I'm a good girl! I'm a proper girl!

    Mrs. Putnam enters with Tituba, and instantly Abigail points at Tituba.

ABIGAIL: She made me do it! She made Betty do it!

TITUBA, *shocked and angry*: Abby!

ABIGAIL: She makes me drink blood!

PARRIS: Blood!!

MRS. PUTNAM: My baby's blood?

TITUBA: No, no, chicken blood. I give she chicken blood!

HALE: Woman, have you <u>enlisted</u>（招募） these children for the Devil?

TITUBA: No, no, sir, I don't <u>truck</u>（交易） with no Devil!

HALE: Why can she not wake? Are you silencing this child?

TITUBA: I love me Betty!

HALE: You have sent your spirit out upon this child, have you not? Are you gathering souls for the Devil?

ABIGAIL: She sends her spirit on me in church; she makes me laugh at prayer!

PARRIS: She have often laughed at prayer!

ABIGAIL: She comes to me every night to go and drink blood!

TITUBA: You beg *me* to conjure! She beg *me* make <u>charm</u>（符咒）—

---

① Lucifer: a proud, rebellious archangel, identified with Satan, who fell from heaven.

ABIGAIL: Don't lie! *To Hale*: She comes to me while I sleep; she's always making me dream corruptions!

TITUBA: Why you say that, Abby?

ABIGAIL: Sometimes I wake and find myself standing in the open doorway and not a stitch on（一丝不挂） my body! I always hear her laughing in my sleep. I hear her singing her Barbados songs and tempting me with—

TITUBA: Mister Reverend, I never—

HALE, *resolved now*: Tituba, I want you to wake this child.

TITUBA: I have no power on this child, sir.

HALE: You most certainly do, and you will free her from it now! When did you compact（订立契约） with the Devil?

TITUBA: I don't compact with no Devil!

PARRIS: You will confess yourself or I will take you out and whip you to your death, Tituba!

PUTNAM: This woman must be hanged! She must be taken and hanged!

TITUBA, *terrified, falls to her knees*: No, no, don't hang Tituba! I tell him I don't desire to work for him, sir.

PARRIS: The Devil?

HALE: Then you saw him! *Tituba weeps.* Now Tituba, I know that when we bind（使……受合同约束） ourselves to Hell it is very hard to break with it. We are going to help you tear yourself free—

TITUBA, *frightened by the coming process*: Mister Reverend, I do believe somebody else be witchin' these children.

HALE: Who?

TITUBA: I don't know, sir, but the Devil got him numerous witches.

HALE: Does he! It is a clue. Tituba, look into my eyes. Come, look into me. *She raises her eyes to his fearfully.* You would be a good Christian woman, would you not, Tituba?

TITUBA: Aye, sir, a good Christian woman.

HALE: And you love these little children?

TITUBA: Oh, yes, sir, I don't desire to hurt little children.

HALE: And you love God, Tituba?

TITUBA: I love God with all my bein'.

HALE: Now, in God's holy name—

TITUBA: Bless Him. Bless Him. *She is rocking on her knees, sobbing in terror.*

HALE: And to His glory—

TITUBA: Eternal glory. Bless Him—bless God...

HALE: Open yourself, Tituba—open yourself and let God's holy light shine on you.

TITUBA: Oh, bless the Lord.

Unit 5

Arthur Miller and *The Crucible*

HALE: When the Devil comes to you does he ever come—with another person? *She stares up into his face,* Perhaps another person in the village? Someone you know.

PARRIS: Who came with him?

PUTNAM: Sarah Good? Did you ever see Sarah Good with him? Or Osburn?

PARRIS: Was it man or woman came with him?

TITUBA: Man or woman. Was—was woman.

PARRIS: What woman? A woman, you said. What woman?

TITUBA: It was black dark, and I—

PARRIS: You could see him, why could you not see her?

TITUBA: Well, they was always talking; they was always runnin' round and carryin' on—

PARRIS: You mean out of Salem? Salem witches?

TITUBA: I believe so, yes, sir.

Now Hale takes her hand. She is surprised.

HALE: Tituba. You must have no fear to tell us who they are, do you understand? We will protect you. The Devil can never overcome a minister. You know that, do you not?

TITUBA, *kisses Hale's hand*: Aye, sir, oh, I do.

HALE: You have confessed yourself to witchcraft, and that speaks a wish to come to Heaven's side. And we will bless you, Tituba.

TITUBA, *deeply relieved*: Oh, God bless you, Mr. Hale!

HALE, *with rising <u>exaltation</u>*（兴奋）: You are God's instrument put in our hands to discover the Devil's agents among us. You are selected, Tituba, you are chosen to help us <u>cleanse</u>（清洗） our village. So speak utterly, Tituba, turn your back on him and face God—face God, Tituba, and God will protect you.

TITUBA, *joining with him*: Oh, God, protect Tituba!

HALE, *kindly*: Who came to you with the Devil? Two? Three? Four? How many?

Tituba pants, and begins rocking back and forth again, staring ahead.

TITUBA: There was four. There was four.

PARRIS, *pressing in on her*: Who? Who? Their names, their names!

TITUBA, *suddenly bursting out*: Oh, how many times he bid me kill you, Mr. Parris!

PARRIS: Kill me!

TITUBA, *in a fury*: He say Mr. Parris must be kill! Mr. Parris no goodly man, Mr. Parris mean man and no gentle man, and he bid me rise out of my bed and cut your throat! *They gasp.* But I tell him "No! I don't hate that man. I don't want kill that man." But he say, "You work for me, Tituba, and I make you free! I give you pretty dress to wear, and put you way high up in the air, and you gone fly back to Barbados!" And I say, "You lie, Devil, you lie!" And then he come one stormy night to me, and he say, "Look! I have *white* people belong to me." And I look—

and there was Goody Good.

PARRIS: Sarah Good!

TITUBA, *rocking and weeping*: Aye, sir, and Goody Osburn.

MRS. PUTNAM: I knew it! Goody Osburn were midwife（产婆） to me three times. I begged you, Thomas, did I not? I begged him not to call Osburn because I feared her. My babies always shriveled in her hands!

HALE: Take courage, you must give us all their names. How can you bear to see this child suffering? Look at her, Tituba. *He is indicating Betty on the bed.* Look at her God-given innocence; her soul is so tender; we must protect her, Tituba; the Devil is out and preying on（折磨） her like a beast upon the flesh of the pure lamb. God will bless you for your help.

Abigail rises, staring as though inspired, and cries out.

ABIGAIL: I want to open myself! *They turn to her, startled. She is* enraptured（狂喜）, *as though in a* pearly（珍珠般的） *light.* I want the light of God, I want the sweet love of Jesus! I danced for the Devil; I saw him; I wrote in his book; I go back to Jesus; I kiss His hand. I saw Sarah Good with the Devil! I saw Goody Osburn with the Devil! I saw Bridget Bishop with the Devil!

As she is speaking, Betty is rising from the bed, a fever in her eyes, and picks up the chant.

BETTY, *staring too*: I saw George Jacobs with the Devil! I saw Goody Howe with the Devil!

PARRIS: She speaks! *He rushes to embrace Betty.* She speaks!

HALE: Glory to God! It is broken, they are free!

BETTY, *calling out hysterically and with great relief*: I saw Martha Bellows with the Devil!

ABIGAIL: I saw Goody Sibber with the Devil! *It is rising to a great* glee（欢乐）.

PUTNAM: The marshal（典狱长）, I'll call the marshal!

Parris is shouting a prayer of thanksgiving.

BETTY: I saw Alice Barrow with the Devil!

The curtain begins to fall.

HALE, *as Putnam goes out*: Let the marshal bring irons!

ABIGAIL: I saw Goody Hawkins with the Devil!

BETTY: I saw Goody Bibber with the Devil!

ABIGAIL: I saw Goody Booth with the Devil!

On their ecstatic（欣喜若狂的） *cries*

THE CURTAIN FALLS

Unit 5

Arthur Miller and *The Crucible*

Excerpt 4 (from Act 2)

Eight days have passed since Abigail and Betty began accusing individuals of witchcraft. Proctor returns late after working in the fields and eats dinner with his wife Elizabeth. They talk about the trials that are going on in Salem. Evidently, there is tension between them.

PROCTOR: I think you're sad again. Are you?

ELIZABETH—*she doesn't want friction（摩擦）, and yet she must*: You come so late I thought you'd gone to Salem this afternoon.

PROCTOR: Why? I have no business in Salem.

ELIZABETH: You did speak of going, earlier this week.

PROCTOR—*he knows what she means*: I thought better of it since.

ELIZABETH: Mary Warren's there today.

PROCTOR: Why'd you let her? You heard me forbid her go to Salem any more!

ELIZABETH: I couldn't stop her.

PROCTOR, *holding back a full condemnation（谴责）of her*: It is a fault, it is a fault, Elizabeth—you're the mistress here, not Mary Warren.

ELIZABETH: She frightened all my strength away.

PROCTOR: How may that mouse frighten you, Elizabeth? You—

ELIZABETH: It is a mouse no more. I forbid her go, and she raises up her chin like the daughter of a prince and says to me, "I must go to Salem, Goody Proctor; I am an official of the court!"

PROCTOR: Court! What court?

ELIZABETH: Aye, it is a proper court they have now. They've sent four judges out of Boston, she says, weighty magistrates（地方法官）of the General Court, and at the head sits the Deputy Governor（副总督）of the Province.

PROCTOR, *astonished*: Why, she's mad.

ELIZABETH: I would to God she were. There be fourteen people in the jail now, she says. *Proctor simply looks at her, unable to grasp it.* And they'll be tried, and the court have power to hang them too, she says.

PROCTOR, *scoffing（嘲笑）, but without conviction*: Ah, they'd never hang—

ELIZABETH: The Deputy Governor promise hangin' if they'll not confess, John. The town's gone wild, I think. She speak of Abigail, and I thought she were a saint, to hear her. Abigail brings the other girls into the court, and where she walks the crowd will part like the sea for Israel[①]. And folks are brought before them, and if they scream and howl and fall to the floor the person's clapped in the jail for

---

① part ... Israel: allusion to the Bible story of Exodus. When Moses and the Israelites arrived at the coast of the Red Sea, he parted the sea with the help of God, so his people were able to cross the sea to the other shore.

bewitchin'（对……施巫术）them.

PROCTOR, *wide-eyed*: Oh, it is a black mischief.

ELIZABETH: I think you must go to Salem, John. *He turns to her.* I think so. You must tell them it is a fraud.

PROCTOR, *thinking beyond this*: Aye, it is, it is surely.

ELIZABETH: Let you go to Ezekiel Cheever—he knows you well. And tell him what she said to you last week in her uncle's house. She said it had naught to do with witchcraft, did she not?

PROCTOR, *in thought*: Aye, she did, she did. *Now, a pause.*

ELIZABETH, *quietly, fearing to anger him by prodding*（敦促）: God forbid you keep that from the court, John. I think they must be told.

PROCTOR, *quietly, struggling with his thought*: Aye, they must, they must. It is a wonder they do believe her.

ELIZABETH: I would go to Salem now, John—let you go tonight.

PROCTOR: I'll think on it.

ELIZABETH, *with her courage now*: You cannot keep it, John.

PROCTOR, *angering*: I know I cannot keep it. I say I will think on it!

ELIZABETH, *hurt, and very coldly*: Good, then, let you think on it. *She stands and starts to walk out of the room.*

PROCTOR: I am only wondering how I may prove what she told me, Elizabeth. If the girl's a saint now, I think it is not easy to prove she's fraud, and the town gone so silly. She told it to me in a room alone—I have no proof for it.

ELIZABETH: You were alone with her?

PROCTOR, *stubbornly*: For a moment alone, aye.

ELIZABETH: Why, then, it is not as you told me.

PROCTOR, *his anger rising*: For a moment, I say. The others come in soon after.

ELIZABETH, *quietly—she has suddenly lost all faith in him*: Do as you wish, then. *She starts to turn.*

PROCTOR: Woman. *She turns to him.* I'll not have your suspicion any more.

ELIZABETH, *a little loftily*（高傲地）: I have no—

PROCTOR: I'll not have it!

ELIZABETH: Then let you not earn it.

PROCTOR, *with a violent undertone*: You doubt me yet?

ELIZABETH, *with a smile, to keep her dignity*: John, if it were not Abigail that you must go to hurt, would you falter now? I think not.

PROCTOR: Now look you—

ELIZABETH: I see what I see, John.

PROCTOR, *with solemn warning*: You will not judge me more, Elizabeth. I have good reason to think before I charge fraud on Abigail, and I will think on it. Let you

Unit 5

Arthur Miller and *The Crucible*

look to your own improvement before you go to judge your husband any more. I have forgot Abigail, and—

ELIZABETH: And I.

PROCTOR: Spare me! You forget nothin' and forgive nothin'. Learn charity, woman. I have gone tiptoe in this house all seven month since she is gone. I have not moved from there to there without I think to please you, and still an everlasting funeral marches round your heart. I cannot speak but I am doubted, every moment judged for lies, as though I come into a court when I come into this house!

ELIZABETH: John, you are not open with me. You saw her with a crowd, you said. Now you—

PROCTOR: I'll plead my honesty no more, Elizabeth.

ELIZABETH—*now she would justify herself*: John, I am only—

PROCTOR: No more! I should have roared you down when first you told me your suspicion. But I wilted（畏缩）, and, like a Christian, I confessed. Confessed! Some dream I had must have mistaken you for God that day. But you're not, you're not, and let you remember it! Let you look sometimes for the goodness in me, and judge me not.

ELIZABETH: I do not judge you. The magistrate sits in your heart that judges you. I never thought you but a good man, John—*with a smile*—only somewhat bewildered.

PROCTOR, *laughing bitterly*: Oh, Elizabeth, your justice would freeze beer! *He turns suddenly toward a sound outside. He starts for the door as Mary Warren enters. As soon as he sees her, he goes directly to her and grabs her by her cloak, furious.* How do you go to Salem when I forbid it? Do you mock me? *Shaking her.* I'll whip you if you dare leave this house again!

Strangely, she doesn't resist him, but hangs limply by his grip.

MARY WARREN: I am sick, I am sick, Mr. Proctor. Pray, pray, hurt me not. *Her strangeness throws him off（使……困窘）, and her evident pallor and weakness. He frees her.* My insides are all shuddery（打战）; I am in the proceedings（诉讼） all day, sir.

PROCTOR, *with draining（逐渐耗尽的） anger—his curiosity is draining it*: And what of these proceedings here? When will you proceed to keep this house, as you are paid nine pound a year to do—and my wife not wholly well?

As though to compensate, Mary Warren goes to Elizabeth with a small rag（碎布） doll.

MARY WARREN: I made a gift for you today, Goody Proctor. I had to sit long hours in a chair, and passed the time with sewing（缝制）.

ELIZABETH, *perplexed, looking at the doll*: Why, thank you, it's a fair poppet（布娃娃）.

MARY WARREN, *with a trembling,* decayed（衰弱的） *voice*: We must all love each other now, Goody Proctor.

ELIZABETH, *amazed at her strangeness*: Aye, indeed we must.

MARY WARREN, *glancing at the room*: I'll get up early in the morning and clean the house. I must sleep now. *She turns and starts off.*

PROCTOR: Mary. *She halts.* Is it true? There be fourteen women arrested?

MARY WARREN: No, sir. There be thirty-nine now—*She suddenly breaks off and sobs and sits down, exhausted.*

ELIZABETH: Why, she's weepin'! What ails you, child?

MARY WARREN: Goody Osburn—will hang!

There is a shocked pause, while she sobs.

PROCTOR: Hang! *He calls into her face.* Hang, y'say?

MARY WARREN, *through her weeping*: Aye.

PROCTOR: The Deputy Governor will permit it?

MARY WARREN: He sentenced her. He must. *To* ameliorate（缓和） *it*: But not Sarah Good. For Sarah Good confessed, y'see.

PROCTOR: Confessed? To what?

MARY WARREN: That she—*in horror at the memory*—she sometimes made a compact with Lucifer, and wrote her name in his black book—with her blood—and bound herself to torment Christians till God's thrown down—and we all must worship Hell forevermore.

Pause.

PROCTOR: But—surely you know what a jabberer（说话荒唐的人） she is. Did you tell them that?

MARY WARREN: Mr. Proctor, in open court she near to choked us all to death.

PROCTOR: How, choked you?

MARY WARREN: She sent her spirit out.

ELIZABETH: Oh, Mary, Mary, surely you—

MARY WARREN, *with an indignant edge*: She tried to kill me many times, Goody Proctor!

ELIZABETH: Why, I never heard you mention that before.

MARY WARREN: I never knew it before. I never knew anything before. When she come into the court I say to myself, I must not accuse this woman, for she sleep in ditches（沟壑）, and so very old and poor. But then—then she sit there, denying and denying, and I feel a misty（朦胧的） coldness climbin' up my back, and the skin on my skull begin to creep（起鸡皮疙瘩）, and I feel a clamp（夹钳） around my neck and I cannot breathe air; and then—*entranced*（着迷一般）—I hear a voice, a screamin' voice, and it were my voice—and all at once I remembered everything she done to me!

Unit 5

Arthur Miller and *The Crucible*

PROCTOR: Why? What did she do to you?

MARY WARREN, *like one awakened to a marvelous secret insight*: So many time, Mr. Proctor, she come to this very door, beggin' bread and a cup of cider—and mark this: whenever I turned her away empty, she *mumbled*.

ELIZABETH: Mumbled! She may mumble if she's hungry.

MARY WARREN: But what does she mumble? You must remember, Goody Proctor. Last month—a Monday, I think—she walked away, and I thought my guts（内脏）would burst for two days after. Do you remember it?

ELIZABETH: Why—I do, I think, but—

MARY WARREN: And so I told that to Judge Hathorne, and he asks her so. "Sarah Good," says he, "what curse do you mumble that this girl must fall sick after turning you away?" And then she replies—*mimicking an old crone*（丑老太婆）—"Why, your excellence, no curse at all. I only say my commandments（戒律）; I hope I may say my commandments," says she!

ELIZABETH: And that's an upright answer.

MARY WARREN: Aye, but then Judge Hathorne say, "Recite for us your commandments!"—*leaning avidly toward them*—and of all the ten she could not say a single one. She never knew no commandments, and they had her in a flat lie!

PROCTOR: And so condemned her?

MARY WARREN, *now a little strained, seeing his stubborn doubt*: Why, they must when she condemned herself.

PROCTOR: But the proof, the proof!

MARY WARREN, *with greater impatience with him*: I told you the proof. It's hard proof, hard as rock, the judges said.

PROCTOR, *pauses an instant, then*: You will not go to court again, Mary Warren.

MARY WARREN: I must tell you, sir, I will be gone every day now. I am amazed you do not see what weighty work we do.

PROCTOR: What work you do! It's strange work for a Christian girl to hang old women!

MARY WARREN: But, Mr. Proctor, they will not hang them if they confess. Sarah Good will only sit in jail some time—*recalling*—and here's a wonder for you; think on this. Goody Good is pregnant!

ELIZABETH: Pregnant! Are they mad? The woman's near to sixty!

MARY WARREN: They had Doctor Griggs examine her, and she's full to the brim（鼓满了）. And smokin' a pipe all these years, and no husband either! But she's safe, thank God, for they'll not hurt the innocent child, But be that not a marvel? You must see it, sir, it's God's work we do. So I'll be gone every day for some time. I'm—I am an official of the court, they say, and I—*She has been edging*（徐徐移动）*toward offstage*（舞台后部）.

PROCTOR: I'll official you! *He strides to the mantel（壁炉架）, takes down the whip hanging there.*

MARY WARREN, *terrified, but coming erect, striving for her authority*: I'll not stand whipping any more!

ELIZABETH, *hurriedly, as Proctor approaches*: Mary, promise now you'll stay at home—

MARY WARREN, *backing from him, but keeping her erect posture, striving, striving for her way*: The Devil's loose（横行）in Salem, Mr. Proctor; we must discover where he's hiding!

PROCTOR: I'll whip the Devil out of you! *With whip raised he reaches out for her, and she streaks（飞跑）away and yells.*

MARY WARREN, *pointing at Elizabeth*: I saved her life today!

    Silence. His whip comes down.

ELIZABETH, *softly*: I am accused?

MARY WARREN, *quaking*: Somewhat mentioned. But I said I never see no sign you ever sent your spirit out to hurt no one, and seeing I do live so closely with you, they dismissed（驳回）it.

ELIZABETH: Who accused me?

MARY WARREN: I am bound by law, I cannot tell it. *To Proctor*: I only hope you'll not be so sarcastical（爱挖苦人的）no more. Four judges and the King's deputy（代表）sat to dinner with us but an hour ago. I—I would have you speak civilly to me, from this out.

PROCTOR, *in horror, muttering in disgust at her*: Go to bed.

MARY WARREN, *with a stamp（跺脚）of her foot*: I'll not be ordered to bed no more, Mr. Proctor! I am eighteen and a woman, however single!

PROCTOR: Do you wish to sit up（熬夜不睡）? Then sit up.

MARY WARREN: I wish to go to bed!

PROCTOR, *in anger*: Good night, then!

MARY WARREN: Good night. *Dissatisfied, uncertain of herself, she goes out. Wide-eyed, both, Proctor and Elizabeth stand staring.*

ELIZABETH, *quietly*: Oh, the noose（绞索）, the noose is up!

PROCTOR: There'll be no noose.

ELIZABETH: She wants me dead. I knew all week it would come to this!

PROCTOR, *without conviction*: They dismissed it. You heard her say—

ELIZABETH: And what of tomorrow? She will cry me out until they take me!

PROCTOR: Sit you down.

ELIZABETH: She wants me dead, John, you know it!

PROCTOR: I say sit down! *She sits, trembling. He speaks quietly, trying to keep his wits.* Now we must be wise, Elizabeth.

Unit 5

Arthur Miller and *The Crucible*

ELIZABETH, *with sarcasm, and a sense of being lost*: Oh, indeed, indeed!

PROCTOR: Fear nothing. I'll find Ezekiel Cheever. I'll tell him she said it were all sport.

ELIZABETH: John, with so many in the jail, more than Cheever's help is needed now, I think. Would you favor me with this? Go to Abigail.

PROCTOR, *his soul hardening as he senses...*: What have I to say to Abigail?

ELIZABETH, <u>delicately</u>（小心翼翼地）: John—grant me this. You have a <u>faulty</u>（错误的） understanding of young girls. There is a promise made in any bed—

PROCTOR, *striving against his anger*: What promise!

ELIZABETH: Spoke or silent, a promise is surely made. And she may <u>dote on</u>（珍视） it now—I am sure she does—and thinks to kill me, then to take my place.

Proctor's anger is rising; he cannot speak.

ELIZABETH: It is her dearest hope, John, I know it. There be a thousand names; why does she call mine? There be a certain danger in calling such a name—I am no Goody Good that sleeps in ditches, nor Osburn, drunk and <u>half-witted</u>（愚笨的）. She'd dare not call out such a farmer's wife but there be <u>monstrous</u>（巨大的） profit in it. She thinks to take my place, John.

PROCTOR: She cannot think it! *He knows it is true.*

ELIZABETH, *"reasonably"*: John, have you ever shown her somewhat of <u>contempt</u>（蔑视）? She cannot pass you in the church but you will blush—

PROCTOR: I may blush for my sin.

ELIZABETH: I think she sees another meaning in that blush.

PROCTOR: And what see you? What see you, Elizabeth?

ELIZABETH, *"<u>conceding</u>"*（让步；承认）: I think you be somewhat ashamed, for I am there, and she so close.

PROCTOR: When will you know me, woman? Were I stone I would have cracked for shame this seven month!

ELIZABETH: Then go and tell her she's a <u>whore</u>（娼妇）. Whatever promise she may sense—break it, John, break it.

PROCTOR, <u>*between his teeth*</u>（咬牙切齿）: Good, then. I'll go. *He starts for his <u>rifle</u>*（步枪）.

ELIZABETH, *trembling, fearfully*: Oh, how unwillingly!

PROCTOR, *turning on her, rifle in hand*: I will curse her hotter than the oldest <u>cinder</u>（炭火） in hell. But pray, <u>begrudge</u>（因为……发牢骚） me not my anger!

ELIZABETH: Your anger! I only ask you—

PROCTOR: Woman, am I so <u>base</u>（卑劣）? Do you truly think me base?

ELIZABETH: I never called you base.

PROCTOR: Then how do you charge me with such a promise? The promise that a stallion gives a <u>mare</u>（母马） I gave that girl!

ELIZABETH: Then why do you anger with me when I bid you break it?

PROCTOR: Because it speaks deceit(欺骗), and I am honest! But I'll plead no more! I see now your spirit twists(纠缠) around the single error of my life, and I will never tear it free!

ELIZABETH, *crying out*: You'll tear it free—when you come to know that I will be your only wife, or no wife at all! She has an arrow in you yet, John Proctor, and you know it well!

Excerpt 5 (from Act 3)

The wives of John Proctor, Francis Nurse and Giles Corey have all been charged with witchcraft. In the Salem meeting house, the court is questioning Martha Corey when Giles Corey interrupts the proceedings by shouting that Putnam is only making a grab for more land. Giles and Francis state that they both have evidence for the court that the girls are pretending.

Then Proctor brings along Mary Warren, who tells Judge Danforth that she and the other girls only pretended to be afflicted by witchcraft. Shocked, Danforth asks Proctor if he is attempting to undermine the court. When Proctor assures him that he just wants to free his wife, Danforth declares that he need not worry about Elizabeth's imminent execution because she claims to be pregnant.

DANFORTH: Mr. Proctor, this morning, your wife send me a claim in which she states that she is pregnant now.

PROCTOR: My wife pregnant!

DANFORTH: There be no sign of it—we have examined her body.

PROCTOR: But if she say she is pregnant, then she must be! That woman will never lie, Mr. Danforth.

DANFORTH: She will not?

PROCTOR: Never, sir, never.

DANFORTH: We have thought it too convenient to be credited(相信). However, if I should tell you now that I will let her be kept another month; and if she begin to show her natural signs, you shall have her living yet another year until she is delivered(给……接生)—what say you to that? *John Proctor is struck silent.* Come now. You say your only purpose is to save your wife. Good, then, she is saved at least this year, and a year is long. What say you, sir? It is done now. *In conflict, Proctor glances at Francis and Giles.* Will you drop this charge?

PROCTOR: I—I think I cannot.

DANFORTH, *now an almost imperceptible(察觉不到的) hardness in his voice*:

Unit 5
Arthur Miller and *The Crucible*

Then your purpose is somewhat larger.

PARRIS: He's come to overthrow this court, Your Honor!

PROCTOR: These are my friends. Their wives are also accused—

DANFORTH, *with a sudden briskness（尖刻）of manner*: I judge you not, sir. I am ready to hear your evidence.

PROCTOR: I come not to hurt the court; I only—

DANFORTH, *cutting him off*: Marshal, go into the court and bid Judge Stoughton and Judge Sewall declare recess（休庭）for one hour. And let them go to the tavern, if they will. All witnesses and prisoners are to be kept in the building.

HERRICK: Aye, sir. *Very deferentially*: If I may say it, sir, I know this man all my life. It is a good man, sir.

DANFORTH—*it is the reflection（影射）on himself he resents*: I am sure of it, Marshal. *Herrick nods, then goes out.* Now, what deposition（证词）do you have for us, Mr. Proctor? And I beg you be clear, open as the sky, and honest.

PROCTOR, *as he takes out several papers*: I am no lawyer, so I'll—

DANFORTH: The pure in heart need no lawyers. Proceed as you will.

PROCTOR, *handing Danforth a paper*: Will you read this first, sir? It's a sort of testament（证明）. The people signing it declare their good opinion of Rebecca, and my wife, and Martha Corey. *Danforth looks down at the paper.*

PARRIS, *to enlist（谋取）Danforth's sarcasm（挖苦）*: Their good opinion! *But Danforth goes on reading, and Proctor is heartened（鼓励）.*

PROCTOR: These are all landholding farmers, members of the church. *Delicately, trying to point out a paragraph*: If you'll notice, sir—they've known the women many years and never saw no sign they had dealings with the Devil.

Parris nervously moves over and reads over Danforth's shoulder.

DANFORTH, *glancing down a long list*: How many names are here?

FRANCIS: Ninety-one, Your Excellency.

PARRIS, *sweating*: These people should be summoned（传唤）. *Danforth looks up at him questioningly.* For questioning.

FRANCIS, *trembling with anger*: Mr. Danforth, I gave them all my word no harm would come to them for signing this.

PARRIS: This is a clear attack upon the court!

HALE, *to Parris, trying to contain（克制）himself*: Is every defense an attack upon the court? Can no one—?

PARRIS: All innocent and Christian people are happy for the courts in Salem! These people are gloomy for it. *To Danforth directly*: And I think you will want to know, from each and every one of them, what discontents them with you!

HATHORNE: I think they ought to be examined, sir.

DANFORTH: It is not necessarily an attack, I think. Yet—

FRANCIS: These are all covenanted Christians, sir.

DANFORTH: Then I am sure they may have nothing to fear. *Hands Cheever the paper*. Mr. Cheever, have warrants（逮捕令） drawn for all of these—arrest for examination. *To Proctor*: Now, Mister, what other information do you have for us? *Francis is still standing, horrified.* You may sit, Mr. Nurse.

FRANCIS: I have brought trouble on these people; I have—

DANFORTH: No, old man, you have not hurt these people if they are of good conscience. But you must understand, sir, that a person is either with this court or he must be counted against it, there be no road between. This is a sharp time, now, a precise time—we live no longer in the dusky（朦胧的） afternoon when evil mixed itself with good and befuddled（迷惑） the world. Now, by God's grace, the shining sun is up, and them that fear not light will surely praise it. I hope you will be one of those. *Mary Warren suddenly sobs.* She's not hearty, I see.

PROCTOR: No, she's not, sir. *To Mary, bending to her, holding her hand, quietly*: Now remember what the angel Raphael said to the boy Tobias[①]. Remember it.

MARY WARREN, *hardly audible*: Aye.

PROCTOR: "Do that which is good, and no harm shall come to thee."

MARY WARREN: Aye.

DANFORTH: Come, man, we wait you.

    Marshal Herrick returns, and takes his post at the door.

GILES: John, my deposition, give him mine.

PROCTOR: Aye. *He hands Danforth another paper.* This is Mr. Corey's deposition.

DANFORTH: Oh? *He looks down at it. Now Hathorne comes behind him and reads with him.*

HATHORNE, *suspiciously*: What lawyer drew this, Corey?

GILES: You know I never hired a lawyer in my life, Hathorne.

DANFORTH, *finishing the reading*: It is very well phrased（措辞）. My compliments. Mr. Parris, if Mr. Putnam is in the court, will you bring him in? *Hathorne takes the deposition, and walks to the window with it. Parris goes into the court.* You have no legal training, Mr. Corey?

GILES, *very pleased*: I have the best, sir—I am thirty-three time in court in my life. And always plaintiff（原告）, too.

DANFORTH: Oh, then you're much put-upon（被占便宜）.

GILES: I am never put-upon; I know my rights, sir, and I will have them. You know, your father tried（审理） a case of mine—might be thirty-five year ago, I think.

DANFORTH: Indeed.

---

① Raphael ... Tobias: In the Bible, the Archangel Raphael helped a young man named Tobias. When Tobias is sent by his blind father to a distant land to collect a debt, the archangel appears in the guise of an older companion and guide.

Unit 5

Arthur Miller and *The Crucible*

GILES: He never spoke to you of it?

DANFORTH: No, I cannot recall it.

GILES: That's strange, he give me nine pound damages. He were a fair judge, your father. Y'see, I had a white mare that time, and this fellow come to borrow the mare—*Enter Parris with Thomas Putnam. When he sees Putnam, Giles' ease（自在）goes; he is hard.* Aye, there he is.

DANFORTH: Mr. Putnam, I have here an accusation by Mr. Corey against you. He states that you coldly prompted（怂恿）your daughter to cry witchery upon George Jacobs that is now in jail.

PUTNAM: It is a lie.

DANFORTH, *turning to Giles*: Mr. Putnam states your charge is a lie. What say you to that?

GILES, *furious, his fists clenched*: A fart on Thomas Putnam, that is what I say to that!

DANFORTH: What proof do you submit for your charge, sir?

GILES: My proof is there! *Pointing to the paper.* If Jacobs hangs for a witch he forfeit（丧失）up his property—that's law! And there is none but Putnam with the coin to buy so great a piece. This man is killing his neighbors for their land!

DANFORTH: But proof, sir, proof.

GILES, *pointing at his deposition*: The proof is there! I have it from an honest man who heard Putnam say it! The day his daughter cried out on Jacobs, he said she'd given him a fair gift of land.

HATHORNE: And the name of this man?

GILES, *taken aback*: What name?

HATHORNE: The man that give you this information.

GILES, *hesitates, then*: Why, I—I cannot give you his name.

HATHORNE: And why not?

GILES, *hesitates, then bursts out*: You know well why not! He'll lay in jail if I give his name!

HATHORNE: This is contempt of the court, Mr. Danforth!

DANFORTH, *to avoid that*: You will surely tell us the name.

GILES: I will not give you no name, I mentioned my wife's name once and I'll burn in hell long enough for that. I stand mute.

DANFORTH: In that case, I have no choice but to arrest you for contempt of this court, do you know that?

GILES: This is a hearing; you cannot clap me for contempt of a hearing.

DANFORTH: Oh, it is a proper lawyer! Do you wish me to declare the court in full session（开庭）here? Or will you give me good reply?

GILES, *faltering*（犹豫）: I cannot give you no name, sir, I cannot.

DANFORTH: You are a foolish old man. Mr. Cheever, begin the record. The court is now in session. I ask you, Mr. Corey—

PROCTOR, *breaking in*: Your Honor—he has the story in confidence（作为秘密）, sir, and he—

PARRIS: The Devil lives on such confidences! *To Danforth*: Without confidences there could be no conspiracy（阴谋）, Your Honor!

HATHORNE. I think it must be broken, sir.

DANFORTH, *to Giles*: Old man, if your informant（告密人）tells the truth let him come here openly like a decent man. But if he hide in anonymity（匿名）I must know why. Now sir, the government and central church demand of you the name of him who reported Mr. Thomas Putnam a common murderer.

HALE: Excellency（阁下）—

DANFORTH: Mr. Hale.

HALE: We cannot blink it more. There is a prodigious fear of this court in the country—

DANFORTH: Then there is a prodigious guilt in the country. Are *you* afraid to be questioned here?

HALE: I may only fear the Lord, sir, but there is fear in the country nevertheless.

DANFORTH, *angered now*: Reproach me not with the fear in the country; there is fear in the country because there is a moving plot to topple Christ in the country!

HALE: But it does not follow that everyone accused is part of it.

DANFORTH: No uncorrupted man may fear this court, Mr. Hale! None! *To Giles*: You are under arrest in contempt of this court. Now sit you down and take counsel（商议）with yourself, or you will be set in the jail until you decide to answer all questions.

Giles Corey makes a rush for Putnam. Proctor lunges（前冲）and holds him.

PROCTOR: No, Giles!

GILES, *over Proctor's shoulder at Putnam*: I'll cut your throat, Putnam, I'll kill you yet!

PROCTOR, *forcing him into a chair*: Peace, Giles, peace. *Releasing him.* We'll prove ourselves. Now we will. *He starts to turn to Danforth.*

GILES: Say nothin' more, John. *Pointing at Danforth*: He's only playin' you! He means to hang us all!

Mary Warren bursts into sobs.

DANFORTH: This is a court of law, Mister. I'll have no effrontery（放肆）here!

PROCTOR: Forgive him, sir, for his old age. Peace, Giles, we'll prove it all now. *He lifts up Mary's chin.* You cannot weep, Mary. Remember the angel, what he say to the boy. Hold to it, now; there is your rock（支柱）. *Mary quiets. He takes out a paper, and turns to Danforth.* This is Mary Warren's deposition. I—I would ask you remember, sir, while you read it, that until two week ago she were no different than the other children are today. *He is speaking reasonably, restraining all his fears, his anger, his anxiety.* You saw her scream, she howled, she swore <u>familiar spirits</u>（女巫的精灵） choked her; she even testified that Satan, in the form of women now in jail, tried to win her soul away, and then when she refused—

DANFORTH: We know all this.

PROCTOR: Aye, sir. She swears now that she never saw Satan; nor any spirit, vague or clear, that Satan may have sent to hurt her. And she declares her friends are lying now.

> *Proctor starts to hand Danforth the deposition, and Hale comes up to Danforth in a trembling state.*

HALE: Excellency, a moment. I think this goes to the heart of the matter.

DANFORTH, *with deep <u>misgivings</u>（担忧）*: It surely does.

HALE: I cannot say he is an honest man; I know him little. But in all justice, sir, a claim so weighty cannot be argued by a farmer. In God's name, sir, stop here; send him home and let him come again with a lawyer—

DANFORTH, *patiently*: Now look you, Mr. Hale—

HALE: Excellency, I have signed seventy-two death warrants; I am a minister of the Lord, and I dare not take a life without there be a proof so <u>immaculate</u>（完美无瑕的） no slightest <u>qualm</u>（疑虑） of conscience may doubt it.

DANFORTH: Mr. Hale, you surely do not doubt my justice.

HALE: I have this morning signed away the soul of Rebecca Nurse, Your Honor. I'll not conceal it, my hand shakes yet as with a wound! I pray you, sir, *this* argument let lawyers present to you.

DANFORTH: Mr. Hale, believe me; for a man of such terrible learning you are most bewildered—I hope you will forgive me. I have been thirty-two year <u>at the bar</u>（做律师）, sir, and I should be <u>confounded</u>（惊慌失措） were I called upon to defend these people. Let you consider, now—*To Proctor and the others*: And I bid you all do likewise. In an ordinary crime, how does one defend the accused? One calls up witnesses to prove his innocence. But witchcraft is *<u>ipso facto</u>*（拉丁语：根据事实本身）, on its face and by its nature, an invisible crime, is it not? Therefore, who may possibly be witness to it? The witch and the victim. None other. Now we cannot hope the witch will accuse herself; granted? Therefore, we must rely upon her victims—and they do testify, the children certainly do testify. As for the witches, none will deny that we are most eager for all their confessions. Therefore, what is left for a lawyer to bring out? I think I have made my point. Have I not?

HALE: But this child claims the girls are not truthful, and if they are not—

DANFORTH: That is precisely what I am about to consider, sir. What more may you ask of me? Unless you doubt my probity?

HALE, *defeated*: I surely do not, sir. Let you consider it, then.
DANFORTH: And let you put your heart to rest. Her deposition, Mr. Proctor.

> **Excerpt 6 (from Act 3, continued)**
> As one of the girls who have instigated the witch trials, Mary Warren provides a deposition that carries great weight. However, as this excerpt shows, it fails to function properly when facing Judge Hathorne's challenge. To save his wife, John Proctor has to resort to a desperate act.

Proctor hands it to him. Hathorne rises, goes beside Danforth, and starts reading. Parris comes to his other side. Danforth looks at John Proctor, then proceeds to read. Hale gets up, finds position near the judge, reads too. Proctor glances at Giles. Francis prays silently, hands pressed together. Cheever waits placidly（平静地）, *the* sublime（庄严的） *official,* dutiful（忠于职守的）. *Mary Warren sobs once. John Proctor touches her head reassuringly. Presently Danforth lifts his eyes, stands up, takes out a kerchief and blows his nose. The others stand aside as he moves in thought toward the window.*

PARRIS, *hardly able to contain his anger and fear*: I should like to question—

DANFORTH—*his first real outburst, in which his contempt for Parris is clear*: Mr. Parris, I bid you be silent! *He stands in silence, looking out the window. Now, having established that he will set the* gait（步调）: Mr. Cheever, will you go into the court and bring the children here? *Cheever gets up and goes out upstage. Danforth now turns to Mary.* Mary Warren, how came you to this turnabout（反悔）? Has Mr. Proctor threatened you for this deposition?

MARY WARREN: No, sir.

DANFORTH: Has he ever threatened you?

MARY WARREN, *weaker*: No, sir.

DANFORTH, *sensing a weakening*: Has he threatened you?

MARY WARREN: No, sir.

DANFORTH: Then you tell me that you sat in my court, callously（冷酷无情地） lying, when you knew that people would hang by your evidence? *She does not answer.* Answer me!

MARY WARREN, *almost inaudibly*: I did, sir.

DANFORTH: How were you instructed in your life? Do you not know that God damns all liars? *She cannot speak.* Or is it now that you lie!

MARY WARREN: No, sir—I am with God now.

DANFORTH: You are with God now.

MARY WARREN: Aye, sir.

DANFORTH, *containing himself*: I will tell you this—you are either lying now, or you were lying in the court, and in either case you have committed perjury（伪证） and you will go to jail for it. You cannot lightly say you lied, Mary. Do you know that?

MARY WARREN: I cannot lie no more. I am with God, I am with God.

But she breaks into sobs at the thought of it, and the right door opens, and enter Susanna Walcott, Mercy Lewis, Betty Parris, and finally Abigail. Cheever comes to Danforth.

CHEEVER: Ruth Putnam's not in the court, sir, nor the other children.

DANFORTH: These will be sufficient. Sit you down, children. *Silently they sit.* Your friend, Mary Warren, has given us a deposition. In which she swears that she never saw familiar spirits, apparitions（幽灵）, nor any manifest（显现） of the Devil. She claims as well that none of you have seen these things either. *Slight pause.* Now, children, this is a court of law. The law, based upon the Bible, and the Bible, writ by Almighty God, forbid the practice of witchcraft, and describe death as the penalty thereof. But likewise, children, the law and Bible damn all bearers of false witness. *Slight pause.* Now then. It does not escape me that this deposition may be devised to blind us; it may well be that Mary Warren has been conquered by Satan, who sends her here to distract our sacred purpose. If so, her neck will break for it. But if she speak true, I bid you now drop your guile（诡计） and confess your pretense, for a quick confession will go easier with you. *Pause.* Abigail Williams, rise. *Abigail slowly rises.* Is there any truth in this?

ABIGAIL: No, sir.

DANFORTH, *thinks, glances at Mary, then back to Abigail*: Children, a very augur bit （钻头） will now be turned into your souls until your honesty is proved. Will either of you change your positions now, or do you force me to hard questioning?

ABIGAIL: I have naught to change, sir. She lies.

DANFORTH, *to Mary*: You would still go on with this?

MARY WARREN, *faintly*: Aye, sir.

DANFORTH, *turning to Abigail*: A poppet were discovered in Mr. Proctor's house, stabbed by a needle. Mary Warren claims that you sat beside her in the court when she made it, and that you saw her make it and witnessed how she herself stuck her needle into it for safe-keeping. What say you to that?

ABIGAIL, *with a slight note of indignation*: It is a lie, sir.

DANFORTH, *after a slight pause*: While you worked for Mr. Proctor, did you see poppets in that house?

ABIGAIL: Goody Proctor always kept poppets.

PROCTOR: Your Honor, my wife never kept no poppets. Mary Warren confesses it was her poppet.

CHEEVER: Your Excellency.

DANFORTH: Mr. Cheever.

CHEEVER: When I spoke with Goody Proctor in that house, she said she never kept no poppets. But she said she did keep poppets when she were a girl.

PROCTOR: She has not been a girl these fifteen years, Your Honor.

HATHORNE: But a poppet will keep fifteen years, will it not?

PROCTOR: It will keep if it is kept, but Mary Warren swears she never saw no poppets in my house, nor anyone else.

PARRIS: Why could there not have been poppets hid where no one ever saw them?

PROCTOR, *furious*: There might also be a dragon with five legs in my house, but no one has ever seen it.

PARRIS: We are here, Your Honor, precisely to discover what no one has ever seen.

PROCTOR: Mr. Danforth, what profit this girl to turn herself about? What may Mary Warren gain but hard questioning and worse?

DANFORTH: You are charging Abigail Williams with a marvelous cool plot to murder, do you understand that?

PROCTOR: I do, sir. I believe she means to murder.

DANFORTH, *pointing at Abigail*, <u>incredulously</u>（不相信地）: This child would murder your wife?

PROCTOR: It is not a child. Now hear me, sir. In the sight of the congregation she were twice this year put out of this meetin' house for laughter during prayer.

DANFORTH, *shocked, turning to Abigail*: What's this? Laughter during—!

PARRIS: Excellency, she were under Tituba's power at that time, but she is solemn now.

GILES: Aye, now she is solemn and goes to hang people!

DANFORTH: Quiet, man.

HATHORNE: Surely it <u>have no bearing on</u>（与……无关） the question, sir. He charges <u>contemplation</u>（意图） of murder.

DANFORTH: Aye. *He studies Abigail for a moment, then*: Continue, Mr. Proctor.

PROCTOR: Mary, Now tell the Governor how you danced in the woods.

PARRIS, *instantly*: Excellency, since I come to Salem this man is blackening my name. He—

DANFORTH: In a moment, sir. *To Mary Warren,* <u>sternly</u>（严厉地）, *and surprised*: What is this dancing?

MARY WARREN: I— *She glances at Abigail, who is staring down at her* <u>remorselessly</u>（冷酷无情地）. *Then, appealing to Proctor*: Mr. Proctor—

PROCTOR, *taking it right up*: Abigail leads the girls to the woods, Your Honor, and they have danced there naked—

Unit 5

Arthur Miller and *The Crucible*

PARRIS: Your Honor, this—

PROCTOR, *at once*: Mr. Parris discovered them himself in the dead of night! There's the "child" she is!

Danforth—*it is growing into a nightmare, and he turns, astonished, to Parris*: Mr. Parris—

PARRIS: I can only say, sir, that I never found any of them naked, and this man is—

DANFORTH: But you discovered them dancing in the woods? *Eyes on Parris, he points at Abigail.* Abigail?

HALE: Excellency, when I first arrived from Beverly, Mr. Parris told me that.

DANFORTH: Do you deny it, Mr. Parris?

PARRIS: I do not, sir, but I never saw any of them naked.

DANFORTH: But she have danced?

PARRIS, *unwillingly*: Aye, sir.

Danforth, as though with new eyes, looks at Abigail.

HATHORNE: Excellency, will you permit me? *He points at Mary Warren.*

DANFORTH, *with great worry*: Pray, proceed.

HATHORNE: You say you never saw no spirits, Mary, were never threatened or afflicted by any manifest of the Devil or the Devil's agents.

MARY WARREN, *very faintly*: No, sir.

HATHORNE, *with a gleam of victory*: And yet, when people accused of witchery <u>confronted</u>（与……对质）you in court, you would faint, saying their spirits came out of their bodies and choked you—

MARY WARREN: That were pretense, sir.

DANFORTH: I cannot hear you.

MARY WARREN: Pretense, sir.

PARRIS: But you did turn cold, did you not? I myself picked you up many times, and your skin were icy, Mr. Danforth, you—

DANFORTH: I saw that many times.

PROCTOR: She only pretended to faint, Your Excellency. They're all marvelous pretenders.

HATHORNE: Then can she pretend to faint now?

PROCTOR: Now?

PARRIS: Why not? Now there are no spirits attacking her, for none in this room is accused of witchcraft. So let her turn herself cold now, let her pretend she is attacked now, let her faint. *He turns to Mary Warren.* Faint!

MARY WARREN: Faint?

PARRIS: Aye, faint. Prove to us how you pretended in the court so many times.

MARY WARREN, *looking to Proctor*: I—cannot faint now, sir.

PROCTOR, *alarmed, quietly*: Can you not pretend it?

MARY WARREN: I— *She looks about as though searching for the passion to faint.* I—have no sense of it now, I—
DANFORTH: Why? What is lacking now?
MARY WARREN: I—cannot tell, sir, I—
DANFORTH: Might it be that here we have no afflicting spirit loose, but in the court there were some?
MARY WARREN: I never saw no spirits.
PARRIS: Then see no spirits now, and prove to us that you can faint by your own will, as you claim.
MARY WARREN, *stares, searching for the emotion of it, and then shakes her head*: I—cannot do it.
PARRIS: Then you will confess, will you not? It were attacking spirits made you faint!
MARY WARREN: No, sir, I—
PARRIS: Your Excellency, this is a trick to blind the court!
MARY WARREN: It's not a trick! *She stands.* I—I used to faint because I—I thought I saw spirits.
DANFORTH: *Thought* you saw them!
MARY WARREN: But I did not, Your Honor.
HATHORNE: How could you think you saw them unless you saw them?
MARY WARREN: I—I cannot tell how, but I did. I—I heard the other girls screaming, and you, Your Honor, you seemed to believe them, and I—It were only sport in the beginning, sir, but then the whole world cried spirits, spirits, and I—I promise you, Mr. Danforth, I only thought I saw them but I did not.
    Danforth peers at her.
PARRIS, *smiling, but nervous because Danforth seems to be struck by Mary Warren's story*: Surely Your Excellency is not taken by this simple lie.
DANFORTH, *turning worriedly to Abigail*: Abigail. I bid you now search your heart and tell me this—and beware of it, child, to God every soul is precious and His vengeance is terrible on them that take life without cause. Is it possible, child, that the spirits you have seen are illusion only, some <u>deception</u>（幻象） that may cross your mind when—
ABIGAIL: Why, this—this—is a base question, sir.
DANFORTH: Child, I would have you consider it—
ABIGAIL: I have been hurt, Mr. Danforth; I have seen my blood runnin' out! I have been near to murdered every day because I done my duty pointing out the Devil's people—and this is my reward? To be mistrusted, denied, questioned like a—
DANFORTH, *weakening*: Child, I do not mistrust you—
ABIGAIL, *in an open threat*: Let *you* beware, Mr. Danforth. Think you to be so mighty that the power of Hell may not <u>turn *your* wits</u>（迷惑……的心智）? Beware of

Unit 5

Arthur Miller and *The Crucible*

it! There is—*Suddenly, from an <u>accusatory</u>（控诉的） attitude, her face turns, looking into the air above—it is truly frightened.*

DANFORTH, *apprehensively*: What is it, child?

ABIGAIL, *looking about in the air, clasping her arms about her as though cold*: I—I know not. A wind, a cold wind, has come. *Her eyes fall on Mary Warren.*

MARY WARREN, *terrified, pleading*: Abby!

MERCY LEWIS, *shivering*: Your Honor, I freeze!

PROCTOR: They're pretending!

HATHORNE, *touching Abigail's hand*: She is cold, Your Honor, touch her!

MERCY LEWIS, *through <u>chattering</u>（颤抖的） teeth*: Mary, do you send this shadow on me?

MARY WARREN: Lord, save me!

SUSANNA WALCOTT: I freeze, I freeze!

ABIGAIL, *shivering visibly*: It is a wind, a wind!

MARY WARREN: Abby, don't do that!

DANFORTH, *himself <u>engaged</u>（被吸引） and entered by Abigail*: Mary Warren, do you witch her? I say to you, do you send your spirit out?

With a hysterical cry Mary Warren starts to run. Proctor catches her.

MARY WARREN, *almost collapsing*: Let me go, Mr. Proctor, I cannot, I cannot—

ABIGAIL, *crying to Heaven*: Oh, Heavenly Father, take away this shadow!

Without warning or hesitation, Proctor leaps at Abigail and, grabbing her by the hair, pulls her to her feet. She screams in pain. Danforth, astonished, cries, "what are you about?" and Hathorne and Parris call, "take your hands off her!" and out of it all comes Proctor's roaring voice.

PROCTOR: How do you call Heaven! Whore! Whore!

Herrick breaks Proctor from her.

HERRICK: John!

DANFORTH: Man! Man, what do you—

PROCTOR, *breathless and in <u>agony</u>（痛苦）*: It is a whore!

DANFORTH, *dumfounded*: You charge—?

ABIGAIL: Mr. Danforth, he is lying!

PROCTOR: Mark her! Now she'll suck a scream to stab me with, but—

DANFORTH: You will prove this! This will not pass!

PROCTOR, *trembling, his life collapsing about him*: I have known her, sir. I have known her.

DANFORTH: You—you are a <u>lecher</u>（私通犯）?

FRANCIS, *horrified*: John, you cannot say such a—

PROCTOR: Oh, Francis, I wish you had some evil in you that you might know me! *To Danforth*: A man will not cast away his good name. You surely know that.

DANFORTH, *dumfounded*: In—in what time? In what place?

PROCTOR, *his voice about to break, and his shame great*: In the proper place—where my beasts are bedded. On the last night of my joy, some eight months past. She used to serve me in my house, sir. *He has to clamp his jaw to keep from weeping.* A man may think God sleeps, but God sees everything, I know it now. I beg you, sir, I beg you—see her what she is. My wife, my dear good wife, took this girl soon after, sir, and put her out on the highroad. And being what she is, a lump of vanity, sir—*He is being overcome.* Excellency, forgive me, forgive me. *Angrily against himself, he turns away from the Governor for a moment. Then, as though to cry out is his only means of speech left*: She thinks to dance with me on my wife's grave! And well she might, for I thought of her softly. God help me, I lusted, and there is a promise in such sweat. But it is a whore's vengeance, and you must see it; I set myself entirely in your hands, I know you must see it now.

DANFORTH, *blanched, in horror, turning to Abigail*: You deny every scrap（点滴） and tittle（毫厘） of this?

ABIGAIL: If I must answer that, I will leave and I will not come back again!

    Danforth seems unsteady.

PROCTOR: I have made a bell of my honor! I have rung the doom of my good name—you will believe me, Mr. Danforth! My wife is innocent, except she knew a whore when she saw one!

ABIGAIL, *stepping up to Danforth*: What look do you give me? *Danforth cannot speak.* I'll not have such looks! *She turns and starts for the door.*

DANFORTH: You will remain where you are! *Herrick steps into her path. She comes up short, fire in her eyes.* Mr. Parris, go into the court and bring Goodwife Proctor out.

PARRIS, *objecting*: Your Honor, this is all a—

DANFORTH, *sharply to Parris*: Bring her out! And tell her not one word of what's been spoken here. And let you knock before you enter. *Parris goes out.* Now we shall touch the bottom of this swamp（沼泽，困境）. *To Proctor*: Your wife, you say, is an honest woman.

PROCTOR: In her life, sir, she have never lied. There are them that cannot sing, and them that cannot weep—my wife cannot lie. I have paid much to learn it, sir.

DANFORTH: And when she put this girl out of your house, she put her out for a harlot（娼妓）?

PROCTOR: Aye, sir.

DANFORTH: And knew her for a harlot?

PROCTOR: Aye, sir, she knew her for a harlot.

DANFORTH: Good then. *To Abigail*: And if she tell me, child, it were for harlotry（淫行）, may God spread His mercy on you! *There is a knock. He calls to the door.*

Hold! *To Abigail*: Turn your back. Turn your back. *To Proctor*: Do likewise. *Both turn their backs—Abigail with indignant slowness.* Now let neither of you turn to face Goody Proctor. No one in this room is to speak one word, or raise a gesture aye（是） or nay（否）. *He turns toward the door, calls*: Enter! *The door opens. Elizabeth enters with Parris. Parris leaves her. She stands alone, her eyes looking for Proctor.* Mr. Cheever, report this testimony in all exactness. Are you ready?

CHEEVER: Ready, sir.

> ### ✂ Excerpt 7 (from Act 3, continued)
> *In this excerpt, we witness the moral test of Elizabeth Proctor and Mary Warren. Both women tell a lie in court, but for completely different purposes. However, both lies lead to the undoing of John Proctor.*

DANFORTH: Come here, woman. *Elizabeth comes to him, glancing at Proctor's back.* Look at me only, not at your husband. In my eyes only.

ELIZABETH, *faintly*: Good, sir.

DANFORTH: We are given to understand that at one time you dismissed（解雇） your servant, Abigail Williams.

ELIZABETH: That is true, sir.

DANFORTH: For what cause did you dismiss her? *Slight pause. Then Elizabeth tries to glance at Proctor.* You will look in my eyes only and not at your husband. The answer is in your memory and you need no help to give it to me. Why did you dismiss Abigail Williams?

ELIZABETH, *not knowing what to say, sensing a situation, wetting her lips to stall（拖延） for time*: She—dissatisfied me. *Pause.* And my husband.

DANFORTH: In what way dissatisfied you?

ELIZABETH: She were—*She glances at Proctor for a cue.*

DANFORTH: Woman, look at me! *Elizabeth does.* Were she slovenly（邋遢，懒散）? Lazy? What disturbance did she cause?

ELIZABETH: Your Honor, I—in that time I were sick. And I—My husband is a good and righteous（正直的） man. He is never drunk as some are, nor wastin' his time at the shovelboard（打圆盘游戏）, but always at his work. But in my sickness—you see, sir, I were a long time sick after my last baby, and I thought I saw my husband somewhat turning from me. And this girl—*She turns to Abigail.*

DANFORTH: Look at me.

ELIZABETH: Aye, sir. Abigail Williams—*She breaks off.*

DANFORTH: What of Abigail Williams?

ELIZABETH: I came to think he fancied her. And so one night I lost my wits, I think, and put her out on the highroad.

DANFORTH: Your husband—did he indeed turn from you?

ELIZABETH, *in agony*: My husband—is a goodly man, sir.

DANFORTH: Then he did not turn from you.

ELIZABETH, *starting to glance at Proctor*: He—

DANFORTH, *reaches out and holds her face, then*: Look at me! To your own knowledge, has John Proctor ever committed the crime of lechery? *In a crisis of indecision she cannot speak,* Answer my question! Is your husband a lecher!

ELIZABETH, *faintly*: No, sir.

DANFORTH: Remove her, Marshal.

PROCTOR: Elizabeth, tell the truth!

DANFORTH: She has spoken. Remove her!

PROCTOR, *crying out*: Elizabeth, I have confessed it!

ELIZABETH: Oh, God! *The door closes behind her.*

PROCTOR: She only thought to save my name!

HALE: Excellency, it is a natural lie to tell; I beg you, stop now before another is condemned! I may shut my conscience to it no more—private vengeance is working through this testimony! From the beginning this man has struck me true. By my oath to Heaven, I believe him now, and I pray you call back his wife before we—

DANFORTH: She spoke nothing of lechery, and this man has lied.

HALE: I believe him! *Pointing at Abigail*: This girl has always struck me false! She has—

> Abigail, with a <u>weird</u>（怪异的）, wild, <u>chilling</u>（令人恐惧的）cry, screams up to the ceiling.

ABIGAIL: You will not! <u>Begone</u>（走开）! Begone, I say!

DANFORTH: What is it, child? *But Abigail, pointing with fear, is now raising up her frightened eyes, her <u>awed</u>（畏怯的）face, toward the ceiling—the girls are doing the same—and now Hathorne, Hale, Putnam, Cheever, Herrick, and Danforth do the same.* What's there? *He lowers his eyes from the ceiling, and now he is frightened; there is real tension in his voice.* Child! *She is <u>transfixed</u>（呆若木鸡）—with all the girls, she is whimpering open-mouthed, <u>agape</u>（目瞪口呆）at the ceiling.* Girls! Why do you—?

MERCY LEWIS, *pointing*: It's on the <u>beam</u>（房梁）! Behind the <u>rafter</u>（椽子）!

DANFORTH, *looking up*: Where!

ABIGAIL: Why—? *She <u>gulps</u>（大口吸气）.* Why do you come, yellow bird?

PROCTOR: Where's a bird? I see no bird!

ABIGAIL, *to the ceiling*: My face? My face?

Unit 5

Arthur Miller and *The Crucible*

PROCTOR: Mr. Hale—

DANFORTH: Be quiet!

PROCTOR, *to Hale*: Do you see a bird?

DANFORTH: Be quiet!

ABIGAIL, *to the ceiling, in a genuine conversation with the "bird" as though trying to talk it out of attacking her*: But God made my face; you cannot want to tear my face. Envy is a deadly sin, Mary.

MARY WARREN, *on her feet with a spring, and horrified, pleading*: Abby!

ABIGAIL, <u>unperturbed</u>（不受干扰）, *continuing to the "bird"*: Oh, Mary, this is a black art to change your shape. No, I cannot, I cannot stop my mouth; it's God's work I do.

MARY WARREN: Abby, I'm here!

PROCTOR, *frantically*: They're pretending, Mr. Danforth!

ABIGAIL—*now she takes a backward step, as though in fear the bird will <u>swoop</u>（猛扑） down <u>momentarily</u>（随时）*: Oh, please, Mary! Don't come down.

SUSANNA WALCOTT: Her claws, she's stretching her claws!

PROCTOR: Lies, lies.

ABIGAIL, *backing further, eyes still fixed above*: Mary, please don't hurt me!

MARY WARREN, *to Danforth*: I'm not hurting her!

DANFORTH, *to Mary Warren*: Why does she see this vision?

MARY WARREN: She sees nothin'!

ABIGAIL, *now staring <u>full front</u>（正前方） as though <u>hypnotized</u>（催眠）, and mimicking the exact tone of Mary Warren's cry*: She sees nothin'!

MARY WARREN, *pleading*: Abby, you mustn't!

ABIGAIL *and all the girls, all transfixed*: Abby, you mustn't!

MARY WARREN, *to all the girls*: I'm here, I'm here!

GIRLS: I'm here, I'm here!

DANFORTH, *horrified*: Mary Warren! Draw back your spirit out of them!

MARY WARREN: Mr. Danforth!

GIRLS, *cutting her off*: Mr. Danforth!

DANFORTH: Have you compacted with the Devil? Have you?

MARY WARREN: Never, never!

GIRLS: Never, never!

DANFORTH, *growing hysterical*: Why can they only repeat you?

PROCTOR: Give me a whip—I'll stop it!

MARY WARREN: They're sporting. They—!

GIRLS: They're sporting!

MARY WARREN, *turning on them all hysterically and stamping her feet*: Abby, stop it!

GIRLS, *stamping their feet*: Abby, stop it!

MARY WARREN: Stop it!

GIRLS: Stop it!

MARY WARREN, *screaming it out at the top of her lungs, and raising her fists*: Stop it!!

GIRLS, *raising their fists*: Stop it!!

> *Mary Warren, utterly confounded, and becoming overwhelmed by Abigail's—and the girls'—utter conviction, starts to whimper, hands half raised, powerless, and all the girls begin whimpering exactly as she does.*

DANFORTH: A little while ago you were afflicted. Now it seems you afflict others; where did you find this power?

MARY WARREN, *staring at Abigail*: I—have no power.

GIRLS: I have no power.

PROCTOR: They're <u>gulling</u>（欺骗） you, Mister!

DANFORTH: Why did you turn about this past two weeks? You have seen the Devil, have you not?

HALE, *indicating Abigail and the girls*: You cannot believe them!—

MARY WARREN: I—

PROCTOR, *sensing her weakening*: Mary, God damns all liars!

DANFORTH, <u>pounding</u>（强行灌输） *it into her*: You have seen the Devil, you have made compact with Lucifer, have you not?

PROCTOR: God damns liars, Mary!

> *MARY utters something <u>unintelligible</u>（不知所云的）, staring at Abigail, who keeps watching the "bird" above.*

DANFORTH: I cannot hear you. What do you say? *Mary utters again unintelligibly.* You will confess yourself or you will hang! *He turns her roughly to face him.* Do you know who I am? I say you will hang if you do not open with me!

PROCTOR: Mary, remember the angel Raphael—do that which is good and—

ABIGAIL, *pointing upward*: The wings! Her wings are spreading! Mary, please, don't, don't—!

HALE: I see nothing, Your Honor!

DANFORTH: Do you confess this power! *He is an inch from her face.* Speak!

ABIGAIL: She's going to come down! She's walking the beam!

DANFORTH: Will you speak!

MARY WARREN, *staring in horror*: I cannot!

GIRLS: I cannot!

PARRIS: Cast the Devil out! Look him in the face! <u>Trample</u>（践踏） him! We'll save you, Mary, only stand <u>fast</u>（坚定地） against him and—

ABIGAIL, *looking up*: Look out! She's coming down!

Unit 5

Arthur Miller and *The Crucible*

She and all the girls run to one wall, shielding their eyes. And now, as though <u>cornered</u>（逼入绝境）, they let out a <u>gigantic</u>（巨大的）scream, and Mary, as though <u>infected</u>（感染）, opens her mouth and screams with them. Gradually Abigail and the girls leave off, until only Mary is left there, staring up at the "bird," screaming madly. All watch her, horrified by this evident <u>fit</u>（神经发作）. Proctor <u>strides</u>（跨步走）to her.

PROCTOR: Mary, tell the Governor what they—*He has hardly got a word out, when, seeing him coming for her, she rushes out of his reach, screaming in horror.*

MARY WARREN: Don't touch me—don't touch me! *At which the girls halt at the door.*

PROCTOR, *astonished*: Mary!

MARY WARREN, *pointing at Proctor*: You're the Devil's man!

  He is stopped <u>in his tracks</u>（当场，即刻）.

PARRIS: Praise God!

GIRLS: Praise God!

PROCTOR, *numbed*: Mary, how—?

MARY WARREN: I'll not hang with you! I love God, I love God.

DANFORTH, *to MARY*: He bid you do the Devil's work?

MARY WARREN, *hysterically, indicating Proctor*: He come at me by night and every day to sign, to sign, to—

DANFORTH: Sign what?

PARRIS: The Devil's book? He come with a book?

MARY WARREN, *hysterically, pointing at Proctor, fearful of him*: My name, he want my name. "I'll murder you," he says, "if my wife hangs! We must go and overthrow the court," he says!

  Danforth's head <u>jerks</u>（猛地转向）toward Proctor, shock and horror in his face.

PROCTOR, *turning, appealing to Hale*: Mr. Hale!

MARY WARREN, *her sobs beginning*: He wake me every night, his eyes were like coals and his fingers claw my neck, and I sign, I sign...

HALE: Excellency, this child's gone wild!

PROCTOR, *as Danforth's wide eyes pour on him*: Mary, Mary!

MARY WARREN, *screaming at him*: No, I love God; I go your way no more. I love God, I bless God. *Sobbing, she rushes to Abigail.* Abby, Abby, I'll never hurt you more! *They all watch, as Abigail, out of her infinite charity, reaches out and draws the sobbing Mary to her, and then looks up to Danforth.*

DANFORTH, *to Proctor*: What are you? *Proctor is beyond speech in his anger.* You are combined with anti-Christ, are you not? I have seen your power; you will not deny it! What say you, Mister?

HALE: Excellency—

DANFORTH: I will have nothing from you, Mr. Hale! *To Proctor*: Will you confess yourself <u>befouled with</u>（与……同流合污） Hell, or do you keep that black <u>allegiance</u>（效忠） yet? What say you?

PROCTOR, *his mind wild, breathless*: I say—I say—God is dead!

PARRIS: Hear it, hear it!

PROCTOR, *laughs <u>insanely</u>（疯癫地）, then*: A fire, a fire is burning! I hear the boot of Lucifer, I see his filthy face! And it is my face, and yours, Danforth! For them that <u>quail</u>（畏缩） to bring men out of ignorance, as I have quailed, and as you quail now when you know in all your black hearts that this be fraud—God damns our kind especially, and we will burn, we will burn together!

DANFORTH: Marshal! Take him and Corey with him to the jail!

HALE, *starting across to the door*: I <u>denounce</u>（谴责） these proceedings!

PROCTOR: You are pulling Heaven down and raising up a whore!

HALE: I denounce these proceedings, I quit this court! *He slams the door to the outside behind him.*

DANFORTH, *calling to him in a fury*: Mr. Hale! Mr. Hale!

THE CURTAIN FALLS

Excerpt 8 (from Act 4)

As time passes, more people are involved in the witch trials, which lay waste to the village. Seeing rising discontent over the court and the accusers, Abigail flees Salem. To prevent a potential uprising, Judge Danforth and Reverend Parris decide to bring John Proctor, who is an influential figure in Salem, to a false confession. They choose to ask Elizabeth to talk with John Proctor and change his mind.

Alone. Proctor walks to her, halts. It is as though they stood in a <u>spinning</u>（天旋地转的） world. It is beyond sorrow, above it. He reaches out his hand as though toward an <u>embodiment</u>（化身） not quite real, and as he touches her, a strange soft sound, half laughter, half amazement, comes from his throat. He pats her hand. She covers his hand with hers. And then, weak, he sits. Then she sits, facing him.

PROCTOR: The child?

ELIZABETH: It grows.

PROCTOR: There is no word of the boys?

ELIZABETH: They're well. Rebecca's Samuel keeps them.

PROCTOR: You have not seen them?

ELIZABETH: I have not. *She catches a weakening in herself and downs it.*

Unit 5

Arthur Miller and *The Crucible*

PROCTOR: You are a—marvel, Elizabeth.

ELIZABETH: You—have been tortured?

PROCTOR: Aye. *Pause. She will not let herself be drowned in the sea that threatens her.* They come for my life now.

ELIZABETH: I know it.

    Pause.

PROCTOR: None—have yet confessed?

ELIZABETH: There be many confessed.

PROCTOR: Who are they?

ELIZABETH: There be a hundred or more, they say. Goody Ballard is one; Isaiah Goodkind is one. There be many.

PROCTOR: Rebecca?

ELIZABETH: Not Rebecca. She is one foot in Heaven now; naught may hurt her more.

PROCTOR: And Giles?

ELIZABETH: You have not heard of it?

PROCTOR: I hear nothin', where I am kept.

ELIZABETH: Giles is dead.

    He looks at her incredulously.

PROCTOR: When were he hanged?

ELIZABETH, *quietly,* factually（据实地）: He were not hanged. He would not answer aye or nay to his indictment（指控）; for if he denied the charge they'd hang him surely, and auction（拍卖） out his property. So he stand mute, and died Christian under the law. And so his sons will have his farm. It is the law, for he could not be condemned a wizard without he answer the indictment, aye or nay.

PROCTOR: Then how does he die?

ELIZABETH, *gently*: They press him, John.

PROCTOR: Press?

ELIZABETH: Great stones they lay upon his chest until he plead aye or nay. *With a tender smile for the old man*: They say he give them but two words. "More weight," he says. And died.

PROCTOR, *numbed—a thread to weave into his agony*: "More weight."

ELIZABETH: Aye. It were a fearsome（令人敬畏的） man, Giles Corey.

    Pause.

PROCTOR, *with great* force of will（意志力）*, but not quite looking at her*: I have been thinking I would confess to them, Elizabeth. *She shows nothing*. What say you? If I give them that?

ELIZABETH: I cannot judge you, John.

    Pause.

PROCTOR, *simply—a pure question*: What would you have me do?

ELIZABETH: <u>As you will</u>（如你所愿）, I would have it. *Slight pause*: I want you living, John. That's sure.

PROCTOR, *pauses, then with a flailing of hope*: Giles' wife? Have she confessed?

ELIZABETH: She will not.

    Pause.

PROCTOR: It is a pretense, Elizabeth.

ELIZABETH: What is?

PROCTOR: I cannot mount the <u>gibbet</u>（绞刑架） like a saint. It is a fraud. I am not that man. *She is silent.* My honesty is broke, Elizabeth; I am no good man. Nothing's spoiled by giving them this lie that were not <u>rotten</u>（腐败的） long before.

ELIZABETH: And yet you've not confessed till now. That speak goodness in you.

PROCTOR: <u>Spite</u>（愤恨） only keeps me silent. It is hard to give a lie to dogs. *Pause, for the first time he turns directly to her.* I would have your forgiveness, Elizabeth.

ELIZABETH: It is not for me to give, John, I am—

PROCTOR: I'd have you see some honesty in it. Let them that never lied die now to keep their souls. It is pretense for me, a vanity that will not blind God nor keep my children out of the wind. *Pause.* What say you?

ELIZABETH, *upon a <u>heaving</u>（起起伏伏的） sob that always <u>threatens</u>（可能发生）*: John, it come to naught that I should forgive you, if you'll not forgive yourself. *Now he turns away a little, in great agony.* It is not my soul, John, it is yours. *He stands, as though in physical pain, slowly rising to his feet with a great <u>immortal</u>（永久的） longing to find his answer. It is difficult to say, and she is on the verge of tears.* Only be sure of this, for I know it now: Whatever you will do, it is a good man does it. *He turns his doubting, searching gaze upon her.* I have read my heart this three month, John. *Pause.* I have sins of my own to count. It needs a cold wife to prompt lechery.

PROCTOR, *in great pain*: Enough, enough—

ELIZABETH, *now pouring out her heart*: Better you should know me!

PROCTOR: I will not hear it! I know you!

ELIZABETH: You take my sins upon you, John—

PROCTOR, *in agony*: No, I take my own, my own!

ELIZABETH: John, I counted myself so plain, so poorly made, no honest love could come to me! Suspicion kissed you when I did; I never knew how I should say my love. It were a cold house I kept! *In fright, she <u>swerves</u>（突然转身）, as Hathorne enters.*

HATHORNE: What say you, Proctor? The sun is soon up.

    Proctor, his chest heaving, stares, turns to Elizabeth. She comes to him as though to plead, her voice quaking.

Unit 5

Arthur Miller and *The Crucible*

ELIZABETH: Do what you will. But let none be your judge. There be no higher judge under Heaven than Proctor is! Forgive me, forgive me, John—I never knew such goodness in the world! *She covers her face, weeping.*

 Proctor turns from her to Hathorne; he is <u>off the earth</u>（恍惚）, *his voice hollow.*

PROCTOR: I want my life.

HATHORNE, <u>electrified</u>（兴奋）, *surprised*: You'll confess yourself?

PROCTOR: I will have my life.

HATHORNE, *with a* <u>mystical</u>（神秘的） *tone*: God be praised! It is a providence! *He rushes out the door, and his voice is heard calling down the corridor*: He will confess! Proctor will confess!

PROCTOR, *with a cry, as he strides to the door*: Why do you cry it? *In great pain he turns back to her.* It is evil, is it not? It is evil.

ELIZABETH, *in terror, weeping*: I cannot judge you, John, I cannot!

PROCTOR: Then who will judge me? *Suddenly clasping his hands*: God in Heaven, what is John Proctor, what is John Proctor? *He moves as an animal, and a fury is riding in him, a* <u>tantalized</u>（令人干着急的） *search.* I think it is honest, I think so; I am no saint. *As though she had denied this he calls angrily at her*: Let Rebecca go like a saint; for me it is fraud!

 Voices are heard in the hall, speaking together in <u>suppressed</u>（忍住的） *excitement.*

ELIZABETH: I am not your judge, I cannot be. *As though giving him release*: Do as you will, do as you will!

PROCTOR: Would you give them such a lie? Say it. Would you ever give them this? *She cannot answer.* You would not; if <u>tongs of fire</u>（火钳） were <u>singeing</u>（烧焦） you you would not! It is evil. Good, then—it is evil, and I do it!

 Hathorne enters with Danforth, and, with them, Cheever, Parris, and Hale. It is a businesslike, rapid entrance, as though the ice had been broken.

DANFORTH, *with great relief and gratitude*: Praise to God, man, praise to God; you shall be blessed in Heaven for this. *Cheever has hurried to the bench with pen, ink, and paper. Proctor watches him.* Now then, let us have it. Are you ready, Mr. Cheever?

PROCTOR, *with a cold, cold horror at their efficiency*: Why must it be written?

DANFORTH: Why, for the good instruction of the village, Mister; this we shall post upon the church door! *To Parris, urgently*: Where is the marshal?

PARRIS, *runs to the door and calls down the corridor*: Marshal! Hurry!

DANFORTH: Now, then, Mister, will you speak slowly, and directly to the point, for Mr. Cheever's sake. *He is* <u>on record</u>（被记录在案） *now, and is really dictating to Cheever, who writes.* Mr. Proctor, have you seen the Devil in your life? *Proctor's jaws lock.* Come, man, there is light in the sky; the town waits at the scaffold（绞刑台）; I would give out this news. Did you see the Devil?

PROCTOR: I did.

PARRIS: Praise God!

DANFORTH: And when he come to you, what were his demand? *Proctor is silent. Danforth helps.* Did he bid you to do his work upon the earth?

PROCTOR: He did.

DANFORTH: And you bound yourself to his service? *Danforth turns, as Rebecca Nurse enters, with Herrick helping to support her. She is barely able to walk.* Come in, come in, woman!

REBECCA, *brightening as she sees Proctor*: Ah, John! You are well, then, eh?
    Proctor turns his face to the wall.

DANFORTH: Courage, man, courage—let her witness your good example that she may come to God herself. Now hear it, Goody Nurse! Say on, Mr, Proctor. Did you bind yourself to the Devil's service?

REBECCA, *astonished*: Why, John!

PROCTOR, *through his teeth, his face turned from Rebecca*: I did.

DANFORTH: Now, woman, you surely see it profit nothin' to keep this conspiracy any further. Will you confess yourself with him?

REBECCA: Oh, John—God send his mercy on you!

DANFORTH: I say, will you confess yourself, Goody Nurse?

REBECCA: Why, it is a lie, it is a lie; how may I damn myself? I cannot, I cannot.

DANFORTH: Mr. Proctor. When the Devil came to you did you see Rebecca Nurse in his company? *Proctor is silent.* Come, man, take courage—did you ever see her with the Devil?

PROCTOR, *almost inaudibly*: No.
    Danforth, now sensing trouble, glances at John and goes to the table, and picks up a sheet—the list of condemned.

DANFORTH: Did you ever see her sister, Mary Easty, with the Devil?

PROCTOR: No, I did not.

DANFORTH, *his eyes narrow on Proctor*: Did you ever see Martha Corey with the Devil?

PROCTOR: I did not.

DANFORTH, *realizing, slowly putting the sheet down*: Did you ever see anyone with the Devil?

PROCTOR: I did not.

DANFORTH: Proctor, you mistake me. I am not empowered（授权）to trade your life for a lie. You have most certainly seen some person with the Devil. *Proctor is silent.* Mr. Proctor, a score of people have already testified they saw this woman with the Devil.

PROCTOR: Then it is proved. Why must I say it?

Unit 5

Arthur Miller and *The Crucible*

DANFORTH: Why "must" you say it! Why, you should <u>rejoice</u>（庆幸） to say it if your soul is truly <u>purged</u>（洗净） of any love for Hell!

PROCTOR: They think to go like saints. I like not to spoil their names.

DANFORTH, *inquiring, incredulous*: Mr. Proctor, do you think they go like saints?

PROCTOR, *evading*: This woman never thought she done the Devil's work.

DANFORTH: Look you, sir. I think you mistake your duty here. It matters nothing what she thought—she is convicted of the unnatural murder of children, and you for sending your spirit out upon Mary Warren. Your soul alone is the issue here, Mister, and you will prove its whiteness or you cannot live in a Christian country. Will you tell me now what persons conspired with you in the Devil's company? *Proctor is silent.* To your knowledge was Rebecca Nurse ever—

PROCTOR: I speak my own sins; I cannot judge another. *Crying out, with hatred*: I have no tongue for it.

HALE, *quickly to Danforth*: Excellency, it is enough he confess himself. Let him sign it, let him sign it.

PARRIS, *feverishly*: It is a great service, sir. It is a weighty name; it will strike the village that Proctor confess. I beg you, let him sign it. The sun is up, Excellency!

DANFORTH, *considers; then with dissatisfaction,* Come, then, sign your testimony. *To Cheever*: Give it to him. *Cheever goes to Proctor, the confession and a pen in hand. Proctor does not look at it.* Come, man, sign it.

PROCTOR, *after glancing at the confession*: You have all witnessed it—it is enough.

DANFORTH: You will not sign it?

PROCTOR: You have all witnessed it; what more is needed?

DANFORTH: Do you sport with me? You will sign your name or it is no confession, Mister! *His breast heaving with agonized breathing, Proctor now lays the paper down and signs his name.*

PARRIS: Praise be to the Lord!

> *Proctor has just finished signing when Danforth reaches for the paper. But Proctor snatches it up, and now a wild terror is rising in him, and a <u>boundless</u>（无边的） anger.*

DANFORTH, *perplexed, but politely <u>extending</u>（伸出） his hand*: If you please, sir.

PROCTOR: No.

DANFORTH, *as though Proctor did not understand*: Mr. Proctor, I must have—

PROCTOR: No, no. I have signed it. You have seen me. It is done! You have no need for this.

PARRIS: Proctor, the village must have proof that—

PROCTOR: Damn the village! I confess to God, and God has seen my name on this! It is enough!

DANFORTH: No, sir, it is—

PROCTOR: You came to save my soul, did you not? Here! I have confessed myself; it is enough!

DANFORTH: You have not con—

PROCTOR: I have confessed myself! Is there no good penitence（悔罪） but it be public? God does not need my name nailed upon the church! God sees my name; God knows how black my sins are! It is enough!

DANFORTH: Mr. Proctor—

PROCTOR: You will not use me! I am no Sarah Good or Tituba, I am John Proctor! You will not use me! It is no part of salvation（救赎） that you should use me!

DANFORTH: I do not wish to—

PROCTOR: I have three children—how may I teach them to walk like men in the world, and I sold my friends?

DANFORTH: You have not sold your friends—

PROCTOR: Beguile（诱骗） me not! I blacken all of them when this is nailed to the church the very day they hang for silence!

DANFORTH: Mr. Proctor, I must have good and legal proof that you—

PROCTOR: You are the high court, your word is good enough! Tell them I confessed myself; say Proctor broke his knees and wept like a woman; say what you will, but my name cannot—

DANFORTH, *with suspicion*: It is the same, is it not? If I report it or you sign to it?

PROCTOR—*he knows it is insane*: No, it is not the same! What others say and what I sign to is not the same!

DANFORTH: Why? Do you mean to deny this confession when you are free?

PROCTOR: I mean to deny nothing!

DANFORTH: Then explain to me, Mr. Proctor, why you will not let—

PROCTOR, *with a cry of his whole soul*: Because it is my name! Because I cannot have another in my life! Because I lie and sign myself to lies! Because I am not worth the dust on the feet of them that hang! How may I live without my name? I have given you my soul; leave me my name!

DANFORTH, *pointing at the confession in Proctor's hand*: Is that document a lie? If it is a lie I will not accept it! What say you? I will not deal in lies, Mister! *Proctor is motionless.* You will give me your honest confession in my hand, or I cannot keep you from the rope. *Proctor does not reply.* Which way do you go, Mister? *His breast heaving, his eyes staring, Proctor tears the paper and* crumples（揉捏） *it, and he is weeping in fury, but* erect（矗立）.

DANFORTH: Marshal!

PARRIS, *hysterically, as though the tearing paper were his life*: Proctor, Proctor!

HALE: Man, you will hang! You cannot!

PROCTOR, *his eyes full of tears*: I can. And there's your first marvel, that I can. You have made your magic now, for now I do think I see some shred of goodness in John Proctor. Not enough to weave a banner（旗帜） with, but white enough to keep it from such dogs. *Elizabeth, in a burst of terror, rushes to him and weeps against his hand.* Give them no tear! Tears pleasure them! Show honor now, show a stony heart and sink them with it! *He has lifted her, and kisses her now with great passion.*

REBECCA: Let you fear nothing! Another judgment waits us all!

DANFORTH: Hang them high over the town! Who weeps for these, weeps for corruption! *He sweeps out past them. Herrick starts to lead Rebecca, who almost collapses, but Proctor catches her, and she glances up at him apologetically（歉疚的）.*

REBECCA: I've had no breakfast.

HERRICK: Come, man.

> *Herrick escorts（押解） them out, Hathorne and Cheever behind them. Elizabeth stands staring at the empty doorway.*

PARRIS, *in deadly fear, to Elizabeth*: Go to him, Goody Proctor! There is yet time!

> *From outside a drumroll（击鼓声） strikes the air. Parris is startled. Elizabeth jerks about toward the window.*

PARRIS: Go to him! *He rushes out the door, as though to hold back（阻挡） his fate.* Proctor! Proctor!

> *Again, a short burst of drums.*

HALE: Woman, plead with（恳求） him! *He starts to rush out the door, and then goes back to her.* Woman! It is pride, it is vanity. *She avoids his eyes, and moves to the window. He drops to his knees.* Be his helper!—What profit him to bleed? Shall the dust praise him? Shall the worms declare his truth? Go to him, take his shame away!

ELIZABETH, *supporting herself against collapse, grips the bars of the window, and with a cry*: He have his goodness now. God forbid I take it from him!

> *The final drumroll crashes（突然响起）, then heightens violently. Hale weeps in frantic prayer, and the new sun is pouring in upon her face, and the drums rattle like bones in the morning air.*

THE CURTAIN FALLS

5.2.4 Exercises

❶ Give a brief answer to each of the following questions.

Act 1

1) What is Parris's initial attitude to witchcraft? Why is it so? Why does he change his opinion later?

2) What does the conversation between Abigail and the other girls reveal about their recent activities?
3) What does Proctor think about his relationship with Abigail? What does Abigail think of it?
4) How does Mrs. Putnam explain Betty's sudden scream? How does Rebecca explain the girl's odd behavior?
5) Why does Reverend Hale come to Salem?
6) What does Tituba confess to? Why does she confess? Why does Abigail confess?

Act 2

7) What does Elizabeth urge Proctor to do? Why does he hesitate? What is the relationship between Proctor and Elizabeth like?
8) What gift does Mary Warren give Elizabeth? What information does she provide about the trial?
9) Why does Hale visit the Proctors? Why does he ask them to recite the Ten Commandments? How well does Proctor do it? Why?
10) What are Rebecca Nurse, Martha Corey and Elizabeth Proctor accused of?

Act 3

11) How do the three husbands (Proctor, Corey, Nurse) plan to save their wives? Why does Danforth tell Proctor that his wife is pregnant?
12) What depositions do Francis Nurse, Giles Corey and John Proctor present to the court? What are the results?
13) What secret does Proctor reveal about himself and Abigail? How does Danforth test Proctor's revelation?
14) What does Mary accuse Proctor of? Why does she do it?

Act 4

15) Why does Abigail flee Salem?
16) Why does Danforth want Proctor to see Elizabeth? Why does he consider it important?
17) How does Hale try to persuade Elizabeth to talk with Proctor? What does this say about the change in his mind?
18) How and for what reason does Giles die?
19) At first, why does Proctor say he will confess? What has kept him from doing that?
20) What does Proctor refuse to do even though he confesses? Why does he tear his confession paper after signing it?

❷ Identify the following characters.

1) _____ seems more concerned with his reputation as town minister than he is about his parishioners or his troubled daughter. He attempts to strengthen his position through the witch trial proceedings.

Unit 5

Arthur Miller and *The Crucible*

2) _____ functions as an example of the downtrodden who are made into an easy target for blame. She is strongly suspected because she knows how to perform pagan rituals.

3) _____ views the world around her as pretense, and is willing to commit murder to get what she wants. She tells lies, manipulates her friends and the entire town, and eventually sends many innocent people to prison or to their deaths.

4) _____ looks for revenge for past grievances. He also attempts to benefit from the accusations made against the other members of the community by attaining their forfeited land at cut-rate prices.

5) _____ tends to reverse her position when she is intimidated. Initially awed by Abigail's threat, she is goaded by Proctor to call the girls frauds in court but then again succumbs to their pressures.

6) _____ is plagued with guilt over a secret, and believes his sin has irreparably damaged him. However, by sacrificing himself to save his wife, and by finally refusing to give up his personal integrity, he is redeemed for his earlier sin.

7) _____ is the ultimate good, religious community member marked for her wisdom, compassion and moral strength. When she is accused of witchcraft, it may be a sign that the town has lapsed into collective madness.

8) _____ is independent and brave, someone who can reinforce the beliefs of Proctor. He is held in contempt of court and is pressed to death with large stones, but his disdain for the trials is illustrated in his last words: "More weight."

9) _____ depends on information from books that he believes hold all the answers. He does not realize the trouble he has helped create until he finds out that Abigail is lying.

10) _____ is grave and intent on upholding the power of the court at all costs. He sees no flexibility in the law, and fears that he will appear weak and irresolute, so he stubbornly refuses to reverse a previous decision—regardless of its injustice.

❸ Plot Review

In the Puritan New England town of Salem, Massachusetts, two girls, Betty Parris and Ruth Putnam, are mysteriously taken ill. Rumors of 1) _____ spread fast, and the local minister, Reverend Parris, sends for Reverend Hale to look into such possibilities. Actually, the night before, Parris discovered a group of teenage girls 2) _____ "like heathens" in the woods, and among them were his daughter Betty, his niece Abigail, and his black slave Tituba. Worried that his enemies may use this 3) _____ him, Parris doesn't reveal what he saw until Hale arrives.

As the girls are questioned, Abigail, to 4) _____ her own name, blames Tituba for enticing her to sin. Then Tituba is fearfully led into confessing complicity with the 5) _____, and pressured to name two other women as witches. Joining in the hysterical atmosphere, Abigail adds more names, as does Betty. The crowd is thrown into an uproar, and frightened teenagers become respected 6) _____. Whoever Abigail and her troop name as they go into hysterics is arrested for 7) _____ the girls. A full-blown investigation is launched, with the deputy governor of the province, Danforth, sitting at the head of the court.

Earlier, Abigail has attributed Betty's sickness to 8) _____ and has revealed the secret to John Proctor, a local farmer with whom she had an 9) _____ while employed as a servant in his household. Proctor is urged by his wife Elizabeth to tell the truth to the court, but he is unwilling. Mary Warren, their current servant and a member of Abigail's group, returns from Salem with news that 10) _____ has been accused of witchcraft, but the court dismissed it when she defended her. Then Hale arrives. He is unsure of the girls' accusations and wants to 11) _____ further. He questions the Proctors about their religious adherence. Then, the Proctors' friends, Giles Corey and Francis Nurse, come to report that their 12) _____ have been arrested on charges of witchcraft. Soon officers of the court arrive and arrest Elizabeth, as well. After they leave, Proctor tells Mary Warren that she must testify in court against Abigail.

The trial of Martha Corey is interrupted when Proctor and his friends storm in, determined to expose Abigail and the other girls as 13) _____. However, Danforth is suspicious of Proctor's 14) _____ and tells him that Elizabeth is found to be 15) _____ and will be spared for a time, but Proctor persists in his charge. He makes Mary Warren tell the court that she only 16) _____ to see spirits in past trials and that Abigail and the other girls were also lying. Abigail, with her friends, denies the charge, and claims that Mary Warren is bewitching them. Furious, Proctor confesses his relationship with Abigail and accuses her of being motivated by 17) _____ of his wife. Abigail denies this, and when Elizabeth is brought in, she does the same, thinking to protect Proctor's 18) _____. Danforth denounces Proctor as a 19) _____. Meanwhile, Abigail and the girls resume their accusation against Mary, who then gives in and takes their 20) _____, and cries out against Proctor. All the judges are convinced by this performance, and have Proctor arrested, but Hale 21) _____ the proceedings.

Three months have passed, and people's attitude to witch trials has been very different. There is rumor of 22) _____ against the court in the neighboring town, and Parris worries that the people of Salem will follow suit. Abigail has 23) _____, taking all of her uncle's savings with her. Parris attempts to convince Danforth to 24) _____ the executions of John Proctor and other respected people, but Danforth is adamant, believing that to pardon others would cast 25) _____ on the guilt of those 12 already hanged. Hale, who has lost faith in the court, begs the accused witches to make 26) _____ confessions in order to save their lives, but they refuse. To extract a confession from Proctor, Danforth suggests using Elizabeth to

27) _____ Proctor into confessing. Left alone, Elizabeth tells Proctor how Giles Corey died under 28) _____. Proctor suggests he may as well confess and live. However, he refuses to 29) _____ anyone else, and when the court insists that his confession must be made 30) _____, Proctor grows angry, tears it up, and retracts his admission of guilt. Parris and Hale beg Elizabeth to get Proctor to change his mind, but she honors his decision and refuses.

❹ Identify the speakers of the following lines, briefly tell the situation in which each of them is uttered, and explain its significance.

1) Let either of you breathe a word, or the edge of a word, about the other things, and I will come to you in the black of some terrible night and I will bring a pointy reckoning that will shudder you.
2) There is prodigious danger in the seeking of loose spirits. I fear it, I fear it. Let us rather blame ourselves and—
3) There are wheels within wheels in this village, and fires within fires!
4) I have trouble enough without I come five mile to hear him preach only hellfire and bloody damnation. Take it to heart, Mr. Parris. There are many others who stay away from church these days because you hardly ever mention God any more.
5) I want to open myself! I want the light of God, I want the sweet love of Jesus! I danced for the Devil; I saw him; I wrote in his book; I go back to Jesus; I kiss His hand. I saw Sarah Good with the Devil! I saw Goody Osburn with the Devil! I saw Bridget Bishop with the Devil!
6) Man, remember, until an hour before the Devil fell, God thought him beautiful in Heaven.
7) I'll tell you what's walking Salem — vengeance is walking Salem. We are what we always were in Salem, but now the little crazy children are jangling the keys of the kingdom, and common vengeance writes the law!
8) Do you know, Mr. Proctor, that the entire contention of the state in these trials is that the voice of Heaven is speaking through the children?
9) But you must understand, sir, that a person is either with this court or he must be counted against it, there be no road between. This is a sharp time, now, a precise time — we live no longer in the dusky afternoon when evil mixed itself with good and befuddled the world. Now, by God's grace, the shining sun is up, and them that fear not light will surely praise it.
10) Excellency, I have signed seventy-two death warrants; I am a minister of the Lord, and I dare not take a life without there be a proof so immaculate no slightest qualm of conscience may doubt it.
11) Let *you* beware, Mr. Danforth. Think you to be so mighty that the power of Hell may not turn *your* wits?

12) She thinks to dance with me on my wife's grave! ... But it is a whore's vengeance, and you must see it; I set myself entirely in your hands, I know you must see it now.
13) I say—I say—God is dead!
14) You are pulling Heaven down and raising up a whore!
15) You cannot hang this sort. There is danger for me. I dare not step outside at night!
16) It is mistaken law that leads you to sacrifice. Life, woman, life is God's most precious gift; no principle, however glorious, may justify the taking of it.
17) Great stones they lay upon his chest until he plead aye or nay. They say he give them but two words. "More weight," he says. And died.
18) I speak my own sins; I cannot judge another. I have no tongue for it.
19) How may I live without my name? I have given you my soul; leave me my name!
20) He have his goodness now. God forbid I take it from him!

❺ Questions for essay or discussion

1) Discuss how the title of the play relates to the story.
2) In *The Crucible*, what role does vengeance play in the witch trial hysteria?
3) What are John Proctor's dilemmas at the beginning of the witch trials, after his wife is charged, and finally, after he is arrested?
4) Discuss the changes that Reverend Hale undergoes in the course of the play.
5) This play cannot be entirely trusted in terms of historical truth. Then what is its significance or value?

Unit 6

Lorraine Hansberry and *A Raisin in the Sun*

6.1 Lorraine Hansberry: Life and Works

6.1.1 About the Playwright

Lorraine Hansberry (1930—1965), is a playwright, essayist, poet, and leading literary figure in the civil rights movement. She became the first black woman to have a play produced on Broadway with *A Raisin in the Sun* (1959). Its success was confirmed when the New York Drama Critics' Circle voted it Best Play of the Year over Tennessee Williams's *Sweet Bird of Youth*, and Eugene O'Neill's *A Touch of the Poet*. Lorraine Hansberry, who was an unknown dramatist, achieved unprecedented success when her play became a Broadway sensation. Not only were successful women playwrights rare at the time, but successful young black women playwrights were virtually unheard of.

Lorraine Vivian Hansberry was born into a family of substantial means on May 19, 1930, in Chicago, Illinois. She was the youngest of four children. Her father, Carl Augustus Hansberry, Sr., was from Gloucester, Mississippi. He moved to Chicago after attending Alcorn College, and became known as the "kitchenette king" after subdividing large homes vacated by whites moving to suburbs and selling these small apartments or kitchenettes to African American migrants from the South. Hansberry's mother, Nannie Perry, a schoolteacher and, later, ward committee woman, was from

Tennessee. At the time of Lorraine's birth, she had become an influential society matron who hosted major cultural and literary figures such as Paul Robeson, Langston Hughes, and Joe Louis. Although Lorraine and her siblings enjoyed privileges unknown to their working-class schoolmates, the parents infused their children with racial pride and civil responsibility. They founded the Hansberry Foundation, an organization designed to inform African Americans of their civil rights, and encouraged their children to challenge the exclusionary policies of local restaurants and stores. Carl and Nannie Hansberry challenged restrictive real estate covenants by moving into an all-white neighborhood. A mob of whites gathered in front of the house and threw a brick through the front window, narrowly missing eight-year-old Lorraine and forcing the family to move out. Her father won a narrow victory over restrictive covenants from the Supreme Court, but the decision failed to set precedent on this issue.

In 1948 Lorraine Hansberry attended the University of Wisconsin, a predominantly white university, to study journalism, but was equally attracted to the visual arts. She integrated into an all-white women's dormitory and became active in the campus chapter of the Young Progressive Association, serving as its president during her sophomore year. She left Wisconsin in 1950 to head for New York, where she transferred to the New School of Social Research and began working for Paul Robeson's radical black monthly, *Freedom*. She wrote articles about conditions in the black community, and reviewed books and plays by blacks. By 1952 she had become an associate editor.

It was in New York that Hansberry became personally involved in the racial struggle, marching in public demonstrations, speaking on street corners, and helping black tenants move back into apartments from which they had been evicted. While participating in a demonstration at New York University, she met Robert Nemiroff, son of progressive Russian Jewish immigrants, and an aspiring writer and graduate student in English and history at New York University. After a short courtship, she married him on 20 June 1953. Having earned his master's degree four months earlier, Nemiroff had begun writing a book on Theodore Dreiser, his thesis topic. The young couple moved to Greenwich Village and Hansberry began to write extensively about the people and lifestyles that she observed around her. She published articles, essays, and poetry in *Freedom*, *New Challenge*, and other leftist magazines. In the late 1950s African American playwriting received a tremendous boost with the highly acclaimed *A Raisin in the Sun*. Hansberry became an overnight celebrity, appearing on numerous talk shows and using these platforms as an opportunity to speak to a wider audience about the need for black social, political, and economic reform. Capturing the spirit of the civil rights movement, *A Raisin in the Sun* won the 1959 New York Drama Critics' Circle Award and made Hansberry the first black, youngest person, and fifth woman to win that prize.

In 1963 she was hospitalized for tests that indicated cancer, but she continued to write and be politically active. At the request of James Baldwin in May 1963, Hansberry joined a meeting of prominent blacks and whites with Attorney General Robert Kennedy to discuss the racial crisis, forcefully arguing for better treatment of black Americans and condemning an American society that allowed such discrimination.

Hansberry's second produced play, *The Sign in Sidney Brustein's Window* (1964), depicting Jews and other whites as well as blacks in Greenwich Village, opened at Longacre Theater in New York three months before she died. Despite mixed reviews, out of respect, the play was kept running up to the day of Hansberry's death, January 12, 1965.

Hansberry left a number of finished and unfinished writings that indicate the breadth of her social and artistic vision. Nemiroff, whom she had quietly divorced in 1964 but designated as her literary executor, worked to bring Hansberry's other writing to public attention. In addition to publishing the unproduced plays and producing *Les Blancs*, he also edited a memoir, *To Be Young, Gifted and Black* (1969), and wrote and produced a play based on this, which was later adapted for television, as well as producing an acclaimed musical version of *A Raisin in the Sun* (1972). Until 1991 when he died, Nemiroff devoted his life to editing, promoting, and producing Hansberry's works on stage and television.

6.1.2 Lorraine Hansberry's Major Plays

A Raisin in the Sun (1959) 《阳光下的葡萄干》
The Sign in Sidney Brustein's Window (1964) 《西德尼·布鲁斯坦窗口的标记》

6.2.1 About the Play

A Raisin in the Sun (1959) was the first Broadway production to be directed by an African American, Lloyd Richards. The play ran for 538 performances on Broadway and was made into a film, which won a special award at the Cannes Film Festival in 1961. Now a classic of the American theater, *A Raisin in the Sun* has been published in several editions since its inaugural production, and has been translated into over thirty languages on every continent.

Set entirely in the Younger living room, the play takes place in Chicago during

英美戏剧与电影
English and American Drama and Film

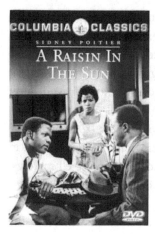

the middle of the twentieth century. Three generations of the African American, working-class family live in this crowded apartment. An insurance benefit of ten thousand dollars paid on the death of Walter, Sr. becomes the source of conflict within the Younger family, as Mama Lena Younger, and her son, Walter Lee Younger, argue over its use. Their debate reveals fundamental differences in values and ponders the relationship of material wealth to human dignity. The play depicts the frustrations of a struggling, working-class black family whose dreams of economic progress have been thwarted. In depicting three generations of the Younger family Hansberry made a lasting contribution to American drama. She rejected lessons of despair, of helplessness, of cynical indifference to the events of modern life, and instead she celebrated the complex humanity of Americans whose hopes and dreams can no longer be deferred.

When Hansberry began *A Raisin in the Sun*, she titled it *The Crystal Stair*, from a line in Langston Hughes's poem "Mother to Son." In the poem, a black mother asserts that "life for me ain't been no crystal stair," as she describes her struggle to provide a better life for her family and encourages her son to continue the fight. Hansberry later changed the title from *The Crystal Stair* to *A Raisin in the Sun*, from a line in Hughes's poem "Harlem" (1951), which warns that a dream deferred might "dry up / like a raisin in the sun" —or "explode." She felt this new title better conveyed the bitterness of the social conditions that conspired to defer the aspirations of the black family in the play.

Harlem
—by Langston Hughes

What happens to a dream deferred?
Does it dry up
Like a raisin in the sun?
Or fester like a sore—
And then run?
Does it stink like rotten meat?
Or crust and sugar over—
Like a syrupy sweet?

Maybe it just sags
Like a heavy load.

Or does it explode?

6.2.2 Characters

Lena Younger, called **Mama,** a retired domestic and the matriarch of the Younger family. In her early sixties, Mama is a religious, optimistic, moral, and proud black woman.

Walter Lee Younger, a chauffeur and Mama's only son. He is a frustrated thirty-five-year-old black man.

Ruth Younger, Walter's wife and Travis's mother. She is about thirty, but is aging quickly because of hard work.

Beneatha (Bennie) Younger, Mama's daughter and Walter's younger sister. A college student, she is intellectual, independent and ambitious.

Travis Younger, Walter and Ruth's loveable young son.

Joseph Asagai, one of Beneatha's fellow students and one of her suitors. He is from Nigeria and is very proud of his African heritage.

George Murchison, a wealthy, African-American man who courts Beneatha.

Mr. Karl Lindner, the only white character in the play. He visits the Youngers' apartment from the Clybourne Park Improvement Association.

Bobo, one of Walter's partners in the liquor store plan.

Willy Harris, a friend of Walter's and a partner in the liquor store plan. Willy does not appear onstage.

Mrs. Johnson, the Youngers' nosy, stingy neighbor who warns them about moving into a white neighborhood. Her role is eliminated in some versions of the play.

6.2.3 Selected Readings from the Play

> **Excerpt 1 (from Act 1, Scene 1)**
> It is morning at the Youngers' apartment in one of the poorer sections of Southside Chicago. It is a cramped place clearly too small for its five occupants. There is only one little window for the living room and the kitchen area, and they share a bathroom in the hall with their neighbors. Ruth gets up first and after some difficulty, rouses Travis and Walter as she makes breakfast. They all seem tired, but they keep mentioning a check.

TRAVIS: Mama, this is Friday. *(gleefully)* Check coming tomorrow, huh?
RUTH: You get your mind off money and eat your breakfast.
TRAVIS *(eating)*: This is the morning we supposed to bring the fifty cents to school.
RUTH: Well, I ain't got no fifty cents this morning.
TRAVIS: Teacher say we have to.
RUTH: I don't care what teacher say. I ain't got it. Eat your breakfast, Travis.

TRAVIS: I *am* eating.

RUTH: Hush up now and just eat!

> The boy gives her an exasperated（恼怒的） look for her lack of understanding, and eats grudgingly（不情愿地）.

TRAVIS: You think Grandmama would have it?

RUTH: No! And I want you to stop asking your grandmother for money, you hear me?

TRAVIS *(outraged)*: Gaaaleee! I don't ask her, she just gimme it sometimes!

RUTH: Travis Willard Younger—I got too much on me this morning to be—

TRAVIS: Maybe Daddy—

RUTH: *Travis!*

> The boy hushes（安静） abruptly. They are both quiet and tense for several seconds.

TRAVIS *(presently)*: Could I maybe go carry some groceries in front of the supermarket for a little while after school then?

RUTH: Just hush, I said. *(Travis jabs〈戳〉 his spoon into his cereal bowl viciously, and rests his head in anger upon his fists.)* If you through eating, you can get over there and make up your bed.

> The boy obeys stiffly and crosses the room, almost mechanically, to the bed and more or less folds the bedding into a heap, then angrily gets his books and cap.

TRAVIS *(sulking and standing apart from her unnaturally)*: I'm gone.

RUTH *(looking up from the stove to inspect him automatically)*: Come here. *(He crosses to her and she studies his head.)* If you don't take this comb and fix this here head, you better! *(Travis puts down his books with a great sigh of oppression〈压抑，苦恼〉, and crosses to the mirror. His mother mutters under her breath about his "slubbornness".)* 'Bout to march out of here with that head looking just like chickens slept in it! I just don't know where you get your slubborn ways... And get your jacket, too. Looks chilly out this morning.

TRAVIS *(with conspicuously〈显著地〉 brushed hair and jacket)*: I'm gone.

RUTH: Get carfare and milk money—*(waving one finger)*—and not a single penny for no caps（玩具枪的火药帽）, you hear me?

TRAVIS *(with sullen politeness)*: Yes'm.

> He turns in outrage to leave. His mother watches after him as in his frustration he approaches the door almost comically. When she speaks to him, her voice has become a very gentle tease.

RUTH *(mocking; as she thinks he would say it)*: Oh, Mama makes me so mad sometimes, I don't know what to do! *(She waits and continues to his back as he stands stock-still〈静止不动〉 in front of the door.)* I wouldn't kiss that woman good-bye for nothing in this world this morning! *(The boy finally turns around and rolls his eyes at her, knowing the mood has changed and he is vindicated〈使……

Unit 6

Lorraine Hansberry and *A Raisin in the Sun*

不受责怪〉; *he does not, however, move toward her yet.*) Not for nothing in this world! (*She finally laughs aloud at him and holds out her arms to him and we see that it is a way between them, very old and practiced. He crosses to her and allows her to embrace him warmly but keeps his face fixed with masculine rigidity. She holds him back from her presently and looks at him and runs her fingers over the features of his face. With utter gentleness—*) Now—whose little old angry man are you?

TRAVIS (*the masculinity and gruffness*〈粗鲁〉 *start to jade*〈疲倦〉 *at last*): Aw gaalee—Mama...

RUTH (*mimicking*): Aw—gaaaaalleeeee, Mama! (*She pushes him, with rough playfulness and finality*〈决断〉*, toward the door.*) Get on out of here or you going to be late.

TRAVIS (*in the face of love, new aggressiveness*): Mama, could I please go carry groceries?

RUTH: Honey, it's starting to get so cold evenings.

WALTER (*coming in from the bathroom and drawing a make-believe*〈假装的〉 *gun from a make-believe holster*〈枪套〉 *and shooting at his son*): What is it he wants to do?

RUTH: Go carry groceries after school at the supermarket.

WALTER: Well, let him go...

TRAVIS (*quickly, to the ally*): I have to—she won't gimme the fifty cents...

WALTER (*to his wife only*): Why not?

RUTH (*simply, and with flavor*): 'Cause we don't have it.

WALTER (*to Ruth only*): What you tell the boy things like that for? (*Reaching down into his pants with a rather important gesture.*) Here, son—(*He hands the boy the coin, but his eyes are directed to his wife's. Travis takes the money happily.*)

TRAVIS: Thanks, Daddy.

> *He starts out. Ruth watches both of them with murder in her eyes. Walter stands and stares back at her with defiance, and suddenly reaches into his pocket again on an afterthought.*

WALTER (*without even looking at his son, still staring hard at his wife*): In fact, here's another fifty cents... Buy yourself some fruit today—or take a taxicab to school or something!

TRAVIS: Whoopee—

> *He leaps up and clasps his father around the middle with his legs, and they face each other in mutual appreciation; slowly Walter Lee peeks*（窥视） *around the boy to catch the violent rays from his wife's eyes and draws his head back as if shot.*

WALTER: You better get down now—and get to school, man.

TRAVIS (*at the door*): O.K. Good-bye. (*He exits.*)

WALTER *(after him, pointing with pride)*: That's my boy. *(She looks at him in disgust and turns back to her work.)* You know what I was thinking 'bout in the bathroom this morning?

RUTH: No.

WALTER: How come you always try to be so pleasant!

RUTH: What is there to be pleasant 'bout!

WALTER: You want to know what I was thinking 'bout in the bathroom or not!

RUTH: I know what you thinking 'bout.

WALTER *(ignoring her)*: 'Bout what me and Willy Harris was talking about last night.

RUTH *(immediately—a refrain〈老调重弹〉)*: Willy Harris is a good-for-nothing（没用的） loudmouth（牛皮大王）.

WALTER: Anybody who talks to me has got to be a good-for-nothing loudmouth, ain't he? And what you know about who is just a good-for-nothing loudmouth? Charlie Atkins was just a "good-for-nothing loudmouth" too, wasn't he! When he wanted me to go in the dry-cleaning business with him. And now—he's grossing（总共收入） a hundred thousand a year. A hundred thousand dollars a year! You still call *him* a loudmouth!

RUTH *(bitterly)*: Oh, Walter Lee...

She folds her head on her arms over the table.

WALTER *(rising and coming to her and standing over her)*: You tired, ain't you? Tired of everything. Me, the boy, the way we live—this beat-up（破旧的） hole（阴暗肮脏的小房屋）—everything. Ain't you? *(She doesn't look up, doesn't answer.)* So tired—moaning and groaning all the time, but you wouldn't do nothing to help, would you? You couldn't be on my side that long for nothing, could you?

RUTH: Walter, please leave me alone.

WALTER: A man needs for a woman to back him up...

RUTH: Walter—

WALTER: Mama would listen to you. You know she listen to you more than she do me and Bennie. She think more of you. All you have to do is just sit down with her when you drinking your coffee one morning and talking 'bout things like you do and—*(He sits down beside her and demonstrates graphically〈活灵活现地〉what he thinks her methods and tone should be.)* —you just sip（小口喝） your coffee, see, and say easy like that you been thinking 'bout that deal Walter Lee is so interested in, 'bout the store and all, and sip some more coffee, like what you saying ain't really that important to you—And the next thing you know, she be listening good and asking you questions and when I come home—I can tell her the details. This ain't no fly-by-night（不可靠的） proposition, baby. I mean we figured it out, me and Willy and Bobo.

RUTH *(with a frown)*: Bobo?

Unit 6

Lorraine Hansberry and *A Raisin in the Sun*

WALTER: Yeah. You see, this little liquor store we got in mind cost seventy-five thousand and we figured the initial investment on the place be 'bout thirty thousand, see. That be ten thousand each. Course, there's a couple of hundred you got to pay so's you don't spend your life just waiting for them clowns to let your license get approved—

RUTH: You mean graft（贿赂）?

WALTER *(frowning impatiently)*: Don't call it that. See there, that just goes to show you what women understand about the world. Baby, don't *nothing* happen for you in this world 'less you pay *somebody* off!

RUTH: Walter, leave me alone! *(She raises her head and stares at him vigorously—then says, more quietly.) Eat* your eggs, they gonna be cold.

WALTER *(straightening up from her and looking off)*: That's it. There you are. Man say to his woman: I got me a dream. His woman say: Eat your eggs. *(Sadly, but gaining in power)* Man say: I got to take hold of this here world, baby! And a woman will say: Eat your eggs and go to work. *(Passionately now)* Man say: I got to change my life, I'm choking to death, baby! And his woman say—*(in utter anguish as he brings his fists down on his thighs)*—Your eggs is getting cold!

RUTH *(softly)*: Walter, that ain't none of our money.

WALTER *(not listening at all or even looking at her)*: This morning, I was lookin' in the mirror and thinking about it ... I'm thirty five years old; I been married eleven years and I got a boy who sleeps in the living room—*(very, very quietly)*—and all I got to give him is stories about how rich white people live...

RUTH: Eat your eggs, Walter.

WALTER *(slams the table and jumps up)*: —DAMN MY EGGS—DAMN ALL THE EGGS THAT EVER WAS!

RUTH: Then go to work.

WALTER *(looking up at her)*: See—I'm trying to talk to you 'bout myself—*(shaking his head with the repetition)*—and all you can say is eat them eggs and go to work.

RUTH *(wearily)*: Honey, you never say nothing new. I listen to you every day, every night and every morning, and you never say nothing new. *(shrugging)* So you would rather *be* Mr. Arnold than be his chauffeur（私家司机）. So—I would *rather* be living in Buckingham Palace.

WALTER: That is just what is wrong with the colored woman in this world... Don't understand about building their men up and making 'em feel like they somebody（大人物）. Like they can do something.

RUTH *(drily, but to hurt.)*: There *are* colored men who do things.

WALTER: No thanks to（并未沾……的光）the colored woman.

RUTH: Well, being a colored woman, I guess I can't help myself none.

She rises and gets the ironing board and sets it up and attacks（动手干）

a huge pile of rough-dried clothes, sprinkling them in preparation for the ironing and then rolling them into tight fat balls.

WALTER *(mumbling)*: We one group of men tied to a race of women with small minds!

His sister Beneatha enters. She is about twenty, as slim and <u>intense</u>（性子烈） as her brother. She is not as pretty as her sister-in-law, but her lean, almost intellectual face has a handsomeness of its own. She wears a bright-red <u>flannel</u>（法兰绒） <u>nightie</u>（女睡衣）, and her thick hair stands wildly about her head. Her speech is a mixture of many things; it is different from the rest of the family's insofar as education has <u>permeated</u>（渗透） her sense of English—and perhaps the Midwest[①] rather than the South has finally—at last—won out in her <u>inflection</u>（词尾变形）; but not altogether, because over all of it is a soft <u>slurring</u>（发音含糊） and transformed use of vowels which is the decided influence of the Southside[②]. She passes through the room without looking at either Ruth or Walter and goes to the outside door and looks, a little blindly, out to the bathroom. She sees that it has been lost to the Johnsons. She closes the door with a sleepy vengeance and crosses to the table and sits down a little defeated.

BENEATHA: I am going to start timing those people.

WALTER: You should get up earlier.

BENEATHA *(her face in her hands. She is still fighting the urge to go back to bed)*: Really—would you suggest dawn? Where's the paper?

WALTER *(pushing the paper across the table to her as he studies her almost <u>clinically</u>〈客观冷静地〉, as though he has never seen her before)*: You a horrible-looking chick at this hour.

BENEATHA *(drily)*: Good morning, everybody.

WALTER *(<u>senselessly</u>〈不带感情地〉)*: How is school coming?

BENEATHA *(in the same spirit)*: Lovely. Lovely. And you know, biology is the greatest. *(looking up at him)* I <u>dissected</u>（解剖） something that looked just like you yesterday.

WALTER: I just wondered if you've made up your mind and everything.

BENEATHA *(gaining in sharpness and impatience)*: And what did I answer yesterday morning—and the day before that?

RUTH *(from the ironing board, like someone <u>disinterested</u>〈不偏不倚的〉 and old)*: Don't be so nasty, Bennie.

BENEATHA *(still to her brother)*: And the day before that and the day before that!

[①] Midwest: also called Middle West, is one of four geographic regions defined by the United States Census Bureau. It occupies the northern central part of the United States of America, and consists of 12 states: Illinois, Indiana, Iowa, Kansas, Michigan, Minnesota, Missouri, Nebraska, North Dakota, Ohio, South Dakota, and Wisconsin.

[②] Southside: a region of the city of Chicago, where there is a large African American population.

Unit 6

Lorraine Hansberry and *A Raisin in the Sun*

WALTER *(defensively)*: I'm interested in you. Something wrong with that? Ain't many girls who decide—

WALTER and BENEATHA *(in unison 〈异口同声〉)*: —"to be a doctor." *(Silence)*

WALTER: Have we figured out yet just exactly how much medical school is going to cost?

RUTH: Walter Lee, why don't you leave that girl alone and get out of here to work?

BENEATHA *(exits to the bathroom and bangs on the door)*: Come on out of there, please! *(She comes back into the room.)*

WALTER *(looking at his sister intently 〈专注地〉)*: You know the check is coming tomorrow.

BENEATHA *(turning on him with a sharpness all her own)*: That money belongs to Mama, Walter, and it's for her to decide how she wants to use it. I don't care if she wants to buy a house or a rocket ship or just nail it up somewhere and look at it. It's hers. Not ours—*hers*.

WALTER *(bitterly)*: Now ain't that fine! You just got your mother's interest at heart, ain't you, girl? You such a nice girl—but if Mama got that money she can always take a few thousand and help you through school too—can't she?

BENEATHA: I have never asked anyone around here to do anything for me!

WALTER: No! And the line between asking and just accepting when the time comes is big and wide—ain't it!

BENEATHA *(with fury)*: What do you want from me, Brother—that I quit school or just drop dead, which!

WALTER: I don't want nothing but for you to stop acting holy 'round here. Me and Ruth done made some sacrifices for you—why can't you do something for the family?

RUTH: Walter, don't be dragging me in it.

WALTER: You are in it—Don't you get up and go work in somebody's kitchen for the last three years to help put clothes on her back?

RUTH: Oh, Walter—that's not fair...

WALTER: It ain't that nobody expects you to get on your knees and say thank you, Brother; thank you, Ruth; thank you, Mama—and thank you, Travis, for wearing the same pair of shoes for two semesters—

BENEATHA *(dropping to her knees)*: Well—I *do*—all right? —thank everybody! And forgive me for ever wanting to be anything at all! *(pursuing him on her knees across the floor)* FORGIVE ME, FORGIVE ME, FORGIVE ME!

RUTH: Please stop it! Your mama'll hear you.

WALTER: Who the hell told you you had to be a doctor? If you so crazy 'bout messing 'round with sick people—then go be a nurse like other women—or just get married and be quiet...

BENEATHA: Well—you finally got it said ... It took you three years but you finally got it said. Walter, give up; leave me alone—it's Mama's money.

WALTER: *He was my father, too!*

BENEATHA: So what? He was mine, too—and Travis' grandfather—but the insurance money belongs to Mama. Picking on me is not going to make her give it to you to invest in any liquor stores—*(underbreath*〈低声〉*, dropping into a chair)*—and I for one say, God bless Mama for that!

WALTER *(to Ruth)*: See—did you hear? Did you hear!

RUTH: Honey, please go to work.

WALTER: Nobody in this house is ever going to understand me.

BENEATHA: Because you're a nut（疯子）.

WALTER: Who's a nut?

BENEATHA: You—you are a nut. Thee is mad, boy.

WALTER *(looking at his wife and his sister from the door, very sadly)*: The world's most backward race of people, and that's a fact.

BENEATHA *(turning slowly in her chair)*: And then there are all those prophets（先知）who would lead us out of the wilderness—*(Walter slams out of the house)*—into the swamps!

RUTH: Bennie, why you always gotta be pickin' on your brother? Can't you be a little sweeter sometimes? *(Door opens. Walter walks in. He fumbles with his cap, starts to speak, clears throat, looks everywhere but at Ruth. Finally:)*

WALTER *(to Ruth)*: I need some money for carfare.

RUTH *(looks at him, then warms; teasing, but tenderly)*: Fifty cents? *(She goes to her bag and gets money.)* Here—take a taxi!

Walter exits.

✂ Excerpt 2 (from Act 1, Scene 1)

After Walter leaves for work, Mama enters and goes directly to a small plant that she keeps just outside the kitchen window—"a feeble little plant growing doggedly." She shows great concern for her children, cautioning Beneatha not to catch cold, and questioning Ruth about the breakfast she has been serving Travis. Then she asks Ruth why Walter and Beneatha quarreled.

MAMA: What was they fighting about?

RUTH: Now you know as well as I do.

MAMA *(shaking her head)*: Brother still worrying hisself sick about that money?

RUTH: You know he is.

MAMA: You had breakfast?

Unit 6

Lorraine Hansberry and *A Raisin in the Sun*

RUTH: Some coffee.

MAMA: Girl, you better start eating and looking after yourself better. You almost thin as Travis.

RUTH: Lena—

MAMA: Un-hunh?

RUTH: What are you going to do with it?

MAMA: Now don't you start, child. It's too early in the morning to be talking about money. It ain't Christian.

RUTH: It's just that he got his heart set on that store—

MAMA: You mean that liquor store that Willy Harris want him to invest in?

RUTH: Yes—

MAMA: We ain't no business people, Ruth. We just plain working folks.

RUTH: Ain't nobody business people till they go into business. Walter Lee say colored people ain't never going to start getting ahead till they start gambling on some different kinds of things in the world—investments and things.

MAMA: What done got into you, girl? Walter Lee done finally sold you on investing.

RUTH: No. Mama, something is happening between Walter and me. I don't know what it is—but he needs something—something I can't give him any more. He needs this chance, Lena.

MAMA *(frowning deeply)*: But liquor, honey

RUTH: Well—like Walter say—I spec people going to always be drinking themselves some liquor.

MAMA: Well—whether they drinks it or not ain't none of my business. But whether I go into business selling it to 'em *is*, and I don't want that on my ledger (账簿) this late in life. *(stopping suddenly and studying her daughter-in-law)* Ruth Younger, what's the matter with you today? You look like you could fall over right there.

RUTH: I'm tired.

MAMA: Then you better stay home from work today.

RUTH: I can't stay home. She'd be calling up the agency and screaming at them, "My girl didn't come in today send me somebody! My girl didn't come in!" Oh, she just have a fit...

MAMA: Well, let her have it. I'll just call her up and say you got the flu—

RUTH *(laughing)*: Why the flu?

MAMA: 'Cause it sounds respectable to 'em. Something white people get, too. They know 'bout the flu. Otherwise they think you been cut up or something when you tell 'em you sick.

RUTH: I got to go in. We need the money.

MAMA: Somebody would of thought my children done all but starved to death the way they talk about money here late. Child, we got a great big old check coming tomorrow.

RUTH *(sincerely, but also self-righteously)*: Now that's your money. It ain't got nothing to do with me. We all feel like that—Walter and Bennie and me—even Travis.

MAMA *(thoughtfully, and suddenly very far away)*: Ten thousand dollars—

RUTH: Sure is wonderful.

MAMA: Ten thousand dollars.

RUTH: You know what you should do, Miss Lena? You should take yourself a trip somewhere. To Europe or South America or someplace—

MAMA *(throwing up her hands at the thought)*: Oh, child!

RUTH: I'm serious. Just pack up and leave! Go on away and enjoy yourself some. Forget about the family and have yourself a ball for once in your life—

MAMA *(drily)*: You sound like I'm just about ready to die. Who'd go with me? What I look like wandering 'round Europe by myself?

RUTH: Shoot—these here rich white women do it all the time. They don't think nothing of packing up they suitcases and piling on one of them big steamships and—swoosh!—they gone, child.

MAMA: Something always told me I wasn't no rich white woman.

RUTH: Well—what are you going to do with it then?

MAMA: I ain't rightly decided. *(Thinking. She speaks now with emphasis.)* Some of it got to be put away for Beneatha and her schoolin'—and ain't nothing going to touch that part of it. Nothing. *(She waits several seconds, trying to make up her mind about something, and looks at Ruth a little tentatively before going on.)* Been thinking that we maybe could meet the <u>notes</u>（票据） on a little old two-story somewhere, with a yard where Travis could play in the summertime, if we use part of the insurance for a <u>down payment</u>（首付，定金）and everybody kind of <u>pitch in</u>（投入）. I could maybe take on a little day work again, few days a week—

RUTH *(studying her mother-in-law furtively and concentrating on her ironing, anxious to encourage without seeming to)*: Well, Lord knows, we've put enough rent into this here <u>rat trap</u>（破屋子） to pay for four houses by now…

MAMA *(looking up at the words "rat trap" and then looking around and leaning back and sighing—in a suddenly reflective mood—)*: "Rat trap"—yes, that's all it is. *(smiling)* I remember just as well the day me and Big Walter moved in here. Hadn't been married but two weeks and wasn't planning on living here no more than a year. *(She shakes her head at the dissolved dream.)* We was going to set away, little by little, don't you know, and buy a little place out in Morgan Park. We had even picked out the house. *(chuckling a little)* Looks right <u>dumpy</u>（丑陋的，破旧的）today. But Lord, child, you should know all the dreams I had 'bout buying that house and fixing it up and making me a little garden in the back—*(She waits and stops smiling.)* And didn't none of it happen. *(dropping her hands in a futile gesture.)*

RUTH *(keeps her head down, ironing)*: Yes, life can be a barrel of disappointments, sometimes.

MAMA: Honey, Big Walter would come in here some nights back then and slump down on that couch there and just look at the rug, and look at me and look at the rug and then back at me—and I'd know he was down then... really down. *(After a second very long and thoughtful pause; she is seeing back to times that only she can see.)* And then, Lord, when I lost that baby—little Claude—I almost thought I was going to lose Big Walter too. Oh, that man grieved hisself! He was one man to love his children.

RUTH: Ain't nothin' can tear at you like losin' your baby.

MAMA: I guess that's how come that man finally worked hisself to death like he done. Like he was fighting his own war with this here world that took his baby from him.

RUTH: He sure was a fine man, all right. I always liked Mr. Younger.

MAMA: Crazy 'bout his children! God knows there was plenty wrong with Walter Younger—hard-headed, mean, kind of wild with women—plenty wrong with him. But he sure loved his children. Always wanted them to have something—be something. That's where Brother gets all these notions, I reckon. Big Walter used to say, he'd get right wet in the eyes sometimes, lean his head back with the water standing in his eyes and say, "Seem like God didn't see fit to give the black man nothing but dreams—but He did give us children to make them dreams seem worth while." *(She smiles.)* He could talk like that, don't you know.

RUTH: Yes, he sure could. He was a good man, Mr. Younger.

MAMA: Yes, a fine man—just couldn't never catch up with his dreams, that's all.

  Beneatha comes in, brushing her hair and looking up to the ceiling, where the sound of a <u>vacuum cleaner</u>（吸尘器） has started up.

BENEATHA: What could be so dirty on that woman's rugs that she has to vacuum them every single day?

RUTH: I wish certain young women 'round here who I could name would take inspiration about certain rugs in a certain apartment I could also mention.

BENEATHA *(shrugging)*: How much cleaning can a house need, for Christ's sakes.

MAMA *(not liking the Lord's name used thus)*: Bennie!

RUTH: Just listen to her—just listen!

BENEATHA: Oh, God!

MAMA: If you use the Lord's name just one more time—

BENEATHA *(a bit of a <u>whine</u>〈牢骚〉)*: Oh, Mama—

RUTH: <u>Fresh</u>（无礼）—just fresh as salt, this girl!

BENEATHA (drily): Well—if the salt loses its savor[①]—

MAMA: Now that will do. I just ain't going to have you 'round here reciting the scriptures（经文）in vain（轻慢）—you hear me?

BENEATHA: How did I manage to get on everybody's wrong side by just walking into a room?

RUTH: If you weren't so fresh—

BENEATHA: Ruth, I'm twenty years old.

MAMA: What time you be home from school today?

BENEATHA: Kind of late. (with enthusiasm) Madeline is going to start my guitar lessons today. (Mama and Ruth look up with the same expression.)

MAMA: Your *what* kind of lessons?

BENEATHA: Guitar.

RUTH: Oh, Father!

MAMA: How come you done taken it in your mind to learn to play the guitar?

BENEATHA: I just want to, that's all.

MAMA (smiling): Lord, child, don't you know what to do with yourself? How long it going to be before you get tired of this now—like you got tired of that little play-acting group you joined last year? (looking at Ruth) And what was it the year before that?

RUTH: The horseback-riding club for which she bought that fifty-five-dollar riding habit（衣装）that's been hanging in the closet ever since!

MAMA (to Beneatha): Why you got to flit（转变）so from one thing to another, baby?

BENEATHA (sharply): I just want to learn to play the guitar. Is there anything wrong with that?

MAMA: Ain't nobody trying to stop you. I just wonders sometimes why you has to flit so from one thing to another all the time. You ain't never done nothing with all that camera equipment you brought home—

BENEATHA: I don't flit! I—I experiment with different forms of expression—

RUTH: Like riding a horse?

BENEATHA: —People have to express themselves one way or another.

MAMA: What is it you want to express?

BENEATHA (angrily): Me! (Mama and Ruth look at each other and burst into raucous〈粗声的〉laughter.) Don't worry—I don't expect you to understand.

MAMA (to change the subject): Who you going out with tomorrow night?

BENEATHA (with displeasure): George Murchison again.

MAMA (pleased): Oh—you getting a little sweet on him?

---

① if ... savor: an allusion to Jesus's words in the Bible, "Salt is good, but if it loses its saltiness, how can you make it salty again? Have salt among yourselves, and be at peace with each other." (Mark 9:50)

Unit 6

Lorraine Hansberry and *A Raisin in the Sun*

RUTH: You ask me, this child ain't sweet on nobody but herself—*(underbreath)* Express herself! *(They laugh.)*

BENEATHA: Oh—I like George all right, Mama. I mean I like him enough to go out with him <u>and stuff</u>（之类的）, but—

RUTH *(for <u>devilment</u>〈恶作剧〉)*: What does "and stuff" mean?

BENEATHA: Mind your own business.

MAMA: Stop <u>picking at</u>（找岔子） her now, Ruth. *(She chuckles—then a suspicious sudden look at her daughter as she turns in her chair for emphasis.)* What DOES it mean?

BENEATHA *(wearily)*: Oh, I just mean I couldn't ever really be serious about George. He's—he's so shallow.

RUTH: Shallow—what do you mean he's shallow? He's *Rich*!

MAMA: Hush, Ruth.

BENEATHA: I know he's rich. He knows he's rich, too.

RUTH: Well—what other qualities a man got to have to satisfy you, little girl?

BENEATHA: You wouldn't even begin to understand. Anybody who married Walter could not possibly understand.

MAMA *(outraged)*: What kind of way is that to talk about your brother?

BENEATHA: Brother is a <u>flip</u>（冒失鬼）—let's face it.

MAMA *(to Ruth, helplessly)*: What's a flip?

RUTH *(glad to add kindling)*: She's saying he's crazy.

BENEATHA: Not crazy. Brother isn't really crazy yet—he—he's an elaborate <u>neurotic</u>（神经质）.

MAMA: Hush your mouth!

BENEATHA: As for George. Well. George looks good—he's got a beautiful car and he takes me to nice places and, as my sister-in-law says, he is probably the richest boy I will ever get to know and I even like him sometimes—but if the Youngers are sitting around waiting to see if their little Bennie is going to tie up the family with the Murchisons, they are wasting their time.

RUTH: You mean you wouldn't marry George Murchison if he asked you someday? That pretty, rich thing? Honey, I knew you was odd—

BENEATHA: No I would not marry him if all I felt for him was what I feel now. Besides, George's family wouldn't really like it.

MAMA: Why not?

BENEATHA: Oh, Mama—The Murchisons are honest-to-God-real-*live*-rich colored people, and the only people in the world who are more <u>snobbish</u>（势利的） than rich white people are rich colored people. I thought everybody knew that. I've met Mrs. Murchison. She's a scene!

MAMA: You must not dislike people 'cause they well off, honey.

BENEATHA: Why not? It makes just as much sense as disliking people 'cause they are poor, and lots of people do that.

RUTH *(a wisdom-of-the-ages manner. To Mama)*: Well, she'll get over some of this—

BENEATHA: Get over it? What are you talking about, Ruth? Listen, I'm going to be a doctor. I'm not worried about who I'm going to marry yet—if I ever get married.

MAMA and RUTH: *If!*

MAMA: Now, Bennie—

BENEATHA: Oh, I probably will ... but first I'm going to be a doctor, and George, for one, still thinks that's pretty funny. I couldn't be bothered with that. I am going to be a doctor and everybody around here better understand that!

MAMA *(kindly)*: 'Course you going to be a doctor, honey, God willing.

BENEATHA *(drily)*: God hasn't got a thing to do with it.

MAMA: Beneatha—that just wasn't necessary.

BENEATHA: Well—neither is God. I get sick of hearing about God.

MAMA: Beneatha!

BENEATHA: I mean it! I'm just tired of hearing about God all the time. What has He got to do with anything? Does he pay tuition?

MAMA: You 'bout to get your fresh little jaw slapped(掴耳光)!

RUTH: That's just what she needs, all right!

BENEATHA: Why? Why can't I say what I want to around here, like everybody else?

MAMA: It don't sound nice for a young girl to say things like that—you wasn't brought up that way. Me and your father went to trouble to get you and Brother to church every Sunday.

BENEATHA: Mama, you don't understand. It's all a matter of ideas, and God is just one idea I don't accept. It's not important. I am not going out and be immoral or commit crimes because I don't believe in God. I don't even think about it. It's just that I get tired of Him getting credit for all the things the human race achieves through its own stubborn effort. There simply is no blasted(该死的) God— there is only man and it is he who makes miracles!

> *Mama absorbs this speech, studies her daughter and rises slowly and crosses to Beneatha and slaps her powerfully across the face. After, there is only silence and the daughter drops her eyes from her mother's face, and Mama is very tall before her.*

MAMA: Now—you say after me, in my mother's house there is still God. *(There is a long pause and Beneatha stares at the floor wordlessly. Mama repeats the phrase with precision and cool emotion.)* In my mother's house there is still God.

BENEATHA: In my mother's house there is still God. *(a long pause)*

MAMA *(walking away from Beneatha, too disturbed for triumphant posture. Stopping and turning back to her daughter.)*: There are some ideas we ain't going to have in this house. Not long as I am at the head of this family.

BENEATHA: Yes, ma'am. *(Mama walks out of the room.)*

RUTH *(almost gently, with profound understanding)*: You think you a woman, Bennie—but you still a little girl. What you did was childish—so you got treated like a child.

BENEATHA: I see. *(quietly)* I also see that everybody thinks it's all right for Mama to be a tyrant（暴君）. But all the tyranny（暴虐） in the world will never put a God in the heavens! *(She picks up her books and goes out. Pause.)*

RUTH *(goes to Mama's door)*: She said she was sorry.

MAMA *(coming out, going to her plant)*: They frightens me, Ruth. My children.

RUTH: You got good children, Lena. They just a little off sometimes—but they're good.

MAMA: No—there's something come down between me and them that don't let us understand each other and I don't know what it is. One done almost lost his mind thinking 'bout money all the time and the other done commence to talk about things I can't seem to understand in no form or fashion. What is it that's changing, Ruth?

RUTH *(soothingly〈安慰地〉, older than her years)*: Now... you taking it all too seriously. You just got strong-willed children and it takes a strong woman like you to keep 'em in hand.

MAMA *(looking at her plant and sprinkling a little water on it)*: They spirited（性子烈的） all right, my children. Got to admit they got spirit—Bennie and Walter. Like this little old plant that ain't never had enough sunshine or nothing—and look at it...

    She has her back to Ruth, who has had to stop ironing and lean against something and put the back of her hand to her forehead.

RUTH *(trying to keep Mama from noticing)*: You... sure... loves that little old thing, don't you? ...

MAMA: Well, I always wanted me a garden like I used to see sometimes at the back of the houses down home. This plant is close as I ever got to having one. *(She looks out of the window as she replaces the plant.)* Lord, ain't nothing as dreary as the view from this window on a dreary day, is there? Why ain't you singing this morning, Ruth? Sing that "No Ways Tired." That song always lifts me up so—*(She turns at last to see that Ruth has slipped quietly to the floor, in a state of semiconsciousness〈半意识〉.)* Ruth! Ruth honey—what's the matter with you... Ruth!

CURTAIN

✂ Excerpt 3 (from Act 1, Scene 2)

The following morning, Saturday, is the time that the check is expected to arrive. Beneatha and Mama are busy doing weekend housecleaning when Ruth comes in, announcing sadly that she is pregnant. Mama is upset when she realizes that Ruth is contemplating an abortion. Ruth suddenly breaks down into tears and Mama takes her into the bedroom. Just then, Joseph Asagai arrives for a visit to Beneatha.

ASAGAI: Hello, Alaiyo—

BENEATHA *(holding the door open and regarding him with pleasure)*: Hello... *(Long pause)* Well—come in. And please excuse everything. My mother was very upset about my letting anyone come here with the place like this.

ASAGAI *(coming into the room)*: You look disturbed too ... Is something wrong?

BENEATHA *(still at the door, absently)*: Yes... we've all got acute ghetto-itus. *(She smiles and comes toward him, finding a cigarette and sitting.)* So—sit down! No! Wait! *(She whips the spraygun〈喷枪〉off sofa where she had left it and puts the cushions back. At last perches〈在高处或边缘暂坐〉on arm of sofa. He sits.)* So, how was Canada?

ASAGAI *(a sophisticate)*: Canadian.

BENEATHA *(looking at him)*: Asagai, I'm very glad you are back.

ASAGAI *(looking back at her in turn)*: Are you really?

BENEATHA: Yes—very.

ASAGAI: Why?—you were quite glad when I went away. What happened?

BENEATHA: You went away.

ASAGAI: Ahhhhhhhh.

BENEATHA: Before—you wanted to be so serious before there was time.

ASAGAI: How much time must there be before one knows what one feels?

BENEATHA *(Stalling this particular conversation. Her hands pressed together, in a deliberately childish gesture.)*: What did you bring me?

ASAGAI *(handing her the package)*: Open it and see.

BENEATHA *(eagerly opening the package and drawing out some records and the colorful robes of a Nigerian woman)*: Oh, Asagai! ... You got them for me! ... How beautiful... and the records too! *(She lifts out the robes and runs to the mirror with them and holds the drapery〈布料〉up in front of herself.)*

ASAGAI *(coming to her at the mirror)*: I shall have to teach you how to drape（披挂）it properly. *(He flings the material about her for the moment and stands back to look at her.)* Ah—Oh-pay-gay-day, oh-gbah-mu-shay. *(a Yoruba[①] exclamation for*

[①] Yoruba: one of the three largest ethnic groups of Nigeria, concentrated in the southwestern part of that country.

admiration) You wear it well... very well... mutilated（残损） hair and all.

BENEATHA *(turning suddenly)*: My hair—what's wrong with my hair?

ASAGAI *(shrugging)*: Were you born with it like that?

BENEATHA *(reaching up to touch it)*: No ... of course not. *(She looks back to the mirror, disturbed.)*

ASAGAI *(smiling)*: How then?

BENEATHA: You know perfectly well how ... as crinkly（卷缩的） as yours... that's how.

ASAGAI: And it is ugly to you that way?

BENEATHA *(quickly)*: Oh, no—not ugly... *(more slowly, apologetically)* But it's so hard to manage when it's, well—raw（自然状态的）.

ASAGAI: And so to accommodate（照顾，考虑） that—you mutilate it every week?

BENEATHA: It's not mutilation!

ASAGAI *(laughing aloud at her seriousness)*: Oh ... please! I am only teasing（逗乐） you because you are so very serious about these things. *(He stands back from her and folds his arms across his chest as he watches her pulling at her hair and frowning in the mirror.)* Do you remember the first time you met me at school? ... *(He laughs.)* You came up to me and you said—and I thought you were the most serious little thing I had ever seen—you said: *(He imitates her.)* "Mr. Asagai—I want very much to talk with you. About Africa. You see, Mr. Asagai, I am looking for my *identity*!" *(He laughs.)*

BENEATHA *(turning to him, not laughing)*: Yes—*(Her face is quizzical〈好奇的〉, profoundly disturbed.)*

ASAGAI *(still teasing and reaching out and taking her face in his hands and turning her profile〈侧面〉 to him)*: Well... it is true that this is not so much a profile of a Hollywood queen as perhaps a queen of the Nile—*(a mock dismissal〈不理会〉 of the importance of the question)* But what does it matter? Assimilationism（民族同化主义） is so popular in your country.

BENEATHA *(wheeling, passionately, sharply)*: I am not an assimilationist!

ASAGAI *(The protest hangs in the room for a moment and Asagai studies her, his laughter fading)*: Such a serious one. *(There is a pause.)* So—you like the robes? You must take excellent care of them—they are from my sister's personal wardrobe.

BENEATHA *(with incredulity)*: You—you sent all the way home—for me?

ASAGAI *(with charm)*: For you—I would do much more... Well, that is what I came for. I must go.

BENEATHA: Will you call me Monday?

ASAGAI: Yes... We have a great deal to talk about. I mean about identity and time and all that.

BENEATHA: Time?

ASAGAI: Yes. About how much time one needs to know what one feels.

BENEATHA: You see! You never understood that there is more than one kind of feeling which can exist between a man and a woman—or, at least, there should be.

ASAGAI *(shaking his head negatively but gently)*: No. Between a man and a woman there need be only one kind of feeling. I have that for you... Now even... right this moment...

BENEATHA: I know—and by itself—it won't do. I can find that anywhere.

ASAGAI: For a woman it should be enough.

BENEATHA: I know—because that's what it says in all the novels that men write. But it isn't. Go ahead and laugh—but I'm not interested in being someone's little episode in America or—*(with feminine vengeance)*—one of them! *(Asagai has burst into laughter again.)* That's funny as hell, huh!

ASAGAI: It's just that every American girl I have known has said that to me. White—black—in this you are all the same. And the same speech, too!

BENEATHA *(angrily)*: Yuk, yuk, yuk[①]!

ASAGAI: It's how you can be sure that the world's most liberated women are not liberated at all. You all talk about it too much!

Mama enters and is immediately all social charm because of the presence of a guest.

BENEATHA: Oh—Mama—this is Mr. Asagai.

MAMA: How do you do?

ASAGAI *(total politeness to an elder)*: How do you do, Mrs. Younger. Please forgive me for coming at such an <u>outrageous</u>（离谱的） hour on a Saturday.

MAMA: Well, you are quite welcome. I just hope you understand that our house don't always look like this. *(chatterish)* You must come again. I would love to hear all about—*(not sure of the name)*—your country. I think it's so sad the way our American Negroes don't know nothing about Africa 'cept Tarzan and all that. And all that money they pour into these churches when they ought to be helping you people over there drive out them French and Englishmen done taken away your land.

The mother flashes a slightly superior look at her daughter upon completion of the <u>recitation</u>（背诵）.

ASAGAI *(taken aback by this sudden and acutely unrelated expression of sympathy)*: Yes ... yes...

MAMA *(smiling at him suddenly and relaxing and looking him over)*: How many miles is it from here to where you come from?

ASAGAI: Many thousands.

MAMA *(looking at him as she would Walter)*: I bet you don't half look after yourself,

---

① Yuk ... yuk: used in repetition to indicate pleasure or amused malice.

being away from your mama either. I spec you better come 'round here from time to time to get yourself some decent home-cooked meals...

ASAGAI *(moved)*: Thank you. Thank you very much. *(They are all quiet, then—)* Well ... I must go. I will call you Monday, Alaiyo.

MAMA: What's that he call you?

ASAGAI: Oh—"Alaiyo." I hope you don't mind. It is what you would call a nickname, I think. It is a Yoruba word. I am a Yoruba.

MAMA *(looking at Beneatha)*: I—I thought he was from—*(uncertain)*

ASAGAI *(understanding)*: Nigeria is my country. Yoruba is my tribal origin—

BENEATHA: You didn't tell us what Alaiyo means... for all I know, you might be calling me Little Idiot or something...

ASAGAI: Well... let me see ... I do not know how just to explain it ... The sense of a thing can be so different when it changes languages.

BENEATHA: You're evading.

ASAGAI: No—really it is difficult... *(thinking)* It means ... it means One for Whom Bread—Food—Is Not Enough. *(He looks at her.)* Is that all right?

BENEATHA *(understanding, softly)*: Thank you.

MAMA: *(looking from one to the other and not understanding any of it)* Well... that's nice... You must come see us again—Mr.—

ASAGAI: Ah-sah-guy...

MAMA: Yes... Do come again.

ASAGAI: Good-bye. *(He exits)*

MAMA *(after him)*: Lord, that's a pretty thing just went out here! *(insinuatingly, to her daughter)* Yes, I guess I see why we done commence to get so interested in Africa 'round here. Missionaries（传教士） my aunt Jenny! *(She exits.)*

BENEATHA: Oh, Mama! ...

> She picks up the Nigerian dress and holds it up to her in front of the mirror again. She sets the headdress（饰头巾） on haphazardly（随意地） and then notices her hair again and clutches at it and then replaces the headdress and frowns at herself. Then she starts to wriggle（扭动） in front of the mirror as she thinks a Nigerian woman might. Travis enters and stands regarding her.

TRAVIS: What's the matter, girl, you cracking up（精神崩溃）?

BENEATHA: Shut up.

> She pulls the headdress off and looks at herself in the mirror and clutches at her hair again and squinches her eyes as if trying to imagine something. Then, suddenly, she gets her raincoat and kerchief and hurriedly prepares for going out.

MAMA *(coming back into the room)*: She's resting now. Travis, baby, run next door and ask Miss Johnson to please let me have a little kitchen cleanser（清洁剂）. This here can is empty as Jacob's kettle.

TRAVIS: I just came in.

MAMA: Do as you told. *(He exits and she looks at her daughter.)* Where you going?

BENEATHA *(halting at the door)*: To become a queen of the Nile!

  She exits in a breathless blaze of glory. Ruth appears in the bedroom doorway.

MAMA: Who told you to get up?

RUTH: Ain't nothing wrong with me to be lying in no bed for. Where did Bennie go?

MAMA *(drumming her fingers)*: Far as I could make out（理解）—to Egypt. *(Ruth just looks at her.)* What time is it getting to?

RUTH: Ten twenty. And the mailman going to ring that bell this morning just like he done every morning for the last umpteen（无数的） years.

  Travis comes in with the cleanser can.

TRAVIS: She say to tell you that she don't have much.

MAMA *(angrily)*: Lord, some people I could name sure is tight-fisted（吝啬的）! *(directing her grandson)* Mark two cans of cleanser down on the list there. If she that hard up for（缺少） kitchen cleanser, I sure don't want to forget to get her none!

RUTH: Lena—maybe the woman is just short on（缺乏） cleanser—

MAMA *(not listening)*: —Much baking powder as she done borrowed from me all these years, she could of done gone into the baking business!

  The bell sounds suddenly and sharply and all three are stunned—serious and silent—mid-speech（说话间）. In spite of all the other conversations and distractions of the morning, this is what they have been waiting for, even Travis, who looks helplessly（不知所措地） from his mother to his grandmother. Ruth is the first to come to life again.

RUTH *(to Travis)*: Get down them steps, boy! *(Travis snaps to life〈迅速回过神来〉and flies out to get the mail.)*

MAMA *(her eyes wide, her hand to her breast)*: You mean it done really come?

RUTH *(excited)*: Oh, Miss Lena!

MAMA *(collecting herself〈镇定下来〉)*: Well ... I don't know what we all so excited about 'round here for. We known it was coming for months.

RUTH: That's a whole lot different from having it come and being able to hold it in your hands... a piece of paper worth ten thousand dollars... *(Travis bursts back into the room. He holds the envelope high above his head, like a little dancer, his face is radiant〈容光焕发〉 and he is breathless. He moves to his grandmother with sudden slow ceremony〈客套〉 and puts the envelope into her hands. She accepts it, and then merely holds it and looks at it.)* Come on! Open it ... Lord have mercy, I wish Walter Lee was here!

TRAVIS: Open it, Grandmama!

Unit 6

Lorraine Hansberry and *A Raisin in the Sun*

MAMA *(staring at it)*: Now you all be quiet. It's just a check.

RUTH: Open it...

MAMA *(still staring at it)*: Now don't act silly ... We ain't never been no people to act silly 'bout no money—

RUTH *(swiftly)*: We ain't never had none before—OPEN IT!

> *Mama finally makes a good strong tear and pulls out the thin blue slice of paper and inspects it closely. The boy and his mother study it* <u>raptly</u>（全神贯注地） *over Mama's shoulders.*

MAMA: Travis! *(She is counting off with doubt.)* Is that the right number of zeros.

TRAVIS: Yes'm... ten thousand dollars. Gaalee, Grandmama, you rich.

MAMA *(She holds the check away from her, still looking at it. Slowly her face <u>sobers</u>〈变得严肃〉 into a mask of unhappiness)*: Ten thousand dollars. *(She hands it to Ruth)* Put it away somewhere, Ruth. *(She does not look at Ruth; her eyes seem to be seeing something somewhere very far off.)* Ten thousand dollars they give you. Ten thousand dollars.

TRAVIS *(to his mother, sincerely)*: What's the matter with Grandmama—don't she want to be rich?

RUTH *(<u>distractedly</u> 〈心神不宁地〉)*: You go on out and play now, baby. *(Travis exits. Mama starts wiping dishes absently, humming intently to herself. Ruth turns to her, with kind exasperation.)* You've gone and got yourself upset.

MAMA *(not looking at her)*: I spec if it wasn't for you all ... I would just put that money away or give it to the church or something.

RUTH: Now what kind of talk is that. Mr. Younger would just be plain mad if he could hear you talking foolish like that.

MAMA *(stopping and staring off)*: Yes... he sure would. *(sighing)* We got enough to do with that money, all right. *(She halts then, and turns and looks at her daughter-in-law hard; Ruth avoids her eyes and Mama wipes her hands with finality and starts to speak firmly to Ruth.)* Where did you go today, girl?

RUTH: To the doctor.

MAMA *(impatiently)*: Now, Ruth… you know better than that. Old Doctor Jones is strange enough in his way but there ain't nothing 'bout him make somebody <u>slip</u>（犯错） and call him "she"—like you done this morning.

RUTH: Well, that's what happened—my tongue slipped.

MAMA: You went to see that woman, didn't you?

RUTH *(defensively, giving herself away)*: What woman you talking about?

MAMA *(angrily)*: That woman who—*(Walter enters in great excitement.)*

WALTER: Did it come?

MAMA *(quietly)*: Can't you give people a Christian greeting before you start asking about money?

WALTER *(to Ruth)*: Did it come? *(Ruth unfolds the check and lays it quietly before *him, watching him intently with thoughts of her own. Walter sits down and grasps it close and counts off the zeros.)* Ten thousand dollars—*(He turns suddenly, frantically to his mother and draws some papers out of his breast pocket.)* Mama—look. Old Willy Harris put everything on paper—

MAMA: Son—I think you ought to talk to your wife... I'll go on out and leave you alone if you want—

WALTER: I can talk to her later—Mama, look—

MAMA: Son—

WALTER: WILL SOMEBODY PLEASE LISTEN TO ME TODAY!

MAMA *(quietly)*: I don't 'low no yellin' in this house, Walter Lee, and you know it— *(Walter stares at them in frustration and starts to speak several times.)* And there ain't going to be no investing in no liquor stores.

WALTER: But, Mama, you ain't even looked at it.

MAMA: I don't aim to have to speak on that again. *(a long pause)*

WALTER: You ain't looked at it and you don't aim to have to speak on that again? You ain't even looked at it and *you* have decided—*(crumpling his papers)* Well, *you* tell that to my boy tonight when you put him to sleep on the living-room couch... *(turning to Mama and speaking directly to her)* Yeah—and tell it to my wife, Mama, tomorrow when she has to go out of here to look after somebody else's kids. And tell it to *me*, Mama, every time we need a new pair of curtains and I have to watch you go out and work in somebody's kitchen. Yeah, you tell me then! *(Walter starts out.)*

RUTH: Where you going?

WALTER: I'm going out!

RUTH: Where?

WALTER: Just out of this house somewhere—

RUTH *(getting her coat)*: I'll come too.

WALTER: I don't want you to come!

RUTH: I got something to talk to you about, Walter.

WALTER: That's too bad.

MAMA *(still quietly)*: Walter Lee—*(She waits and he finally turns and looks at her.)* Sit down.

WALTER: I'm a grown man, Mama.

MAMA: Ain't nobody said you wasn't grown. But you still in my house and my presence. And as long as you are—you'll talk to your wife civil. Now sit down.

RUTH *(suddenly)*: Oh, let him go on out and drink himself to death! He makes me sick to my stomach! *(She flings her coat against him and exits to bedroom.)*

WALTER *(violently flinging the coat after her)* And you turn mine too, baby! *(The door slams behind her.)* That was my biggest mistake—

MAMA *(still quietly)*: Walter, what is the matter with you?

WALTER: Matter with me? Ain't nothing the matter with *me*!

MAMA: Yes there is. Something eating you up like a crazy man. Something more than me not giving you this money. The past few years I been watching it happen to you. You get all nervous acting and kind of wild in the eyes—*(Walter jumps up impatiently at her words.)* I said sit there now, I'm talking to you!

WALTER: Mama—I don't need no nagging at me today.

MAMA: Seem like you getting to a place where you always tied up in some kind of knot about something. But if anybody ask you 'bout it you just yell at 'em and bust out the house and go out and drink somewheres. Walter Lee, people can't live with that. Ruth's a good, patient girl in her way—but you getting to be too much. Boy, don't make the mistake of driving that girl away from you.

WALTER: Why—what she do for me?

MAMA: She loves you.

WALTER: Mama—I'm going out. I want to go off somewhere and be by myself for a while.

MAMA: I'm sorry 'bout your liquor store, son. It just wasn't the thing for us to do. That's what I want to tell you about—

WALTER: I got to go out, Mama—*(He rises.)*

MAMA: It's dangerous, son.

WALTER: What's dangerous?

MAMA: When a man goes outside his home to look for peace.

WALTER *(beseechingly〈恳求地〉)*: Then why can't there never be no peace in this house then?

MAMA: You done found it in some other house?

WALTER: No—there ain't no woman! Why do women always think there's a woman somewhere when a man gets restless（焦躁不安）. *(picks up the check)* Do you know what this money means to me? Do you know what this money can do for us? *(puts it back)* Mama—Mama—I want so many things...

MAMA: Yes, son—

WALTER: I want so many things that they are driving me kind of crazy... Mama—look at me.

MAMA: I'm looking at you. You a good-looking boy. You got a job, a nice wife, a fine boy and—

WALTER: A job. *(looks at her)* Mama, a job? I open and close car doors all day long. I drive a man around in his limousine（豪华轿车） and I say, "Yes, sir; no, sir; very good, sir; shall I take the Drive, sir?" Mama, that ain't no kind of job... that ain't nothing at all. *(very quietly)* Mama, I don't know if I can make you understand.

MAMA: Understand what, baby?

WALTER (quietly): Sometimes it's like I can see the future stretched out in front of me—just plain as day. The future, Mama. Hanging over there at the edge of my days. Just waiting for me—a big, looming blank space—full of *nothing*. Just waiting for *me*. But it don't have to be. (*Pause. Kneeling beside her chair*) Mama—sometimes when I'm downtown and I pass them cool, quiet-looking restaurants where them white boys are sitting back and talking 'bout things... sitting there turning deals worth millions of dollars... sometimes I see guys don't look much older than me—

MAMA: Son—how come you talk so much 'bout money?

WALTER (*with* immense 〈极大的〉 *passion*): Because it is life, Mama!

MAMA (*quietly*): Oh—(*very quietly*) So now it's life. Money is life. Once upon a time freedom used to be life—now it's money. I guess the world really do change...

WALTER: No—it was always money, Mama. We just didn't know about it.

MAMA: No ... something has changed. (*She looks at him.*) You something new, boy. In my time we was worried about not being lynched（私刑处死）and getting to the North if we could and how to stay alive and still have a pinch of（一丁点儿）dignity too... Now here come you and Beneatha—talking 'bout things we ain't never even thought about hardly, me and your daddy. You ain't satisfied or proud of nothing we done. I mean that you had a home; that we kept you out of trouble till you was grown; that you don't have to ride to work on the back of nobody's streetcar—You my children—but how different we done become.

WALTER (*A long* beat 〈停顿〉. *He pats her hand and gets up*): You just don't understand, Mama, you just don't understand.

MAMA: Son—do you know your wife is expecting another baby? (*Walter stands, stunned, and absorbs what his mother has said.*) That's what she wanted to talk to you about. (*Walter sinks down into a chair.*) This ain't for me to be telling—but you ought to know. (*She waits.*) I think Ruth is thinking 'bout getting rid of that child.

WALTER (*slowly understanding*): —No—no—Ruth wouldn't do that.

MAMA: When the world gets ugly enough—a woman will do anything for her family. *The part that's already living.*

WALTER: You don't know Ruth, Mama, if you think she would do that.

Ruth opens the bedroom door and stands there a little limp（虚弱无力）.

RUTH (beaten 〈沮丧的〉): Yes I would too, Walter. (*Pause.*) I gave her a five-dollar down payment.

There is total silence as the man stares at his wife and the mother stares at her son.

MAMA (*presently*): Well—(*tightly*) Well—son, I'm waiting to hear you say something... (*She waits.*) I'm waiting to hear how you be your father's son. Be the man he was... *(Pause. The silence shouts.)* Your wife say she going to destroy your child. And I'm waiting to hear you talk like him and say we a people who give children life, not who destroys them—*(She rises.)* I'm waiting to see you stand up and look like your daddy and say we done give up one baby to poverty and that we ain't going to give up nary another one... I'm waiting.

WALTER: Ruth—*(He can say nothing.)*

MAMA: If you a son of mine, tell her! *(Walter picks up his keys and his coat and walks out. She continues, bitterly.)* You... you are a disgrace to your father's memory. Somebody get me my hat!

CURTAIN

Excerpt 4 (from Act 2, Scene 1)

Later that Saturday, dressed in her new Nigerian robes and headdress, Beneatha dances to African music as a way to explore her African roots. Ruth finds it silly, but Walter, returned from drinking, joins her in acting out some made-up tribal rituals. George arrives for a date with Beneatha, but is upset by Beneatha's new appearance: she has cut off most of her hair to appear more African. She accuses him of being an assimilationist, while he mocks their African heritage.

Walter sounds George out for a loan, then verbally attacks him for his indifference. After Beneatha and George leave, Ruth tries to get Walter to talk; they do begin to make up, and then Mama returns.

WALTER: Mama, where have you been?

MAMA: My—them steps is longer than they used to be. Whew! *(She sits down and ignores him.)* How you feeling this evening, Ruth?

  Ruth shrugs, disturbed at having been interrupted and watching her husband <u>knowingly</u>（会意地）.

WALTER: Mama, where have you been all day?

MAMA *(still ignoring him and leaning on the table and changing to more comfortable shoes)*: Where's Travis?

RUTH: I let him go out earlier and he ain't come back yet. Boy, is he going to get it!

WALTER: Mama!

MAMA *(as if she has heard him for the first time)*: Yes, son?

WALTER: Where did you go this afternoon?

MAMA: I went downtown to tend to some business that I had to tend to.

WALTER: What kind of business?

MAMA: You know better than to question me like a child, Brother.

WALTER *(rising and bending over the table)*: Where were you, Mama? *(bringing his fists down and shouting)* Mama, you didn't go do something with that insurance money, something crazy?

> *The front door opens slowly, interrupting him, and Travis peeks his head in, less than hopefully.*

TRAVIS *(to his mother)*: Mama, I—

RUTH: "Mama I" nothing! You're going to get it, boy! Get on in that bedroom and get yourself ready!

TRAVIS: But I—

MAMA: Why don't you all never let the child explain hisself.

RUTH: Keep out of it now, Lena.

> *Mama clamps her lips together, and Ruth advances toward her son menacingly.*

RUTH: A thousand times I have told you not to go off like that—

MAMA *(holding out her arms to her grandson)*: Well—at least let me tell him something. I want him to be the first one to hear... Come here, Travis. *(The boy obeys, gladly.)* Travis—*(She takes him by the shoulder and looks into his face.)* —you know that money we got in the mail this morning?

TRAVIS: Yes'm—

MAMA: Well—what you think your grandmama gone and done with that money?

TRAVIS: I don't know, Grandmama.

MAMA *(putting her finger on his nose for emphasis)*: She went out and she bought you a house! *(The explosion comes from Walter at the end of the revelation and he jumps up and turns away from all of them in a fury. Mama continues, to Travis.)* You glad about the house? It's going to be yours when you get to be a man.

TRAVIS: Yeah—I always wanted to live in a house.

MAMA: All right, gimme some sugar then—*(Travis puts his arms around her neck as she watches her son over the boy's shoulder. Then, to Travis, after the embrace.)* Now when you say your prayers tonight, you thank God and your grandfather—'cause it was him who give you the house—in his way.

RUTH *(taking the boy from Mama and pushing him toward the bedroom)*: Now you get out of here and get ready for your beating.

TRAVIS: Aw, Mama—

RUTH: Get on in there—*(closing the door behind him and turning radiantly to her mother-in-law)* So you went and did it!

MAMA *(quietly, looking at her son with pain)*: Yes, I did.

RUTH *(raising both arms classically)*: PRAISE GOD! *(Looks at Walter a moment, who says nothing. She crosses rapidly to her husband.)* Please, honey—let me be glad... you be glad too. (She has laid her hands on his shoulders, but he shakes

Unit 6

Lorraine Hansberry and *A Raisin in the Sun*

himself free of her roughly, without turning to face her.) Oh, Walter... a home... *a home. (She comes back to Mama.)* Well—where is it? How big is it? How much it going to cost?

MAMA: Well—

RUTH: When we moving?

MAMA *(smiling at her)*: First of the month.

RUTH *(throwing back her head with jubilance*〈喜悦〉*)*: Praise God!

MAMA *(tentatively*〈试探性地〉*, still looking at her son's back turned against her and Ruth)*: It's—it's a nice house too ... *(She cannot help speaking directly to him. An imploring*〈恳求的〉 *quality in her voice, her manner, makes her almost like a girl now.)* Three bedrooms—nice big one for you and Ruth.... Me and Beneatha still have to share our room, but Travis have one of his own—and *(with difficulty)* I figure if the—new baby—is a boy, we could get one of them double-decker outfits... And there's a yard with a little patch of dirt where I could maybe get to grow me a few flowers… And a nice big basement...

RUTH: Walter honey, be glad—

MAMA *(still to his back, fingering things on the table)*: 'Course I don't want to make it sound fancier than it is ... It's just a plain little old house—but it's made good and solid—and it will be *ours*. Walter Lee—it makes a difference in a man when he can walk on floors that belong to *him*...

RUTH: Where is it?

MAMA *(frightened at this telling)*: Well—well—it's out there in Clybourne Park—
> Ruth's radiance jades abruptly, and Walter finally turns slowly to face his mother with incredulity（不相信） and hostility（敌意）.

RUTH: Where?

MAMA *(matter-of-factly*〈平淡地〉*)*: Four o six Clybourne Street, Clybourne Park.

RUTH: Clybourne Park? Mama, there ain't no colored people living in Clybourne Park.

MAMA *(almost idiotically*〈呆呆地〉*)*: Well, I guess there's going to be some now.

WALTER *(bitterly)*: So that's the peace and comfort you went out and bought for us today!

MAMA *(raising her eyes to meet his finally)*: Son—I just tried to find the nicest place for the least amount of money for my family.

RUTH *(trying to recover from the shock)*: Well—well—'course I ain't one never been 'fraid of no crackers（白人穷鬼）, mind you—but—well, wasn't there no other houses nowhere?

MAMA: Them houses they put up for colored in them areas way out all seem to cost twice as much as other houses. I did the best I could.

RUTH *(Struck senseless with the news, in its various degrees of goodness and trouble, she sits a moment, her fists propping*〈支撑〉 *her chin in thought, and then she starts to rise, bringing her fists down with vigor, the radiance spreading from cheek to cheek again)*: Well—well! —All I can say is—if this is my time in life— MY TIME—to say good-bye—*(and she builds with <u>momentum</u>〈动力〉 as she starts to circle the room with an <u>exuberant</u>〈旺盛的〉, almost tearfully happy release)* —to these Goddamned cracking walls! *(She <u>pounds</u>〈揭，重击〉 the walls.)*—and these marching <u>roaches</u>（蟑螂）! —*(She wipes at an imaginary army of marching roaches.)*—and this cramped little closet which ain't now or never was no kitchen! ... then I say it loud and good, HALLELUJAH（感谢上帝）! AND GOOD-BYE MISERY ... I DON'T NEVER WANT TO SEE YOUR UGLY FACE AGAIN! *(She laughs joyously, having practically destroyed the apartment, and flings her arms up and lets them come down happily, slowly, <u>reflectively</u>〈沉思地〉, over her <u>abdomen</u>〈腹部〉, aware for the first time perhaps that the life therein pulses with happiness and not despair.)* Lena?

MAMA *(moved, watching her happiness)*: Yes, honey?

RUTH *(<u>looking off</u>〈看向别处〉)*: Is there—is there a whole lot of sunlight?

MAMA *(understanding)*: Yes, child, there's a whole lot of sunlight. *(long pause)*

RUTH *(collecting herself and going to the door of the room Travis is in)*: Well—I guess I better see 'bout Travis. *(to Mama)* Lord, I sure don't feel like whipping nobody today! *(She exits.)*

MAMA: *(The mother and son are left alone now and the mother waits a long time, considering deeply, before she speaks.)* Son—you—you understand what I done, don't you? *(Walter is silent and <u>sullen</u>〈愠怒〉.)* I—I just seen my family falling apart today... just falling to pieces in front of my eyes... We couldn't of gone on like we was today. We was going backwards 'stead of forwards—talking 'bout killing babies and wishing each other was dead... When it gets like that in life—you just got to do something different, push on out and do something bigger... *(She waits.)* I wish you say something, son... I wish you'd say how deep inside you you think I done the right thing—

WALTER *(crossing slowly to his bedroom door and finally turning there and speaking <u>measuredly</u>〈慢而稳地〉)*: What you need me to say you done right for? *You* the head of this family. You run our lives like you want to. It was your money and you did what you wanted with it. So what you need for me to say it was all right for? *(bitterly, to hurt her as deeply as he knows is possible)* So you <u>butcher</u>ed（屠杀） up a dream of mine—you—who always talking 'bout your children's dreams...

MAMA: Walter Lee—

He just closes the door behind him. Mama sits alone, thinking heavily.

CURTAIN

Unit 6

Lorraine Hansberry and *A Raisin in the Sun*

> ### Excerpt 5 (from Act 2, Scene 2)
> It is a Friday night a few weeks later. Packing crates fill the Younger apartment in preparation for the move. Beneatha and George are arguing after an evening out again; he just wants a pretty girl and is getting tired of her intellectuality. Beneatha ends the date angrily. Then Mrs. Johnson, the Youngers' neighbor, visits.

Mama is silent and someone knocks on the door. Mama and Ruth exchange weary and knowing glances and Ruth opens it to admit the neighbor, Mrs. Johnson, who is a rather <u>squeaky</u>（声音尖细的） wide-eyed（大眼圆睁的） lady of no particular age, with a newspaper under her arm.

MAMA (*changing her expression to acute delight and a ringing cheerful greeting*): Oh—hello there, Johnson.

JOHNSON (*This is a woman who decided long ago to be enthusiastic about EVERYTHING in life and she is inclined to wave her wrist vigorously at the height of her <u>exclamatory</u>〈感叹的〉 comments.*): Hello there, yourself! H'you this evening, Ruth?

RUTH (*not much of a <u>deceptive</u>〈骗人的〉 type*): Fine, Mis' Johnson, h'you?

JOHNSON: Fine. (*reaching out quickly, playfully, and patting Ruth's stomach*) Ain't you starting to <u>poke out</u>（凸出） none yet! (*She <u>mugs</u>〈扮鬼脸〉 with delight at the <u>over-familiar</u>〈过于亲昵的〉 remark and her eyes dart around looking at the <u>crates</u>〈板条箱〉 and packing preparation; Mama's face is a cold sheet of <u>endurance</u>〈忍耐〉.*) Oh, ain't we getting ready round here, though! Yessir! Lookathere! I'm telling you the Youngers is really getting ready to "move on up a little higher!"—Bless God!

MAMA (*a little drily, doubting the total sincerity of the Blesser*): Bless God.

JOHNSON: He's good, ain't He?

MAMA: Oh yes, He's good.

JOHNSON: I mean sometimes He works in mysterious ways... but He works, don't He!

MAMA (*the same*): Yes, he does.

JOHNSON: I'm just soooooo happy for y'all. And this here child—(*about Ruth*) looks like she could just <u>pop open</u>（啪的一声裂开） with happiness, don't she. Where's all the rest of the family?

MAMA: Bennie's gone to bed—

JOHNSON: Ain't no... (*The implication is pregnancy.*) sickness done hit you—I hope...?

MAMA: No—she just tired. She was out this evening.

JOHNSON (*All is a <u>coo</u>〈低语〉, an <u>emphatic</u>〈加强语气的〉 coo.*): Aw—ain't that lovely. She still going out with the little Murchison boy?

MAMA *(drily)*: Ummmm huh.

JOHNSON: That's lovely. You sure got lovely children, Younger. Me and Isaiah talks all the time 'bout what fine children you was blessed with. We sure do.

MAMA: Ruth, give Mis' Johnson a piece of sweet potato pie and some milk.

JOHNSON: Oh honey, I can't stay hardly a minute—I just dropped in to see if there was anything I could do. *(accepting the food easily)* I guess y'all seen the news what's all over the colored paper this week...

MAMA: No—didn't get mine yet this week.

JOHNSON *(lifting her head and blinking 〈眨眼〉 with the spirit of catastrophe 〈大灾难〉)*: You mean you ain't read 'bout them colored people that was bombed out their place out there?

> Ruth straightens with concern and takes the paper and reads it. Johnson notices her and feeds commentary.

JOHNSON: Ain't it something how bad these here white folks is getting here in Chicago! Lord, getting so you think you right down in Mississippi! *(with a tremendous and rather insincere sense of melodrama 〈夸张的情节剧〉)* 'Course I thinks it's wonderful how our folks keeps on pushing out. You hear some of these Negroes round here talking 'bout how they don't go where they ain't wanted and all that—but not me, honey! *(This is a lie.)* Wilhemenia Othella Johnson goes anywhere, any time she feels like it! *(with head movement for emphasis)* Yes I do! Why if we left it up to these here crackers, the poor niggers wouldn't have nothing—*(She clasps her hand over her mouth.)* Oh, I always forgets you don't 'low that word in your house.

MAMA *(quietly, looking at her)*: No—I don't 'low it.

JOHNSON *(vigorously again)*: Me neither! I was just telling Isaiah yesterday when he come using it in front of me—I said, "Isaiah, it's just like Mis' Younger says all the time—"

MAMA: Don't you want some more pie?

JOHNSON: No—no thank you; this was lovely. I got to get on over home and have my midnight coffee. I hear some people say it don't let them sleep but I finds I can't close my eyes right lessen I done had that laaaast cup of coffee... *(She waits. A beat. Undaunted 〈不屈不挠的〉.)* My Goodnight coffee, I calls it!

MAMA *(with much eye-rolling and communication between herself and Ruth)*: Ruth, why don't you give Mis' Johnson some coffee.

> Ruth gives Mama an unpleasant look for her kindness.

JOHNSON *(accepting the coffee)*: Where's Brother tonight?

MAMA: He's lying down.

JOHNSON: MMmmmmm, he sure gets his beauty rest, don't he? Good-looking man. Sure is a good-looking man! *(reaching out to pat Ruth's stomach again)* I guess that's how come we keep on having babies around here. *(She winks at Mama.)* One thing 'bout Brother, he always know how to have a *good* time. And sooooo ambitious! I bet it was his idea y'all moving out to Clybourne Park. Lord—I bet this time next month y'all's names will have been in the papers plenty—*(holding up her hands to mark off each word of the headline she can see in front of her)* "NEGROES INVADE CLYBOURNE PARK—BOMBED!"

MAMA *(She and Ruth look at the woman in amazement)*: We ain't exactly moving out there to get bombed.

JOHNSON: Oh, honey—you know I'm praying to God every day that don't nothing like that happen! But you have to think of life like it is—and these here Chicago peckerwoods（白人穷鬼）is some baaaad peckerwoods.

MAMA *(wearily)*: We done thought about all that Mis' Johnson.

  Beneatha comes out of the bedroom in her robe and passes through to the bathroom. Mrs. Johnson turns.

JOHNSON: Hello there, Bennie!

BENEATHA *(crisply〈干净利落地〉)*: Hello, Mrs. Johnson.

JOHNSON: How is school?

BENEATHA *(crisply)*: Fine, thank you. *(She goes out.)*

JOHNSON *(insulted)*: Getting so she don't have much to say to nobody.

MAMA: The child was on her way to the bathroom.

JOHNSON: I know—but sometimes she act like ain't got time to pass the time of day with nobody ain't been to college. Oh—I ain't criticizing her none. It's just— you know how some of our young people gets when they get a little education. *(Mama and Ruth say nothing, just look at her)* Yes—well. Well, I guess I better get on home. *(unmoving)* 'Course I can understand how she must be proud and everything—being the only one in the family to make something of herself. I know just being a chauffeur ain't never satisfied Brother none. He shouldn't feel like that, though. Ain't nothing wrong with being a chauffeur.

MAMA: There's plenty wrong with it.

JOHNSON: What?

MAMA: Plenty. My husband always said being any kind of a servant wasn't a fit thing for a man to have to be. He always said a man's hands was made to make things, or to turn the earth with—not to drive nobody's car for 'em—or—*(She looks at her own hands.)* carry they slop（泔水）jars. And my boy is just like him—he wasn't meant to wait on（服侍）nobody.

JOHNSON *(rising, somewhat offended)*: Mmmmmmmmm. The Youngers is too much for me! *(She looks around.)* You sure one proud acting bunch of colored folks.

Well—I always thinks like Booker T. Washington① said that time—"Education has spoiled many a good plow hand"—

MAMA: Is that what old Booker T. said?

JOHNSON: He sure did.

MAMA: Well, it sounds just like him. The fool.

JOHNSON *(indignantly)*: Well—he was one of our great men.

MAMA: Who said so?

JOHNSON *(nonplussed*〈困惑的〉*)*: You know, me and you ain't never agreed about some things, Lena Younger. I guess I better be going—

RUTH *(quickly)*: Good night.

JOHNSON: Good night. Oh—*(thrusting it at her)* You can keep the paper! *(with a trill)* 'Night.

MAMA: Good night, Mis' Johnson. *(Mrs. Johnson exits.)*

RUTH: If ignorance was gold…

MAMA: Shush（嘘）. Don't talk about folks behind their backs.

RUTH: You do.

MAMA: I'm old and corrupted. *(Beneatha enters.)* You was rude to Mis' Johnson, Beneatha, and I don't like it at all.

BENEATHA *(at her door)*: Mama, if there are two things we, as a people, have got to overcome, one is the Ku Klux Klan②—and the other is Mrs. Johnson. *(She exits.)*

MAMA: Smart aleck（傻瓜）.

(The phone rings.)

RUTH: I'll get it.

MAMA: Lord, ain't this a popular place tonight.

RUTH *(at the phone)*: Hello—Just a minute. *(goes to door)* Walter, it's Mrs. Arnold. *(Waits. Goes back to the phone. Tense.)* Hello. Yes, this is his wife speaking… He's lying down now. Yes… well, he'll be in tomorrow. He's been very sick. Yes—I know we should have called, but we were so sure he'd be able to come in today. Yes—yes, I'm very sorry. Yes… Thank you very much. *(She hangs up. Walter is standing in the doorway of the bedroom behind her.)* That was Mrs. Arnold.

WALTER *(indifferently)*: Was it?

RUTH: She said if you don't come in tomorrow that they are getting a new man…

WALTER: Ain't that sad—ain't that crying sad.

---

① Booker T. Washington: 1856—1915, is one of the dominant leaders in the African-American community in the late 19th and 20th century. He preached self-reliance and urged blacks to accept discrimination for the time being. He believed in the cultivation of virtues through education in the crafts, industrial and farming skills. Some of his ideas were considered too conservative and thus challenged by radical critics.

② Ku Klux Klan: commonly called the KKK or simply the Klan, is a secret hate group active across the U.S., especially in the South. It has advocated white supremacy and is directed against blacks, Muslims, Jews, Catholics, immigrants, and other groups.

Unit 6

Lorraine Hansberry and *A Raisin in the Sun*

RUTH: She said Mr. Arnold has had to take a cab for three days... Walter, you ain't been to work for three days! *(This is a revelation to her.)* Where you been, Walter Lee Younger? *(Walter looks at her and starts to laugh.)* You're going to lose your job.

WALTER: That's right... *(He turns on the radio.)*

RUTH: Oh, Walter, and with your mother working like a dog every day—

A steamy, deep blues pours into the room.

WALTER: That's sad too—Everything is sad.

MAMA: What you been doing for these three days, son?

WALTER: Mama—you don't know all the things a man what got leisure can find to do in this city... What's this—Friday night? Well—Wednesday I borrowed Willy Harris' car and I went for a drive... just me and myself and I drove and drove... Way out... way past South Chicago, and I parked the car and I sat and looked at the steel mills all day long. I just sat in the car and looked at them big black chimneys for hours. Then I drove back and I went to the Green Hat. *(pause)* And Thursday—Thursday I borrowed the car again and I got in it and I pointed it the other way and I drove the other way—for hours—way, way up to Wisconsin, and I looked at the farms. I just drove and looked at the farms. Then I drove back and I went to the Green Hat. *(pause)* And today—today I didn't get the car. Today I just walked. All over the Southside. And I looked at the Negroes and they looked at me and finally I just sat down on the curb at Thirty-ninth and South Parkway and I just sat there and watched the Negroes go by. And then I went to the Green Hat. You all sad? You all depressed? And you know where I am going right now—

Ruth goes out quietly.

MAMA: Oh, Big Walter, is this the harvest of our days?

WALTER: You know what I like about the Green Hat? I like this little cat they got there who blows a sax... He blows. He talks to me. He ain't but 'bout five feet tall and he's got a <u>conked</u>（用药剂把卷发弄直） head and his eyes is always closed and he's all music—

MAMA *(rising and getting some papers out of her handbag)*: Walter—

WALTER: And there's this other guy who plays the piano... and they got a sound. I mean they can work on some music... They got the best little <u>combo</u>（小型爵士乐团） in the world in the Green Hat... You can just sit there and drink and listen to them three men play and you realize that don't nothing matter worth a damn, but just being there—

MAMA: I've helped do it to you, haven't I, son? Walter, I been wrong.

WALTER: Naw—you ain't never been wrong about nothing, Mama.

MAMA: Listen to me, now. I say I been wrong, son. That I been doing to you what the rest of the world been doing to you. *(She turns off the radio.)* Walter—*(She stops*

337

and he looks up slowly at her and she meets his eyes pleadingly.) What you ain't never understood is that I ain't got nothing, don't own nothing, ain't never really wanted nothing that wasn't for you. There ain't nothing as precious to me... There ain't nothing worth holding on to, money, dreams, nothing else—if it means—if it means it's going to destroy my boy. *(She takes an envelope out of her handbag and puts it in front of him and he watches her without speaking or moving.)* I paid the man thirty-five hundred dollars down on the house. That leaves sixty-five hundred dollars. Monday morning I want you to take this money and take three thousand dollars and put it in a savings account for Beneatha's medical schooling. The rest you put in a checking account—with your name on it. And from now on any penny that come out of it or that go in it is for you to look after. For you to decide. *(She drops her hands a little helplessly.)* It ain't much, but it's all I got in the world and I'm putting it in your hands. I'm telling you to be the head of this family from now on like you supposed to be.

WALTER *(stares at the money)*: You trust me like that. Mama?

MAMA: I ain't never stop trusting you. Like I ain't never stop loving you.

> *She goes out, and Walter sits looking at the money on the table. Finally, in a decisive gesture, he gets up, and, in mingled joy and desperation, picks up the money.*

✂ Excerpt 6 (from Act 2, Scene 3)

Saturday, a week later. This is the day when the family will move to their new neighborhood. Ruth and Beneatha are in good spirits; Ruth reveals that on the previous evening, she and Walter even went on a date to the movies. Then Walter comes in.

> *Walter enters with a large package. His happiness is deep in him; he cannot keep still with his new-found <u>exuberance</u>（兴高采烈）. He is singing and <u>wiggling</u>（扭动） and snapping his fingers. He puts his package in a corner and puts a <u>phonograph</u>（留声机） record, which he has brought in with him, on the record player. As the music, <u>soulful</u>（深情的） and <u>sensuous</u>（悦耳的）, comes up he dances over to Ruth and tries to get her to dance with him. She gives in at last to his raunchiness and in a fit of <u>giggling</u>（咯咯笑） allows herself to be drawn into his mood. They <u>dip</u>（倾斜） and she melts into his arms in a classic, <u>body-melding</u>（身体紧贴的） "<u>slow drag</u>（慢步舞）."*

BENEATHA *(regarding them a long time as they dance, then drawing in her breath for a deeply exaggerated comment which she does not particularly mean)*: Talk about—olddddddddddd-fashioneddddddd—Negroes!

Unit 6

Lorraine Hansberry and *A Raisin in the Sun*

WALTER *(stopping momentarily〈即刻〉)*: What kind of Negroes? *(He says this in fun. He is not angry with her today, nor with anyone. He starts to dance with his wife again.)*

BENEATHA: Old-fashioned.

WALTER *(as he dances with Ruth)*: You know, when these *New Negroes* have their convention（大会）—*(pointing at his sister)*—that is going to be the chairman of the Committee on Unending Agitation（骚动）. *(He goes on dancing, then stops.)* Race, race, race! ... Girl, I do believe you are the first person in the history of the entire human race to successfully brainwash yourself. *(Beneatha breaks up and he goes on dancing. He stops again, enjoying his tease.)* Damn, even the N double A C P[①] takes a holiday sometimes! *(Beneatha and Ruth laugh. He dances with Ruth some more and starts to laugh and stops and pantomimes〈演哑剧, 打手势〉 someone over an operating table.)* I can just see that chick someday looking down at some poor cat on an operating table and before she starts to slice him, she says... *(pulling his sleeves back maliciously)* "By the way, what are your views on civil rights down there? ..." *(He laughs at her again and starts to dance happily. The bell sounds.)*

BENEATHA: Sticks and stones may break my bones but... words will never hurt me!

Beneatha goes to the door and opens it as Walter and Ruth go on with the clowning. Beneatha is somewhat surprised to see a quiet-looking middle-aged white man in a business suit holding his hat and a briefcase in his hand and consulting a small piece of paper.

MAN: Uh—how do you do, miss. I am looking for a Mrs. —*(He looks at the slip of paper.)* Mrs. Lena Younger? *(He stops short, struck dumb at the sight of the oblivious〈忘我的〉 Walter and Ruth.)*

BENEATHA *(smoothing her hair with slight embarrassment)*: Oh—yes, that's my mother. Excuse me *(She closes the door and turns to quiet the other two.)* Ruth! Brother! *(Enunciating〈吐字清晰〉 precisely but soundlessly: "There's a white man at the door!" They stop dancing, Ruth cuts off the phonograph, Beneatha opens the door. The man casts a curious quick glance at all of them.)* Uh—come in please.

MAN *(coming in)*: Thank you.

BENEATHA: My mother isn't here just now. Is it business?

MAN: Yes... well, of a sort.

WALTER *(freely, the Man of the House)*: Have a seat. I'm Mrs. Younger's son. I look after most of her business matters.

Ruth and Beneatha exchange amused glances.

---

① N ... P: NAACP, or National Association for the Advancement of Colored People, was established in 1909 and is America's oldest and largest civil rights organization.

MAN (*regarding Walter, and sitting*): Well—My name is Karl Lindner...

WALTER (*stretching out his hand*): Walter Younger. This is my wife—(*Ruth nods politely*) —and my sister.

LINDNER: How do you do.

WALTER (*amiably, as he sits himself easily on a chair, leaning forward on his knees with interest and looking expectantly into the newcomer's face*): What can we do for you, Mr. Lindner!

LINDNER (*some minor shuffling of the hat and briefcase on his knees*): Well—I am a representative of the Clybourne Park Improvement Association—

WALTER (*pointing*): Why don't you sit your things on the floor?

LINDNER: Oh—yes. Thank you. (*He slides the briefcase and hat under the chair.*) And as I was saying—I am from the Clybourne Park Improvement Association and we have had it brought to our attention at the last meeting that you people—or at least your mother—has bought a piece of residential <u>property</u>（地产） at—(*He <u>digs</u>〈掏〉 for the slip of paper again.*)—four o six Clybourne Street...

WALTER: That's right. Care for something to drink? Ruth, get Mr. Lindner a beer.

LINDNER (*upset for some reason*): Oh—no, really. I mean thank you very much, but no thank you.

RUTH (*innocently*): Some coffee?

LINDNER: Thank you, nothing at all.

  Beneatha is watching the man carefully.

LINDNER: Well, I don't know how much you folks know about our organization. (*He is a gentle man; thoughtful and somewhat <u>labored</u>〈不自然的〉 in his manner.*) It is one of these community organizations set up to look after —oh, you know, things like block <u>upkeep</u>（维护） and special projects and we also have what we call our New Neighbors Orientation Committee...

BENEATHA: *(drily)* Yes—and what do they do?

LINDNER (*turning a little to her and then returning the main force to Walter*): Well—it's what you might call a sort of welcoming committee, I guess. I mean they, we—I'm the chairman of the committee—go around and see the new people who move into the neighborhood and sort of give them the <u>lowdown</u>（真相，内幕） on the way we do things out in Clybourne Park.

BENEATHA (*with <u>appreciation</u>〈领会〉 of the two meanings, which escape Ruth and Walter*): Un-huh.

LINDNER: And we also have the category of what the association calls—(*He looks elsewhere*) —uh—special community problems...

BENEATHA: Yes and what are some of those?

WALTER: Girl, let the man talk.

LINDNER (*with <u>understated</u>〈不动声色的〉 relief*): Thank you. I would sort of like to explain this thing in my own way. I mean I want to explain to you in a certain way.

WALTER: Go ahead.

LINDNER: Yes. Well. I'm going to try to get right to the point. I'm sure we'll all appreciate that in the long run.

BENEATHA: Yes.

WALTER: Be still now!

LINDNER: Well—

RUTH *(still innocently)*: Would you like another chair—you don't look comfortable.

LINDNER *(more frustrated than annoyed)*: No, thank you very much. Please. Well—to get right to the point I—*(A great breath, and he is off at last)* I am sure you people must be aware of some of the incidents which have happened in various parts of the city when colored people have moved into certain areas *(Beneatha exhales〈呼气〉heavily and starts tossing a piece of fruit up and down in the air.)* Well—because we have what I think is going to be a unique type of organization in American community life—not only do we deplore（谴责）that kind of thing—but we are trying to do something about it. *(Beneatha stops tossing and turns with a new and quizzical interest to the man.)* We feel—*(gaining confidence in his mission because of the interest in the faces of the people he is talking to)*—we feel that most of the trouble in this world, when you come right down to it *(He hits his knee for emphasis.)*—most of the trouble exists because people just don't sit down and talk to each other.

RUTH *(nodding as she might in church, pleased with the remark)*: You can say that again, mister.

LINDNER *(more encouraged by such affirmation〈肯定〉)*: That we don't try hard enough in this world to understand the other fellow's problem. The other guy's point of view.

RUTH: Now that's right.

Beneatha and Walter merely watch and listen with genuine interest.

LINDNER: Yes—that's the way we feel out in Clybourne Park. And that's why I was elected to come here this afternoon and talk to you people. Friendly like, you know, the way people should talk to each other and see if we couldn't find some way to work this thing out. As I say, the whole business is a matter of *caring* about the other fellow. Anybody can see that you are a nice family of folks, hard working and honest I'm sure. *(Beneatha frowns slightly, quizzically, her head tilted regarding〈注视〉him.)* Today everybody knows what it means to be on the outside of *something*. And of course, there is always somebody who is out to take advantage of people who don't always understand.

WALTER: What do you mean?

LINDNER: Well—you see our community is made up of people who've worked hard as the dickens for years to build up that little community. They're not rich and fancy people; just hard-working, honest people who don't really have much but those little homes and a dream of the kind of community they want to raise their children in. Now, I don't say we are perfect and there is a lot wrong in some of the things they want. But you've got to admit that a man, right or wrong, has the right to want to have the neighborhood he lives in a certain kind of way. And at the moment the overwhelming majority of our people out there feel that people get along better, take more of a common interest in the life of the community, when they share a common background. I want you to believe me when I tell you that race prejudice simply doesn't enter into it. It is a matter of the people of Clybourne Park believing, rightly or wrongly, as I say, that for the happiness of all concerned that our Negro families are happier when they live in their *own* communities.

BENEATHA *(with a grand and bitter gesture)*: This, friends, is the Welcoming Committee!

WALTER *(dumfounded, looking at Lindner)*: Is this what you came marching all the way over here to tell us?

LINDNER: Well, now we've been having a fine conversation. I hope you'll hear me all the way through.

WALTER *(tightly)*: Go ahead, man.

LINDNER: You see—in the face of all the things I have said, we are prepared to make your family a very generous offer...

BENEATHA: Thirty pieces① and not a coin less!

WALTER: Yeah?

LINDNER *(putting on his glasses and drawing a form out of the briefcase)*: Our association is prepared, through the collective（集体的） effort of our people, to buy the house from you at a financial gain to your family.

RUTH: Lord have mercy, ain't this the living gall（无耻）!

WALTER: All right, you through?

LINDNER: Well, I want to give you the exact terms of the financial arrangement—

WALTER: We don't want to hear no exact terms of no arrangements. I want to know if you got any more to tell us 'bout getting together?

LINDNER *(taking off his glasses)*: Well—I don't suppose that you feel...

WALTER: Never mind how I feel—you got any more to say 'bout how people ought to sit down and talk to each other? ... Get out of my house, man. *(He turns his back and walks to the door.)*

LINDNER *(looking around at the hostile faces and reaching and assembling〈收拾〉 his hat and briefcase)*: Well—I don't understand why you people are reacting this

---

① Thirty pieces: a Biblical allusion. Thirty pieces of silver was the price of a slave; later, Judas Iscariot betrayed Jesus for the same price.

way. What do you think you are going to gain by moving into a neighborhood where you just aren't wanted and where some elements—well—people can get awful worked up when they feel that their whole way of life and everything they've ever worked for is threatened.

WALTER: Get out.

LINDNER: *(at the door, holding a small card)* Well—I'm sorry it went like this.

WALTER: Get out.

LINDNER *(almost sadly regarding Walter)*: You just can't force people to change their hearts, son.

> *He turns and put his card on a table and exits. Walter pushes the door to with <u>stinging</u>（刺痛的） hatred, and stands looking at it. Ruth just sits and Beneatha just stands. They say nothing.*

Excerpt 7 (from Act 3)

When Mama comes home, Walter, Ruth, and Beneatha tell her about Mr. Lindner's visit. It shocks and worries her, but she supports their decision to refuse the buyout offer. Then, the rest of the family surprise her with gifts of gardening tools and a huge gardening hat. In the midst of their celebration, Bobo arrives to tell Walter that Willy has run off with their money. They learn Walter gave his friend Willy Mama's money to get the liquor store, and Walter never banked a portion for Beneatha's schooling as Mama had asked.

An hour later, the family remains stunned by their financial reversals. Asagai comes to help them pack, but is greeted by a changed Beneatha.

ASAGAI: I came over ... I had some free time. I thought I might help with the packing. Ah, I like the look of packing crates! A household in preparation for a journey! It depresses some people... but for me ... it is another feeling. Something full of the flow of life, do you understand? Movement, progress ... It makes me think of Africa.

BENEATHA: Africa!

ASAGAI: What kind of a mood is this? Have I told you how deeply you move me?

BENEATHA: He gave away the money, Asagai...

ASAGAI: Who gave away what money?

BENEATHA: The insurance money. My brother gave it away.

ASAGAI: Gave it away?

BENEATHA: He made an investment! With a man even Travis wouldn't have <u>trusted</u>（托付） with his most worn-out <u>marbles</u>（弹珠）.

ASAGAI: And it's gone?

BENEATHA: Gone!

ASAGAI: I'm very sorry... And you, now?

BENEATHA: Me? ... Me? ... Me, I'm nothing... Me. When I was very small ... we used to take our sleds out in the wintertime and the only hills we had were the ice-covered stone steps of some houses down the street. And we used to fill them in with snow and make them smooth and slide down them all day... and it was very dangerous, you know ... far too steep... and sure enough one day a kid named Rufus came down too fast and hit the sidewalk and we saw his face just split open right there in front of us ... And I remember standing there looking at his bloody open face thinking that was the end of Rufus. But the ambulance came and they took him to the hospital and they fixed the broken bones and they sewed it all up ... and the next time I saw Rufus he just had a little line down the middle of his face ... I never got over（忘怀）that...

ASAGAI: What?

BENEATHA: That that was what one person could do for another, fix him up—sew up the problem, make him all right again. That was the most marvelous thing in the world ... I wanted to do that. I always thought it was the one concrete thing in the world that a human being could do. Fix up the sick, you know—and make them whole again. This was truly being God...

ASAGAI: You wanted to be God?

BENEATHA: No—I wanted to cure. It used to be so important to me. I wanted to cure. It used to matter. I used to care. I mean about people and how their bodies hurt...

ASAGAI: And you've stopped caring?

BENEATHA: Yes—I think so.

ASAGAI: Why?

BENEATHA *(bitterly)*: Because it doesn't seem deep enough, close enough to what ails mankind! It was a child's way of seeing things—or an idealist's（理想主义者）.

ASAGAI: Children see things very well sometimes—and idealists even better.

BENEATHA: I know that's what you think. Because you are still where I left off. You with all your talk and dreams about Africa! You still think you can patch up（修补）the world. Cure the Great Sore of Colonialism（殖民主义）—*(loftily, mocking it)* with the Penicillin（青霉素）of Independence—!

ASAGAI: Yes!

BENEATHA: Independence *and then what*? What about all the crooks（骗子，坏蛋）and thieves and just plain idiots who will come into power and steal and plunder（掠夺）the same as before—only now they will be black and do it in the name of the new Independence—WHAT ABOUT THEM?!

ASAGAI: That will be the problem for another time. First we must get there.

BENEATHA: And where does it end?

ASAGAI: End? Who even spoke of an end? To life? To living?

BENEATHA: An end to misery! To stupidity! Don't you see there isn't any real progress, Asagai, there is only one large circle that we march in, around and around, each of us with our own little picture in front of us—our own little mirage（幻想）that we think is the future.

ASAGAI: That is the mistake.

BENEATHA: What?

ASAGAI: What you just said about the circle. It isn't a circle—it is simply a long line—as in geometry, you know, one that reaches into infinity. And because we cannot see the end—we also cannot see how it changes. And it is very odd but those who see the changes—who dream, who will not give up are called idealists... and those who see only the circle—we call *them* the "realists"!

BENEATHA: Asagai, while I was sleeping in that bed in there, people went out and took the future right out of my hands! And nobody asked me, nobody consulted me—they just went out and changed my life!

ASAGAI: Was it your money?

BENEATHA: What?

ASAGAI: Was it your money he gave away?

BENEATHA: It belonged to all of us.

ASAGAI: But did you earn it? Would you have had it at all if your father had not died?

BENEATHA: No.

ASAGAI: Then isn't there something wrong in a house—in a world—where all dreams, good or bad, must depend on the death of a man? I never thought to see *you* like this, Alaiyo. You! Your brother made a mistake and you are grateful to him so that now you can give up the ailing（生病的）human race on account of it! You talk about what good is struggle, what good is anything! Where are we all going and why are we bothering!

BENEATHA: AND YOU CANNOT ANSWER IT!

ASAGAI *(shouting over her)*: *I LIVE THE ANSWER!* (pause) In my village at home it is the exceptional man who can even read a newspaper ... or who ever sees a book at all. I will go home and much of what I will have to say will seem strange to the people of my village. But I will teach and work and things will happen, slowly and swiftly. At times it will seem that nothing changes at all ... and then again the sudden dramatic events which make history leap into the future. And then quiet again. Retrogression（退化）even. Guns, murder, revolution. And I even will have moments when I wonder if the quiet was not better than all that death and hatred. But I will look about my village at the illiteracy（文盲，无知）and disease and ignorance and I will not wonder long. And perhaps... perhaps I will be a great man ... I mean perhaps I will hold on to the substance of truth and find my way always with the right course... and perhaps for it I will be butchered in my bed some night by the servants of empire...

BENEATHA: *The <u>martyr</u>（殉道者）!*

ASAGAI *(He smiles.)*: ... or perhaps I shall live to be a very old man, respected and esteemed in my new nation... And perhaps I shall hold office and this is what I'm trying to tell you, Alaiyo: Perhaps the things I believe now for my country will be wrong and <u>outmoded</u>（过时的）, and I will not understand and do terrible things to have things my way or merely to keep my power. Don't you see that there will be young men and women—not British soldiers then, but my own black countrymen—to step out of the shadows some evening and <u>slit</u>（切开） my then useless throat? Don't you see they have always been there... that they always will be. And that such a thing as my own death will be an advance? They who might kill me even... actually <u>replenish</u>（使……圆满） all that I was.

BENEATHA: Oh, Asagai, I know all that.

ASAGAI: Good! Then stop moaning and groaning and tell me what you plan to do.

BENEATHA: Do?

ASAGAI: I have a bit of a suggestion.

BENEATHA: What?

ASAGAI *(rather quietly for him)*: That when it is all over—that you come home with me—

BENEATHA *(staring at him and crossing away with exasperation)*: Oh—Asagai—at this moment you decide to be romantic!

ASAGAI *(quickly understanding the misunderstanding)*: My dear, young creature of the New World—I do not mean across the city—I mean across the ocean: home—to Africa.

BENEATHA *(slowly understanding and turning to him with murmured amazement)*: To Africa?

ASAGAI: Yes! ... *(smiling and lifting his arms playfully)* Three hundred years later the African Prince rose up out of the seas and swept the maiden back across the middle passage[①] over which her ancestors had come—

BENEATHA *(unable to play)*: To—to Nigeria?

ASAGIA: Nigeria. Home. *(coming to her with genuine romantic <u>flippancy</u>〈轻浮〉)* I will show you our mountains and our stars; and give you cool drinks from <u>gourds</u>（瓢）and teach you the old songs and the ways of our people—and, in time, we will pretend that—*(very softly)*—you have only been away for a day. Say that you'll come—*(He swings her around and takes her full in his arms in a kiss which proceeds to passion.)*

BENEATHA *(pulling away suddenly)*: You're getting me all mixed up—

---

① middle passage: the forced voyage of enslaved Africans across the Atlantic Ocean to the New World.

ASAGAI: Why?

BENEATHA: Too many things—too many things have happened today. I must sit down and think. I don't know what I feel about anything right this minute. *(She promptly 〈迅速〉 sits down and props her chin on her fist.)*

ASAGAI *(charmed)*: All right, I shall leave you. No—don't get up. *(touching her, gently, sweetly)* Just sit awhile and think... Never be afraid to sit awhile and think. *(He goes to door and looks at her.)* How often I have looked at you and said, "Ah—so this is what the New World hath finally wrought..."

> *He exits. Beneatha sits on alone. Presently Walter enters from his room and starts to rummage 〈翻找〉 through things, feverishly looking for something. She looks up and turns in her seat.*

BENEATHA *(hissingly 〈发嘘声〉)*: Yes—just look at what the New World hath wrought! ... Just look! *(She gestures with bitter disgust.)* There he is! *Monsieur le petit bourgeois noir*[①]—himself! There he is—Symbol of a Rising Class! Entrepreneur! Titan 〈巨人〉 of the system! *(Walter ignores her completely and continues frantically and destructively looking for something and hurling 〈用力投掷〉 things to floor and tearing things out of their place in his search. Beneatha ignores the eccentricity 〈古怪〉 of his actions and goes on with the monologue 〈独白〉 of insult.)* Did you dream of yachts on Lake Michigan, Brother? Did you see yourself on that Great Day sitting down at the Conference Table, surrounded by all the mighty bald-headed men in America? All halted, waiting, breathless, waiting for your pronouncements on industry? Waiting for you—Chairman of the Board 〈董事会〉! *(Walter finds what he is looking for—a small piece of white paper—and pushes it in his pocket and puts on his coat and rushes out without ever having looked at her. She shouts after him.)* I look at you and I see the final triumph of stupidity in the world!

⚘ Excerpt 8 (from Act 3)

After Walter leaves the room, Mama enters. She suggests that they give up their dream of moving and that they make themselves satisfied with the apartment in which they are presently living, a suggestion that seems to upset Ruth more than anyone else.

MAMA: Well—ain't it a mess in here, though? *(a false cheerfulness, a beginning of something)* I guess we all better stop moping 〈闷闷不乐〉 around and get some work done. All this unpacking and everything we got to do. *(Ruth raises her head*

---

① *Monsieur ... noir*: (French) Mister [black] small bourgeois.

slowly in response to the sense of the line; and Beneatha in similar manner turns very slowly to look at her mother.) One of you all better call the moving people and tell 'em not to come.

RUTH: Tell 'em not to come?

MAMA: Of course, baby. Ain't no need in 'em coming all the way here and having to go back. They charges for that too. *(She sits down, fingers to her brow, thinking.)* Lord, ever since I was a little girl, I always remembers people saying, "Lena—Lena Eggleston, you aims too high all the time. You needs to slow down and see life a little more like it is. Just slow down some." That's what they always used to say down home—"Lord, that Lena Eggleston is a high-minded thing. She'll get her due one day!"

RUTH: No, Lena...

MAMA: Me and Big Walter just didn't never learn right.

RUTH: Lena, no! We gotta go. Bennie—tell her ... *(She rises and crosses to Beneatha with her arms outstretched. Beneatha doesn't respond.)* Tell her we can still move... the notes ain't but a hundred and twenty-five a month. We got four grown people in this house—we can work...

MAMA *(to herself)*: Just aimed too high all the time—

RUTH *(turning and going to Mama fast—the words pouring out with urgency and desperation)*: Lena—I'll work... I'll work twenty hours a day in all the kitchens in Chicago. . . I'll strap my baby on my back if I have to and scrub all the floors in America and wash all the sheets in America if I have to—but we got to MOVE! We got to get OUT OF HERE!!

Mama reaches out absently and pats Ruth's hand.

MAMA: No—I sees things differently now. Been thinking 'bout some of the things we could do to fix this place up some. I seen a second-hand bureau over on Maxwell Street just the other day that could fit right there. *(She points to where the new furniture might go. Ruth wanders away from her.)* Would need some new handles on it and then a little <u>varnish</u>（清漆） and it look like something brand-new. And—we can put up them new curtains in the kitchen... Why this place be looking fine. Cheer us all up so that we forget trouble ever come... *(to Ruth)* And you could get some nice screens to put up in your room round the baby's <u>bassinet</u>（摇篮） ... *(She looks at both of them, pleadingly.)* Sometimes you just got to know when to give up some things... and hold on to what you got....

Walter enters from the outside, looking <u>spent</u>（筋疲力尽的） and leaning against the door, his coat hanging from him.

MAMA: Where you been, son?

WALTER *(breathing hard)*: Made a call.

MAMA: To who, son?

Unit 6

Lorraine Hansberry and *A Raisin in the Sun*

WALTER: To The Man. *(He heads for his room.)*

MAMA: What man, baby?

WALTER *(stops in the door)*: The Man, Mama. Don't you know who The Man is?

RUTH: Walter Lee?

WALTER: The Man. Like the guys in the streets say—The Man. Captain Boss—Mistuh Charley... Old Cap'n Please Mr. Bossman...

BENEATHA *(suddenly)*: Lindner!

WALTER: That's right! That's good. I told him to come right over.

BENEATHA *(fiercely〈凶恶地〉, understanding)*: For what? What do you want to see him for!

WALTER *(looking at his sister)*: We going to do business with him.

MAMA: What you talking 'bout, son?

WALTER: Talking 'bout life, Mama. You all always telling me to see life like it is. Well—I laid in there on my back today... and I figured it out. Life just like it is. Who gets and who don't get. *(He sits down with his coat on and laughs.)* Mama, you know it's all divided up. Life is. Sure enough. Between the takers and the "tooken." *(He laughs.)* I've figured it out finally. *(He looks around at them.)* Yeah. Some of us always getting "tooken." *(He laughs.)* People like Willy Harris, they don't never get "tooken." And you know why the rest of us do? 'Cause we all mixed up. Mixed up bad. We get to looking 'round for the right and the wrong; and we worry about it and cry about it and stay up nights trying to figure out 'bout the wrong and the right of things all the time... And all the time, man, them takers is out there operating, just taking and taking. Willy Harris? Shoot—Willy Harris don't even count. He don't even count in the big scheme of things. But I'll say one thing for old Willy Harris... he's taught me something. He's taught me to keep my eye on what counts in this world. Yeah—*(shouting out a little)* Thanks, Willy!

RUTH: What did you call that man for, Walter Lee?

WALTER: Called him to tell him to come on over to the show. Gonna put on a show for the man. Just what he wants to see. You see, Mama, the man came here today and he told us that them people out there where you want us to move—well they so upset they willing to pay us *not* to move! *(He laughs again.)* And—and oh, Mama—you would of been proud of the way me and Ruth and Bennie acted. We told him to get out... Lord have mercy! We told the man to get out! Oh, we was some proud folks this afternoon, yeah. *(He lights a cigarette.)* We were still full of that old-time stuff...

RUTH *(coming toward him slowly)*: You talking 'bout taking them people's money to keep us from moving in that house?

WALTER: I ain't just talking 'bout it, baby—I'm telling you that's what's going to happen!

BENEATHA: Oh, God! Where is the bottom! Where is the real honest-to-God bottom so he can't go any farther!

WALTER: See—that's the old stuff. You and that boy that was here today. You all want everybody to carry a flag and a spear and sing some marching songs（进行曲）, huh? You wanna spend your life looking into things and trying to find the right and the wrong part, huh? Yeah. You know what's going to happen to that boy someday—he'll find himself sitting in a dungeon（地牢）, locked in forever—and the takers will have the key! Forget it, baby! There ain't no causes（事业）—there ain't nothing but taking in this world, and he who takes most is smartest—and it don't make a damn bit of difference *how.*

MAMA: You making something inside me cry, son. Some awful pain inside me.

WALTER: Don't cry, Mama. Understand. That white man is going to walk in that door able to write checks for more money than we ever had. It's important to him and I'm going to help him... I'm going to put on the show, Mama.

MAMA: Son—I come from five generations of people who was slaves and sharecroppers（佃农）—but ain't nobody in my family never let nobody pay 'em no money that was a way of telling us we wasn't fit to walk the earth. We ain't never been that poor. *(raising her eyes and looking at him)* We ain't never been that dead inside.

BENEATHA: Well—we are dead now. All the talk about dreams and sunlight that goes on in this house. It's all dead now.

WALTER: What's the matter with you all! I didn't make this world! It was give to me this way! Hell, yes, I want me some yachts someday! Yes, I want to hang some real pearls 'round my wife's neck. Ain't she supposed to wear no pearls? Somebody tell me—tell me, who decides which women is suppose to wear pearls in this world. I tell you I am a *man* —and I think my wife should wear some pearls in this world!

> *This last line hangs（停留） a good while and Walter begins to move about the room. The word "Man" has penetrated（渗透） his consciousness; he mumbles it to himself repeatedly between strange agitated（焦躁不安的） pauses as he moves about.*

MAMA: Baby, how you going to feel on the inside?

WALTER: Fine! ... Going to feel fine... a man...

MAMA: You won't have nothing left then, Walter Lee.

WALTER *(coming to her)*: I'm going to feel fine, Mama. I'm going to look that son-of-a-bitch in the eyes and say—*(He falters*〈踌躇，支吾〉*.)*—and say, "All right, Mr. Lindner—*(He falters even more.)* —that's *your* neighborhood out there! You got the right to keep it like you want! You got the right to have it like you want! Just write the check and—the house is yours." And—and I am going to say—

(His voice almost breaks.) "And you—you people just put the money in my hand and you won't have to live next to this bunch of <u>stinking</u>（发臭的）niggers! ..." *(He straightens up and moves away from his mother, walking around the room.)* And maybe—maybe I'll just get down on my black knees... *(He does so; Ruth and Bennie and Mama watch him in frozen horror.)* "Captain, Mistuh, Bossman—*(<u>groveling</u>〈匍匐〉 and grinning and wringing his hands in profoundly anguished imitation of the <u>slow-witted</u>〈头脑迟钝的〉 movie <u>stereotype</u>〈模式化形象〉)* A-hee-hee-hee! Oh, yassuh boss! Yassssssuh! Great white—*(Voice breaking, he forces himself to go on.)*—Father, just gi' ussen de money, fo' God's sake, and we's—we's ain't gwine come out deh and dirty up yo' white folks neighborhood..." *(He breaks down completely.)* And I'll feel fine! Fine! FINE! *(He gets up and goes into the bedroom.)*

BENEATHA: That is not a man. That is nothing but a toothless rat.

MAMA: Yes—death done come in this here house. *(She is nodding, slowly, reflectively.)* Done come walking in my house on the lips of my children. You what supposed to be my beginning again. You—what supposed to be my harvest. *(to Beneatha)* You—you mourning your brother?

BENEATHA: He's no brother of mine.

MAMA: What you say?

BENEATHA: I said that that individual in that room is no brother of mine.

MAMA: That's what I thought you said. You feeling like you better than he is today? *(Beneatha does not answer.)* Yes? What you tell him a minute ago? That he wasn't a man? Yes? You give him up for me? You done wrote his <u>epitaph</u>（墓志铭）too—like the rest of the world? Well, who give you the <u>privilege</u>（特权）?

BENEATHA: Be on my side for once! You saw what he just did, Mama! You saw him—down on his knees. Wasn't it you who taught me to <u>despise</u>（鄙视） any man who would do that? Do what he's going to do?

MAMA: Yes—I taught you that. Me and your daddy. But I thought I taught you something else too ... I thought I taught you to love him.

BENEATHA: Love him? There is nothing left to love.

MAMA: There is *always* something left to love. And if you ain't learned that, you ain't learned nothing. *(looking at her)* Have you cried for that boy today? I don't mean for yourself and for the family 'cause we lost the money. I mean for him: what he been through and what it done to him. Child, when do you think is the time to love somebody the most? When they done good and made things easy for everybody? Well then, you ain't through learning—because that ain't the time at all. It's when he's at his lowest and can't believe in hisself 'cause the world done whipped him so! When you starts measuring somebody, measure him right, child, measure him right. Make sure you done taken into account what hills and valleys he come through before he got to wherever he is.

Travis bursts into the room at the end of the speech, leaving the door open.

TRAVIS: Grandmama—the moving men are downstairs! The truck just <u>pulled up</u>（停车）.

MAMA *(turning and looking at him)*: Are they, baby? They downstairs?

  She sighs and sits. Lindner appears in the doorway. He peers in and knocks lightly, to gain attention, and comes in. All turn to look at him.

LINDNER *(hat and briefcase in hand)*: Uh—hello...

  Ruth crosses mechanically to the bedroom door and opens it and lets it <u>swing</u>（旋转） open freely and slowly as the lights come up on Walter within, still in his coat, sitting at the far corner of the room. He looks up and out through the room to Lindner.

RUTH: He's here. *(A long minute passes and Walter slowly gets up.)*

LINDNER *(coming to the table with efficiency, putting his briefcase on the table and starting to unfold papers and <u>unscrew</u>〈旋开〉 fountain pens)*: Well, I certainly was glad to hear from you people. *(Walter has begun the <u>trek</u>〈艰苦跋涉〉 out of the room, slowly and awkwardly, rather like a small boy, passing the back of his sleeve across his mouth from time to time.)* Life can really be so much simpler than people let it be most of the time. Well—with whom do I negotiate? You, Mrs. Younger, or your son here? *(Mama sits with her hands folded on her lap and her eyes closed as Walter advances. Travis goes closer to Lindner and looks at the papers curiously.)* Just some official papers, sonny.

RUTH: Travis, you go downstairs—

MAMA *(opening her eyes and looking into Walter's)*: No. Travis, you stay right here. And you make him understand what you doing, Walter Lee. You teach him good. Like Willy Harris taught you. You show where our five generations done come to. *(Walter looks from her to the boy, who grins at him innocently.)* Go ahead, son— *(She folds her hands and closes her eyes.)* Go ahead.

WALTER *(at last crosses to Lindner, who is reviewing the contract)*: Well, Mr. Lindner. *(Beneatha turns away.)* We called you—*(There is a profound, simple <u>groping</u>〈探索性的〉 quality in his speech.)* because, well, me and my family *(He looks around and shifts from one foot to the other.)* Well—we are very plain people...

LINDNER: Yes—

WALTER: I mean—I have worked as a chauffeur most of my life—and my wife here, she does domestic work in people's kitchens. So does my mother. I mean—we are plain people...

LINDNER: Yes, Mr. Younger—

WALTER *(really like a small boy, looking down at his shoes and then up at the man)*: And—uh—well, my father, well, he was a laborer most of his life....

Unit 6

Lorraine Hansberry and *A Raisin in the Sun*

LINDNER *(absolutely confused)*: Uh, yes—yes, I understand. *(He turns back to the contract.)*

WALTER *(a beat; staring at him)*: And my father—*(with sudden intensity)* My father almost *beat a man to death* once because this man called him a bad name or something, you know what I mean?

LINDNER *(looking up, frozen)*: No, no, I'm afraid I don't—

WALTER *(A beat. The tension hangs; then Walter steps back from it.)*: Yeah. Well—what I mean is that we come from people who had a lot of *pride*. I mean—we are very proud people. And that's my sister over there and she's going to be a doctor—and we are very proud—

LINDNER: Well—I am sure that is very nice, but—

WALTER: What I am telling you is that we called you over here to tell you that we are very proud and that this—*(signaling to Travis)* Travis, come here. *(Travis crosses and Walter draws him before him facing the man.)* This is my son, and he makes the sixth generation our family in this country. And we have all thought about your offer—

LINDNER: Well, good... good—

WALTER: And we have decided to move into our house because my father—my father —he earned it for us brick by brick. *(Mama has her eyes closed and is* rocking〈摇摆〉 *back and forth as though she were in church, with her head nodding the* Amen〈阿门，表示衷心赞成〉 *yes.)* We don't want to make no trouble for nobody or fight no causes, and we will try to be good neighbors. And that's *all* we got to say about that. *(He looks the man absolutely in the eyes.)* We don't want your money. *(He turns and walks away.)*

LINDNER *(looking around at all of them)*: I take it then—that you have decided to occupy...

BENEATHA: That's what the man said.

LINDNER *(to Mama in her* reverie〈沉思，遐想〉*)*: Then I would like to appeal to you, Mrs. Younger. You are older and wiser and understand things better I am sure…

MAMA: I am afraid you don't understand. My son said we was going to move and there ain't nothing left for me to say, *(briskly)* You know how these young folks is nowadays, mister. Can't do a thing with 'em! *(As he opens his mouth, she rises.)* Good-bye.

LINDNER *(folding up his materials)*: Well—if you are that final（坚决的） about it… there is nothing left for me to say. *(He finishes, almost ignored by the family, who are concentrating on Walter Lee. At the door Lindner halts and looks around.)* I sure hope you people know what you're getting into. *(He shakes his head and exits.)*

RUTH *(looking around and coming to life)*: Well, for God's sake—if the moving men are here—LETS GET THE HELL OUT OF HERE!

MAMA *(into action)*: Ain't it the truth! Look at all this here mess. Ruth, put Travis' good jacket on him... Walter Lee, fix your tie and tuck（把衣物的边塞起来）your shirt in, you look like somebody's hoodlum（流氓）! Lord have mercy, where is my plant? *(She flies to get it amid the general bustling of the family, who are deliberately trying to ignore the nobility〈崇高〉of the past moment.)* You all start on down... Travis child, don't go empty-handed... Ruth, where did I put that box with my skillets（长柄平底煎锅）in it? I want to be in charge of it myself... I'm going to make us the biggest dinner we ever ate tonight... Beneatha, what's the matter with them stockings? Pull them things up, girl...

The family starts to file（列队行进）out as two moving men appear and begin to carry out the heavier pieces of furniture, bumping（撞击）into the family as they move about.

BENEATHA: Mama, Asagai asked me to marry him today and go to Africa—

MAMA *(in the middle of her getting-ready activity)*: He did? You ain't old enough to marry nobody—*(seeing the moving men lifting one of her chairs precariously〈不牢靠地〉)* Darling, that ain't no bale（包，捆）of cotton, please handle it so we can sit in it again! I had that chair twenty-five years...

The movers sigh with exasperation and go on with their work.

BENEATHA *(girlishly and unreasonably trying to pursue the conversation)*: To go to Africa, Mama—be a doctor in Africa...

MAMA *(distracted)*: Yes, baby—

WALTER: *Africa!* What he want you to go to Africa for?

BENEATHA: To practice（行医）there...

WALTER: Girl, if you don't get all them silly ideas out your head! You better marry yourself a man with some loot（钱）...

BENEATHA *(angrily, precisely as in the first scene of the play)*: What have you got to do with who I marry!

WALTER: Plenty. Now I think George Murchison—

BENEATHA: *George Murchison!* I wouldn't marry him if he was Adam and I was Eve!

Walter and Beneatha go out yelling at each other vigorously and the anger is loud and real till their voices diminish. Ruth stands at the door and turns to Mama and smiles knowingly.

MAMA *(fixing her hat at last)*: Yeah—they something all right, my children...

RUTH: Yeah—they're something. Let's go, Lena.

MAMA *(stalling, starting to look around at the house)*: Yes—I'm coming. Ruth—

RUTH: Yes?

MAMA *(quietly, woman to woman)*: He finally come into his manhood today, didn't he? Kind of like a rainbow after the rain...

Unit 6

Lorraine Hansberry and *A Raisin in the Sun*

RUTH *(biting her lip lest her own pride explode in front of Mama)*: Yes, Lena.
    Walter's voice calls for them raucously.
WALTER *(off stage)*: Y'all come on! These people charges by the hour, you know!
MAMA *(waving Ruth out vaguely)*: All right, honey—go on down. I be down directly.
    Ruth hesitates, then exits. Mama stands, at last alone in the living room, her plant on the table before her as the lights start to come down. She looks around at all the walls and ceilings and suddenly, despite herself（不由自主）, while the children call below, a great heaving（起伏，汹涌）thing rises in her and she puts her fist to her mouth to stifle（压制）it, takes a final desperate look, pulls her coat about her, pats her hat and goes out. The lights dim down. The door opens and she comes back in, grabs her plant, and goes out for the last time.
                    CURTAIN

6.2.4 Exercises

① Give a brief answer to each of the following questions.

The title
1) How do you understand the title "A Raisin in the Sun"?

Act 1
Scene 1
2) What does Walter intend to do with the coming check? How does Ruth react to it?
3) What is the relationship between Walter and Beneatha like? Why is it so?
4) What suggestion does Ruth give Mama about how to use the insurance money? How does Mama want to use it?
5) What does Beneatha do that angers Mama? How do they view God differently?

Scene 2
6) What is Beneatha's standpoint on her cultural identity?
7) How does Walter explain his business plan to Mama? What does Mama think of him?

Act 2
Scene 1
8) How do Beneatha and George view their African heritage differently?
9) What has Mama done with the insurance money? How do Ruth and Walter respond differently? Why?
10) Where is their new house located? Why are Ruth and Walter upset when they hear the address?

Scene 2
11) Who is Mrs. Johnson? Why has she come to visit?

12) Why does Mama give Walter the remaining money? What does she ask him to do with it?

Scene 3

13) How is the mood of the Youngers changed after they buy a new house?
14) What's Mr. Lindner's real purpose in visiting the Youngers? What does he offer them in order to achieve his purpose?
15) What gifts does Mama receive on the moving day? How does she feel?
16) What news does Bobo bring? How much money has Walter lost?

Act 3

17) To what extent has Beneatha's mood been affected by the loss of the insurance money? How does Asagai renew her courage and hope?
18) What does Walter say he has learned from Willy Harris? What does he decide to do next?
19) What lesson does Mama give Beneatha?
20) What does Walter say to Mr. Lindner? What has brought about the change in him?

❷ Identify the following characters.

1) _____ has integrated into white culture, and has no interest in African heritage. He courts Beneatha but wants her to be a traditional, submissive woman.
2) _____ aims to bring progress to his country in Africa. He appreciates Beneatha's quest for her African identity, and inspires her with his own dream when she is disillusioned.
3) _____ likes to take advantage of the Youngers' generosity. She tries to dampen the spirits of the Youngers when they are preparing to move into a new neighborhood.
4) _____ brings the Youngers the bad news that his and Walter's mutual friend Willy Harris has absconded with their money. He seems as distraught as Walter about the misfortune.
5) _____ represents the future of the Younger family. Mama and Ruth disagree over how to parent him, and Walter feels obliged to be a role model in his presence.
6) _____ does not have much material wealth, but she walks tall and exudes dignity. She is the backbone of the Youngers. Her moral strength and wisdom win her the respect of all the family, while her loving care guides their growth.
7) _____ is the spokesman for the white community into which the Youngers plan to move. He has been authorized by his community to offer the Youngers a monetary incentive not to move in.
8) _____ loves her husband and family. Poverty and the problems between her and Walter exhaust her energies, but her pragmatism and emotional strength are revealed when she learns of the possibility of moving into a house.

Unit 6

Lorraine Hansberry and *A Raisin in the Sun*

9) _____ has great ambition but lacks the means and talent to realize it. He believes wealth to be the answer to his desperation and spends most of the play obsessed with money; by the end, however, he regains his pride and integrity.

10) _____ dares to pursue her identity or express herself by engaging in different activities considered frivolous in a traditional, black, working-class household. She also challenges conventional expectations of women.

❸ Plot Review

The Youngers are a poor African American family living in a crowded and worn-out 1) _____ in Chicago. They are about to receive an 2) _____ check for ten thousand dollars, which comes from the 3) _____ of the children's old father, Big Walter. This windfall, however, sets the family quarreling, as they all depend on it to realize their different 4) _____.

Mama longs to buy a 5) _____, which she has always wanted to do but never succeeded. Her idea also pleases Ruth, her daughter-in-law, who is now 6) _____ with another baby. Beneatha, Mama's daughter, is a college student and needs the money for her 7) _____ schooling. Walter, Beneatha's elder brother, wants the money to start a 8) _____ store with his friends. He views his business plan as a way to get the family out of 9) _____, but all the women in the family 10) _____ of it. Annoyed, he blames them for being 11) _____.

When the check does arrive, however, Mama's joy is diminished because she discovers that Ruth has actually planned to have an 12) _____ so as to lessen the family's burden, and that Walter, in his 13) _____, seems to consent to his wife's decision. From Mama's perspective, the family needs a bigger space to stay together, so she spends part of the money making a 14) _____ payment on a house. After she learns that Walter has not been to 15) _____ for days, she reconsiders her position and decides to ask him to take care of the remaining money as the 16) _____ of the family, which finally raises his 17) _____.

However, the house Mama has bought is located in a(n) 18) _____ neighborhood. On the moving day, Mr. Lindner, one of their future neighbors, comes for a visit, attempting to 19) _____ the house back from the Youngers, but they refuse because it means an 20) _____. Then they face another setback: without telling his family, Walter has invested all the money Mama gave him in his business venture and now that money is 21) _____ — one of his business partners has 22) _____ with it. As a result, the family sinks into despair.

Earlier, Beneatha has rejected one of her suitors, George Murchison, a wealthy middle-class African-American man whom she considers 23) _____. Instead, she favors Joseph Asagai, who is from Nigeria, because he can understand her 24) _____ pursuits and appreciate her quest for her African 25) _____. Now that Beneatha is dejected, Asagai comforts her, encourages her to remain 26) _____, and even 27) _____ to her. Meanwhile, Walter considers taking Mr. Lindner's 28) _____. However, Mama reminds him of the family's long tradition of 29) _____, and he finally decides that the Youngers should move into their new house. Mama is delighted to see her son finally reach his 30) _____.

❹ **Identify the speakers of the following lines, briefly tell the situation in which each of them is uttered, and explain its significance.**

1) — The world's most backward race of people, and that's a fact.
   — And then there are all those prophets who would lead us out of the wilderness— into the swamps!
2) Mama, something is happening between Walter and me. I don't know what it is— but he needs something—something I can't give him any more. He needs this chance, Lena.
3) Seem like God didn't see fit to give the black man nothing but dreams—but He did give us children to make them dreams seem worth while.
4) Now—you say after me, in my mother's house there is still God.
5) — Assimilationism is so popular in your country.
   — I am not an assimilationist!
6) Sometimes it's like I can see the future stretched out in front of me—just plain as day. The future, Mama. Hanging over there at the edge of my days. Just waiting for me—a big, looming blank space—full of *nothing*. Just waiting for *me*. But it don't have to be.
7) So now it's life. Money is life. Once upon a time freedom used to be life—now it's money. I guess the world really do change.
8) See there… you are standing there in your splendid ignorance talking about people who were the first to smelt iron on the face of the earth! The Ashanti were performing surgical operations when the English—were still tattooing themselves with blue dragons!
9) So you butchered up a dream of mine—you—who always talking 'bout your children's dreams…
10) There ain't nothing as precious to me… There ain't nothing worth holding on to, money, dreams, nothing else—if it means—if it means it's going to destroy my boy.
11) — You see—in the face of all the things I have said, we are prepared to make your family a very generous offer…
    — Thirty pieces and not a coin less!
12) Man … I trusted you… Man, I put my life in your hands…Man… THAT MONEY IS MADE OUT OF MY FATHER'S FLESH—
13) Oh, God…Look down here— and show me the strength!

14) And it is very odd but those who see the changes—who dream, who will not give up are called idealists... and those who see only the circle—we call *them* the "realists"!

15) Then isn't there something wrong in a house—in a world—where all dreams, good or bad, must depend on the death of a man?

16) I'll work twenty hours a day in all the kitchens in Chicago... I'll strap my baby on my back if I have to and scrub all the floors in America and wash all the sheets in America if I have to—but we got to MOVE!

17) Some of us always getting "tooken." People like Willy Harris, they don't never get "tooken." And you know why the rest of us do? 'Cause we all mixed up. Mixed up bad.

18) Child, when do you think is the time to love somebody the most? When they done good and made things easy for everybody? Well then, you ain't through learning—because that ain't the time at all. It's when he's at his lowest and can't believe in hisself 'cause the world done whipped him so! When you starts measuring somebody, measure him right, child, measure him right. Make sure you done taken into account what hills and valleys he come through before he got to wherever he is.

19) And we have decided to move into our house because my father—my father—he earned it for us brick by brick. We don't want to make no trouble for nobody or fight no causes, and we will try to be good neighbors. And that's all we got to say about that. We don't want your money.

20) He finally come into his manhood today, didn't he? Kind of like a rainbow after the rain...

❺ Questions for essay or discussion

1) What are the dreams of the Youngers? Why have they been deferred? Are they still deferred at the end of the play?
2) What is the significance of the following names or objects: the Youngers, Ruth, Beneatha, the furniture, Mama's plant, and Beneatha's hair?
3) Discuss how minor characters such as George Murchison, Mrs. Johnson, Willy Harris, and Mr. Lindner represent the ideas against which the main characters react.
4) What do you think will happen after the Youngers move to Clybourne Park?
5) What impresses you most about the play?

主要参考书目

Abbotson, Susan C. W. *Masterpieces of 20th-Century American Drama.* Westport and London: Greenwood Press, 2005.

Abrams, M. H. *A Glossary of Literary Terms, Seventh Edition.* Boston: Thomson Learning, Inc., 1999.

Adler, Thomas P. *A Streetcar Named Desire: The Moth and the Lantern.* Boston: Twayne Publishers, 1990.

Adler, Thomas P. *Tennessee Williams: A Streetcar Named Desire / Cat on a Hot Tin Roof—A Reader's Guide to Essential Criticism.* London: Palgrave Macmillan, 2012.

Ajtony, Zsuzsanna. *Britain and Britishness in G. G. Shaw's Plays: A Linguistic Perspective.* Newcastle upon Tyne: Cambridge Scholars Publishing, 2012.

Baldick, Chris. *Oxford Concise Dictionary of Literary Terms, Second Edition.* Oxford and New York: Oxford University Press, 2001.

Baym, Nina, ed. *The Norton Anthology of American Literature, Seventh Edition.* New York and London: W. W. Norton & Company, 2007.

Bloom, Harold, ed. *Bloom's Modern Critical Views: George Bernard Shaw—New Edition.* New York: Infobase Publishing, 2011.

Bloom, Harold, ed. *Bloom's Modern Critical Interpretations: William Shakespeare's Romeo and Juliet—New Edition.* New York: Infobase Publishing, 2009.

Bloom, Harold, ed. *Bloom's Modern Critical Interpretations: Tennessee Williams's A Streetcar Named Desire—New Edition.* New York: Infobase Publishing, 2009.

Bloom, Harold, ed. *Bloom's Modern Critical Interpretations: Arthur Miller's The Crucible—New Edition.* New York: Infobase Publishing, 2008.

Bloom, Harold, ed. *Bloom's Guides: Lorraine Hansberry's A Raisin in the Sun.* New York: Infobase Publishing, 2009.

Christopher Innes, ed. *The Cambridge Companion to George Bernard Shaw.* New York: Cambridge University Press, 1998.

Drabble, Margaret. *The Oxford Companion to English Literature.* Oxford: Oxford University Press, 2000.

Galens, David, and Lynn Spampinato, eds. *Drama for Students.* Detroit: Gale Research, 1998.

Greenblatt, Stephen, and M. H. Abrams, eds. *The Norton Anthology of English Literature, Eighth Edition.* New York and London: W. W. Norton & Company, 2005.

Greenblatt, Stephen, ed. *The Norton Shakespeare: Based on the Oxford Edition.* New York and London: W. W. Norton & Company, 1997.

Halio, Jay L. *Romeo and Juliet: A Guide to the Play*. Westport and London: Greenwood Press, 1998.

Harper, Marilynn O. *Cliffs Notes on Shaw's Pygmalion & Arms and the Man*. New York: Hungry Minds, Inc., 1981.

Hart, James D. *The Oxford Companion to American Literature*. Oxford: Oxford University Press, 1995

Hochman, Stanley. *McGraw-Hill Encyclopedia of World Drama*, Salem Press, Inc. 2015

Holroyd, Michael. *Bernard Shaw: The One-Volume Definitive Edition*. New York: Random House, 1997.

Hunt, Maurice, ed. *Approaches to Teaching Shakespeare's Romeo and Juliet*. New York: Modern Language Association of America, 2000.

James, Rosetta. *Cliffs Notes on Hansberry's A Raisin in the Sun*. New York: Hungry Minds, Inc., 1992.

Jacobus, Lee A. *The Bedford Introduction to Drama, Second Edition*. Boston: Bedford Books of St. Martin's Press, 1993.

Keeble, N. H. *Romeo and Juliet: York Notes Advanced*. London: York Press, 2004.

Lauter, Paul et al, eds. *Heath Anthology of American Literature*. Lexington: D. C. Heath and Company, 1990.

McMichael, George et al, eds. *Anthology of American Literature*. New Jersey: Prentice-Hall, 2000.

Miller, Arthur, and Gerald Weales. *The Crucible: Text and Criticism*. New York: Viking Press, 1971.

Palfrey, Simon. *The Connell Guide to Shakespeare's Romeo & Juliet*. London: Connell Guides, 2012.

Raby, Peter, ed. *The Cambridge Companion to Oscar Wilde*. New York: Cambridge University Press, 1997.

Sambrook, Hana. *A Streetcar Named Desire: York Notes for A-level*. London: York Press, 2015.

Shaw, George Bernard, and Nicholas Greene. *Pygmalion (Penguin Classics)*. New York and London: Penguin Books Ltd., 2000.

Siebold, Thomas. *Readings on The Crucible*. San Diego: Greenhaven Press, 1999.

SparkNotes Editors. *SparkNote on The Crucible*. Spark Publishing Group, 2002.

Trudeau, Lawrence J. *Drama Criticism*. Gale Research Inc., 1991

Varty, Anne. *A Preface to Oscar Wilde*. Beijing: Peking University Press, 2005.

Wilde, Oscar, and Peter Raby. *The Importance of Being Earnest and Other Plays (Oxford World's Classics)*. Oxford: Oxford University Press, 1995.

Williams, Tennessee. *A Streetcar Named Desire*. New York: New Directions Books, 1947.

Woods, Gillian. *Shakespeare: Romeo and Juliet—A Reader's Guide to Essential Criticism*. London: Palgrave Macmillan, 2013.